The Windows Internet Tour Guide™

The Windows Internet Tour Guide™

Cruising the Internet the Easy Way

Michael Fraase

VENTANA
PRESS

The Windows Internet Tour Guide™: Cruising the Internet the Easy Way

Library of Congress Cataloging-in-Publication Data
Fraase, Michael.
The Windows Internet tour guide : cruising the Internet the easy way / Michael Fraase. -- 1st ed.
p. cm.
Includes index.
ISBN 1-56604-081-7
1. Microsoft Windows (Computer file) 2. Internet (Computer network) I. Title
TK5105.875.I57F76 1994
384.3--dc20 94-2024
CIP

Book design: Karen Wysocki
Cover design and icons: John Nedwidek, emDesign
Index service: Dianne Bertsch, Answers Plus
Technical review: Darren A. Rousseau
Editorial staff: Diana Merelman, Pam Richardson, Jessica Ryan
Production staff: John Cotterman, Terri March, Marcia Webb
Proofreader: Sue Versenyi

First Edition 9 8
Printed in the United States of America

Ventana Press, Inc.
P.O. Box 2468
Chapel Hill, NC 27515
919/942-0220
FAX 919/942-1140

Trademarks

Trademarked names appear throughout this book. Rather than list the names and entities that own the trademarks or insert a trademark symbol with each mention of the trademarked name, the publisher states that it is using the names only for editorial purposes and to the benefit of the trademark owner with no intention of infringing upon that trademark.

About the Author

Michael Fraase is the proprietor of Arts & Farces, a multifaceted communications and professional services business specializing in hypermedia production, technical writing, desktop/electronic publishing, general consulting and software interface design.

Fraase is the author of numerous books, including the three-volume *Macintosh Hypermedia* series (ScottForesman, 1990–1991), *Farallon's MediaTracks* (Business One Irwin, 1991), *Groupware for the Macintosh* (Business One Irwin, 1991), *Structured Publishing From the Desktop: Frame Technology's FrameMaker* (Business One Irwin, 1992), the 15-volume *Rapid Reference Series* (Business One Irwin, 1992–1993), *The Mac Internet Tour Guide* (Ventana Press, 1993) and *The PC Internet Tour Guide* (Ventana Press, 1994).

Michael Fraase, proprietor
Arts & Farces
2285 Stewart Avenue
Suite 1315
Saint Paul, MN 55116
mfraase@farces.com

Acknowledgments

While the task of writing is a solitary one, the act of creating a book isn't. Thanks to everyone at Ventana Press for again proving what I suspected: small publishers can make a Big Difference. You've truly exceeded all my expectations in a publisher.

I didn't want to do this book; I'm a Mac user and was brought kicking and screaming into the world of MS-DOS and Windows. Thanks to Joe Woodman for seeing the potential in this project and for helping me see it as well.

Thanks to Elizabeth Woodman for her unseen editing hand.

Thanks to Pam Richardson for routing and scheduling everything with patience.

Thanks to Diane Lennox for publicity and promotion.

Thanks to Fran Phillips, Jamie Jaeger and Laura Wenzel for sales.

Thanks to Karen Wysocki for the interior page design and to Marcia Webb for managing a feverish production schedule.

Thanks to John Cotterman for the desktop publishing.

Thanks to John Nedwidek, of emDesign for the cover design and icons. After three iterations, this is still the best computer book cover I've ever seen.

Thanks to Dennis Fazio and Dave Bergum at Minnesota Regional Network (MRNet) for support and advice on all things Internet.

A big thanks to Ruffin Prevost, my editor. Writers' nightmares are populated with bad editors. Ruffin is the exception that proves the rule; he's a real writer's editor, and approached this project as a true collaboration. Ruffin made this a better book with a reasoned, even hand. The world would be a better place if there were more editors like Ruffin. If it weren't for Ruffin, none of the books in this series would have happened.

Thanks to Jessica Ryan for picking up where Ruffin left off.

Finally, thanks yet again to my wife, Karen Caldwell Fraase, for everything.

About the Images in this Book

The graphic images shown on the opening pages of each chapter of *The Windows Internet Tour Guide* are from the OTIS ("The Operative Term is STIMULATE") Project. OTIS is an electronic art gallery containing hundreds of images and animations. According to OTIS Project founder, Ed Stastny, OTIS exists "to distribute original creative images over the world's computer networks for public perusal, scrutiny, and retransmission, and to facilitate communication, inspiration, critique, and to set the foundations for digital immortality."

According to Stastny, "The basic idea behind 'digital immortality' is that computer networks are here to stay and that anything interesting you deposit on them will be around for near-forever. The images of today will be the artifacts of an information-laded future. Perhaps the images will be converted into newer formats when the current formats become obsolete—perhaps only surviving on forgotten backup reels—but they'll be there, and someone will dig them up. Data-archeologists sifting through the cobwebs of an old storage room."

The OTIS Project is currently accessible by anonymous FTP at three sites:

- no-name-broadband.med.umich.edu in the /projects/otis/ directory
- sunsite.unc.edu in the /pub/multimedia/pictures/OTIS/ directory
- aql.gatech.edu in the /pub/OTIS/ directory

For more information about the OTIS Project, contact:

OTIS Project
Ed Stastny
P.O. Box 241113 ed@cwis.unomaha.edu
Omaha, NE 68124 ed@sunsite.unc.edu

A special thanks goes out to those OTIS artists who generously allowed us to reproduce their images. Thanks to: Ed Stastny (Information Web, Chapter 1; VR2, Chapter 5; ©1993 Ed Stastny, used with permission); Tom Nawara (Stigmata, Chapter 2; Eye See U, Chapter 8; ©1993 Tom Nawara, used with permission); Michael Maier (Future Culture, Chapter 3; ©1993 Michael Maier, used with permission); David Anjo (No Roof, Chapter 4; ©1993 David Anjo, used with permission); Barrett Ryker (Fractal Moon, Chapter 6; Castle Spirit, Chapter 7; ©1993 Barrett Ryker, used with permission).

Contents

Chapter 4

Chapter 7 Using Gopher 211

Chapter 8 Other Internet Resources 241

Introduction

These are the days of lasers in the jungle
Lasers in the jungle somewhere
Staccato signals of constant information...
—Paul Simon

Part of the experience of using a PC connected to other computers is a sense that there's a collection of actual places behind the screen—places you can't see, but know are in there. Or, rather, out there. This feeling really hit home for me when I saw a photo a friend used to replace his usual Macintosh desktop pattern. (This was before you could do similar tricks with PCs running Windows.) It showed his face and hands scrunched up against a window pane, creating the illusion of someone *out there* trying to get *in here*. If you've ever used your PC to connect to another computer—either by network or modem—you know this experience, and you know it's real. Tapping into the Internet not only confirms, but *validates*, this feeling.

These days it's hip to call this collection of not-quite-real places *cyberspace*. Cyberspace is a term created by William Gibson in his novel, *Neuromancer*, to represent a universe sustained by a vast network of computers and telecommunications lines.

> People jacked in so they could hustle. Put the trodes on and they were out there, all the data in the world stacked up like one big neon city, so you could cruise around and have a kind of grip on it, visually anyway, because if you didn't, it was too complicated, trying to find your way to a particular piece of data you needed.
> —William Gibson

But cyberspace isn't some wild future dream; it's here now. John Perry Barlow—sometimes Wyoming cattle rancher and sometimes lyricist for the Grateful Dead—describes cyberspace as where you are when you are on the telephone. Think about that for a minute—and then realize that cyberspace is also where your bank accounts, credit history and tax records are. And in the near future, cyberspace is also likely to be where you earn a good portion of your income.

This book is about the Internet—a vast computer network of many component networks. Think of it as a web. Think of it as the first *really real* cyberspace.

For too many years the Internet has been the playground of propeller-heads and spooks, inaccessible to mere mortals. But lately, the Internet has changed, becoming a critical tool for millions of computer users. Powerful but simple software tools have made the Net accessible to practically anyone. And that's what this book is all about: making the Internet as friendly and familiar as everything else you do with your PC.

Explosive Growth

The past few years have seen the Internet expand at an astonishing rate. Individuals and businesses are rushing to the Internet in droves for a good reason: it's an invaluable resource for anyone who works with information. Its power and potential are practically limitless. Just a few of the most popular features of the Internet include:

- **Electronic mail**. Send electronic mail (e-mail) to virtually any networked computer user. Internet e-mail reaches its destination—practically anywhere on the planet—in a matter of a few minutes.
- **Network news**. Participate in a wide variety of electronic discussion groups on just about any topic you can think of. There are literally thousands of in-depth discussions on topics ranging from the essential to the arcane. Molecular biology, politics, comic books, the stock market, computers and practically anything else you can think of are all covered in the Internet's network news.
- **File transfer**. Transfer any kind of file between your computer and any other computer on the Internet. The Internet boasts the largest collection of MS-DOS software and shareware in the world, and its libraries are growing at an unprecedented rate every minute of every day.
- **Information browsing**. You can browse through a never-ending collection of information resources available throughout the

Internet. Weather reports, electronic information databases, and electronic journals (and much more) are available—free to anyone with access to the Internet.

Who Can Use The Windows Internet Tour Guide?

If you use a PC with Windows and already have Internet access, or if you're interested in obtaining Internet access in the future, this book is for you. If you subscribe to one of the commercial information services (such as CompuServe or America Online), you can use this book for exchanging electronic mail with Internet users, subscribing to mailing lists and retrieving files available on the Internet by electronic mail.

This *Tour Guide* is written for Internet newcomers. No knowledge of the Internet is assumed (although experienced Internet users are sure to find plenty of interest here as well). I do assume, however, that you're comfortable finding your way around a PC. You should be able to copy files from a floppy to your hard drive, launch application programs, work with AUTOEXEC.BAT and the various .INI files, and connect peripherals to your PC. If you haven't yet mastered these simple skills, don't despair. A couple of hours with your PC manuals (or a beginning PC tutorial) will bring you up to speed.

Although the *Tour Guide* will help you navigate the Internet and lead you through its vast resources, regardless of what hardware or software you have, you'll need a few things in order to get the most out of this book:

- An IBM PC or compatible with at least 4mb of RAM and at least an 80386 processor running DOS 5.0 or later and Microsoft Windows v3.1 or later.
- An Internet account (or an account on one of the commercial information services if you want to exchange electronic mail with Internet users).
- An appropriate network connection. To make the most of the tools and techniques discussed in this book, you should have a SLIP or PPP connection or direct connection to the Internet. If you have a dial-up connection, you will find many of the tips and resources useful, but you won't be able to make full use of the companion software.

- The floppy disk that comes with this book.
- **Important Note**: The software provided on the disk that comes with this book provides complete Internet connectivity for SLIP and PPP users. **If you enjoy a direct connection to the Internet, you must contact your network administrator or service provider for appropriate network connectivity software. Connectivity software for direct Internet connections is not included on the disk that comes with this book.**

If some of this sounds Greek to you, don't despair. Information on joining the Internet can be found throughout these pages, with specifics in Chapter 2.

The Windows Internet Tour Guide will not only show you the most fascinating and helpful places on the Internet, it will also give you the tools and techniques you need to navigate the vast landscape of information out there. The software on the enclosed companion disk will bring new power and simplicity to everything you do on the Internet. Best of all, every detail of configuring and using the companion software is discussed in detail throughout the book—using real-world examples to show you how to get the most out of your time on the Net. Here's a brief look at what you'll find inside the *Tour Guide*:

What's Inside

Chapter 1: **"What is the Internet?"** (Any Why I Should Use It?) covers network benefits for the average user and provides a general overview of the Internet for beginners. It also includes information about the history, growth and future of the Internet.

Chapter 2, **"Getting Connected"** (The Big Plug-In) provides information for all different types of users about how to physically connect to the Internet. If you work for a medium or large organization, you may want to talk with your system administrator; you may already have an Internet account and not even know it. If you're with a smaller firm, or simply an individual looking to "plug in," this chapter also covers the basics of the various kinds of Internet connections.

Chapter 3, **"Network Infrastructure"** (Electronic Alphabet Soup) offers a background on how the Internet is organized, what you need to know about networking protocols and the parts of an Internet address. We'll also go over some basic information about being a good

Internet citizen. This chapter is a must-read before venturing out into the Net—it will make future chapters easier to understand.

Chapter 4, **"Electronic Mail"** (The Pony Express Goes Digital) covers everything you need to know about sending, receiving and replying to electronic mail (e-mail). You'll learn how to send e-mail from the Internet to virtually any other networked computer. You'll also learn how to use Chameleon Mail (an invaluable e-mail program included on the *Tour Guide* companion disk) and Eudora. Finally, you'll also learn how to find addresses, participate in mailing lists, and send and receive attached files with your e-mail messages.

Chapter 5, **"Network News & Newsgroups"** (Broadsheets of the Broadband) offers information on reading, posting and replying to the tens of thousands of news articles available via the Internet. This chapter shows you how to quickly and effectively browse, track and search newsgroups and articles using Trumpet (a program you'll download as part of a step-by-step tutorial). A brief discussion of posting etiquette and a general overview of available newsgroups are also provided.

Chapter 6, **"Transferring Files"** (The Mother Download) provides complete instructions for using the File Transfer Protocol (FTP) for downloading and uploading files on any of the thousands of publicly accessible file archives on the Net. We'll also cover the basics of computer viruses and how to use the popular SCAN antivirus shareware program.

Chapter 7, **"Using Gopher"** (Burrowing for Information) covers the details of using the powerful and user-friendly HGopher software to browse information resources and download files on any Gopher server on the Internet. Information on creating and sharing Gopher bookmarks (electronic crumb trails through vast amounts of information) is also included.

Chapter 8, **"Other Internet Resources"** (Geez, what is all this stuff?) offers information on various Internet resources, both human and electronic. Just as the Internet promises something for everyone, so will this eclectic chapter. The Electronic Frontier Foundation (EFF) and Internet Society, for instance, are bountiful organizations that provide a wealth of information for Internet users of any level of expertise. This chapter also includes information about relatively "minor" or esoteric Internet services that sometimes get overlooked, including time- and money-saving gems like: knowbots, Netfind, Network Information

Centers, Finger, the Internet Business Pages, Archie, RFCs, FAQs, and the World Wide Web (WWW). This chapter also features an overview of dozens of other fascinating information sources.

A complete glossary, bibliography and index are also included in the last sections of the book.

But perhaps the best thing about *The Windows Internet Tour Guide* is that you can't get lost or left behind—just follow along at your own pace. Everything is covered in simple, step-by-step detail. Even if you've never used the Internet before, you'll find the software and instructions in this *Tour Guide* as easy to use as all your other favorite Windows applications.

Everything you need to connect to the Internet—via SLIP or PPP but not a direct connection—is included on the disk that comes with this book. Chameleon is an integrated set of programs that provides Internet electronic mail, file transfer and TELNET. Chameleon also allows you to establish a SLIP or PPP connection to the Net with a modem over ordinary telephone lines.

And to keep the trip interesting, our tour will take frequent sidetrips to visit some of the most fascinating people, places and resources throughout the Internet. Keep an eye out for these "scenic route sidebars"—they'll feature people profiles, file reviews, resources listings and fun and intriguing examples of the kinds of information you'll find (by chance or design) as you cruise the Internet (for more details on sidebars, see "Finding Your Way Around" on page 3).

So forget what you've heard about how complicated and frustrating the Internet can be. With the right software and a few pointers from a pro, it's a lot easier than you think—in fact, it's actually fun. Hop aboard, our tour is about to begin!

Michael Fraase
Saint Paul, Minnesota
December 1993

CHAPTER 1

WHAT IS THE INTERNET?
And Why Should I Use It?

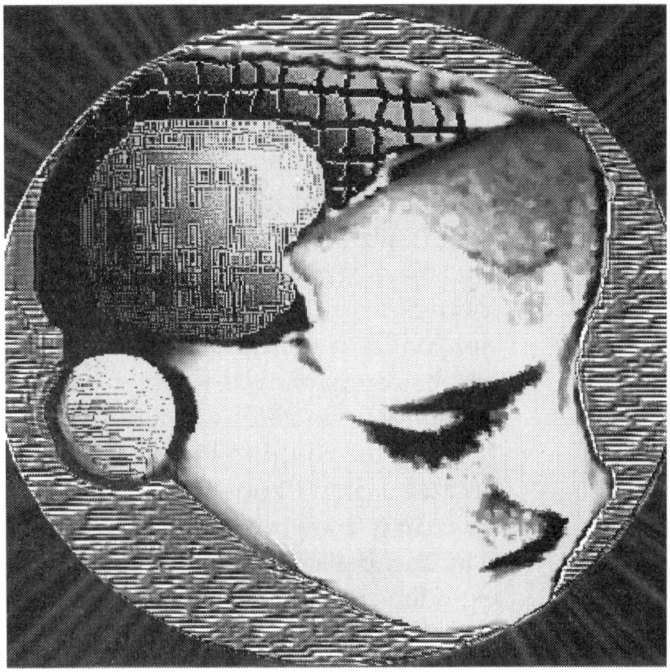

Imagine downloading Dante's *Inferno* from a computer in Massachusetts or California, just as quickly as if you were copying the file from a floppy disk. Imagine corresponding with anyone on almost a billion different computers, anywhere in the world, as easily as typing a letter with a word processor. Imagine reading the latest news practically as soon as it's written, or cruising through a web of connected computer networks and information resources so vast that no one knows for sure how big it is, or how many people it reaches.

Need to know what the weather is like for your trip to New England this weekend? No problem—weather reports and even weather maps are only a few mouse clicks away. Want to find out who wrote a particular book or article? You don't even have to leave your chair to browse the holdings of the Library of Congress. This isn't a scenario from some commercial for a futuristic telephone company or a guess at what television will be like in the year 2050. This is a snapshot of the Internet as it exists *right now*.

It's Easier Than You Think

Forget everything you've heard about how complicated it is to use the Internet. Tools with a Windows interface are available for just about every Internet service. You don't need to know any arcane UNIX commands or have an office next-door to a mainframe computer. The myth is still there, but it's all smoke and no fire. Oh, sure, you can still plod around the Net the hard way, pecking out abbreviated gibberish on your keyboard like so much secret code. But there's a much easier and more powerful way to cruise the Internet—one that will make your time online more fun and more productive—and that's what this book and its companion disk are all about.

I grew up in cities when I was a kid, and my cousins all grew up on farms in the country. Whenever I went to visit, they would tease me because I didn't know much about driving a tractor, saddling a horse or tossing a cowpie. I couldn't tease them about not knowing how to play stickball or dodge traffic because I was on their turf—my city experiences weren't relevant. It's sort of like that on the Internet, but the turf is common to everyone. If the UNIX fans and command-line aficionados want to pump water by hand, that's fine. Since your PC is capable of using a host of powerful software tools to make navigating the Net a breeze, you can just smile at the water-pumpers politely while you turn on your PC faucet.

The main reason my country cousins teased me was because I wasn't familiar with their turf. I didn't have a tour guide or a map of the territory. The same is true for new Internet users. It's a daunting task to navigate new terrain without a guide to point out the landmarks.

This book is a tour guide to the Internet, designed to provide you with the tools and information you need to effectively navigate its vast information resources. You'll also find step-by-step tutorials for using a wide array of Windows software tools that help you effectively communicate with people and travel to both the "cities" and the "rural areas" that make up this vast information resource. In fact, many of these tools are included on *The Windows Internet Tour Guide Companion Disk.*

Finding Your Way Around

Also included in our *Tour Guide* are what information designers and cartographers humbly call *wayfinding elements*, little signs that help you find locations of interest. Being a computer user, you'll know them simply as icons. Look for these four icons for interesting landmarks and tidbits of information.

People profiles are snapshots of how real people use the Internet. These are the true stories of real people, not techno-nerds. With luck, these vignettes will stimulate you to use the Internet in ways you may have never thought of. Look for them to provide insight about the general workings of the Internet, not necessarily relevant to the surrounding text.

Software reviews are brief overviews of some of the best public domain, freeware and shareware software programs available on the Internet. Because space is limited, only the best or most interesting software is mentioned. The archive location and pathname for each program is also provided. All of the programs mentioned can be downloaded to your computer using FTP. (For information on FTP, see Chapter 6, "Transferring Files.")

Hot spots and cool resources are short descriptions of both the most popular and the more offbeat information resources available on the Internet. Complete connection information is provided. These resources usually require you to use a specific software program or Internet client for access. Refer to the appropriate chapter for more information on using the right software tool for the job. Any passwords required to access these resources are provided in the sidebar.

Found text excerpts are brief passages of network news exchanges, electronic mailing list information, amusing conversations, general tips and tricks, and other information morsels that may not fit within the context of a chapter, but are interesting nonetheless.

Cruising the Easy Way

Neal Cassady was one of the most tenacious drivers of his generation. He'd think nothing of hopping in a Buick and driving Jack Kerouac coast to coast—stopping only for gas—with just a hip flask and a pack of smokes. Cassady was a pretty lousy guide though, especially when he was trundling along in the big Merry Prankster bus, Further, on one of Ken Kesey's intrepid trips.

This book is a tour guide of the Internet, but my pace is a little less frantic than Cassady's (then again, I'm still alive). Since getting there is half the fun, we'll be making frequent stops to wander the nooks and crannies of cyberspace. And the great thing about this bus trip is that, although I'm driving, you can take things at your own pace. If you're anxious to get moving, you can bail out and catch up with the group at the next stop. If you're a slow starter, you can slow things down to a more leisurely pace. So, before we leave the station, let's take a couple minutes to check the map and itinerary for a quick overview of where we're headed and what we'll see.

A Sense of Place

People often describe the Internet as a worldwide network of computer networks. That's as good a description as anything I can come up with, but the experience of using the Internet—*being in the Net*—is something completely different. For instance, when I login to the simple local area network in my office, I'm pretty certain of what I'll find there; it doesn't really feel like a place. Instead it's sort of like insipid American hotel chains. There's hardly ever anything different—never a surprise—the same bedspreads, brown Formica, loud air conditioner and view of the interstate.

But when I login to the Internet, it feels like a real place, just as real as the bar on the corner or the deli down the street. There's always something new to explore, and usually an interesting message or two in my e-mail box. And you can no more explore the entire Internet than you could visit every country on the globe. Things change too quickly and dramatically for you to ever become bored.

In this chapter, we'll take a look at what the Internet is, what kinds of information it contains, and how you can use that information to your advantage. We'll also explore a little of the history of the Internet, and speculate about what the future might hold for network users. But best of all, we'll take a look at the places, people and things you'll discover on your tour through the Net.

If you're already familiar with the Internet and how it works, or if you're just anxious to get connected and start exploring, you may want to skip ahead to Chapter 2, "Getting Connected."

Internet Benefits for the Average User

The Internet is much more than a network of networks. It's also much more than a huge repository of information. The Internet is a virtual community, existing only ephemerally in physical reality. While all this philosophical mumbo jumbo is a great mental exercise—something interesting to think about while you're waiting in the dentist's office or the airport—it probably doesn't have much impact on your daily life.

But the Internet provides several very real benefits that can have an enormous impact on your daily life:

- **Electronic mail**. You can use the Internet to send electronic mail (e-mail) to virtually any networked computer user on the planet. Traditional post office mail ("snail mail" or "the paper net" to e-mail users) may take several days to reach its destination. Internet e-mail can be delivered anywhere on the planet in a matter of minutes, or at the most a few hours. I used e-mail to correspond with my editor (who is also on the Internet), sending chapters back and forth during the entire writing cycle of this book. When the manuscript was finished, I used e-mail to correspond with the publisher's marketing and publicity staff—and they weren't even on the Internet.
- **Network news**. You can participate in a wide variety of electronic discussion groups on just about any topic imaginable, from investment strategies to molecular biology, from comic books to politics. If you can think of a topic that isn't already represented by a *newsgroup*, you can start your own. As of the fall of 1993, there were more than 4,000 active newsgroups accessible through the Internet. That number continues to grow steadily, and there are hundreds of additional commercial news groups that are

available for a fee. As I was writing this book, Microsoft announced its intent to open a publicly accessible FTP server. This bit of news, accompanied by discussion and analysis, was posted to several network newsgroups and electronic mailing lists within a few minutes of its announcement—days ahead of the trade press. Similarly, when the Clinton administration voiced its support for the Clipper encryption chip, lively and informative discussions on all sides of the issue were taking place in various newsgroups and mailing lists within minutes of the announcement.

- **File transfer**. You can use the Internet's standard protocols to transfer computer files between your PC and just about any other computer on the Internet. It doesn't matter where the other computer is located, how it's attached to the network or even if it uses the same operating system as yours. You can just as easily download a file from a UNIX-based mainframe in Tokyo as you can copy it from another PC in the next room.
- **Information browsing**. You can use specialized software tools to browse through an almost limitless collection of information resources. Everything from weather reports and electronic journals to university and government databases is available. Shortly after I began work on this book, for example, the Clinton administration made its plan for universal health care available on the Internet.

And that's just the beginning of what the Internet has to offer. As you explore, you'll discover people, places and other resources that will become invaluable to you. Because of its size, depth and diversity, the Internet can truly be all things to all people. But if you're new to the Net, you may be still wondering exactly what it *is*. The answer is at the same time simple and complicated. And the Internet changes so quickly, it's become something of a moving target—like a lemon seed on your kitchen counter—just when you think you have it in your grasp, it slips away.

A General Overview of the Internet

If you're a technophobe and don't much care about how things work, feel free to skip this section. It contains information about the plumbing of the Internet, and you can always read it later.

The Internet is a collection of various computer networks, linked together and communicating by a common protocol known as TCP/IP (Transmission Control Protocol/Internet Protocol). Because every computer on the Internet agrees to communicate using this protocol, it doesn't matter what kinds of computers you travel to, or even what operating system they are running.

In order for your PC to communicate with other computers using TCP/IP, you must have the appropriate TCP/IP software installed and properly configured. This process is discussed in more detail in the next chapter.

Although most of the computers that are connected to the Internet run some form of UNIX (the software that controls the computers), as a Windows user, you don't need to know one whit about UNIX. Though it probably wouldn't kill you to know a little UNIX, it's important to understand that, for the purposes of basic Internet activity, you don't need to know anything about UNIX—especially if you follow the advice and step-by-step instructions in this book.

The Internet is often defined as that group of computer networks that cooperatively form a seamless network using TCP/IP. But what about those computer systems that don't use TCP/IP but appear to be part of the Internet? For example, I can send electronic mail and even file enclosures from my Internet account to any user on MCI Mail. Yet MCI Mail's computers technically aren't on the Internet. MCI Mail maintains a *gateway* that's used to transfer electronic mail between their computers and the Internet. So, if you have an MCI Mail account, you can be reached from the Internet even though you don't have a computer on the Internet.

Internet Governance

Consensual anarchy best describes the governance of the Internet. While the individual networks that make up the Internet are likely to have executive officers, there's no such person running the entire Internet. The closest thing to an absolute governing authority is the Internet Society. The Internet Society is a group of volunteers whose charter is to promote the exchange of information using Internet technology. The Internet Society appoints a subgroup, the Internet Architecture Board, that authorizes standards and allocates and keeps track of Internet resources (such as unique computer addresses).

Another volunteer group, the Internet Engineering Task Force, handles acute operational and technical problems.

If you've ever driven in Paris, you'll understand this notion of consensual anarchy. The French have traffic lights, but they don't pay much attention to them. The traffic sort of develops a rhythm of its own without regard to the traffic lights. Drivers take account of the weather, the time of day, the number of vehicles, but not the traffic lights. If you come to a dead stop at a red light in Paris, people will honk their horns and shout silly sounding French epithets at you. It's hard for an American mind to grasp a situation where there's a sense of everyone doing the right thing without external rules or order. But that's the way it is with the Internet. There are only two "rules" for life on the Internet, and they're unwritten:

- Don't waste bandwidth.
- Don't do anything that threatens the Net.

You can do just about anything you like on the Internet, as long as you keep these two guidelines in mind. Would that the rest of life were as easy.

Each member network maintains its own Network Operations Center. These centers communicate with each other and arrive at a consensus on how to facilitate communications and resolve problems.

Since the Internet doesn't really exist in physical reality, there's nowhere to send a check for access. Each of the component networks that make up the Internet pays for its own operations. I send payment for my organization's connection to a regional network, which in turn pays a national provider for its connection. In theory, everyone on the Internet pays for his or her share, and in practice, this actually works amazingly well.

A Brief History of the Internet

The Internet began in the early 1970s as a U.S. Defense Department network called ARPAnet. The ARPAnet was originally implemented to support military research about how to build networks that could withstand partial outages and still function properly.

This network design approach assumed that the network itself was unreliable—a very realistic approach in hindsight, bomb attacks notwithstanding. Because the original ARPAnet model called for all communication to occur between two computers directly, any segment of the network could suffer an outage and the communication would still take place using any available alternative route across the network. The *computers* on the network—rather than the *network* itself—were responsible for correctly addressing and verifying communications. In network lingo, this is called *peer-to-peer* networking.

All that was needed for two computers to communicate on the ARPAnet was a message enclosed in a standard envelope—called an Internet Protocol (IP) packet—with a correct "address" for the destination computer.

In the early 1980s, Ethernet-based local area networks were developed. Most of the workstations that made up a local area network (LAN) in the early 1980s ran the UNIX operating system. The UNIX operating system came with IP networking capabilities built-in. Organizations using these workstations wanted to connect their LANs to the ARPAnet, rather than connecting to one large timesharing computer at each site. Since all of the networks were speaking IP, the benefits of enabling users on one network to communicate with those on any other network became obvious.

In the late 1980s, the National Science Foundation (NSF) created five regional supercomputer centers, making the resources of the world's fastest computers available for academic research. Because the supercomputer centers were so expensive, only five could be created and the resources were to be shared. A communications problem became immediately apparent: researchers and administrators at the different supercomputer sites needed to connect their centers together and also had to provide access for their clients. The ARPAnet seemed to be the solution to the communications problem, but it was abandoned, mostly because of bureaucratic problems.

The NSF built its own network—NSFNET— based on the ARPAnet's IP technology, with connections running at 56,000 bits per second (56 kbps) over specially conditioned telephone lines. This kind of connection was capable of sending about two pages per second to be transferred across the network—slow by today's standards. Because these special telephone lines were expensive (the telephone companies charge for these lines by the mile) the NSF decided to create regional networks, allowing sites to connect to their nearest neighbor, in daisy-chain fashion. Each daisy chain was connected to one of the regional supercomputer centers, and the centers themselves were linked together. This strategy allowed any computer to communicate with any other computer by passing messages up and down the daisy chain.

This strategy was successful—too successful, actually, and the network quickly became overloaded when the researchers discovered that the network was also useful for sharing resources not directly related to the supercomputer centers. In 1987, Merit Network, Inc., received a contract to maintain and upgrade the network. Merit, in conjunction with IBM and MCI, ran Michigan's educational network. The original NSF network was replaced with telephone lines that were 20 times faster, and quicker computers were also installed. The network was subsequently opened to most academic researchers, government employees and contractors. Access was extended to international research organizations in countries that were allies of the United States.

In the early 1990s the network was opened up to a few large commercial sites, and international Internet access has also started expanding rapidly.

Today, the Internet is a collection of high-speed networks composed of the national backbone network provided by the National Science Foundation and a hierarchy of more than 5,000 attached regional, state, federal agency, campus and corporate networks. Links to networks in Canada, Europe, Japan, Australia, Central America and South America are in place. There are more than 2,000,000 computers and workstations of various sizes connected to the Internet with millions of users. Even the U.S. research station in Antarctica has an Internet connection.

The Future of the Internet

The Internet is growing at a rate of about 10 percent per month as more colleges, universities, and businesses come online. As of February 1993, observers estimated the total Internet population at about 20 million people. The future of the Internet lies in three key areas: *commercialization*, *privatization* and *bandwidth*.

Commercialization

Lots of large multinational corporations have been on the Internet for years, although their access has been limited to research and engineering departments.

Corporations have recently discovered how expensive running multiple networks can be and have begun to look for ways to consolidate their separate networks. Many have discovered that the Internet is at least part of the answer to their problems. In 1992, many of the restrictions on commercial use of the Net began to change. In fact, there are already more commercial sites on the Internet than educational and research sites combined.

Privatization

Internet proponents have always wanted the various telephone companies—or other commercial organizations—to provide Internet connections. They claim you should be able to order an Internet connection just like you order call waiting or a second line for your telephone service. The telephone companies haven't jumped on this idea right away, but the recent corporate interest in the Internet has not gone unheeded, and this attitude is (slowly) changing.

But before the Internet can be fully privatized, users must find a method for funding the connections that are already in place. As soon as enough small businesses and individuals—the driving force of our economy—decide that connection to the Internet is an important asset, privatization of the Internet will occur very quickly.

One of the short-term changes likely to be brought about by commercialization and privatization is that transactions will become commonplace on the Internet. You will soon be able to order and pay for software and information via e-mail. More important, people will actually begin to make their livings in cyberspace.

Bandwidth

Bandwidth is the range of transmission frequencies a network can use. What this means is that as bandwidth increases (which it will dramatically in the next few years), you can transfer *more* information *faster*.

Increasing available bandwidth will not necessarily change the way many people currently use the Internet, but it will improve certain aspects of the way we use it:

- Electronic mail will be richer in media type and benefit from faster delivery.
- File transfers will take much less time—a mere fraction of their current rate.

- Electronic publications—telepublications—will be richer in media type and benefit from faster delivery.
- Telecommuting (working from home via phone, fax and modem) will be more enjoyable and effective.
- Remote collaboration will become easier, more rewarding and more effective.

In short, the way we use and work with information will change drastically. More than ever before, information will take on new value and urgency, while at the same time become more accessible and more readily available.

Moving On

This chapter has introduced you to the basic aspects of the Internet as well as its history and future. By now you're probably ready to get connected and see for yourself what the Internet is all about. Don't worry, we'll get there. But first, you should know how to establish an Internet account and learn a little bit about the mechanics of the Net. The next chapter explains how to establish your account on the Internet.

The road ahead is long and winding, and it's not without its pitfalls. But if you stick with the group and follow instructions, you're guaranteed to enjoy every second of the journey. Let's get started!

CHAPTER 2

GETTING CONNECTED
The Big Plug-In

Before actually starting our tour of the Internet, we'll spend this chapter covering the details of how to get connected. If you already have an Internet connection, you can probably skip all this and go straight to Chapter 3, "Network Infrastructure" where you'll learn about how the places and pathways of the Internet are constructed and connected. Getting connected to the Internet traditionally has been either exceptionally easy or almost impossible. If you're with a university, government agency or corporation that already has computers connected to the Internet—or "on the Net," as veteran netters say—your task is remarkably easy: sweet-talk the folks in your computer support department to create an account for you. It will take them less than 15 minutes, but they'll probably tell you it will take anywhere from a few hours to a few weeks. Don't argue; bite your tongue, smile pleasantly, thank them for their time and efforts, and count your blessings—you are one of the lucky few. If you're not part of an organization that's already on the Net, don't worry; it's not nearly as hard to get connected as it was just a few years ago.

Where to Sign Up

Because the Internet is not a single computer system—it's not even centrally managed—there is literally no "where" to sign up. For years it was nearly impossible to get connected to the Internet. Most people talked to a friend of a friend or found someone inside an organization who could provide them with a news and mail *feed*, sending packets of electronic mail and a limited number of newsgroups.

PGP v2.2 encryption software.
Encryption is an important way to assure privacy and authentication of e-mail messages. PGP v2.2 uses the non-NSA approved IDEA cipher patented in Switzerland.
You can download the current version of PGP by FTP at soda.berkeley.edu in the /pub/ directory.

In those days, when "real people" could only wheedle their way onto the Internet, there was always a feeling of dealing with an "information black market." People passed around secret tips and covert instructions for bluffing your way into getting an account on the sly. Invariably, these instructions were to approach a sympathetic librarian in the musty basement of the local university computer center and imply that you were either a student or on the faculty. (The feeling was always one of begging for an audience with a scribe in the Holy Roman catacomb.) If luck was with you, your account would be activated later that day, and you were off to explore the nether regions of the Net, hoping nothing would go wrong and you wouldn't be found out.

These days, it's much easier. The following four sections provide general instructions about who to befriend and what arcane terms to utter so you'll sound like a seasoned expert. You'll be able to obtain your very own Internet connection, regardless of what type of user you are—academic, government, business or individual.

University Users

If you're a university user—faculty, staff or student—you're in luck. Chances are, your college or university is already directly connected to the Internet. Contact anyone in the computing center and ask them for—or perhaps tell them you *must have*—access to the Net. After you've been shuttled to the right person, he or she will probably ask you a series of questions like the ones shown in Table 2-1. Note that these questions are general in nature and the responses are merely examples, so your mileage will surely vary depending on your situation. But since half the game of getting the kind of Internet connection you want is just knowing what to ask for, the table shows you how to ask for the most and best of everything. If you sound like you know what you're talking about, most people will assume that you do. Don't worry about what it means; that's all explained later.

Table 2-1: University users Internet information.

They'll Ask:	Your Response:
Do you want a full or partial connection?	I need a connection to both my department's local area network, the campus wide area network and the Internet.
What kind of computer do you have?	I have a 486-based PC with 8mb of RAM running DOS 6.2 and Windows 3.1.
Do you want a dedicated, SLIP/PPP, UUCP or dial-in connection.	Preferably both a dedicated and a SLIP/PPP connection. I have a second PC in my home office, and I'd like to have a PPP or SLIP connection to the network.
Do you have an Ethernet card for your dedicated connection?	No, please install and configure one.
What speed modem do you need for your home office connection?	I need a V.32bis/V.42/V.42bis modem and the appropriate software to make the network connection.
Do you want a PPP or a SLIP connection?	I'd prefer a PPP connection.
What do you want for your username?	I'd like my username to be jsmith, which is my first initial and last name with no punctuation.

After all that, the odds are in your favor that you'll get at least some of what you asked for; and at this point you'll probably be scheduled to have your office computer network connection upgraded. Your account should be activated in a day or two. You will probably be given a packet of software, an instruction manual, and the name, telephone number, and e-mail address of your network administrator (often known as a "net ghod"). Most important, you'll probably get the telephone number of the campus help desk for any problems you have while using your Internet connection. That's it—you're now an Internet citizen.

Today's baseball schedule.

You can get today's schedule for any major league baseball team by TELNET to culine.colorado.edu port 862. Press the Enter key for today's schedules. You'll be prompted to enter a team. Here are sample schedules for the Minnesota Twins and the Chicago Cubs:

MLB schedule for Minnesota on Wednesday, 5/12 . . .
Minnesota at California
MLB schedule for Cubs on Wednesday, 5/12 . . .
Los Angeles at Cubs

Government Users

If you work for a government agency, it's likely your agency is already connected to the Internet. Begin by asking your supervisor (or the appropriate computer techie) if your office has an Internet connection. He or she may not know, but will probably be able to point you toward someone who can help. The person responsible for maintaining Internet accounts within your agency may or may not be affiliated with your local office.

In any case, finding the right person to help set up your connection is probably the hardest part. The questions—and your responses—will likely be very similar to the ones shown in Table 2-1. It's not likely that you'll be able to request a dial-in connection—government agencies are fairly stingy with that type of connection, which is usually reserved for work-at-home types or people who travel extensively. But who knows, maybe you'll get lucky.

You'll probably have duplicate requisition forms to fill out, you may have to demonstrate that you have a direct need for an Internet account (a little creativity goes a long way here), and it will probably take you several attempts to fill out all the forms properly.

When your forms are correct and complete and your access has been authorized, someone will come and wire your computer for the network connection. This person will install a network card if necessary and provide you with software and an instruction manual. Here's an important tip: try to get the installer to test the connection for you. The installation person will also give you the name, telephone number and e-mail address of your local network administrator. You probably won't be provided with a help desk telephone number (but you can always call the nearest university help desk and try to sound professorial). You'll also be instructed where to report network problems. Once that's done, you're all set.

Business Users

Many large businesses—especially those involved with the computer industry—are old-timers when it comes to the Internet. Here you may find one person (or even a whole department) in charge of maintaining Internet connections. These are the people you want to seek out: ask your supervisor or refer to your corporate employee manual or interoffice directory. If you've been using a local area network within your department, ask the person who comes to fix your computer when it breaks or when the network goes down. (Odds are, they'll be so happy to hear from someone who isn't reporting a problem, they'll be happy to hook you up to the Net.) The procedure for acquiring an Internet connection within most businesses usually falls somewhere between the looseness of a university connection and the structure of a government connection. You may be able to get a dial-in connection, depending on your organization and its corporate culture. But as a starting point, you should be able to use the responses from Table 2-1.

If the company you work for isn't on the Internet, you may have to look into opening an individual account on your own, and seek reimbursement from the company (for more information on this approach, see "Individual Users" beginning on page 18). Alternatively, you may be able to generate enough interest within your workgroup or department to have management look into connecting existing local and wide area networks to the Internet.

Flame wars, affirmative action and babies (oh my!).

People love to carry out heated debates via the electronic messages they can post throughout the Internet. Here's a great "net.story" from Mikki Barry:

"In 1991, a huge flame war (a heated debate carried out via electronic messages) erupted over affirmative action in the soc.women newsgroup. The flames were exchanged for many months, tensions getting higher and higher. Not being one to let anyone else have the 'last word,' I helped fuel this war with my obviously eloquent articles, made increasingly virile through the evil hormones prevalent through late pregnancy. However, nobody on the net knew I was pregnant, since I was at work until the day I went into labor.

"Just as the flame war reached it's peak, however, I had the strange feeling that I wasn't going to be able to participate for awhile. So I posted a message saying, in effect, 'Sorry, I can't respond to this thread anymore. I have to go have a baby now.' Morgan Elizabeth Baumann was born later that night."

The procedure for establishing an Internet account varies widely from business to business. Some firms create an account for all new employees, while others offer accounts only to "critical" employees. In most medium and large businesses, there will be a help desk (or at least an MIS specialist) available if you have any questions or problems with your Internet account.

Individual Users

Unlike universities and large companies, individuals and small business users rarely need a full-time connection and are well served with only a dial-in connection. With a *dial-in* connection, you use your PC and a modem to dial another computer or server where your Internet account is stationed. This is less convenient (but usually cheaper) than a standard connection, where your computer is always connected directly to the Internet. For more information on the advantages and disadvantages of a dial-in connection, see "Types of Connections" beginning on page 19.

Individuals and small businesses typically have the hardest time establishing an Internet account. Until recently, the Internet has been geared for users within large organizations communicating only with users inside other large organizations. Thankfully, this is changing rapidly, and now it's fairly common to find individuals and small businesses with full Internet access.

The main difference in individuals and small businesses using the Internet is that *you (or your business) have to foot the complete bill for your account*. Needless to say, this affects the kind of connection and level of service you select. But Internet access is not nearly as expensive as it used to be and is now usually well within the means of most small businesses.

Take a quick look at the next two sections, "Types of Connections" and "Resource Requirements," before you jump in and order the most extensive Internet connection offered by your service provider. You run the risk of buying a fully loaded Cadillac with power windows, sunroof and Corinthian leather interior when a more sensible Saturn or even a VW microbus will do.

Types of Connections

This book assumes that your Internet connection is a "full" connection—one that includes electronic mail, TELNET, FTP, network news, and all the other network niceties. "Partial" connections with only some of the features of a full connection are also available from some institutions and service providers, but they are not powerful enough to be of much use to the dedicated Internet cybernaut. With that understanding, there are only two types of individual or small business connections you need concern yourself with: a dedicated connection and a SLIP (Serial Line Internet Protocol) or PPP (Point-to-Point Protocol) connection.

Dedicated Connection

If you have a dedicated Internet connection, your computer—or the local area network to which your PC is connected—is directly connected to the Internet. These connections are most common for users within universities, government agencies and large corporations; they're usually too expensive for individuals and small businesses.

Dedicated connections offer three distinct advantages over SLIP or PPP connections:

- You can set up an FTP server, allowing anyone else on the Internet to access your files when it is most convenient for them (be careful, this can also be seen as a disadvantage in some organizations).

- You don't have to connect to the network each time you want to use it—you're always connected—whenever you go, there you are.
- Your file transfers (and any other work you do on the Internet) will be accomplished much faster.

When you contract for a dedicated Internet connection, your service provider will lease a dedicated telephone line at the speed you specify and will install a *router* at your site. The faster the telephone line you specify, the more you'll pay.

The only disadvantage to a dedicated connection is that it's expensive; but like most everything else, you get what you pay for. If you need convenient, constant access or lightning-fast file transfer and data throughput, you won't be happy with anything less than a dedicated connection. But that performance comes at a great cost. As of winter 1993, a dedicated Internet connection would cost most small businesses between $15,000 and $20,000 for the first year and about $5,000 to $10,000 each subsequent year. Organizations with more than 50 employees pay fees tied more directly to their usage rates, but the average per-employee cost is as much or more than for small businesses.

SLIP & PPP Connection

Luckily, access to the Internet needn't cost several thousands of dollars. Using a modem, you can get most of the benefits of a dedicated connection at only a fraction of the cost. SLIP and PPP allow you to establish an Internet connection over standard telephone lines via high-speed modems. If you have a SLIP or PPP Internet connection, your PC is also directly connected to the Internet—*but only while the SLIP or PPP link is active.*

Although SLIP is currently the more common protocol, PPP will probably surpass SLIP in the near future. PPP offers more features and better throughput during interactive sessions where small bits of information are passed in both directions. Additionally, PPP is a recognized Internet standard for transferring IP information over serial lines (SLIP isn't). If you're given a choice, you're better off to go with a PPP connection—it's the up-and-coming standard.

SCap v1.3.
Allty Systems Inc.'s SCap is a $10 shareware screen capture utility for Windows 3.1. The program lets you capture the entire screen, a selected area, the active window or the client area of a window (the active window without the border, menu bar or title). You can download it by FTP from ftp.cica.indiana.edu in the /pub/pc/win3/desktop/ directory. The filename is SCAP13.ZIP.

All the software you need to establish a SLIP connection to the Internet is provided on *The Windows Internet Tour Guide Companion Disk.*

- **Important Note:** The software provided on the disk that comes with this book provides complete Internet connectivity for SLIP users. *If you enjoy a direct connection to the Internet, you must contact your network administrator or service provider for appropriate network connectivity software. Connectivity software for direct Internet connections is not included on the disk that comes with this book.*

SLIP or PPP connections lack many of the features of a dedicated connection:

- Because you're using a modem rather than a direct network connection, getting files from here to there (and back again) take significantly longer over a SLIP or PPP connection than with a dedicated connection.
- You cannot offer a reliable, constant FTP archive, so other users can't directly access your files at any time.
- Your connection to the Internet is active only while the modem connection is active; when you hang up the modem, you are no longer on the Internet.
- The connection isn't fast enough to support more than two or three users.
- You have to pay for at least one high-speed modem.

The biggest advantages to a SLIP or PPP connection is that you pay much lower connection costs. And unlike a less powerful dial-in connection, you are actually on the Internet while the connection is active. With the exception of offering a full-time FTP archive (something most individuals and small businesses would have limited use for anyway), you can do anything on the Internet with a SLIP or PPP connection that you can do with a dedicated connection at a literal fraction of the cost.

As of winter 1993, an individual commercial user can get SLIP or PPP access for a one-time startup fee of about $150 and monthly charges of about $65 for 80 hours of service. If you use more than 80 hours of connect time per month, you can expect to pay about $2 per hour for each additional hour. Shop around, though, access fees in general are falling. SLIP or PPP access is usually the best alternative for individuals, and is the method I use to connect myself and my very small business to the Internet.

Other Types of Connections

You can dial in to gain access to the Internet if you have an account on a computer that has a dedicated connection to the Internet (a university mainframe, for instance). Dial-in access to another computer is not as useful, powerful or easy to use as a SLIP or PPP connection, but it's much easier (and usually cheaper—sometimes free) to set up. Unfortunately for PC users, dial-in access methods most often require you to use the archaic UNIX commands to traverse the Internet. And your dial-in connection may limit what Internet services you can use.

UUCP (UNIX-to-UNIX Copy Protocol) can also be considered as an alternative type of connection. Every UNIX system supports UUCP as a method of moving information across standard telephone lines. You can usually find a service provider or an existing UUCP site that will allow you to use UUCP to transfer Internet mail and network news to your PC—via a modem—but you won't really be "connected" to the Internet.

While this *Tour Guide* is geared for users with dedicated or SLIP/PPP connections, if you only have limited dial-in access, you'll still find much of the information on electronic mail, network news and other Internet resources highly useful.

Service Providers

The following table shows contact information for some of the major service providers in the United States.

Table 2-2: Internet service providers in the United States.

Service Provider	Region	Connections Offered
Advanced Networks and Services (ANS) 1875 Campus Commons Drive Reston, VA 22091 800/456-8267 info@ans.net	World	High-speed dedicated connections
BARRNET Pine Hall, Room 115 Stanford, CA 94305 415/723-3104 gd.why@forsythe.stanford.edu	San Francisco, Calif.	Dedicated connections; SLIP/PPP
CERFnet P.O. Box 85608 San Diego, CA 92186 800/876-2373 or 619/455-3900 help@cerf.net	Southern Calif.	Low- and medium-speed dedicated connections; SLIP/PPP
CICNET 2901 Hubbard Drive ITI Building, Pod A Ann Arbor, MI 48105 313/998-6103 info@cic.net	Midwest	Medium- and high-speed dedicated connections
Colorado Supernet Colorado School of Mines 1500 Illinois Street Golden, CO 80401 800/748-0800 info@csn.org	National	Low- and medium-speed dedicated connections; SLIP/PPP
CONCERT P.O. Box 12889 3021 Cornwallis Road Research Triangle Park, NC 27709 919/248-1999 jrr@concert.net	North Carolina	Medium-speed dedicated connections; SLIP/PPP
Express Access Digital Express Group 6006 Greenbelt Road, Suite 228 Greenbelt, MD 20770 301/220-2020 info@access.digex.net	Mid-Atlantic, California, Pennsylvania, Minnesota, Georgia, Illinois	Low- to high-speed dedicated connections; SLIP/PPP

Service Provider	Region	Connections Offered
JVNCnet Global Enterprise Services 3 Independence Way Princeton, NJ 08540 609/897-7300 market@jvnc.net	National	Low- and medium-speed dedicated connections; SLIP
Merit 2200 Bonisteel Boulevard Ann Arbor, MI 48109 313/764-9430 jogden@merit.edu	Michigan	Low- and high-speed dedicated connections; SLIP/PPP
MIDnet 29 WSEC University of Nebraska Lincoln, NE 68588 402/472-8971 dmf@westie.unl.edu	Lower Midwest	Low- and medium-speed dedicated connections
Minnesota Regional Network (MRNet) 511 11th Avenue South, Box 212 Minneapolis, MN 55415 612/342-2570 info@mr.net	Minnesota	Low- and medium-speed dedicated connections; SLIP
MSEN 628 Brooks Street Ann Arbor, MI 48103 313/998-4562 info@msen.com	Michigan	Low- and medium-speed dedicated connections; SLIP/PPP
BBN Systems and Technologies (NEARnet) 10 Moulton Street Cambridge, MA 02138 617/873-8730 nearnet-join@nic.near.net	New England	Low- to high-speed dedicated connections; SLIP/PPP
NETCOM On-Line Communication Services 4000 Moorpark Avenue Suite 209 San Jose, CA 95117 408/554-8649 info@netcom.com	National	Low- and medium-speed dedicated connections; SLIP/PPP

Service Provider	Region	Connections Offered
netIllinois Bradley University 1501 West Bradley Avenue Peoria, IL 61625 309/677-3100 joel@bradley.edu	Illinois	Low- and medium-speed dedicated connections
NorthWestNet 15400 SE 30th Place Bellevue, WA 98007 206/562-3000 info@nwnet.net	Pacific Northwest/ Northern Plains/ Alaska	Low- and medium-speed dedicated connections
NYSERNet 200 Elwood Davis Road Suite 103 Liverpool, NY 13088-6147 luckett@nysernet.org	New York State; National	Low- and medium-speed dedicated connections; SLIP/PPP
OARnet 1224 Kinnear Road Columbus, OH 43212 614/292-9248 alison@oar.net	Ohio	Low- and medium-speed dedicated connections; SLIP/PPP
Performance Systems International (PSI) 11800 Sunrise Valley Drive, Suite 1100 Reston, VA 22019 703/620-6651 info@psi.com	World	Low- and medium-speed dedicated connections; SLIP/PPP
PREPnet 305 South Craig, 2nd Floor Pittsburgh, PA 15213 412/268-7870 twb+@andrew.cmu.edu	Pennsylvania	Low- and medium-speed dedicated connections; SLIP/PPP
PSCnet 4400 Fifth Avenue Pittsburgh, PA 15213 412/268-4960 hastings@psc.edu	National	Low- to high-speed dedicated connections

Service Provider	Region	Connections Offered
Sprint International 13221 Woodland Park Road Herndon, VA 22071 703/904-2156 mkiser@icm1.icp.net	World	Low- and medium-speed dedicated connections
SURAnet 8400 Baltimore Boulevard, Suite 101 College Park, MD 20740 301/982-4600 info@sura.net	Southeast	Medium- and high-speed dedicated connections
THEnet Texas Higher Education NIC c/o UT System-Office of Telecommunication Services Service Building 319 Austin, TX 78712 512/471-2400 info@nic.the.net	Texas	Low- and medium-speed dedicated connections; SLIP
UUNET 3110 Fairview Park Drive, Suite 570 Falls Church, VA 22042 703/204-8000 info@uunet.uu.net	World	Low- and medium-speed dedicated connections; SLIP/PPP
VERnet Academic Computing Center, Gilmer Hall University of Virginia Charlottesville, VA 22903 804/924-0616 jaj@virginia.edu	Virginia	Low- and medium-speed dedicated connections
VNET Internet Access, Inc. 229 E. 8th Street Charlotte, NC 28202 704/374-0779 info@char.vnet.net	North Carolina	Low- and medium-speed connections; SLIP/PPP
Westnet 601 South Howes, 6th Floor South Fort Collins, CO 80523 303/491-7260 pburns@yuma.acns.colostate.edu	West	Low- and medium-speed dedicated connections; SLIP/PPP

Service Provider	Region	Connections Offered
WiscNet 1210 West Dayton Street Madison, WI 53706 608/262-8874 dorl@macc.wisc.edu	Wisconsin	Low- and medium-speed dedicated connections; SLIP/PPP

Resource Requirements

Hang on, you're almost there! Now that you know about the different types of available connections, and assuming you have an appropriate network connection, and your account has been activated, let's explore exactly what hardware and software resources are required to connect to the Internet.

Library of Congress Information System (LOCIS).

It's a great spectator sport to watch Congress in action, and you can do it if you have an IBM 3270-compatible terminal emulator. Telnet to locis.loc.gov and browse through the legislation that has been introduced.

Sometimes it's rather alarming:

OFFICIAL TITLE(S):
AS INTRODUCED: (DATA FURNISHED BY THE HOUSE)

A concurrent resolution stating that Congress supports the suspension, with respect to the leadership of Iraq, of the prohibition of Executive Order 12333 on assassinations until Iraq has complied fully with all United Nations Security Council resolutions concerning the withdrawal of Iraqi military forces from Kuwait.

COMMITTEE(S) OF REFERRAL: House Foreign Affairs
SUBCOMMITTEE(S) OF REFERRAL:
Hsc International Security and Scientific Affairs
Hsc Europe and the Middle East

COSPONSORS: Rep. Holloway, Rep. Solomon, Rep. Paxon, Rep. Inhofe, Rep. Santorum, Rep. Barton, Rep. Rohrabacher, Rep. Spence, Rep. Ravenel

IBM PC or Compatible

You'll need a PC of course. Almost any PC will do, so long as it has an 80386 or faster processor, a hard disk drive and at least 4mb of RAM. As in all things related to computers, you can never have too much hard drive space or memory. You'll also need to have DOS 5.0 or later and Windows 3.1 or later installed and properly configured.

Network Interface Card or Modem

You'll also need a way of connecting to the Internet: either a high-speed modem or a network interface card. If you're with a large organization, someone will probably install and configure your network card hardware for you. If you're on your own, simply refer to the instructions that came with the card.

If you plan to access the Internet by SLIP or PPP, use at least a V.32 (9600 baud) modem, although I'd highly recommend a V.32bis/V.42bis (14,400 baud) modem, assuming your service provider supports the higher speed (and most do).

Buying a modem is simple in theory but difficult in practice: purchase the modem supporting the fastest *standard* modulation protocol and the best error correction and data compression you can afford.

SLIP or PPP

If you're connecting to the Internet with either SLIP or PPP, you'll need the appropriate LAP (Link Access Protocol) driver. In most cases, your service provider or network administrator will configure and install this software for you.

All the software you need to establish a SLIP or PPP connection to the Internet is provided on *The Windows Internet Tour Guide Companion Disk.*

- **Important Note:** The software provided on the disk that comes with this book provides complete Internet connectivity for SLIP and PPP users. *If you enjoy a direct connection to the Internet, you must contact your network administrator or service provider for appropriate network connectivity software. Connectivity software for direct Internet connections is not included on the disk that comes with this book.*

  If you have a dedicated Internet connection you do not need either of these drivers; you can skip the rest of this section and continue with "TCP/IP" (located below).

Several commercial PPP drivers are available from Windows TCP/IP connectivity vendors. In addition, several freeware and shareware alternatives are available. The best source for freeware and shareware PPP drivers is the anonymous FTP archive at merit.edu (look in the /pub/ppp/pc/ directory). For information on using FTP, see "Downloading Files With Chameleon FTP" beginning on page 199.

TCP/IP

If you enjoy a direct connection to the Internet, you'll also need to acquire, install and properly configure TCP/IP, the software that allows your PC to communicate with other computers on the Net. If you're dying to know the technicalities of it all, this software enables your PC to use Transmission Control Protocol/Internet Protocol (TCP/IP) to communicate with available devices on the Internet.

If you're using the Chameleon Sampler software (provided on *The Windows Internet Tour Guide Companion Disk*) to connect to the Internet via a SLIP or PPP connection, all the required translation capabilities are built into the driver software. There is no need to install or configure TCP/IP software for use with a SLIP or PPP connection on a PC. TCP/IP capabilities for SLIP and PPP connections are built into the software that comes with this book.

Alice in Wonderland.
The complete text of *Alice in Wonderland* has been made available by Project Gutenberg. Project Gutenberg was formed to encourage the creation and distribution of electronic text.

You can download the complete text of this and other works by FTP at mrcnext.cso.uiuc.edu in the /etext/ directory.

Client Application Software

Unless you're part of a large organization, getting a network connection and an account on the Internet is only half the battle. You'll also need some client application software (software that lets you navigate and take advantage of the Internet). This can be something of a chicken-and-the-egg situation since no such software is built into Windows or provided with your PC when you buy it. If you need a special program to transfer other software programs to your PC (*and you do*), how do you download a program that you need the program to download?

The Windows Internet Tour Guide Companion Disk is the best place to start. This disk is packed with powerful programs and utilities for both *establishing* and *using* your Internet connection. The basic software needed for e-mail, file transfers and remote login is provided on the disk that comes with this book. In the next two sections, I'll discuss how to install and configure the Chameleon Sampler software. Chameleon is an integrated suite of programs that provides an easy-to-use graphical interface for navigating some of the major Internet services: e-mail, file transfer and TELNET.

But this is just the beginning. Once you've installed and configured the companion software, I'll cover in step-by-step detail how to use all the powerful features of the companion software. Best of all, this *Tour Guide* also covers the high points of finding and using tons of other hot software available on the Internet.

Installing Chameleon Sampler

Installing NetManage's Chameleon Sampler software package is straightforward and very simple. The Chameleon software allows you to route Internet information over a standard telephone line with a modem and provides all the basic client services you need to access the Internet in a suite of programs. The Chamelon Sampler is licensed from NetManage, Inc. for educational and testing purposes only. It is not shareware, but is licensed to purchasers of this book.

Note that the Chameleon Sampler provided on the companion disk is a subset of a prior version of the full Chameleon software package and is fully functional, but limited to support for SLIP and PPP connections only. If you enjoy a direct connection to the Internet, you'll need to obtain the appropriate software from your network administrator or service provider to establish your connection to the Internet and navigate the available services on the Net. *Connectivity software for direct Internet connections is not included on the companion disk.*

For information on ordering the full Chameleon software package from NetManage, at a significant discount, see the NetManage contact information in the back of this book. The full version of the software has over two dozen applications including both LAN and dial-up TCP/IP support, MIME support of multimedia email attachments, modem speeds of up to 115.2, a Gopher Client, NewsReader, FTP Server, WhoIs, Finger, LPR/LPD, optional NFS client and Server, and more.

NetManage's Chameleon Sampler software allows you to establish a high-speed SLIP connection to the Internet over the phone lines using only your PC and a modem. The Chameleon Sampler, like the full Chameleon software package, is a native Windows implementation (a 100% DLL if you're wondering) of the TCP/IP protocols and is fully compliant with the WinSock standard. This means that you can run software from other vendors (including freeware and shareware products) that supports the WinSock standard.

Configuration files for five popular Internet service providers—ANS CO+RE, AlterNet, CERFNet, NetCom and PSINet—are also included on *The Windows Internet Tour Guide Companion Disk.* For information about establishing an Internet account, talk to your network administrator or one of the Internet service providers in your geographic area.

I know you're anxious to install the Chameleon software and jack-in to the Net. But before you install the software, you'll need to ask your service provider or network administrator for some address and configuration information. It looks a lot more complicated than it is, and rest assured that—at least for now—you don't need to know what any of this stuff means. You just have to plug the information into the right slots. Think of it as a secret code; a rite of passage into the realms of cyberspace.

An example of the secret decoder ring information you must have is provided in Table 2-3.

Table 2-3: Example Configuration information for Chameleon.

Configuration Information	Example
Your IP Address	134.84.101.1
IP Mask	255.255.0.0
Gateway IP Address	134.84.101.254
Domain Name Server(s)	137.192.2.5
Your Host Name	moriarity
Your Domain Name	farces.com
Port	COM1, 9600
Modem	Hayes
Access Telephone Number	1-612-555-1212
Login Name	mfraase
Password	***************
Startup Command	SLIP
Mailbox Name	mfraase
Mailbox Password	*****************
Mail Server/Gateway Name	mr.net

Important note: The information provided in the table is valid for my Internet connection. Everyone's information will be different and this information is provided only as an example. It is absolutely imperative that you use valid IP addressing information. You can cause all sorts of Net problems if you use bogus IP addressing information. Trust me; the surest way to bring the wrath of your network administrator or service provider about your ears is to use invalid IP addressing information. Don't do it.

OK, we're almost ready. Before installing the Chameleon Sampler software, it's a good idea to make backup copies of your system files. The Chameleon Sampler installation process modifies the AUTOEXEC.BAT and WIN.INI files. See the manuals that came with your computer for information about backing up these files.

To install the Chameleon Sampler software:

1. Start Windows. The Windows Program Manager appears.
2. Insert *The Windows Internet Tour Guide Companion Disk* in your floppy drive. This book assumes that your floppy drive is the A: drive and that your hard drive is the C: drive.
3. From the File menu, select the Run command. The Command Line dialog box is displayed, as shown in Figure 2-1.

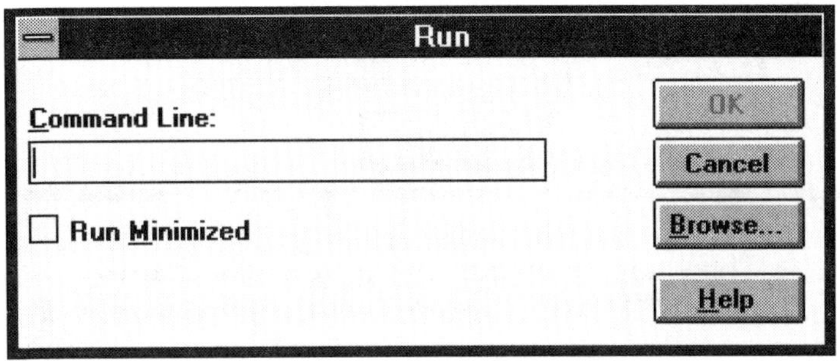

Figure 2-1: Windows 3.1 Command Line dialog box.

4. In the Command Line dialog box, enter **a:\setup** and press **Enter**. The Chameleon setup program will run, and a Setup dialog box instructing you to consult the manuals that came with any network software or hardware you may be running appears, as shown in Figure 2-2.

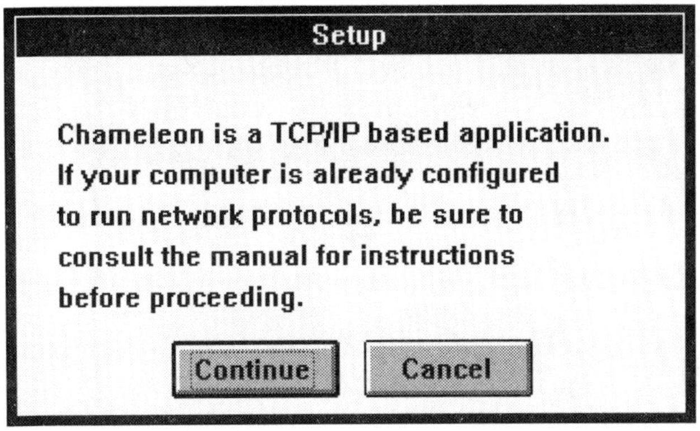

Figure 2-2: Chameleon Setup dialog box.

5. Click the **Continue** button. A progress dialog box appears, providing feedback on the status of the installation process, as shown in Figure 2-3.

Figure 2-3: Chameleon Sampler Setup progress dialog box.

- The Chameleon Sample suite of programs are copied to the C:\NETMANAG directory, the necessary modifications are made to your system files and a new program group and set of icons are created.
- The Chameleon Sampler Setup progress dialog box will notify you when the installation process is complete and an **OK** button appears in the dialog box.

6. When the Chameleon Sampler Setup progress dialog box indicates that the installation process is complete, click the **OK** button.
7. Reboot your computer. The Chameleon Sampler program group will be available, as shown in Figure 2-4.

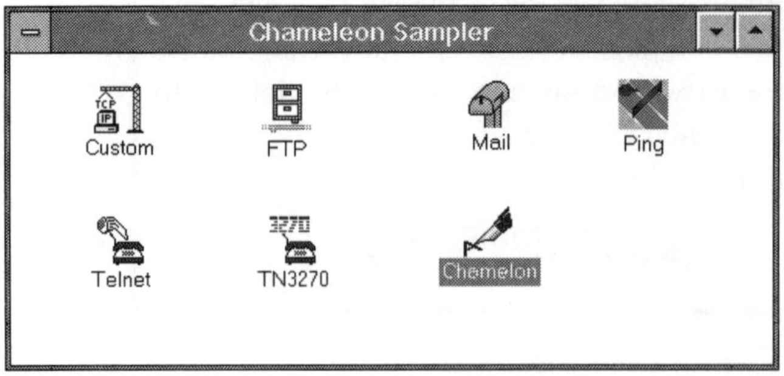

Figure 2-4: Chameleon Sampler program group.

Congratulations. You've successfully installed the Chameleon Sampler software. Before you can use it to establish a connection to the Internet, though, you've got to configure it.

Configuring Chameleon Sampler

NetManage's Chameleon Sampler software is a powerful suite of tools for exploiting the full potential of the Internet. Using Chameleon, you can send and read electronic mail, download and upload files and perform a host of other crucial Net tasks. Chameleon uses a custom TCP/IP communications stack called NEWT (included on *The Windows Internet Tour Guide Companion Disk*) to communicate with other computers on the Internet.

If you enjoy a direct connection to the Internet, skip the remainder of this section and follow the instructions that came with your network software to properly configure your Internet access.

There are three separate procedures to completely configure Chameleon for use with the Internet, and this section provides step-by-step instructions for the complete process:

- First you have to tell NEWT about your computer and the kind of Internet connection you'll be using.
- Next you have to tell NEWT how to communicate with your modem and serial port.
- Finally you have to tell NEWT about the computers used by your Internet service provider.

To configure NEWT for use with your computer and a SLIP or PPP connection:

1. With Windows running and the Chameleon Sampler program group window open, double-click on the **Custom** icon, shown in Figure 2-4. The Custom window appears, as shown in Figure 2-5.

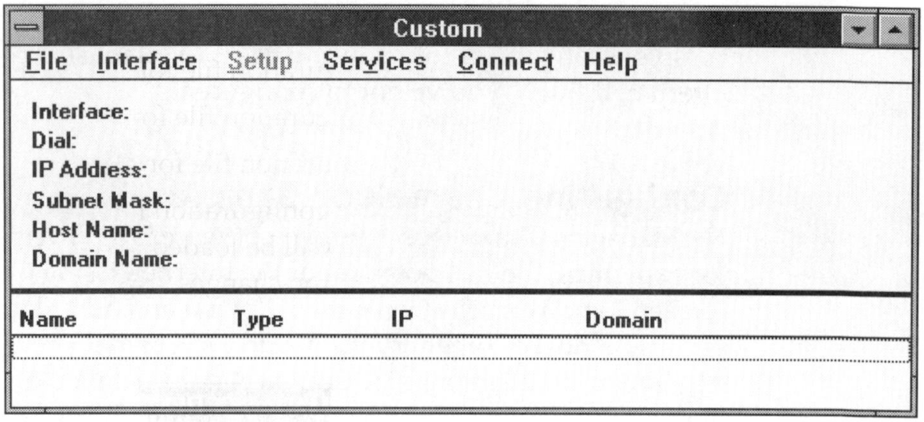

Figure 2-5: Chameleon Custom window.

- Additionally, the Chameleon NEWT icon appears in the lower left corner of your monitor, indicating that the TCP/IP communications stack has been successfully loaded.

2. From the File menu, select the Open command. A standard Open Configuration File dialog box appears, as shown in Figure 2-6.

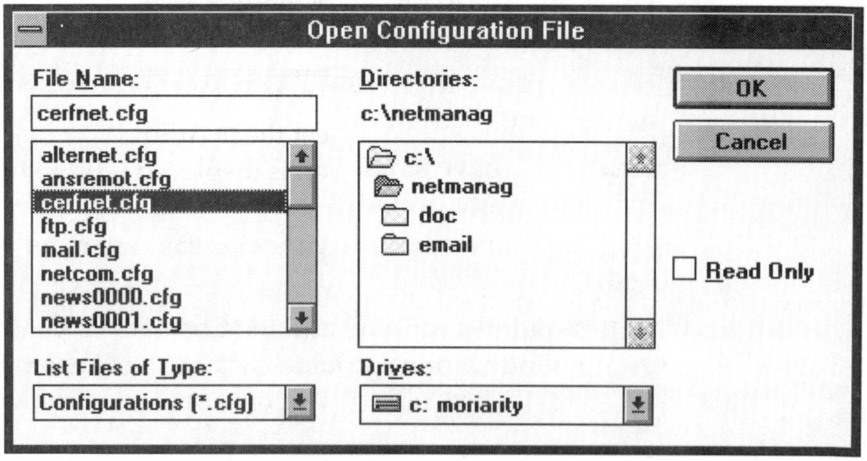

Figure 2-6: Chameleon Open Configuration File dialog box.

3. Select the Configuration file associated with your Internet service provider, if one is available. If a Configuration file for your service provider is not available, advance to step 5.
   - alternet.cfg is the Configuration file for AlterNet.
   - ansremot.cfg is the Configuration file for ANS CO+RE.

- mrnet.cfg is the Configuration file for MRNet.
- cerfnet.cfg is the Configuration file for CERFNet.
- netcom.cfg is the Configuration file for NetCom.
- psinet.cfg is the Configuration file for PSINet.

4. Click the **OK** button. The configuration information for the selected service provider will be loaded and the Custom window will be updated to reflect the changes, as shown in the CERFNet example in Figure 2-7.

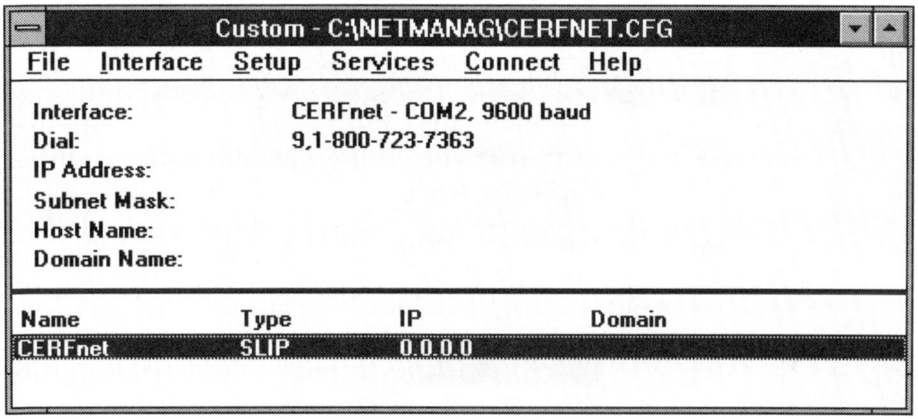

Figure 2-7: Chameleon Custom window with CERFNet configuration information.

5. From the Setup menu, select the IP Address... command. The Internet Address dialog box is displayed, as shown in Figure 2-8.

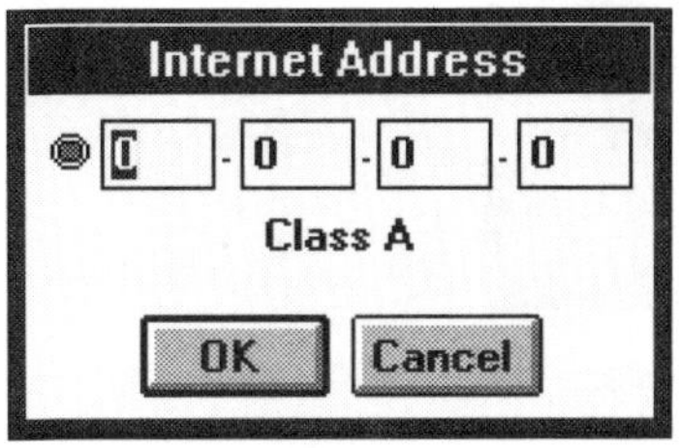

Figure 2-8: Chameleon Internet Address dialog box.

6. Enter your IP address in the Internet Address dialog box, using leading zeros if necessary. For example, my IP address is 134.84.101.1, so I would enter **134084101001** in the Internet Address dialog box.

- It is absolutely imperative that you use valid IP addressing information. You can cause all sorts of Net problems if you use bogus IP addressing information. Trust me; the surest way to bring the wrath of your network administrator or service provider about your ears is to use invalid IP addressing information. Don't do it.

7. Click the **OK** button. Your IP Address information will be added to the Custom window.
8. From the Setup menu, select the Host Name... command. The Host Name dialog box appears, as shown in Figure 2-9.

Figure 2-9: Chameleon Host Name dialog box.

9. Enter the name of your computer in the Host Name dialog box.
10. Click the **OK** button. Your host name will be added to the Custom window.
11. From the Setup menu, select the Domain Name... command. The Domain Name dialog box is displayed, as shown in Figure 2-10.

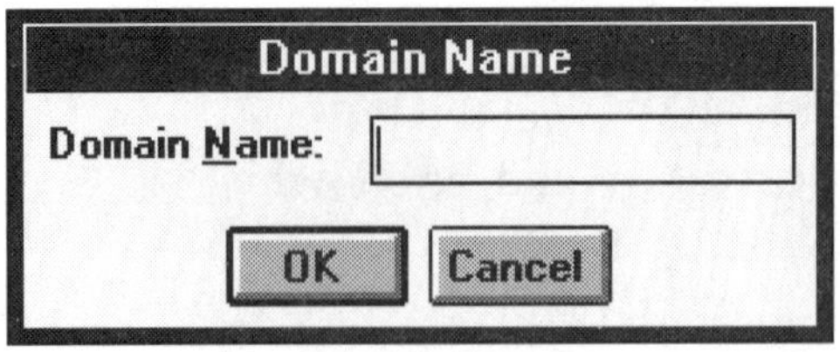

Figure 2-10: Chameleon Domain Name dialog box.

12. Enter your domain name—in the domain.top-domain format—in the Domain Name dialog box.
13. Click the **OK** button. Your domain name will be added to the Custom window.
14. From the File menu, select the Save command. Your settings will be saved to disk.

You've successfully configured the Internet connectivity portion of Chameleon that identifies your computer to the rest of the Internet. An example Custom window, fully configured for use with CERFNet, is shown in Figure 2-11.

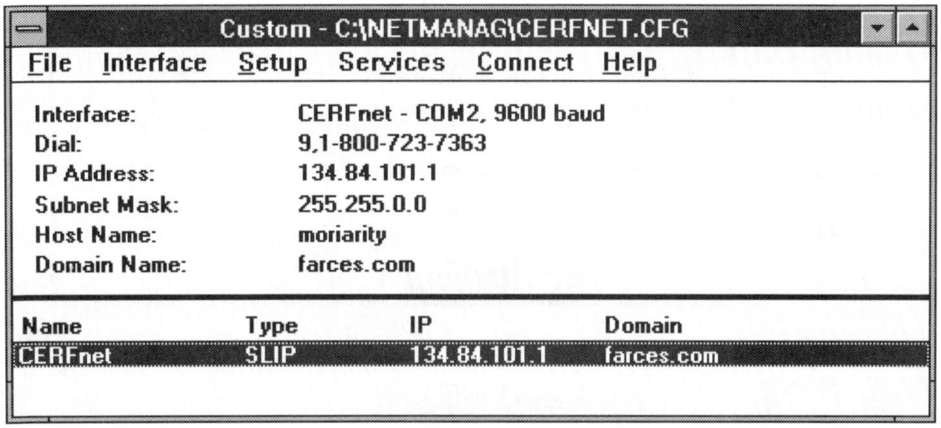

Figure 2-11: Chameleon Custom window, fully configured for use with CERFNet.

The next step is to configure Chameleon for use with your modem. Use this procedure:

1. With Windows running and the Chameleon Sampler program group window open, double-click on the **Custom** icon, shown in Figure 2-4. The Custom window appears, as shown in Figure 2-5.
   - Additionally, the Chameleon NEWT icon appears in the lower left corner of your monitor, indicating that the TCP/IP communications stack has been successfully loaded.
2. From the Setup menu, select the Port... command. The Port Settings dialog box is displayed, as shown in Figure 2-12.

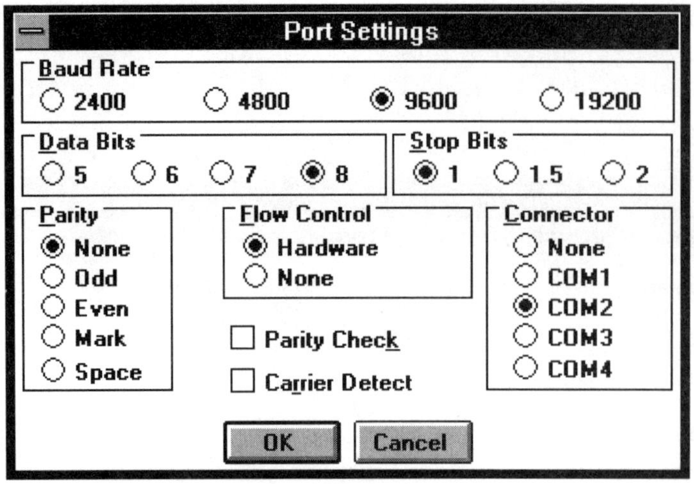

Figure 2-12: Chameleon Port Settings dialog box.

3. Configure Chameleon's port settings as appropriate for your modem and serial port.
   - Click the **Baud Rate** radio button representing the highest communications speed supported by your modem and serial port. This is not necessarily the highest connection speed, but rather the speed at which the serial port communicates with the modem.
   - Click the **8** Data Bits radio button.
   - Select the **1** Stop Bits radio button.
   - Click the **None** Parity radio button.
   - Click the appropriate **Flow Control** radio button for your modem and serial port configuration. Hardware flow control is generally the best option, especially for high-speed modems.
   - Click the **Connector** radio button representing the serial port to which your modem is connected.
4. Click the **OK** button. The port settings you specified will be added to the configuration.
5. From the Setup menu, select the Modem... command. The Modem Settings dialog box appears, as shown in Figure 2-13.

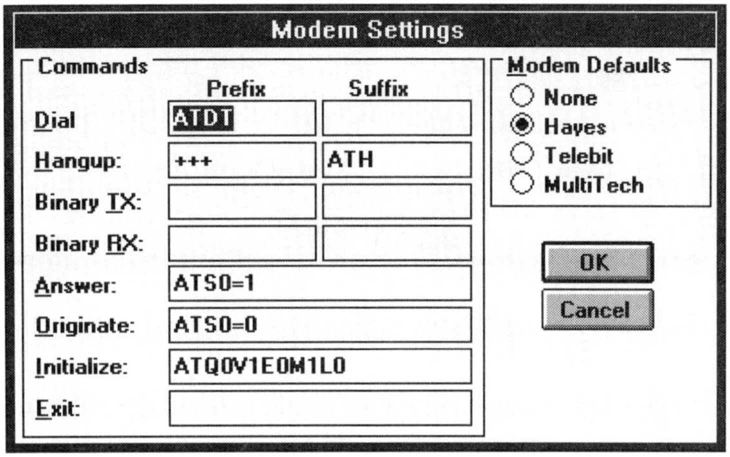

Figure 2-13: Chameleon Modem Settings dialog box.

6. Click the **Modem Defaults** radio button for your modem.
7. Enter the appropriate commands for your modem in the available fields. In most cases the default settings are your best option, although here are three exceptions that I find work best for my modem (I use a Hayes Optima 144 modem):
   - I set the Originate command to **ATS0=0S37-11N0**. This forces the connection to the highest speed supported by my modem.
   - I set the Initialize command to **ATQ0V1E0X0**. This sets the modem to return result codes as words, suppress echo characters during command state and return only the basic call progress result codes.
   - I set the Exit command to **ATZ**. This forces the modem to reset after I disconnect.
8. Click the **OK** button. The modem commands you specified will be added to the configuration.
9. From the Setup menu, select the Dial... command. The Dial Settings dialog box appears, as shown in Figure 2-14.

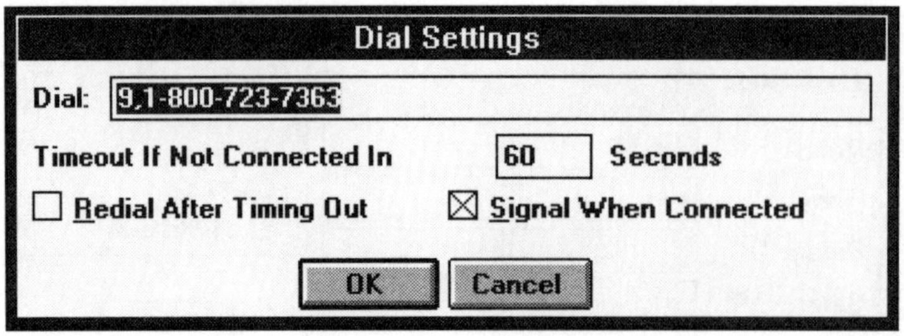

Figure 2-14: Chameleon Dial Settings dialog box.

10. Enter the telephone access number for your service provider in the Dial field.
    - The Dial Settings example shown causes the modem to dial a "9" to get an outside line, a comma (",") to pause for a second dial tone and finally the CERFNet access number.
    - Optionally, change the number of seconds to wait for a connection.
    - Optionally, check the **Redial After Timing Out** check box to automatically redial until a connection is established.
    - Optionally, check the **Signal When Connected** check box to have NEWT alert you when a connection is established.
11. Click the **OK** button. The Dial Settings you specified will be added to the configuration.
12. From the Setup menu, select the Login... command. The Login Settings dialog box appears, as shown in Figure 2-15.

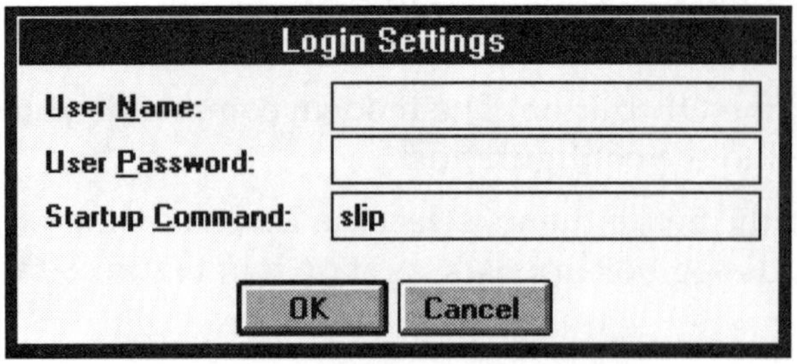

Figure 2-15: Chameleon Login Settings dialog box.

13. Enter the appropriate settings for your account and service provider in the available fields.
    - Enter your username—using the username@domain.top-domain format—in the User Name: field.

- Enter your account password in the User Password: field.
- Enter the appropriate startup command to complete the login process for your service provider in the Startup Command: field.

14. Click the **OK** button. The Login Settings you specified will be added to the configuration.
15. From the File menu, select the Save command. Your settings will be saved to disk.

You've successfully configured Chameleon's modem and serial port settings for use with the NEWT TCP/IP protocol stack.

The final step is to configure Chameleon for use with your Internet service provider's computers. Here's how:

1. With Windows running and the Chameleon Sampler program group window open, double-click on the **Custom** icon, shown in Figure 2-4. The Custom window appears, as shown in Figure 2-5.
   - Additionally, the Chameleon NEWT icon appears in the lower left corner of your monitor, indicating that the TCP/IP communications stack has been successfully loaded.
2. From the Services menu, select the Domain Servers... command. The Domain Servers dialog box appears, as shown in Figure 2-16.

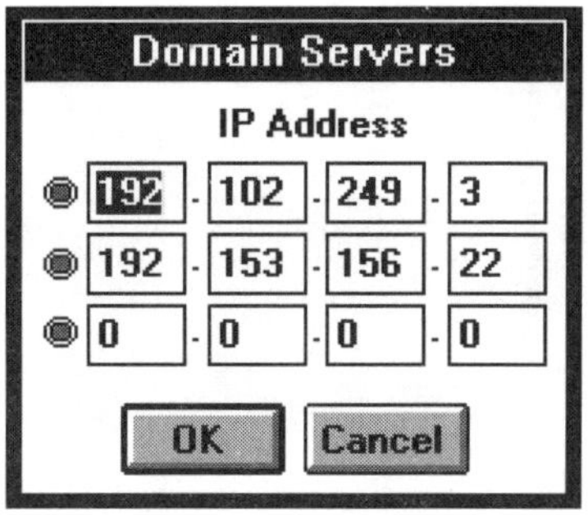

Figure 2-16: Chameleon Domain Servers dialog box.

3. Enter the IP address(es) for your service provider's domain name servers in the Domain Servers dialog box, using leading zeros if necessary. For example, my domain name servers' IP addresses are 137.192.2.5 and 137.192.240.5, so I would enter **137192002005** and **137192240005** in the Domain Servers dialog box.

4. Click the **OK** button. The IP address for the domain name servers you specified will be added to the configuration.
5. From the Services menu, select the Host Table... command. The Host Table dialog box appears, as shown in Figure 2-17.

Figure 2-17: Chameleon Host Table dialog box.

6. Enter the domain name—using the domain.top-domain format—for your mail server in the Official Name field.
7. Click the **Add** button. The Host Table IP Address dialog box for the entry is displayed, as shown in Figure 2-18.

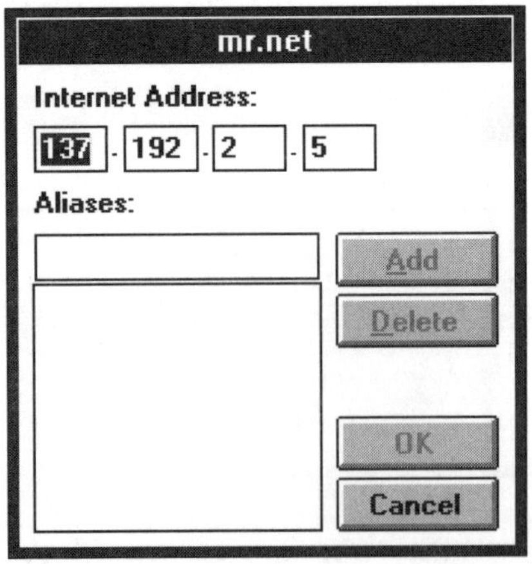

Figure 2-18: Chameleon Host Table IP Address dialog box.

8. Enter the IP address for your mail server in the Host Table IP Address dialog box, using leading zeros if necessary. For example, my mail server's IP address is 137.192.2.5, so I would enter **137192002005** in the dialog box.

9. Click the **OK** button. The IP address for the mail server you specified will be added to the configuration.
10. Repeat steps 6–9 for any additional servers you need to define. Most users will also have to define a network news server and possibly a server for directory services.
11. From the File menu, select the Save command. Your settings will be saved to disk.

Congratulations! You've successfully configured Chameleon to identify your computer to the rest of the Internet, communicate with your modem and serial port and identify the computers used by your service provider.

That's it. You've successfully configured your SLIP connection. Don't despair if you're still trying to figure out the difference between TCP, FTP and UUCP. The important thing to keep in mind is that you've laid the foundation for exploring the Internet with a set of powerful tools, which we'll cover one at a time in upcoming chapters.

Making the Leap

OK, you've got your account established, you've got your network connection or modem configured and you've got your software installed and configured. Congratulations! You're finally ready to make the leap and make your first Internet connection.

If you enjoy a dedicated Internet connection, simply launch the client software program you want to use.

If you use a PPP or SLIP Internet connection, you will have to establish a modem connection to the network before you can launch any of the client software programs you may want to use. Establish your modem connection to the Internet with these steps:

1. With Windows running and the Chameleon Sampler program group window open, double-click on the **Custom** icon, shown in Figure 2-4. The Custom window appears, as shown in Figure 2-5.
   - Additionally, the Chameleon NEWT icon appears in the lower left corner of your monitor, indicating that the TCP/IP communications stack has been successfully loaded.
2. Click the **Connect** menu item. The Connect dialog box appears, and your SLIP or PPP connection will be automatically established, as shown in Figure 2-19.

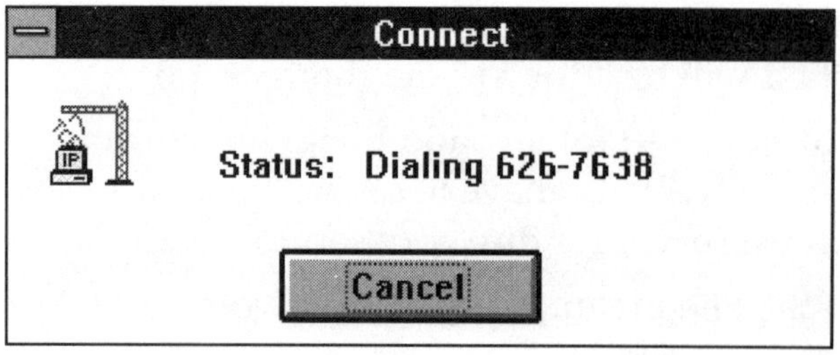

Figure 2-19: Chameleon Connect dialog box.

- Before you click on **Connect**, be sure to open the log by selecting the **Log...** command from the **Setup** menu. This opens a window that lets you monitor your progress and determine when your connection is complete.

3. Launch the client software program you want to use.
4. When you want to sever your Internet connection, click the **Disconnect** menu item. The Disconnect dialog box is displayed, as shown in Figure 2-20.

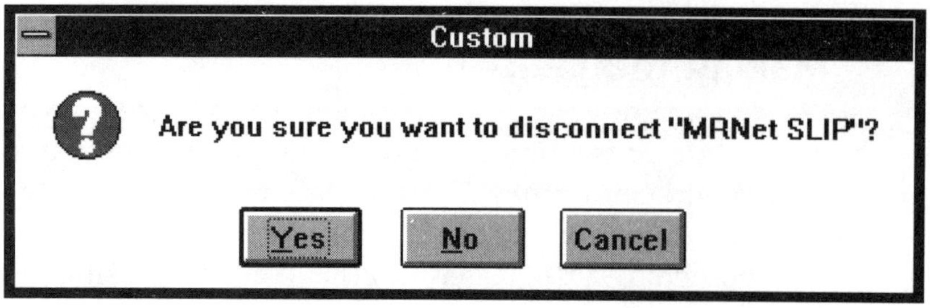

Figure 2-20: Chameleon Disconnect dialog box.

5. Click the **Yes** button. Your modem will hang up and your connection to the Internet will be dropped.

Moving On

Now you know how to get an Internet account—who to talk to and what to ask for—and a little bit about what you need to actually establish the connection.

As the bus pulls out of the station, go ahead and stretch your legs as we get up to speed; that was a long time to spend in the terminal waiting for our old bus to be gassed up and made roadworthy. But the weather ahead looks favorable—feels like we may even have a bit of a tail wind.

If you're anxious to get on the road and take a quick sidetrip on your own, feel free to skip ahead to Chapter 4, "Electronic Mail" where you'll learn how to send e-mail, search for addresses and even subscribe to mailing lists. Or, you can jump to Chapter 6, "Transferring Files" and download some software. But if you want to stay with the main group, we're heading for Chapter 3, where we'll learn what we need to know about the terrain and the natives we're likely to encounter.

CHAPTER 3

NETWORK INFRASTRUCTURE

Electronic Alphabet Soup

As the bus wends its way along the back-roads route (I hate the interstates—they all look the same—so this tour will follow the roads less traveled), now might be a good time to talk about the customs of the people you'll be meeting and the places you'll be visiting as we continue to explore the Internet.

I know you're eager to begin prowling the Internet, but reading this brief chapter before resuming our tour will pay off down the road. This chapter covers what absolute beginners need to know about how the Internet works. One of the most crucial aspects of navigating and using the Internet is understanding the complex and sometimes confusing addressing schemes used throughout the Net. It's important to know how Internet addresses work, not only for sending e-mail, but for locating and using the vast resources available throughout the Net. This chapter explores all you need to know about network addresses to find your way to any resource on the Internet.

We'll also cover what it means to be a good Internet citizen.

An Information Democracy

The Internet's strongest single organizing principle is the democratization of information. As open and untamed as the Wild West, the Internet has no formal organization.

What organization there is can be thought of as a sort of "consensual information anarchy"; a network of networks connected by everything from standard telephone lines to high-speed, dedicated, leased lines to fiber-optic links. Think of each component network as a fiefdom with its own organizational structure.

When someone talks about being "on" the Internet, their computer is connected to one of the interconnected networks that make up the Internet. Computers on the Internet talk to each other by passing notes to each other—just like we all did when we were in grade school. Only the computers on the Internet are a lot more particular about the whole process, as I'll explain shortly.

The Internet has only two practical organizing principles:

1. It serves to democratize information. Your network communications are handled in exactly the same manner, whether you are the chief executive of a Fortune 100 corporation or a junior high student.
2. Every computer on the Internet agrees to follow the same protocol—to speak a common language: TCP/IP, which is short for Transmission Control Protocol/Internet Protocol.

The CICA Indiana archive.
The CICA FTP archive is provided as a service of Indiana University's Center for Innovative Computer Applications, and has become one of the best Windows software archives on the Internet. Just about any public domain, freeware or shareware software for computers running Microsoft Windows is available here. The archive is accessible with Gopher, so use that whenever you can. Point your Gopher at cica_gopher.cica.indiana.edu port 70. Alternatively, all files are available by anonymous FTP at ftp.cica.indiana.edu. A text file containing abstracts of all available files is available in the pub/pc/win3/ directory.

The Internet Rosetta Stone

To understand how your communications on the Internet are handled, you have to know a little bit about TCP/IP, the network's common language. Rather than bore you with unnecessary details, I'll only discuss the main points of TCP/IP. You need to know a good bit about TCP/IP to *administer* an Internet connection, but not to *use* one.

As I mentioned earlier, computers on the Internet talk to each other by passing notes, just like we did in grade school. Unfortunately, the Internet's component networks—and the computers that use the Net to communicate—aren't as intelligent as grade-schoolers. Grade-school kids can decipher just about any kind of note, folded any which way. Computers on the Internet are like a picky penmanship teacher; they require the message to be in a very specific language, and the note has to be folded just so. If the Internet note doesn't comply with the TCP/IP standard, it gets tossed faster than a school love poem intercepted by a lunchroom monitor.

So, if you want to communicate on the Internet, the software you use has to pass properly worded, carefully formatted notes. You can't just shout across the lunchroom, *"Hey! Augie! Pass me those peas!"* You have to use the proper decorum. You have to quietly pass your message in a note to your neighbor closest to Augie.

Transmission Control Protocol (TCP)

The Transmission Control Protocol (TCP)—the first piece of the protocol puzzle—controls the information you want to send across the Internet and separates it into smaller pieces that are easily managed. This allows you to send virtually any type of information, from text and graphics to sounds and video, or even actual shareware and software programs. And that information can range in size from a brief e-mail message to the complete works of William Shakespeare.

As TCP separates your information into manageable chunks, it numbers each piece, so the receiving end can put the pieces back together again in the proper order. As soon as each piece of information is received at the destination, TCP verifies it. If some pieces of your information are missing or garbled, TCP requests the originator to resend the missing or garbled pieces. When TCP has assembled all the information in the correct order, it sends it to the software program using its services. But remember, all this is going on at several thousands of bits per second (bps), even if you're working over a modem, so the whole process is transparent to you.

Going back to Augie in the lunchroom, Augie would number each pea before putting them in a bowl and then pass you the bowl. You'd then take the bowl and eat each pea in numerical sequence. If you found a squished or missing pea, you'd pass a note back to Augie asking for a specific replacement pea. Hey now, I've seen stranger things in a lunchroom.

Internet Protocol (IP)

When you mail a paper message to a friend via the U.S. Postal Service, you seal your message in an envelope containing both a destination and return address. When you drop your message in the mailbox, a mail carrier transports the message to a local post office, where your message is combined with others bound for the same general destination. The messages are then loaded on trucks and planes and shipped off to their destinations. Once there, the sorting process is reversed, and your message is delivered.

Messages sent on the Internet (and everything you do on the Internet is basically a message) work in roughly the same way, thanks to the Internet Protocol (IP). The networks that make up the Internet are connected by special-purpose computers, called *routers*. These routers are the network equivalent of post offices; they determine how to route the information traffic on the Internet. Each router need only know what different connections are available and which is the best next destination to get a message closer to its final destination. The routers are physically linked by Ethernet networks and telephone lines—the network equivalents of the Postal Service's trucks and planes.

The Internet Protocol manages each message's addressing, working just like an addressed envelope for your paper mail.

Once again returning to the lunchroom metaphor—and I promise this is the last time—think of the Internet Protocol (IP) as the lunchroom monitor. The monitor makes sure the bowl of peas Augie passes down the line gets routed most efficiently among all the schoolmates between the two of you, including the class bully, until it finally reaches you.

Travel advisories.

The State Department of the United States provides foreign travel advisories by FTP from world.std.com in the /obi/US.StateDept/Travel/ directory. I've always wanted to go to Belize; let's check out the travel advisory:

Belize—Consular Information Sheet—December 15, 1992

Embassy Location: The U.S. Embassy in Belize is located at the intersection of Gabourel Lane and Hutson Street in Belize City; telephone (501-2) 77161.

Country Description: Belize is a developing country. Its tourism facilities vary in quality.

Entry Requirements: A passport, a return/onward ticket and sufficient funds are required for travel to Belize. U.S. citizens who stay less than three months do not need visas. However, for visits exceeding one month, travelers must obtain permits from the immigration authorities in Belize. For further information, the traveler can contact the Embassy of Belize at 2535 Massachusetts Avenue N.W., Washington, D.C. 20008 tel: (202) 332-9636 or the Belize Mission to the U.N. in New York.

Medical Facilities: Medical care is limited. Doctors and hospitals often expect immediate cash payment for health services.

Crime Information: Petty crime, including pickpocketing and mugging, occurs. Visitors who walk alone on city streets, especially at night, or travel alone to a remote tourist site, are particularly at risk.

Drug Penalties: Penalties for possession and trafficking in drugs are strict, and convicted offenders can expect jail sentences and fines.

Where.Is.That.Thing@On.the.Net?

While messages sent across the Internet may travel in a fashion similar to regular letters, the Internet addressing system looks nothing like a street address. Many beginners are intimidated by the complex and seemingly arcane—or apparently random—way Internet sites are named, or addressed. But a closer look at the process reveals a method to the madness, and learning that method will help you avoid plenty of confusion, panic and frustration.

Each computer on the Internet has two unique addresses:

- IP address like 134.84.101.1 (always four numbers—each less than 256—separated by periods).

- Domain name like moriarity.farces.com (always at least two words—or numbers—separated by periods).

All you really have to know is the domain name (the nonnumeric one) of any computer on the Internet you want to communicate with. The Internet addressing schemes were designed so that people only had to use the domain name address, while the computers would use the IP address.

Each person on the Internet has his or her own unique address: username@domain.top-domain. My Internet address, for example, is mfraase@farces.com. My machine name address is deeper.farces.com or moriarity.farces.com ("deeper" is the name of my Macintosh; "moriarity" is the name of my PC, both of which connect to the Net via SLIP). An example of this domain name address and its structure is shown in Figure 3-1.

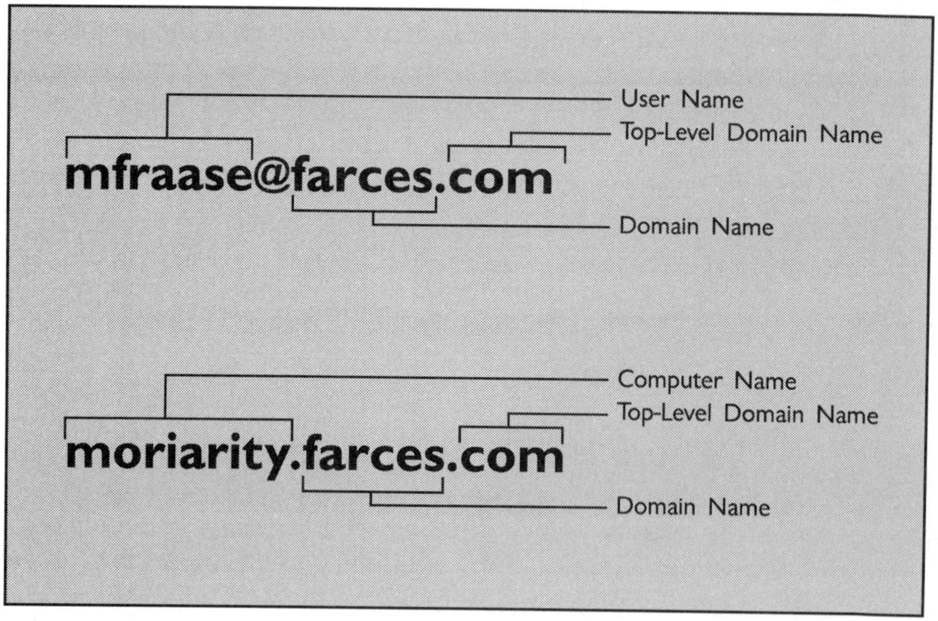

Figure 3-1: Example domain name address and structure.

'Zine scene.
Lots of electronic 'zines are available at the Electronic Frontier Foundation's Gopher server and FTP archive. *Athene, CORE, Quanta, Unplastic News* and *ScreamBaby* are all available. Point your Gopher at gopher.eff.org port 70. Alternatively, you can FTP to ftp.eff.org and browse through the /pub/journals/ directory.

Domain name addresses have special pronunciation rules:

- mfraase@farces.com is pronounced "em-frazy at farces dot com"
- moriarity.farces.com is pronounced "moriarity dot farces dot com"
- deeper.farces.com is pronounced "deeper dot farces dot com"

Usernames aren't always a first initial followed by the last name, as mine is. Sometimes they're a first and last name separated by an underscore, like Ida_Jones@idacorp.com. Others may be almost indecipherable, like mx121bc@cowcollege.edu. If you get a chance to choose your own username, remember that people who send you e-mail will have to remember it. So pick something that's meaningful to other people as well as yourself.

Similarly, domain names aren't always a recognizable company or organization name. Domain names can be virtually anything, so long as they're unique, and they don't always refer to a specific business or other organization.

Generally, you can refer to computers on the Internet with either their IP address or their domain name address (although it's usually much easier to remember a domain name address), and you always refer to people with their domain name address.

Have Your .Org Call My .Gov About that .Com

The last portion of a domain name address is called the top-level domain. It provides a clue about the computer or the person you're addressing. Top-level domain names are standardized throughout the Internet, as shown in Table 3-1.

Table 3-1: U.S. top-level domain names.

Domain	Represents
com	Businesses and commercial organizations
edu	Educational institutions
gov	Government institutions
mil	Military organizations
net	Network resources
org	Other (usually non-profit) organizations

All Internet sites outside of the United States are identified by a unique two-character top-level domain name, as shown by the examples in Table 3-2.

Table 3-2: International top-level domain names.

Domain	Represents
au	Australia
at	Austria
bz	Belize
ca	Canada
dk	Denmark
fi	Finland
fr	France
de	Germany
it	Italy
jp	Japan
no	Norway

The top-level domain name for the United States is "us," although it's not used very often. Some Internet users identify themselves by their geographic location in their domain names. For example, the domain name username@well.sf.ca.us indicates a user on the Whole Earth 'Lectronic Link (WELL) located in San Francisco, California, United States.

Finger.
Finger is a command you can execute from your keyboard during any TELNET (remote login) session to a UNIX-based host. Type finger and the name of the user or machine you want information about. For example, the command finger @riverside.mr.net would return information about the computer named riverside at the mr.net host.

Here are a few tips to help you deal with this alphabet soup of Internet domain-name addresses:

- The example addresses used in this chapter are very simple. My editor's Internet address, for example, is ruffin@gibbs.oit.unc.edu. Ruffin's account is on a computer named Gibbs (gibbs) in the Office of Information and Technology (oit) at the University of North Carolina (unc), an educational facility (edu).
- The computer networks on the Internet aren't picky about case-sensitivity. For instance, mFraase@Farces.COM, Mfraase@farces.Com, MFRAASE@FARCES.COM will all reach me just as efficiently. Consequently, most veteran netters stick to just lowercase letters when typing addresses because it's the easiest option.
- Make sure to write down important e-mail addresses. I can't tell you the number of times I thought I could remember an e-mail address only to have forgotten it by the time I needed it. Keep a hard-copy record of your e-mail address book. You never know when it might be accidentally deleted from the computer that maintains your account.

Eudora.
Eudora is one of the best Internet e-mail programs available. It comes in both commercial and freeware versions for both Windows and Macintosh. You can always download the latest release of the freeware version of the program and its associated documentation by FTP from ftp.qualcomm.com in the /pceudora/windows/ directory. The freeware version of Eudora is covered in Chapter 4, "Electronic Mail."

When in Rome... Don't Tie Up the Phone Lines

If your friend Augie invites you to dinner, you have to know more than just how to get to his house. You also need to know things like which water glass is yours (is it the one on the left or the one on the right) and which fork to use for the salad. Before you set out on your Internet explorations, take a moment to review a few tips that may keep you from alienating anyone or making a fool out of yourself right away. We all make fools of ourselves on the Net at one time or another; here's hoping you can delay your fool debut for a while.

Acceptable Use Policies

Although the acceptable use policies of the various networks that make up the Internet are rapidly changing, we'll all probably have to deal with them at least until the mid-1990s. Instead of reprinting all of the different acceptable use policies, I'll just go over the main points.

To some extent, your category of Internet connection determines how you can use the Internet. If you're classified as an educational, research or noncommercial user your Internet activities must be restricted to the purpose of research, education, charitable activities, government affairs, individual professional development or public service. If you're classified as a commercial user, your Internet activities are unrestricted (except, of course, for activities that are specified as unacceptable). Research and educational network traffic is routed over connections subsidized by taxpayers; commercial network traffic is routed over private connections. You don't have to worry about how your network traffic is routed; that's the responsibility of your service provider.

Most service providers specify these uses as unacceptable:

- Distribution of unsolicited advertising.
- Transmission of anything that causes disruption of service to others.
- Propagation of computer worms or viruses.
- Use of the network to make unauthorized entry to any resource.

In addition, most service providers require you to abide by some general common-sense usage guidelines:

- Respect the privacy of other users.

- Usage must be consistent with common ethical practice and community standards.
- Respect copyright and licenses of programs, information and documents.

Trumpet.
Trumpet is a network news reader for PCs running Windows (an MS-DOS version is also available) that employs an easy-to-use interface. It uses the NNTP protocol and allows you to follow message threads within the various newsgroups. The program is available by FTP from ftp.utas.edu.au in the /pc/trumpet/wintrump/ directory. Trumpet is covered in Chapter 5, "Network News & Newsgroups."

Finally, some service providers may require you to comply with the NSFNET Backbone Services Acceptable Use Policy. Ask your service provider or network administrator if your Internet activity is affected by this policy.

And if your idea of a good time is to wade through pages of legalese, you can always retrieve the complete documents from various archives on the Internet. For more information on how and where to get these documents, refer to "Downloading Files With Chameleon FTP" beginning on page 199 and "Downloading Files With HGopher" beginning on page 227.

Security Issues

With the rapid growth of the Internet, computer security becomes a more serious issue each year, especially when you're sharing resources across the Net. While your Internet connection is active, your computer—and perhaps more important, any other resources attached to your computer via a local area network—are all on the Internet. It is your responsibility to protect your own system.

You also have a responsibility to be a good Internet citizen. You have been granted access to a worldwide resource and should respect the privacy and property of others.

If we, as Internet inhabitants, don't manage our own security wisely, it's likely that some less-than-benevolent government agency will take it upon itself to manage things for us.

Windows Sockets FTP.
FTP is an Internet acronym for File Transfer Protocol, and it's used to upload and download files on the Net. The best freeware FTP client for Windows currently available is ws_ftp. You can always download the latest release of the software and its associated documentation by FTP from ftp.cica.indiana.edu in the /pub/pc/win3/winsock/ directory. The ws_ftp program has garnered an enthusiastic following because of its ability to display long file names.

First Names Are Lousy Passwords

Your login password is your security key and is the most likely way someone will gain unauthorized access to your Internet account. Guard your password with care, don't write it down, don't allow others to use it and change it often.

A good password:

- Is made up of at least six characters that do not form a word.
- Includes both upper- and lowercase letters and numerals.
- Is easily remembered but something no one can guess.

If you think your Internet account is being hacked—or if you suspect that your computer has been broken into—talk to your network administrator or service provider immediately.

HGopher.
Gopher lets you burrow through information resources using a series of easy-to-navigate menus that appear on your screen. You can use HGopher to navigate huge dataspaces with just a few keypresses. The current version of HGopher is always available by FTP from lister.cc.ic.ac.uk in the /pub/wingopher/ directory. The current version of the program is also available by Gopher at gopher.ic.ac.uk port 70. Using HGopher is covered in Chapter 7, "Using Gopher."

Usage Courtesy

Everything you do on the Internet has potential ramifications beyond the Net. The unwritten rule underlying all Internet activity is simple: *The Internet is a good thing and it must be protected*. While unwritten, this rule is enforced with impartial severity. If you screw up badly enough, you can expect to lose your access privileges. While there are no etiquette handbooks or Internet finishing schools, the same common sense and social grace you use in the real world will generally be enough to get you through most potentially sticky Internet situations.

While some of the tips and advice in this section may mean little to you now, they'll become second nature once you get your Internet legs:

- **Anonymous FTP isn't**. Always use your e-mail address as your login password when accessing remote FTP servers as an anonymous user. (See Chapter 6, "Transferring Files," for more information on accessing FTP sites.) You can always make up a phony e-mail address when you visit far-flung spots on the Net, but don't bother. Cookie-crumb trails will lead back to your site, if not directly to you.
- **Leave your ethnocentricity at the door**. Many juicy Internet resources reside in foreign countries. Be careful with the cultural references you use.
- **Don't tie up popular sites at busy times**. Be aware that shared resources on the Internet may actually be in use by real people trying to do real work. Try to access the busiest resources during off-peak hours whenever possible (unless, of course, you're a real person doing real work). Be sensitive to time zones; think about what time it is where you're *going* rather than where you *are*. Try to find alternative routes to the busiest and most popular resources. Many popular archives have less crowded "mirror" sites elsewhere on the Net. Learn where they are and use them when possible.
- **Try to find the closest source for what you need**. Don't FTP or Gopher to Finland for a file you know is available one or two hops away from your local site.
- **Don't use remote resources when you can use local ones**. Don't use archive space clear across the world for your personal files just because you can't afford a bigger hard drive.

- **Log off properly**. Make sure you leave all resources in the same condition and state in which you found them. If you log off improperly, you may leave certain tasks or processes running in the background of the host machine, causing problems for other users or worse, network administrators.

Keep in mind that nothing on the Internet is really free. Somebody is paying for it. And if everyone takes a "free ride" on the most popular and expensive Net resources, it won't be long before those same resources are protected, restricted or closed to public access.

You'll find more Internet etiquette advice in the chapters that deal with specific network services.

Moving On

Now you know how the Internet works and how computers and people are identified. You've also looked at how to best get along with your fellow Internet inhabitants. The next chapter guides you through the wonders of using electronic mail on the Internet. We'll cover how to use some of the most powerful tools available for sending, receiving, reading and sorting electronic mail, and how to communicate via e-mail with people who aren't even on the Internet.

CHAPTER 4

ELECTRONIC MAIL

The Pony Express Goes Digital

Our tour bus has been making pretty good time, sticking to the back roads. But we've been rolling along for some time now, and some of you may want to send a message to your friends and family back home, just to let them know you're having a great time. So let's take a look at how to use electronic mail to communicate privately with individuals and small groups on the Internet.

With the exception of gestures, e-mail is arguably the most efficient means of communication yet devised by humans. Because it uses recycled phosphors on your computer screen, e-mail is ecological—nary a tree and very little energy is used to create, deliver and read e-mail messages. You can choose to read your e-mail whenever it's most convenient for you, not when it's convenient for someone else. You can scan an electronic inbox full of e-mail faster than you can open a single paper mail envelope. You can easily forward, store or reply to e-mail messages with the touch of a button. Sending messages to dozens of people is a snap with the multiple-addressing capabilities of e-mail. And there are a host of other features that make e-mail one of the most powerful and convenient ways to communicate.

But lots of people never get the most from their e-mail systems because they have to wrestle with arcane and obscure commands and abbreviations, just to send a simple message. There are a host of powerful tools available for Windows that provide an easy-to-use interface for the Internet's electronic mail services. After all, electronic mail is only effective if you actually use it, and who wants to put up with a UNIX-based e-mail program with practically no features or options, when simple, Windows-specific alternatives are available?

E-mail is an incredibly powerful form of communication, and there are plenty of Internet users who do little on the Net besides send mail. Consequently, we'll be spending more time discussing e-mail than any other topic in the course of our tour. So before we get started, let's pull off to the side of the road and take a look at the map of what we'll be covering in this chapter:

- What Is E-Mail & How Does it Work?
- E-Mail Etiquette & Courtesy
- How to Send E-Mail Anywhere
- Quick Guide to Using Chameleon Mail (included on the companion disk)
- Quick Guide to Using Eudora
- Finding Addresses
- Electronic Mailing Lists
- E-Mail & Attached Files

We've got a long road ahead, so buckle up and let's get started!

What Is E-Mail & How Does it Work?

Most people who have never used e-mail have trouble understanding why it's touted over regular mail, fax or even phone conversations. It takes anywhere from a few seconds to a few minutes to deliver an e-mail message (complete with attached files) anywhere in the world. A postal delivery usually takes several days to reach its destination, and the telephone system is immediate, but both parties have to be on the phone at the same time. Fax was the rage in the '80s because it was fairly easy to use and didn't require a computer. But this chapter shows why so many people prefer e-mail to phone, fax or paper mail.

You can use e-mail to:

- **Send text-based messages to any other Internet user**. You can also send messages to users on commercial electronic mail and information services. Soon you'll be able to send messages that contain fully formatted text, pictures, sound and even video—*between different types of computers and operating systems.*

- **Attach computer files to text messages**. You can send binary files—complete software programs or fully formatted files—to any other Internet user and users on most of the commercial electronic mail and information services. (Why send a static, dead document via fax when you can work with a live one via e-mail?)
- **Send messages and files to multiple recipients**. Where telephones tend to be useful for one-to-one communications, e-mail is useful for both one-to-one and one-to-many communications.
- **Reply to or forward messages you receive**. You can quickly and easily dash off a reply to a message, or forward it to other users around the world.
- **Subscribe to electronic mailing lists**. You can add your name to any of thousands of mailing lists whose topics range from PC hardware and software to political debates and discussions.
- **Communicate with mail list servers**. By sending e-mail queries to special addresses, you can query list servers that automatically respond to special commands by returning to you specific information, documents or other files.

Electronic mail is different from other Internet services in one important way—the sending and the receiving computers need not be able to connect directly with each other. You create e-mail messages on your computer and send them to a *mail server*. The mail server determines the best route to reach the recipient and passes the e-mail to the next closest mail server. The e-mail is passed through any number of mail servers and is eventually delivered to the final recipient's mail server. This is called a *store-and-forward* service, and it happens much faster than it took you to read about the process.

Smithsonian Institution photograph archive.

The Smithsonian Institution has begun to archive electronic versions of its photographs and art collections. The archive is accessible by FTP at photo1.si.edu in the directory /pub/images/. Unfortunately, this machine has a poor network connection. Daily updates are mirrored at the University of North Carolina and accessible by FTP at sunsite.unc.edu in the /pub/multimedia/pictures/smithsonian/ directory.

Like the phone system and the Postal Service, e-mail isn't infallible. Occasionally, an e-mail message doesn't reach its intended destination. Any e-mail that does not reach its recipient is returned to the sender as undeliverable mail. This is called a *bounced* e-mail message. Reasons for bounced mail include (in order of likelihood):

- **User unknown** (incorrect address in the username portion of the address).
- **Host unknown** (incorrect address in the domain or top-domain portions of the address).
- **Network unreachable** (gateway limitations or problems with the network backbone).
- **Connection timed out** (software problem on the destination mail server).
- **Connection refused** (problem with the destination mail server).

The important point here is, if your e-mail message is undeliverable—for whatever reason—it will be bounced back to you. Many first-time e-mail users waste countless hours worrying if their messages are delivered, often following e-mail transmissions with faxes and phone calls to the effect of "Did you get my e-mail?" As a general rule, assume that your e-mail efforts are successful rather than figuring they don't work at all.

E-Mail Etiquette & Courtesy

Electronic mail eliminates a lot of subtle impediments to effective communication. Judgments based on appearance, voice or social position are impossible in electronic communications. E-mail's asynchronous nature—the ability to deal with a message when it's most convenient for all parties involved—is truly a boon to communications among individuals and groups.

One of the most amazing things about e-mail is the immediacy of its delivery. When you click that **Send** button, your message is delivered in seconds. This is a great advantage in most cases, but can work as a disadvantage if you have a short fuse. Unlike a letter, which may sit on a desk for hours or days before being mailed, electronic communications are usually dashed off as soon as they're completed. If you've been using e-mail for a while, you'll notice that a lot of the messages you receive (and perhaps a few you've written) shouldn't have been sent. It pays to ponder the ramifications of an e-mail message before launching it into the electronic ether—once it's gone out, there's no way to get it back.

The price that you pay for e-mail's convenience and speed is a fairly high potential for misunderstanding. The best way to avoid e-mail misinterpretations and mixed signals is to follow three simple, common-sense rules of etiquette and courtesy.

1. *Don't send anything via e-mail that you wouldn't want to read in your hometown newspaper*. Invariably, that juicy e-mail message is read by the one person who was never meant to read it. There are lots of stories about the politics of e-mail, and until the law catches up with the technology, you're better off playing it safe. Assume your e-mail messages are available to anyone who wants to read them. Some companies even have a policy making e-mail the property of the company, not the individual correspondents. In early 1993, the Georgia Institute of Technology announced that it would no longer consider e-mail delivered to any of its systems on the Internet to be private. Already, landmark legal cases about trade secrets, corporate espionage and e-mail are filtering through the courts. E-mail *should* enjoy all the rights and securities of paper mail, but don't make the mistake of assuming that it *does*.
2. *Facial expressions and body language don't fit through the narrow bandwidth of e-mail*. Statements that you intend as pithy may come across as condescending or sarcastic. Some people approach e-mail as conversational; others don't. Some people never take e-mail personally, others always do. Unless you're close friends with an e-mail recipient, never expect that he or she will understand your sense of humor, wry wit or playful repartee.
3. *You can't control when your message will be delivered, so assume it will arrive at the worst possible time*. Be careful with your wording. What may seem funny or cute today may be inappropriate or rude when e-mail is read tomorrow. Just because e-mail is delivered at warp speed doesn't mean it's read at the same rate. Lots of people get more e-mail than they can keep up with; keep that in mind as you compose your missive. If you only read three e-mail messages a day, you'll probably remember them all for a few days. But people who receive dozens of messages need reminders (or forwarded messages) to help clue them in to the context of previous correspondence.

Auto-Advice From EmilyPost.

If you think you get some perplexing junk paper mail, consider receiving this automated e-mail message:

Dear Net-Mail User [EweR-635-78-2267-3 aSp]:

Your mailbox has just been rifled by EmilyPost, an autonomous courtesy-worm chain program released in October 2036 by an anonymous group of net subscribers in western Alaska. [ref: sequestered confession 592864 -2376298.98634, deposited with Bank Leumi 10/23/36:20:34:21. Expiration-disclosure 10 years.] Under the civil disobedience sections of the Charter of Rio, we accept in advance the fines and penalties that will come due when our confession is released in 2046. However we feel that's a small price to pay for the message brought to you by EmilyPost.

In brief, dear friend, you are not a very polite person. EmilyPost's syntax analysis subroutines show that a very high fraction of your net exchanges are heated, vituperative, even obscene.

Of course you enjoy free speech. But EmilyPost has been designed by people who are concerned about the recent trend toward excessive nastiness in some parts of the net. EmilyPost homes in on folks like you and begins by asking them to please consider the advantages of politeness.

For one thing, your credibility ratings would rise. (EmilyPost has checked your favorite bulletin boards, and finds your ratings aren't high at all. Nobody is listening to you, sir!) Moreover, consider that courtesy can foster calm reason, turning shrill antagonism into useful debate and even consensus.

We suggest introducing an automatic delay to your mail system. Communications are so fast these days, people seldom stop and think. Some net users act like mental patients who shout out anything that comes to mind, rather than as functioning citizens with the human gift of tact.

If you wish, you may use one of the public-domain delay programs included in this version of EmilyPost, free of charge.

Of course, should you insist on continuing as before, disseminating nastiness in all directions, we have equipped EmilyPost with other options you'll soon find out about....

—From David Brin's *Earth* (Bantam, 1990).

E-Mail Privacy

If I took a paper letter from your mailbox, opened it and read it, I'd be guilty of a federal offense. If I did the same thing by intercepting or retrieving your e-mail, chances are I would not be committing a crime.

Electronic communications are not given the same protection as first class mail. As the rapid rate of change outpaces the social and legal conventions that govern how we use technology, we continue to suppose that we have freedoms and rights that simply do not exist. For example, in the past, wiretapping had to be physically carried out. A spook had to be near the person under surveillance. A tape recorder had to be in the immediate vicinity of persons recorded. With advancements in telephone switching technology, this is no longer the case. Anyone can now easily eavesdrop on conversations simply by sending the proper signal tones down the telephone wire—from anywhere.

In 1986, President Ronald Reagan signed into law the Electronic Communications Privacy Act (ECPA). The act is designed to expand the scope of telecommunications covered under the protection of the 1968 federal wiretapping laws. The ECPA protects electronic mail, cellular telephones, pagers and electronic data transmission. It also requires government agencies to obtain a court order before intercepting electronic communications.

The ECPA, as currently written, has two main goals:

1. Protecting all electronic communications systems, including e-mail, from outside intrusion.
2. Protecting the privacy of certain messages transmitted over public-service e-mail systems.

The ECPA makes it a federal crime to intercept certain electronic communications, but makes a distinction between public and internal electronic communications systems. Most important, electronic mail messages transmitted within internal e-mail systems that are used solely for interoffice communications are not subject to the privacy provisions of the ECPA. That means that a company can read such messages without invading the privacy of employees. Electronic mail messages transmitted within internal e-mail systems that allow outside access can be read by a company if either the sender or receiver grants permission. Reading electronic mail messages exchanged over public e-mail systems by anyone other than the sender and receiver is a felony under the ECPA. To make matters more confusing, it's not clear whether the Internet is considered a public e-mail system under the ECPA.

If this all seems a little vague and you're wondering how it relates to you as an e-mail user, a recent poll conducted by *Macworld* magazine might bring the issue into clearer focus. In its July 1993 issue, *Macworld* published the results of a nationwide poll of top corporate managers from 301 businesses of varying sizes. The poll found that 21 percent of respondents have "engaged in searches of employee computer files, voice mail, electronic mail, or other networking communications." The figure was even higher—30 percent—among large companies.

E-Mail Horror Stories.

Linda Ellerbee's infamous Associated Press e-mail incident didn't so much involve eavesdropping or invasion of privacy as it did the simple misrouting of electronic communications. Ellerbee, so the story goes, sent a note to a friend through the Associated Press e-mail system. The note included some very nasty comments about her boss and the Dallas city council, as well as other Texas luminaries. An accident in the network caused the message to be distributed to every AP outlet in four states. Ellerbee lost her job over the incident, and the potential for legal action by everyone involved—including Ellerbee, her boss and the AP—was gigantic.

In the summer of 1990, the members of the city council of Colorado Springs became outraged when they discovered the mayor was secretly intercepting and reading their private e-mail messages.

In August of 1990, Alana Shoars, a network administrator in charge of electronic mail at Epson America Inc. filed a lawsuit against the company. Shoars' lawsuit alleged that her supervisor, Robert Hillseth, manager of data communications for Epson America Inc., had intercepted her MCI Mail messages on a regular basis as they were passing through the company's network gateway. Shoars claims that when she complained about Hillseth's activities, he fired her. Shoars filed an individual suit for wrongful termination and also filed a class action suit with 2,500 other current and former Epson employees asking for unspecified damages of up to $3,000 per violation. That's $3,000 for each message that was intercepted. The class action suit was filed as an invasion of privacy under Section 631 of the California Penal Code.

Secret Service Director John Simpson admitted in a letter to California State Representative Don Edwards that the U.S. government has been intercepting private e-mail and surreptitiously monitoring computer bulletin boards in order to track the activities of suspected hackers.

While there are various techniques for encrypting or otherwise protecting e-mail messages, they are not always practical or convenient, and no system is completely foolproof. So until specific laws are passed and sweeping policy changes are enacted by government and business alike, the lesson here is clear: assume that your e-mail messages are being read by people other than their intended recipients.

How to Send E-Mail Anywhere

You can do anything with e-mail that you can do with postal mail, except mail physical objects. With an Internet account you can even send e-mail to people who have accounts on one of the commercial electronic mail or information services like MCI Mail or CompuServe.

Addressing e-mail on the Internet is standardized and simple, despite how arcane or inscrutable some Internet addresses may seem. Everyone's Internet e-mail address, as explained in "Where.Is.That.Thing@On.the.Net?" on page 53, is formatted the same:

username@domain.top-domain.

To send e-mail to someone on the Internet, just address the message to their Internet address.

The next six sections detail how to send and receive mail from most of the common commercial information services that provide an *e-mail gateway* to the Internet.

An e-mail gateway is software or hardware that connects networks that use different protocols. In effect, it translates between the protocols so that computers on the connected networks can exchange data. Be careful with the size of the files you send by e-mail. Most of the e-mail gateways provided by the commercial information services like CompuServe and America Online have severe file-size limitations, as indicated in Table 4-1.

E-mail addresses are not case-sensitive, and most people don't care how you capitalize their name or domain name, as long as their e-mail gets to them.

Internet to UUCP & Back

UUCP, the UNIX-to-UNIX Copy Program, is a protocol used by UNIX workstations to communicate with each other over telephone lines. UUCP is also commonly referred to as a network, because e-mail and files can be sent to any UUCP-capable computer by specifying which intermediate computers the e-mail must pass through to reach the final recipient. Since many UUCP sites are switching over to full domain name registration, you might first check to see if your recipient has a standard Internet domain name address.

To send e-mail to a UUCP user, use the format:

user@host.uucp

or

user%host.uucp@gateway

For example, to send e-mail to Peter Piper (whose user ID is ppiper) at his Megacorp (megacorp.uucp) host, use the format:

ppiper@megacorp.uucp

Alternatively, if Megacorp uses the Performance Systems International (PSI) gateway to receive e-mail (check with Peter or his assistant if you aren't sure), use the address format:

ppiper%megacorp.uucp@uu.psi.com

Sometimes UUCP users will provide you with what's called a *bang-path address*. Bang-path addresses are easily spotted because they contain exclamation marks (!):

...!uunet!megacorp!ppiper

The exclamation marks are pronounced as "bang." The above address would be pronounced as "from bang uunet bang megacorp bang ppiper."

You can always convert bang-path addresses to this format:

user%host.uucp@gateway

UUCP users with access to an e-mail gateway send e-mail messages to colleagues on the Internet using the standard domain name addressing:

user@domain.top-domain

For example, UUCP users with access to a gateway address e-mail to my Internet address as:

mfraase@farces.com

UUCP users without access to a gateway must route Internet e-mail using whatever paths are appropriate to reach a computer that is connected to the Internet.

Internet to CompuServe & Back

CompuServe is a commercial information service that opened an e-mail gateway to the Internet in July 1989. CompuServe subscribers are assigned a unique identification number as a username, in the format:

71234,5678

To send e-mail to a CompuServe subscriber, use the format:

useridentification.number@compuserve.com

For example, to send e-mail to Peter Piper (whose CompuServe ID number is 71234,5678) use the address format:

71234.5678@compuserve.com

Note that the comma in the recipient's user identification number is translated to a period.

You should also remember that there is a 50,000-character limit on e-mail messages that pass through CompuServe's Internet gateway.

CompuServe subscribers send e-mail to the Internet using the format:

>Internet:user@domain.top-domain

For example, CompuServe subscribers address e-mail to my Internet address as:

>Internet:mfraase@farces.com

"Dear Sysadmin, Punish your user for what he said!"

In mid-April 1993, Carl Kadie asked a variety of system administrators how they respond to the above request from Internet users. The responses were very interesting:

Ten respondents explained the value of free expression or replied that punishing users wasn't their job.

Seven respondents told the accused to "cool it" (or else).

Four respondents said the situation has never come up.

Two respondents said they judge the article and punish the user if the posting is found to violate policy.

One respondent removed the entire newsgroup in which the article was posted.

One respondent told the complainer "we'll handle it," but didn't do anything to follow up.

One respondent passed the complaint up the chain of command.

Internet to MCI Mail & Back

MCI Mail is a commercial electronic mail service that has offered an experimental Internet gateway since the late 1980s; the gateway is no longer considered experimental. MCI Mail subscribers are assigned a unique MCI ID number, an MCI ID name and a full username, in the following respective formats:

557-4126
mfraase
Michael Fraase

To send e-mail to an MCI Mail subscriber, use any of the three following formats:

idnumber@mcimail.com
idname@mcimail.com
full_user_name@mcimail.com

For example, to send e-mail to any of the above three MCI Mail address formats, use the three following formats respectively:

5574126@mcimail.com
mfraase@mcimail.com
michael_fraase@mcimail.com

Note that when you use the idnumber@mcimail.com format, the dash separating the numbers is eliminated. Also, spaces—like those between first and last names—are translated to the underscore (_) character.

There is no limit on the size of e-mail messages that pass through the MCI Mail Internet gateway.

MCI Mail subscribers send e-mail to the Internet with the following steps:

1. At the **Command**: prompt, type **create** and press **Enter**.
2. At the **TO**: prompt, type the full name of the recipient followed by **(EMS)** and press **Enter**.
3. At the **EMS**: prompt, type **Internet** and press **Enter**.
4. At the **MBX**: prompt, type the recipient's Internet domain name address in the format **user@domain.top-domain** and press **Enter**.

For example, MCI Mail subscribers address e-mail to my Internet address as follows:

1. At the **Command**: prompt, type **create** and press **Enter**.
2. At the **TO**: prompt, type **Michael Fraase (EMS)** and press **Enter**.
3. At the **EMS**: prompt, type **Internet** and press **Enter**.
4. At the **MBX**: prompt, type **mfraase@farces.com** and press **Enter**.

Internet to America Online & Back

America Online is a commercial information service that maintains an e-mail gateway to the Internet. Each America Online subscriber has a unique "screen name" as a username, at least three and no more than ten characters long.

To send e-mail to an America Online subscriber, use the format:

screenname@aol.com

For example, to send e-mail to Peter Piper (PetePiper) use the address format:

petepiper@aol.com

Note that there is a 27,000-character limit on e-mail messages that pass through America Online's Internet gateway.

America Online subscribers send e-mail to the Internet using the standard domain name addressing:

user@domain.top-domain

For example, America Online subscribers address e-mail to my Internet address as:

mfraase@farces.com

Internet to AT&T Mail & Back

AT&T Mail is a commercial electronic mail service that opened an e-mail gateway to the Internet in June 1990. Each AT&T Mail subscriber is assigned a unique username.

To send e-mail to an AT&T Mail subscriber, use the format:

username@attmail.com

For example, to send e-mail to Peter Piper (ppiper) use the address format:

ppiper@attmail.com

AT&T Mail subscribers send e-mail to the Internet using the standard domain name addressing:

user@domain.top-domain

For example, AT&T Mail subscribers address e-mail to my Internet address as:

mfraase@farces.com

"Dear Sysadmin, Punish your user for what he said!" Revisited.

In mid-April 1993, Carl Kadie asked a variety of system administrators how they respond to the above request from Internet users. Here's one of the responses he received:

"I believe you need a short lesson in the operation of free speech. I have no particular opinions on the subject of this newsgroup, but I took the trouble to read some of the 'belligerent and harassing' postings of which you speak, and, frankly, they weren't."

"It seems to me that your attempt to characterize them as such stems from a desire to stifle ideas with which you disagree. I have no intention of cooperating with you in this. The remedy for speech with which you disagree is more speech, not a silencing (the rather low signal-to-noise ratio on USENET notwithstanding)."

"If these postings offend you, I suggest you find out how 'kill files' work, rather than wasting the time of overworked system administrators who aren't being underpaid to deal with this sort of childishness."

Cross-Network E-Mail Addressing Quick Reference

The addressing information presented in the previous six sections is distilled for quick reference in Table 4-1.

Table 4-1: Cross-network e-mail addressing at a glance.

Service	From Internet	To Internet
UUCP	user@host.uucp user%host.uucp@gateway ....!gateway!host!user	user@domain.top-domain[1]
CompuServe	user.number@compuserve.com[2]	>Internet:user@domain.top-domain
MCI Mail	idnumber@mcimail.com[3] idname@mcimail.com full_user_name@mcimail.com	TO: recipient's full name (EMS) EMS: Internet MBX: user@domain.top-domain
America Online	screenname@aol.com[4]	user@domain.top-domain
AT&T Mail	username@attmail.com	user@domain.top-domain

[1] Requires access to a gateway.

[2] The comma in the recipient's user identification number is translated to a period. There is a 50,000-character limit on e-mail messages that pass through CompuServe's Internet gateway.

[3] The dash separating the numbers is eliminated.

[4] There is a 27,000-character limit on e-mail messages that pass through America Online's Internet gateway.

Quick Guide to Using Chameleon Mail

The Chameleon Sampler software included on *The Windows Internet Tour Guide Companion Disk* includes an e-mail program for Windows that is fully compatible with the POP3 mail server offered by most Internet service providers. (If you're not sure whether Chameleon Mail is compatible with your mail server, ask your network administrator.) The commercial version of Chameleon Mail includes support for Multipurpose Internet Mail Extensions (MIME), which basically allows you to include multimedia attachments to your e-mail messages.

The Chameleon Mail program is packaged in a self-extracting archive file on the disk and is automatically decompressed and properly installed as part of the installation process described in Chapter 2, "Getting Connected."

Configuring Chameleon Mail

Chameleon Mail must be properly configured before you can begin using it to send e-mail. To use Chameleon Mail, you must have an account on a computer that runs a POP3 (Post Office Protocol version 3) mail server. Use the sequences in this section to configure the Chameleon Mail software.

Note: This section assumes that you have installed the Chameleon Sampler software as part of the installation process outlined in Chapter 2, "Getting Connected."

Before you can use Chameleon Mail to send or receive messages, you have to set up a mail account for yourself (and any other users that may be logging in from your computer).

Use these steps to create an e-mail account for yourself in Chameleon Mail.

1. With Windows running and the Chameleon Sampler program group window open, double-click on the **Mail** icon. The User Login dialog box appears, as shown in Figure 4-1.

Figure 4-1: Chameleon Mail User Login dialog box.

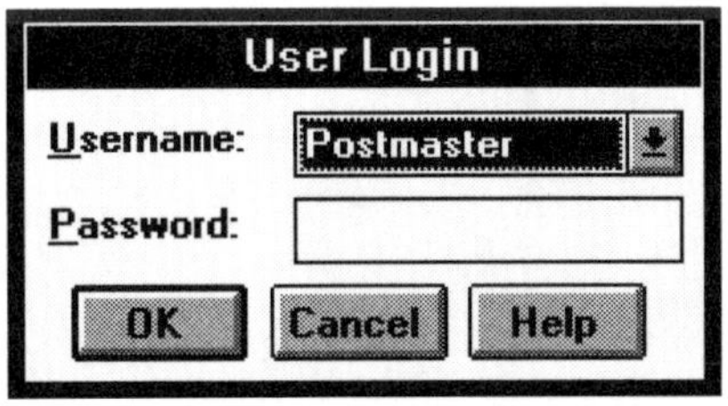

- Additionally, the Chameleon NEWT icon appears in the lower left corner of your monitor, indicating that the TCP/IP communications stack has been successfully loaded.

2. Select the Postmaster item from the Username pop-up menu.
3. Click the **OK** button. (The default state for the Postmaster account is no password, so the Password field should be empty.) The Mail-Postmaster window is displayed, as shown in Figure 4-2.

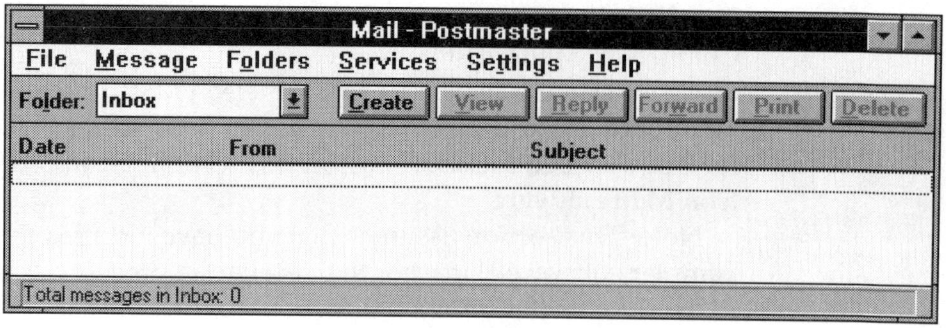

Figure 4-2: Chameleon Mail-Postmaster window.

4. From the Services menu, select the Mailboxes... command. The Mailboxes window appears, as shown in Figure 4-3.

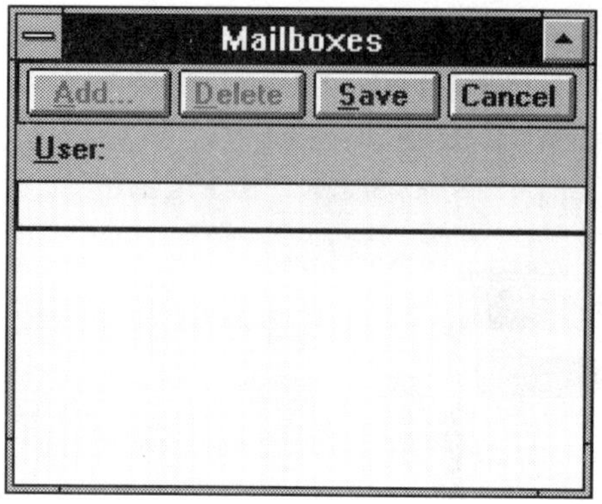

Figure 4-3: Chameleon Mailboxes window.

5. Enter your username in the User: field. For example, I would enter **mfraase** in the User: field. Enter only your username on the host computer, not your entire e-mail address.
6. Click the **Add** button. The User dialog box appears as shown in Figure 4-4.

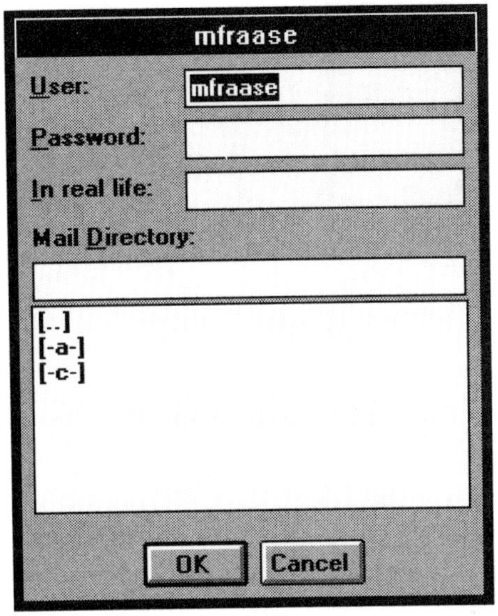

Figure 4-4: Chameleon User dialog box.

7. Enter a password in the Password: field. **Note:** This is a password to gain access to Chameleon Mail, not necessarily your e-mail server.
8. Enter your full name in the In real life: field.
9. Enter the complete pathname for your mail directory. For example, **c:\netmanag\email\mfraase** (where **mfraase** is your username) would be appropriate if you installed Chameleon using the default setup configuration.
   - All configuration files and e-mail messages are stored in the mail directory. Each user should have a separate mail directory. A sample User dialog box with settings appropriate for my account is shown in Figure 4-5.

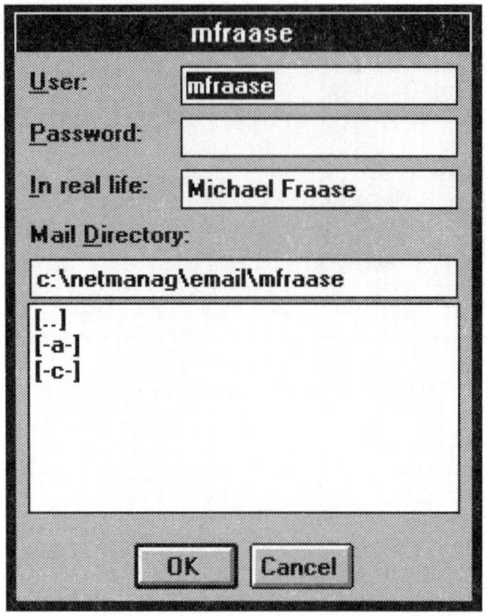

Figure 4-5: Chameleon User dialog box, configured for the user mfraase.

10. Click the **OK** button. The User dialog box is dismissed.
11. Click the **Save** button in the Mailboxes window. A new mail directory for the specified username will be created and the configuration information will be saved.
12. If additional users will be sharing your computer, or if you are configuring your computer for use as a mail server, repeat steps 5–11 for each additional user.
13. When you're finished creating your mail account(s), close the Mailboxes window.

You've successfully created your mail account. Now you can configure Chameleon Mail for use with your mail server with these steps:

1. With Windows running and the Chameleon Sampler program group window open, double-click on the **Mail** icon. The User Login dialog box appears, as shown in Figure 4-1.
   - Additionally, the Chameleon NEWT icon appears in the lower left corner of your monitor, indicating that the TCP/IP communications stack has been successfully loaded.
2. Select your username from the Username pop-up menu.
3. Enter your password in the Password: field.
4. Click the **OK** button. The main Mail window with Inbox folder open appears, as shown in Figure 4-6.

Figure 4-6: Chameleon main Mail window with Inbox folder open.

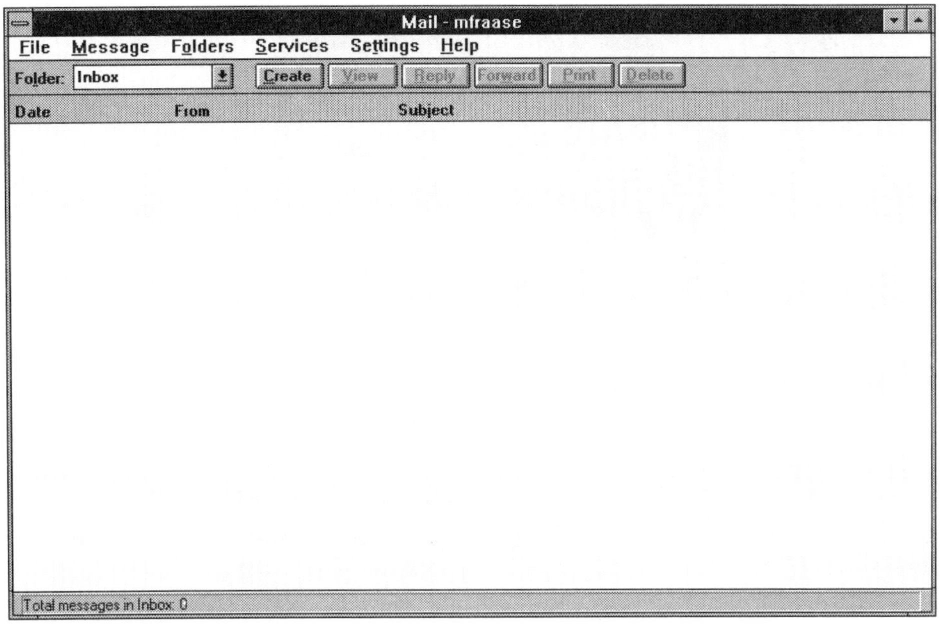

5. From the Settings menu, select the Mail Gateway... command from the Network submenu. The Mail Gateway dialog box is displayed, as shown in Figure 4-7.

Figure 4-7: Chameleon Mail Gateway dialog box.

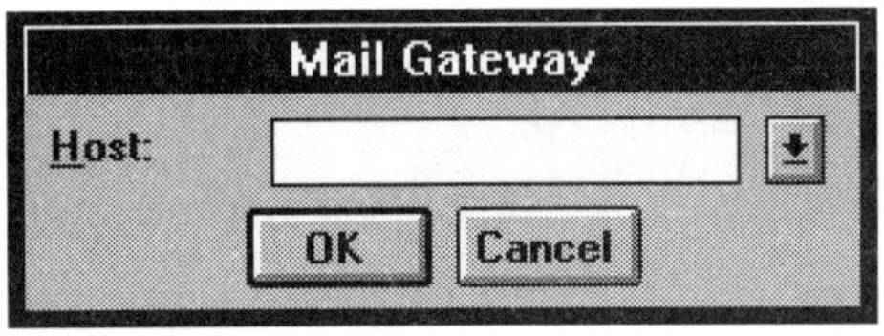

6. Select the domain name of your mail server from the Host: pop-up menu.
   - If no items are available on the pop-up menu, you haven't configured Chameleon properly; see "Configuring Chameleon Sampler" beginning on page 35.
7. Click the **OK** button.
8. From the Settings menu, select the Mail Server... command from the Network submenu. The Mail Server dialog box is displayed, as shown in Figure 4-8.

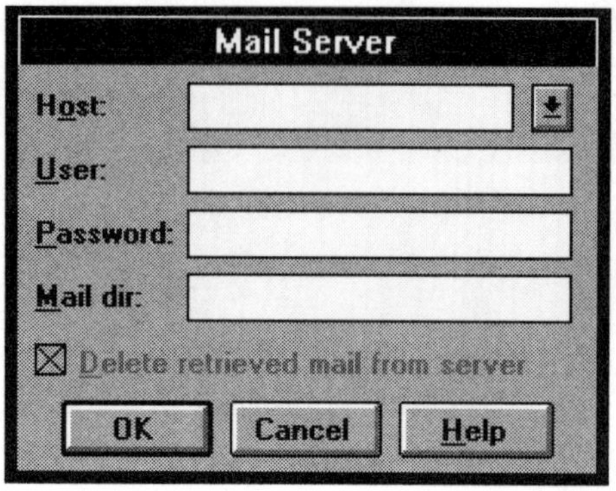

Figure 4-8: Chameleon Mail Server dialog box.

9. Select the domain name of your mail server from the Host: pop-up menu.
   - If no items are available on the pop-up menu, you haven't configured Chameleon properly; see "Configuring Chameleon Sampler" beginning on page 49.
10. Enter your username on the remote mail server in the User: field.
    - Note this username is usually (but not always) the same as your Chameleon Mail username.
11. Enter your password on the remote mail server in the Password: field.
    - Note this password is usually (but not always) the same as your Chameleon Mail password.
12. Check the **Delete retrieved mail from server** check box.
    - This deletes e-mail messages addressed to you from the remote mail server once they have been successfully delivered to your Chameleon Mail Inbox.
13. Click the **OK** button. The Mail Server dialog box is dismissed.
14. From the File menu, select the **Exit** command. The Chameleon Mail program will close.

You've successfully configured Chameleon Mail to communicate with your mail server.

There are several other convenient features Chameleon Mail offers that you might want to take advantage of. Or, you can begin using the program to compose and send e-mail messages. If you want to begin using Chameleon without configuring it for your own personal preferences, you can skip the rest of this section and advance to "Using Chameleon Mail" on page 87.

Follow these steps to further customize Chameleon Mail to your own personal preferences.

1. With Windows running and the Chameleon Sampler program group window open, double-click on the **Mail** icon. The User Login dialog box appears, as shown in Figure 4-1.
   - Additionally, the Chameleon NEWT icon appears in the lower left corner of your monitor, indicating that the TCP/IP communications stack has been successfully loaded.
2. Select your username from the Username pop-up menu.
3. Enter your password in the Password: field.
4. Click the **OK** button. The main Mail window with Inbox folder open appears, as shown in Figure 4-6.
5. From the Settings menu, select the Preferences... command. The Preferences dialog box appears, as shown in Figure 4-9.

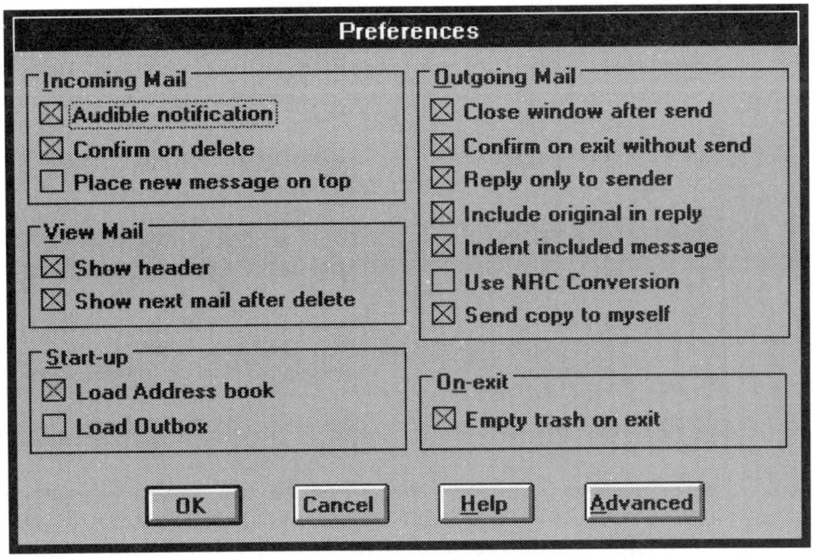

Figure 4-9: Chameleon Mail Preferences dialog box.

6. Based on the information presented in Table 4-2, check or uncheck the available check boxes to suit your personal preferences.

Table 4-2: Chameleon Mail Preferences settings.

Check Box	Function When Enabled
Audible notification	Beeps the speaker when new e-mail is received.
Confirm on delete	Prompts for confirmation when e-mail is deleted.
Place new message on top	Lists e-mail messages in folders with newest messages on top.
Show header	Displays header information for e-mail messages.
Show next mail after delete	Automatically displays next e-mail message in folder when current message is deleted.
Load Address book	Automatically loads address book when Mail program is launched.
Load Outbox	Automatically loads Outbox folder when Mail program is launched.
Close window after send	Closes message window automatically after it is sent.
Confirm on exit without send	Prompts for confirmation when Mail program is closed with e-mail messages waiting to be sent.
Reply only to sender	Addresses e-mail reply to only the sender of an e-mail message, ignoring cc and bcc addresses.
Include original in reply	Automatically pastes a copy of the original message in your reply message.
Indent included message	Automatically indents (and sets off with a bracket [>] character) the copy of the original message in your reply message.
Use NRC conversion	Provides limited support for international character sets.
Send copy to myself	Archives copies of all messages you send.
Empty trash on exit	Permanently removes all messages that have been marked as deleted.

7. Click the **Advanced** button in the Preferences dialog box. The Advanced Preferences dialog box appears, as shown in Figure 4-10.

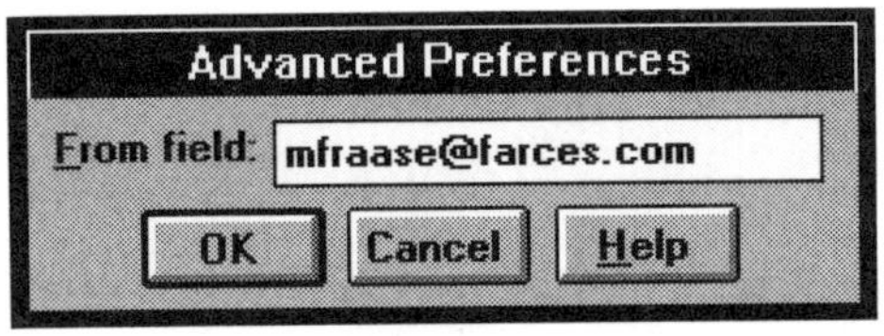

Figure 4-10: Chameleon Mail Advanced Preferences dialog box.

8. Enter your e-mail address—using the username@domain.top-domain format—in the From field:.
9. Click the **OK** button in the Advanced Preferences dialog box. The Advanced Preferences dialog box is dismissed.
10. Click the **OK** button in the Preferences dialog box. The Preferences dialog box is dismissed, saving your settings and leaving the main Mail window active.
11. From the Settings menu, use the Fonts... command to specify a typeface for use in displaying and printing your e-mail, as shown in Figure 4-11.

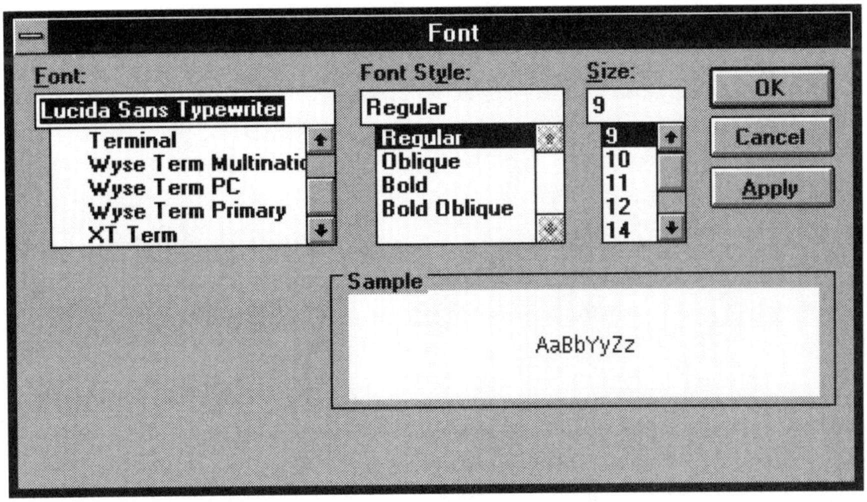

Figure 4-11: Chameleon Mail Font dialog box.

- It's best to select a monospaced font—like Lucida Sans Typewriter or Courier—because each character occupies a set amount of space on each line, resulting in a consistent appearance regardless of the kind of computer used to read your e-mail messages.

12. From the Settings menu, use the Colors... command to specify foreground and background colors for various interface elements within the program, as shown in Figure 4-12.

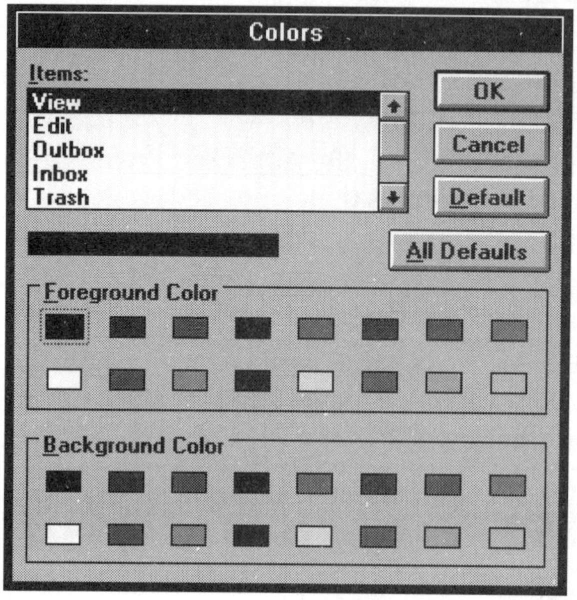

Figure 4-12: Chameleon Mail Colors dialog box.

13. From the Settings menu, use the Signature... command to specify a signature to be attached to your outgoing e-mail messages.
    - A signature is a three- or four-line text file containing your contact information. An example is shown in Figure 4-13. (For more information on using signatures, see the Signatures sidebar later in this chapter.)

TeX.

It's pronounced "tech," and if you're an academician you probably already know about it. TeX is a very specialized typesetting software program. It's notoriously difficult to learn, and painful to use, but for some things—like typesetting mathematical equations—it's indispensable. Several versions of TeX, sample files and utilities are available by anonymous FTP at ftp.cica.indiana.edu in the /pub/pc/win3/util/ directory.

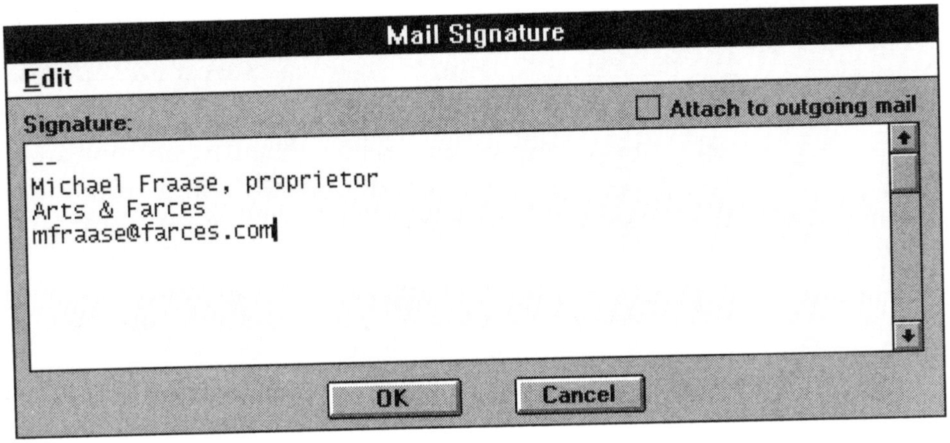

Figure 4-13: Chameleon Mail Signature dialog box.

14. Click the **OK** button in each open dialog box to dismiss them and save your settings.
15. From the File menu, select the Exit command. The Chameleon Mail program will close.

You have now completely configured Chameleon Mail and are ready to use it to send and receive e-mail.

Internet/NREN Business Journal.
The *Internet/NREN Business Journal* is a new hardcopy newsletter from Michael Strangelove. Internet/Bitnet/NREN topics will include case studies of business ventures, legislation news, advertising strategy and ethics, net-based public relations, university-industry activity, resource directories and emerging opportunities. Bimonthly plus six annual special supplements, $75–$149. For information contact 441495@acadvm1.uottawa.ca

Using Chameleon Mail

Chameleon Mail uses the Post Office Protocol (POP) to retrieve e-mail and the Simple Mail Transfer Protocol (SMTP) to send mail. All e-mail you send and receive with Chameleon Mail is handled automatically.

Retrieving & Reading E-Mail With Chameleon

Use these steps to login to your mail server and automatically retrieve any waiting e-mail.

1. With Windows running and the Chameleon Sampler program group window open, double-click on the **Custom** icon. The Custom window appears, as shown in Figure 4-14.

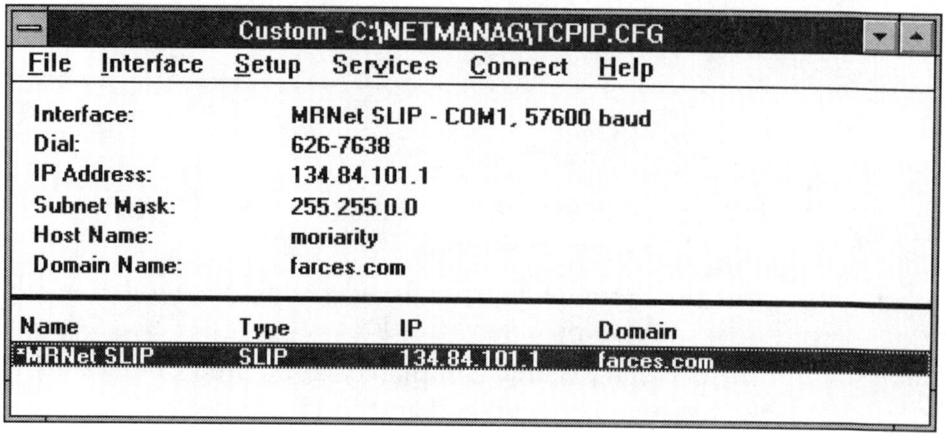

Figure 4-14: Chameleon Custom window.

- Additionally, the Chameleon NEWT icon appears in the lower left corner of your monitor, indicating that the TCP/IP communications stack has been successfully loaded.

2. Click the **Connect** menu. Chameleon attempts to establish a connection using the configuration information you supplied in Chapter 2, and the Connect dialog box is displayed, as shown in Figure 4-15.

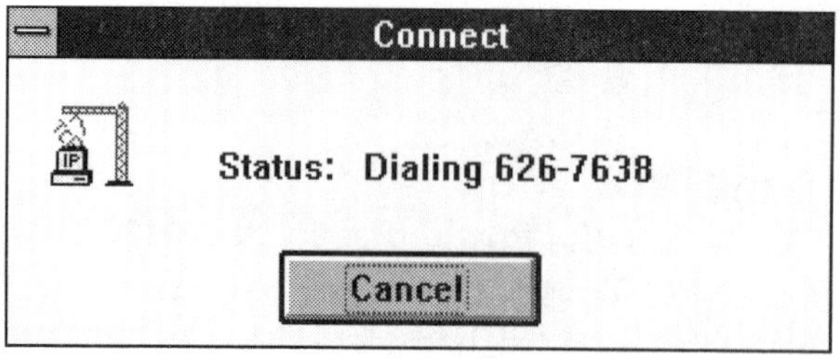

Figure 4-15: Chameleon Connect dialog box.

- When the connection has been successfully established, the Connect dialog box is dismissed and the Custom program's Connect menu changes to a Disconnect menu.

3. In the Chameleon Sampler program group window, double-click on the **Mail** icon. The User Login dialog box appears, as shown in Figure 4-16.

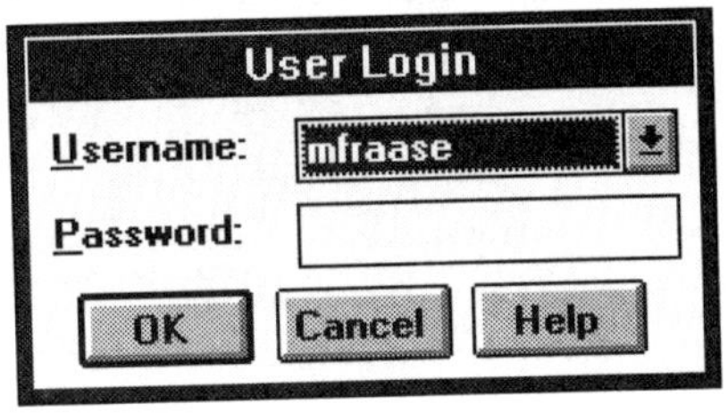

Figure 4-16: Chameleon Mail User Login dialog box.

4. Select your username from the Username menu, if necessary.
5. Enter your password in the Password: field.
6. Click the **OK** button. The main Mail window with Inbox folder open appears, as shown in Figure 4-17.

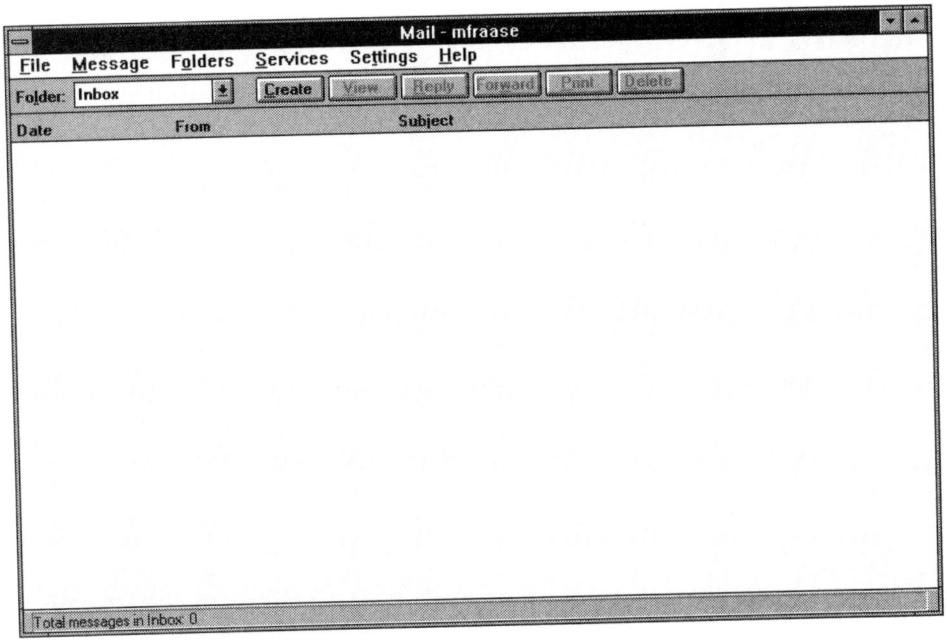

Figure 4-17: Chameleon Mail main Mail window with Inbox folder open.

7. From the Message menu, select the Retrieve Mail command. Chameleon Mail will automatically login to the mail server and download any e-mail addressed to you. The downloaded e-mail

messages appear as a list of items in the Inbox folder within the main Mail window, as shown in Figure 4-18.

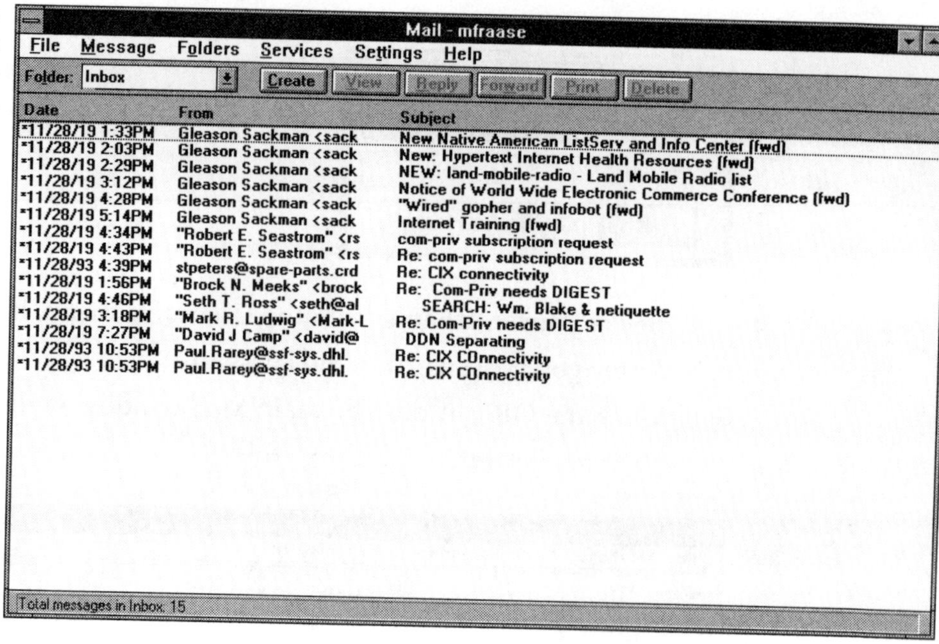

Figure 4-18: Chameleon main Mail window with Inbox folder items.

8. Double-click on the subject line of the message you want to read. The message appears, as shown in the example in Figure 4-19.

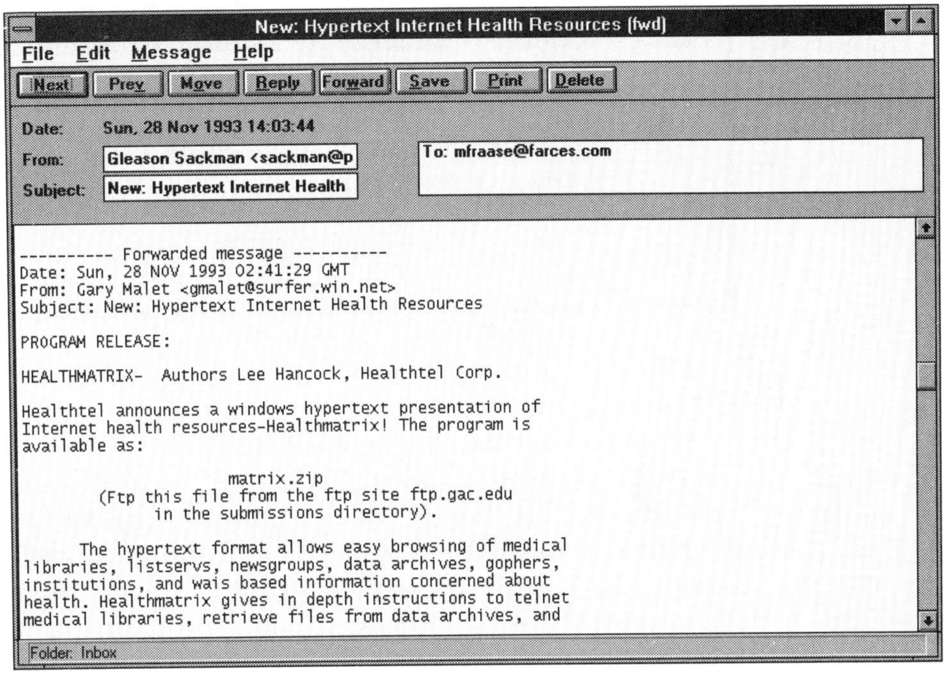

Figure 4-19: Chameleon Mail message example.

9. Close the message window by double-clicking the window's **Control** menu icon.
10. Repeat steps 8–9 for each additional message you want to read.
    - Incoming e-mail messages are stored in the Inbox folder until they are deleted or transferred to another mail folder. See "Managing E-Mail With Chameleon" beginning on page 99 for more information.

Occasionally, you may receive an e-mail message that is too big for Chameleon Mail to handle. If this happens, a Mail dialog box reporting the error is displayed, as shown in Figure 4-20.

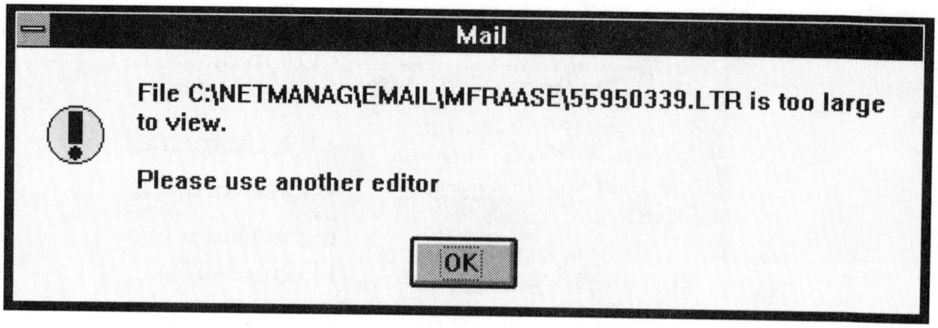

Figure 4-20: Chameleon Mail dialog box reporting an error with a message too large to view.

When this happens, make a note of the pathname for the message and use a text editor or word processor to view the message.

Another limitation of Chameleon Mail is its inability to send or receive binary files as e-mail attachments or enclosures. The commercial version of Chameleon Mail includes support for Multipurpose Internet Mail Extensions (MIME), which basically allows you to include multimedia attachments to your e-mail messages. For information about using a freeware Windows e-mail program that allows you to send and receive binary files as e-mail attachments, see "E-Mail & Attached Files" beginning on page 142.

Creating & Sending an E-Mail Message With Chameleon Mail

Use these steps to create and send an e-mail message with Chameleon Mail.

1. With Windows running and the Chameleon Sampler program group window open, double-click on the **Custom** icon. The Custom window appears, as shown in Figure 4-14.
   - Additionally, the Chameleon NEWT icon appears in the lower left corner of your monitor, indicating that the TCP/IP communications stack has been successfully loaded.
2. Click the **Connect** menu. Chameleon attempts to establish a connection using the configuration information you supplied in Chapter 2, and the Connect dialog box is displayed, as shown in Figure 4-15.
   - When the connection has been successfully established, the Connect dialog box is dismissed and the Custom program's Connect menu changes to a Disconnect menu.

3. In the Chameleon Sampler program group window, double-click on the **Mail** icon. The User Login dialog box appears, as shown in Figure 4-16.
4. Select your username from the Username menu, if necessary.
5. Enter your password in the Password: field.
6. Click the **OK** button. The main Mail window with Inbox folder open appears, as shown in Figure 4-21.

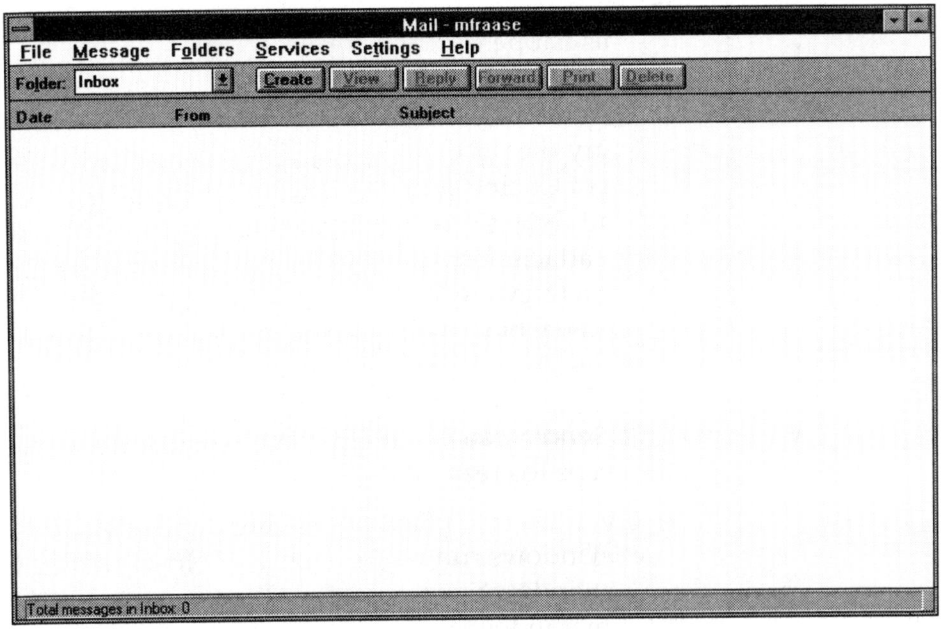

Figure 4-21: Chameleon Mail main Mail window with Inbox folder open.

7. Click the **Create** button in the main Mail window. A New Mail window opens, as shown in Figure 4-22.

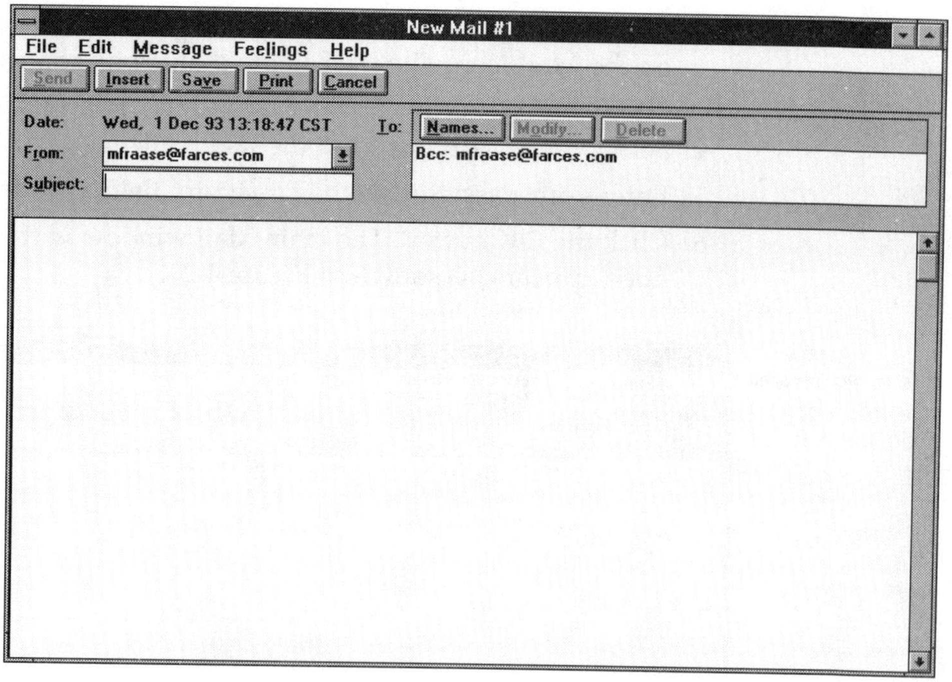

Figure 4-22: Chameleon Mail New Mail window.

8. Enter the subject of your e-mail message in the Subject: field.
9. Enter the body of your e-mail message. You can type or paste text into the message.
   - If you want to place an existing text file into an e-mail message, click the **Insert** button. The File to Insert dialog box appears, within which you can select the file you want to place in your e-mail message, as shown in Figure 4-23.

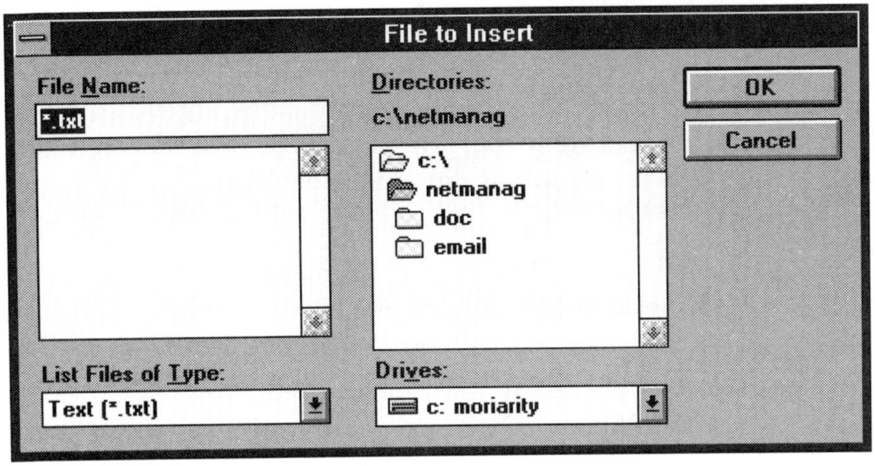

Figure 4-23: Chameleon Mail File to Insert dialog box.

10. Click the **Names...** button. The Names dialog box appears, as shown in Figure 4-24.

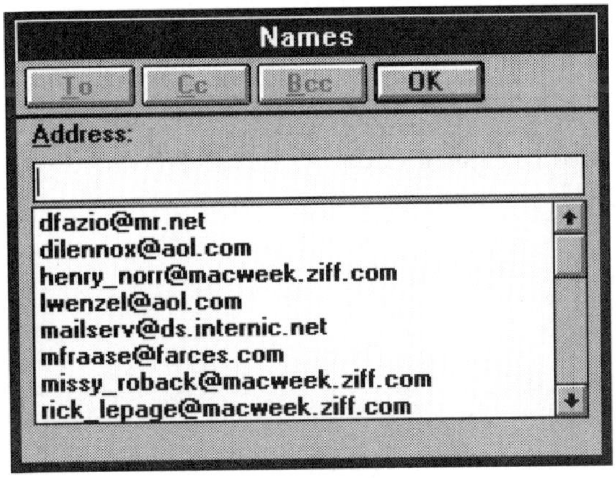

Figure 4-24: Chameleon Mail Names dialog box.

11. Select the e-mail address to which you want to send your e-mail message by clicking on the address in the Names dialog box. (See "Using the Chameleon Mail Address Book" beginning on page 104 for more information on adding frequently used e-mail addresses.)
    - Alternatively, you can enter the e-mail addresses of the recipients—in the username@domain.top-domain format—directly in the Address: box.
12. Click the **To** button. The address will be added to the To: box in the New Mail window.

13. Select the e-mail address to which you want to send a courtesy copy of your e-mail by clicking on the address in the Names dialog box.
    - Courtesy copies are copies of your message sent to third parties *with* a notification to the addressee.
14. Click the **Cc** button. The address will be added to the To: box in the New Mail window as a Cc recipient.
15. Select the e-mail address to which you want to send a blind courtesy copy of your e-mail by clicking on the address in the Names dialog box.
    - Blind courtesy copies are copies of your message sent to third parties *without* a notification to the addressee.
    - For more information on courtesy copies and blind courtesy copies, see the Blind Courtesy Copy sidebar.
16. Click the **Bcc** button. The address will be added to the To: box in the New Mail window as a Bcc recipient.
17. Click the **OK** button when you are done adding your recipients' e-mail addresses. The New Mail window will be updated to reflect your addressing changes, as shown in the example in Figure 4-25.

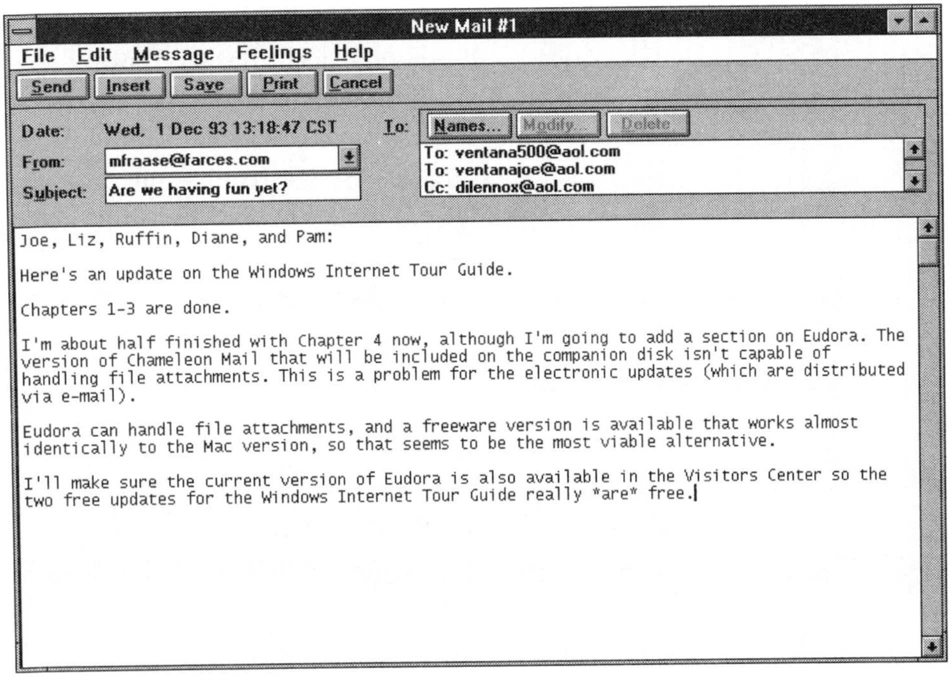

Figure 4-25: Chameleon Mail New Mail window with sample message and addressing.

18. Click the **Send** button in the New Mail window. Your e-mail message will be sent to the recipients you specified.

Blind Courtesy Copies.

Courtesy copies used to be called carbon copies. But since we don't use carbon paper anymore, they're now called courtesy copies by the high-tech, in-the-know crowd. They're useful for distributing identical messages to a number of people.

Most people don't consider *blind* courtesy copies very nice, because they're secretive. They're generally used by someone who is either trying to cover a mistake or by someone who has something to hide. Privacy is a good thing. Secrecy isn't.

Blind courtesy copies are useful for very large mailing lists because sending letters using the blind courtesy copy addressing feature prevents the names of all the recipients from appearing in the message header and overwhelming the actual message.

The distribution list for the electronic updates for this book is handled with blind courtesy copies. I could be altruistic and say that I do it that way to keep the header short, but that would not be completely true. If I used courtesy copies instead of blind courtesy copies, anyone on the list would have access to the entire list. That's not a good thing for your privacy. Nor is it a good thing for my bank account. I'm not sure how to balance the tension between privacy and secrecy. Let me know if you've figured it out.

Replying to E-Mail Messages With Chameleon Mail

Replying to an e-mail message is similar to creating a new message, although it's partially automated. To use Chameleon Mail to reply to an e-mail message:

1. Double-click on the subject line of the message you want to read. The message appears, as shown in the example in Figure 4-19.
2. Click the **Reply** button in the Mail window. A new Mail window is opened with the subject and addressing information automatically copied from the original message. Additionally, the new Mail window may contain the original message as a quote, depending on your Chameleon Mail preferences settings, as shown in the example in Figure 4-26.

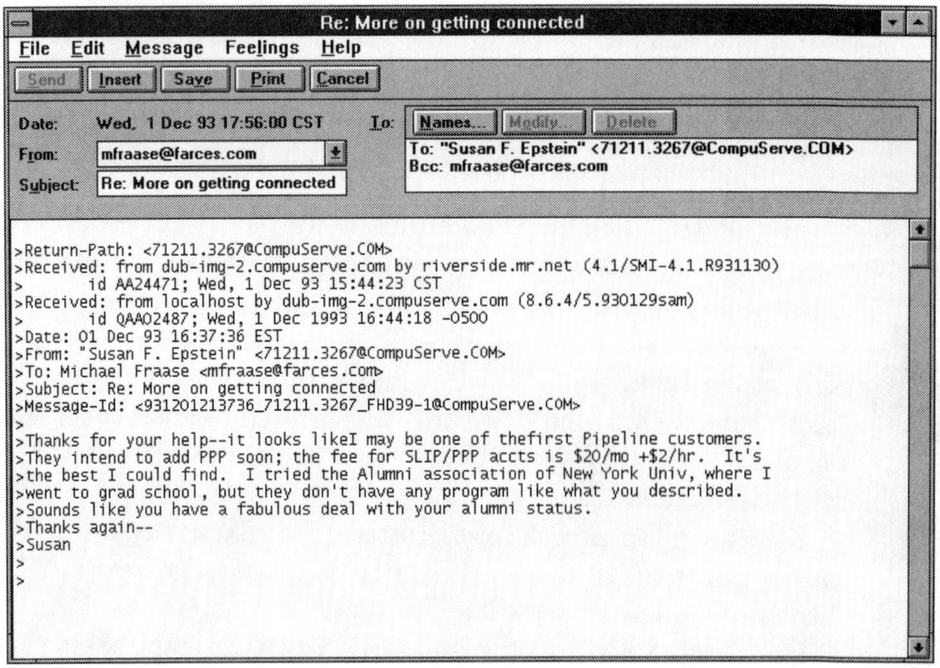

Figure 4-26: Chameleon Mail new Mail window with quoted message.

- For more information on quoting existing messages, see the Internet Quoting Conventions sidebar.

3. Enter the body of your e-mail message. You can type or paste text into the message.

4. If you want to place an existing text file into an e-mail message, click the **Insert** button. The File to Insert dialog box appears, within which you can select the file you want to place in your e-mail message, as shown in Figure 4-23.
5. Click the **Send** button in the New Mail window. Your e-mail message will be sent to the recipients you specified.

Internet Quoting Conventions.
The ">" that precedes each line of a message is the Internet convention for quoted text. There are several variations, but ">" is the most common.

Second hand quotes—quoted replies to quotes—are shown with a ">>" preceding each line.

This can soon get ridiculous. I've seen heated *flame wars* (vitriolic online debates) erupt into five or six levels of ">"s. It's not a pretty sight, and it's impossible to figure out who said what to whom.

A good rule of thumb when replying to e-mail or responding to a message posting is to quote only material that is necessary to further the understanding of the letter or message thread. Don't, for instance, quote a 300-line message in its entirety and add only "I agree" at the end.

Managing E-Mail With Chameleon

Chameleon Mail lets you organize your incoming e-mail by creating new mail folders for storing and moving messages. Chameleon Mail defaults to routing all incoming e-mail to a single mail folder named Inbox. In Chameleon Mail, a "mail folder" is a collection of e-mail messages.

To create new mail folders:

1. In the Chameleon Sampler program group window, double-click on the **Mail** icon. The User Login dialog box appears, as shown in Figure 4-16.
2. Select your username from the Username menu, if necessary.
3. Enter your password in the Password: field.
4. Click the **OK** button. The main Mail window with Inbox folder open appears, as shown in Figure 4-21.
5. From the Folders menu, select the Create... command. The Create Folder dialog box is displayed, as shown in Figure 4-27.

Figure 4-27: Chameleon Mail Create Folder dialog box.

6. Enter a name for the new mail folder.
7. Click the **OK** button. The new mail folder will be created and its name and status will be added to the Folder List.
8. From the Folders menu, select the Folder List... command. The Folder List window appears, containing a list of mail folders you've defined, as shown in Figure 4-28.

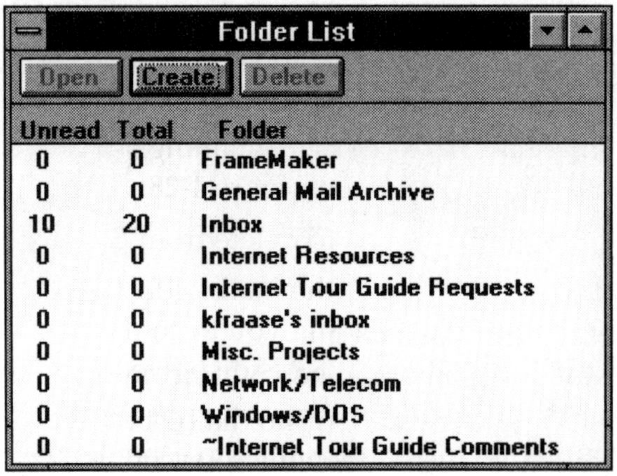

Figure 4-28: Chameleon Mail Folder List window.

9. Select the mail folder you want to open from the list.
10. Click the **Open** button. The selected mail folder will be opened.

To move e-mail messages between mail folders:

1. Select the e-mail message you want to move from the list.
2. From the Message menu, select the Move to Folder... command. The Move To Folder dialog box is displayed, as shown in the example in Figure 4-29.

Figure 4-29: Chameleon Mail Move To Folder dialog box.

3. Select the folder to which you want to move the selected message (or messages) from the list.
4. Click the **OK** button. The selected message (or messages) will be moved to the mailbox you specified.

To delete any unneeded mail folders:

1. From the Folders menu, select the Folder List... command. The Folder List window appears, containing a list of mail folders you've defined, as shown in Figure 4-28.
2. Select the folder you want to delete from the list.
3. Click the **Delete** button. If the mail folder contains any e-mail messages, a dialog box asking you to confirm that you want to delete the selected mail folder is displayed.
   - If the mail folder is empty, no dialog box is displayed and the mail folder is deleted without your confirmation.
4. Click the **OK** button. The selected mail folder—*and its contents, if any*—will be deleted and no longer available.

For more information on managing your e-mail with different mailboxes, see the Mail Folder Strategies sidebar below.

Mail Folder Strategies.

You can create mail folders for any number of filing and organization strategies. Some people like to create folders for each month or week, filing their messages by date. Others like to create a folder for each person they regularly correspond with, organizing messages based on contact.

The strategy that works best for me is to create folders for various topics or projects I'm working on. When new e-mail messages come in, I sort them by content. Many e-mail programs have intelligent *filters* that can be used to automatically sort incoming e-mail based on a wide range of criteria including sender, addressee or even the site from which the message was sent.

You can forward an e-mail message to an associate with these steps.

1. Double-click on the subject line of the message you want to read. The message appears, as shown in the example in Figure 4-19.
2. Click the **Forward** button in the Mail window. A new Mail window is opened with the subject information automatically copied from the original message with a FW: prefix. Additionally, the new Mail window will contain the original message as a quote, as shown in the example in Figure 4-30.

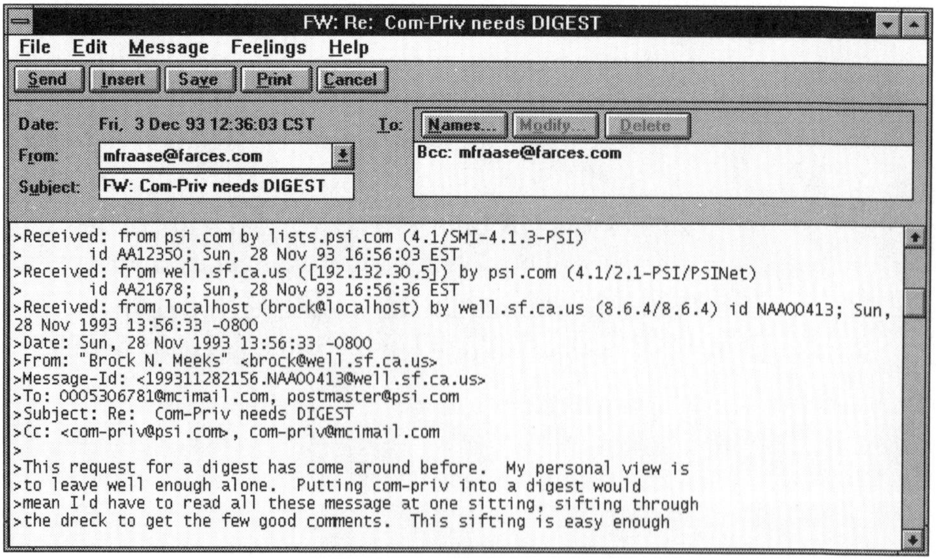

Figure 4-30: Chameleon Mail Forwarded Mail window with quoted message.

- For more information on quoting existing messages, see the Internet Quoting Conventions sidebar.

3. Enter the body of any information you want to include with the forwarded message. You can type or paste text into the message.
    - It's usually a good idea to include a brief preface to your recipient describing why you're forwarding the message.
4. If you want to place an existing text file into an e-mail message, click the **Insert** button. The File to Insert dialog box appears, within which you can select the file you want to place in your e-mail message, as shown in Figure 4-23.
5. Click the **Names...** button. The Names dialog box appears, as shown in Figure 4-24.
6. Select the e-mail address to which you want to send your e-mail message by clicking on the address in the Names dialog box. (See "Using the Chameleon Mail Address Book" beginning on page 104 for more information on adding frequently used e-mail addresses.)
    - Alternatively, you can enter the e-mail addresses of the recipients—in the username@domain.top-domain format—directly in the Address: box.
7. Click the **To** button. The address will be added to the To: box in the New Mail window.
8. Select the e-mail address to which you want to send a courtesy copy of your e-mail by clicking on the address in the Names dialog box.
    - Courtesy copies are copies of your message sent to third parties *with* a notification to the addressee.
9. Click the **Cc** button. The address will be added to the To: box in the New Mail window as a Cc recipient.
10. Select the e-mail address to which you want to send a blind courtesy copy of your e-mail by clicking on the address in the Names dialog box.
    - Blind courtesy copies are copies of your message sent to third parties *without* a notification to the addressee.
    - For more information on courtesy copies and blind courtesy copies, see the Blind Courtesy Copy sidebar.

11. Click the **Bcc** button. The address will be added to the To: box in the New Mail window as a Bcc recipient.
12. Click the **OK** button when you are done adding your recipients' e-mail addresses. The New Mail window will be updated to reflect your addressing changes.
13. Click the **Send** button in the mail window. Your e-mail message will be forwarded to the recipients you specified.

Deleted e-mail messages are removed but not erased from your disk. To permanently erase e-mail messages you have deleted, select the Empty Trash command from the Services menu. This command will be active only if there are messages that have been deleted but not erased from your disk.

Using the Chameleon Mail Address Book

Adding the e-mail addresses of people you correspond with regularly to your Chameleon Mail Address Book helps you communicate quickly and assures that your messages reach their intended recipients. Additionally, if you regularly send the same message to a group of people, it's a straightforward procedure to create an automatic distribution list. Use these steps to create a personal Address Book in Chameleon Mail.

1. In the Chameleon Sampler program group window, double-click on the **Mail** icon. The User Login dialog box appears, as shown in Figure 4-16.
2. Select your username from the Username menu, if necessary.
3. Enter your password in the Password: field.
4. Click the **OK** button. The main Mail window with Inbox folder open appears, as shown in Figure 4-21.
5. From the Settings menu, select the Address Book... command. The Address Book window appears, as shown in Figure 4-31.

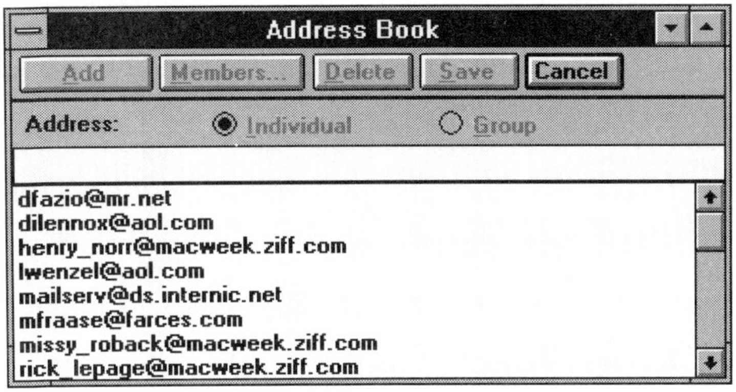

Figure 4-31: Chameleon Mail Address Book window.

6. Enter the e-mail address you want to add to the Address Book, using the username@domain.top-domain format. Note that the **Individual** and **Group** radio buttons become active.
7. Make sure the **Individual** radio button is selected. If not, click the button to select it.
8. Click the **Add** button. The e-mail address you entered will be added to your personal Address Book and will be available from the To: pop-up menu.
9. Double-click on the **Control Menu** icon to close the Address Book window.

Sometimes you may find it useful to create a distribution list for sending the same e-mail message to a group of recipients. Here's how to create an automated distribution list in Chameleon Mail.

1. From the Settings menu, select the Address Book... command. The Address Book window appears, as shown in Figure 4-31.
2. Enter the name of the distribution list you want to create. Note that the **Individual** and **Group** radio buttons become active.
3. Click the **Group** radio button.
4. Click the **Add** button. The Group window appears, bearing the name of the distribution list you entered in step 2. A sample Group window (named Ventana) is shown in Figure 4-32.

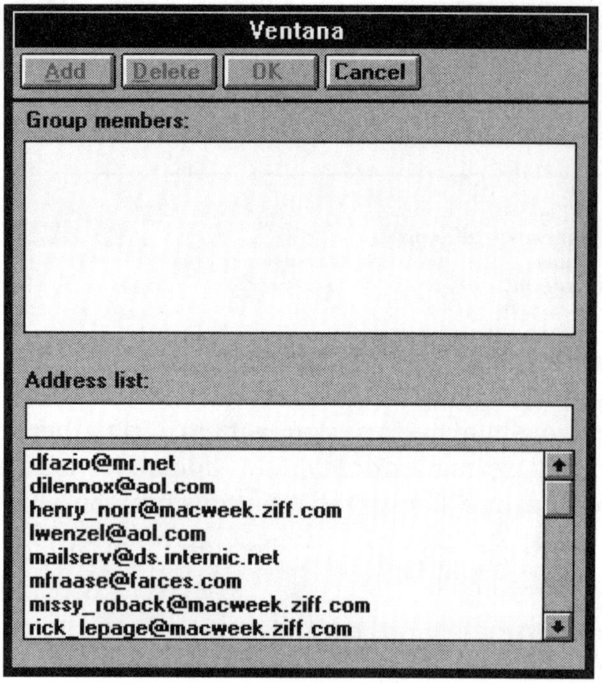

Figure 4-32: Chameleon Mail Group window.

5. Select the e-mail address you want to add to the distribution list from the Address list in the lower portion of the Group window.
   - Alternatively, enter the e-mail address—in the username@domain.top-domain format—of the person you want to add to the distribution list manually in the available field.
6. Click the **Add** button. The selected e-mail address is added to the Group members list in the upper portion of the Group window.
7. Repeat steps 5–6 for each additional address you want to add to the distribution list.
8. Click the **OK** button. The distribution list will be added to your personal Address book, with its name in brackets, as shown in the example in Figure 4-33.

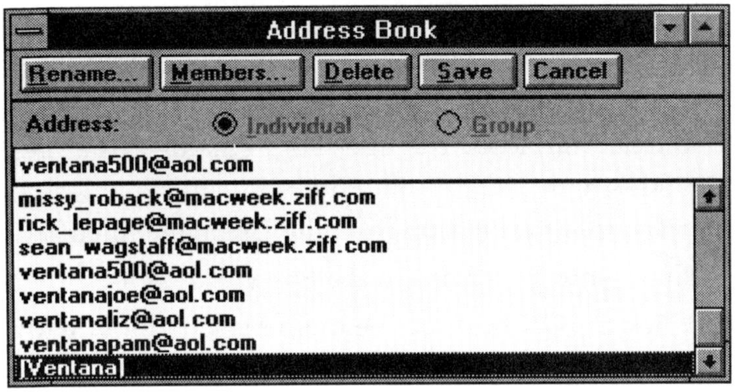

Figure 4-33: Chameleon Mail Address Book with distribution list selected.

- The distribution list will be available from the To: pop-up menu in all Mail windows.

9. Double-click on the **Control Menu** icon to close the Address Book window.

Using Chameleon Mail Filters

Filing important e-mail messages after you've read them is a good way to manage incoming e-mail. But wouldn't it be wonderful if you could file incoming e-mail messages *before* you read them? Well, if you use Chameleon Mail, you can. Chameleon Mail's *filter rules* allow you to automatically manage your e-mail in a number of ways, including routing e-mail to specific mailboxes. The commercial version of Eudora also provides e-mail message filter rules.

Filters can be thought of as "almost-intelligent processors" that look at all incoming e-mail messages and manipulate those messages based on a set of rules you have defined. If you don't want to use Chameleon Mail's filters, or if you want to experiment with e-mail a little before setting up filters, feel free to skip this section.

Chameleon Mail provides global filters for all incoming e-mail messages. You can set up a filter that automatically moves messages you receive from a mailing list to a mail folder you have set up specifically for that list or topic. Or, you can define a filter that automatically forwards messages received from a particular person to a distribution list you have defined.

To create local filter actions to automatically route e-mail messages to appropriate mail folders, follow these steps. The example used in this sequence routes all e-mail messages from the Commercialization and Privatization of the Internet mailing list (com-priv) to a mail folder named Network/Telecom.

1. In the Chameleon Sampler program group window, double-click on the **Mail** icon. The User Login dialog box appears, as shown in Figure 4-16.
2. Select your username from the Username menu, if necessary.
3. Enter your password in the Password: field.
4. Click the **OK** button. The main Mail window with Inbox folder open appears, as shown in Figure 4-21.
5. From the Services menu, select the Rules... command. The Mail rules dialog box appears, as shown in Figure 4-34.

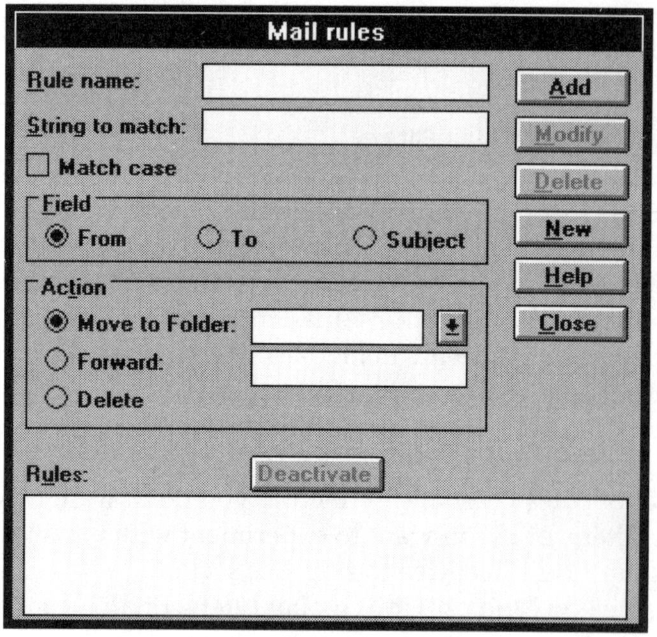

Figure 4-34: Chameleon Mail rules dialog box.

6. Enter a name for the rule you want to create in the Rule name: field.
   - For this example, I'll name the rule **Com-Priv Mailing List**.
7. Enter the text to look for in the String to match: field.

8. Click the appropriate **Field** radio button representing the field of the e-mail message's header in which to search:
   - Click the **From** radio button to search in each message's From field.
   - Click the **To** radio button to search in each message's To field.
   - Click the **Subject** radio button to search in each message's Subject field.
   - For this example, I'll search for any messages that contain **com-priv** in the **To** field. This is somewhat counter-intuitive, because you would expect to search for messages in the From field. In the case of mailing lists, however, it's generally a better idea to search in the To field because it remains consistent from message to message.
9. Click the appropriate **Action** radio button representing the action you want to perform on each e-mail message that meets the search criteria you specified.
   - Click the **Move to Folder**: radio button if you want to route the message to a specific Chameleon mail folder.
   - Click the **Forward**: radio button if you want the message to be forwarded to a specific distribution list you have defined in your personal Address Book.
   - Click the **Delete** radio button if you want to create a sort of "bozo" filter, automatically deleting messages from a particular person or pertaining to a specific subject.
   - For this example, I'll click the **Move to Folder**: radio button because I want all messages from the com-priv mailing list routed to a specific mail folder.
10. From the pop-up menu, select the mail folder you want to use to contain the re-routed e-mail messages.
    - For this example, I'll select the Network/Telecom mail folder.
    - Alternatively, if you're defining a rule to forward e-mail to a distribution list, enter the name of the Address Book group in the Forward: field.
11. Click the **Add** button. The Mail rules dialog box will be updated to reflect the new rule you have defined. An example is shown in Figure 4-35.

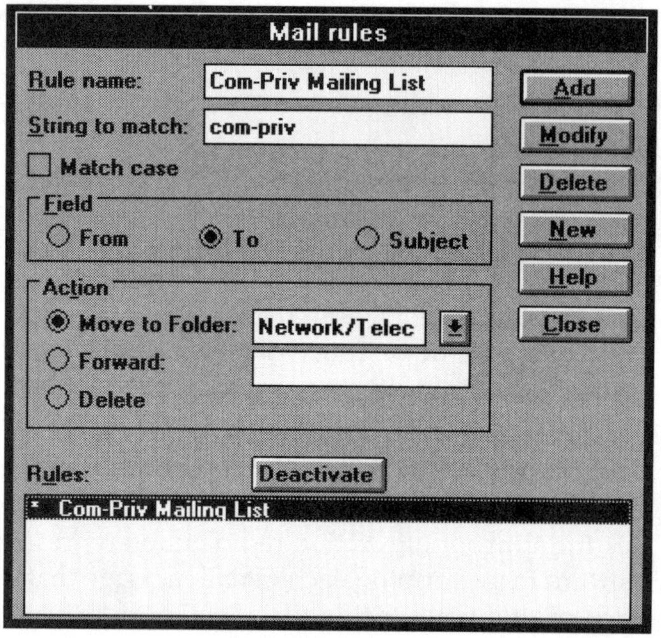

Figure 4-35: Chameleon Mail rules dialog box with a defined rule.

12. Click the **New** button and repeat steps 6–11 for each additional rule you want to define.
13. Click the **Close** button to dismiss the Mail rules dialog box and save your set of rules to disk.

Note that if you define multiple rules that contain the identical text to match, Chameleon Mail will apply only the first rule in the list.

Quick Guide to Using Eudora

Qualcomm Inc.'s Eudora is an electronic mail program for Windows that is fully compatible with the POP3 mail server offered by most Internet service providers. (If you're not sure whether Eudora is compatible with your mail server, ask your network administrator.) Eudora is available in both freeware and commercial versions.

The current release of the freeware version of Eudora is available in the Visitors Center and by anonymous ftp at ftp.qualcomm.com in the /pceudora/windows/ directory. The freeware version of Eudora lacks Chameleon Mail's filtering capabilities but is capable of handling file attachments in e-mail messages. Note that your two free electronic updates (and subsequent subscription editions) to *The Windows Internet*

Tour Guide will be sent to you via e-mail. *You must use an e-mail program capable of handling file attachments to receive these electronic updates.*

The commercial version of Eudora supports both file attachments and filtering rules. Both versions of Eudora are completely compatible with the Chameleon WINSOCK.DLL.

Eudora is available from:

Qualcomm Inc.
10555 Sorrento Valley Road
San Diego, CA 92121
800/238-3672619/587-1121619/587-8276 (Fax)
info@qualcomm.com

Compressing space and time.

Ralph Brandi uses the Internet to compress space and time and to meet people that he would otherwise never encounter. Here is his story of how he uses the Internet:

"The net demolishes the barriers of time and location. If you've got some kind of fairly obscure interest, you can be pretty sure there is someone else on the net who shares it. The fact that they don't live in your neighborhood doesn't prevent you from carrying on an extended conversation. They can even live on the other side of the world and you don't have to worry about waking them up.

The best thing about the net that I've encountered in my 6 or so years connected has nothing to do with computers: it's the people. By communicating with people I share interests with, I've made a number of good friends.

I had a net.friend from New Zealand visit me for a week last year after a couple of years of corresponding over the net. I had a great time showing him New York City and the east coast, and he brought some books and records for me from New Zealand that I couldn't find for love nor money here in the U.S. I'm going to be visiting him in London, where he lives now, this summer.

Some months ago, I was receiving a couple of low-powered radio stations from Australia on my shortwave radio. I had been trying to receive these stations literally for years, and they're highly sought-after targets among shortwave listeners. I posted a note to the rec.radio.shortwave newsgroup. The following morning I had e-mail from a couple of people in Boston who had followed up on that tip and been rewarded with their first receptions of the stations. I later met them at a convention of shortwave enthusiasts, and had a very enjoyable lunch with them and some of their friends.

The common thread here is the interactions with *people*, not computers."

Configuring Eudora E-Mail

Eudora must be properly configured before you can begin using it to send e-mail. To use Eudora, you must have an account on a computer that runs a POP3 (Post Office Protocol version 3) mail server. Use these steps to configure Eudora for use with your mail server.

1. Launch Eudora by double-clicking on its icon in the Program Manager.
2. From the Special menu, select the Configuration... command. The Configuration dialog box appears, as shown in Figure 4-36.

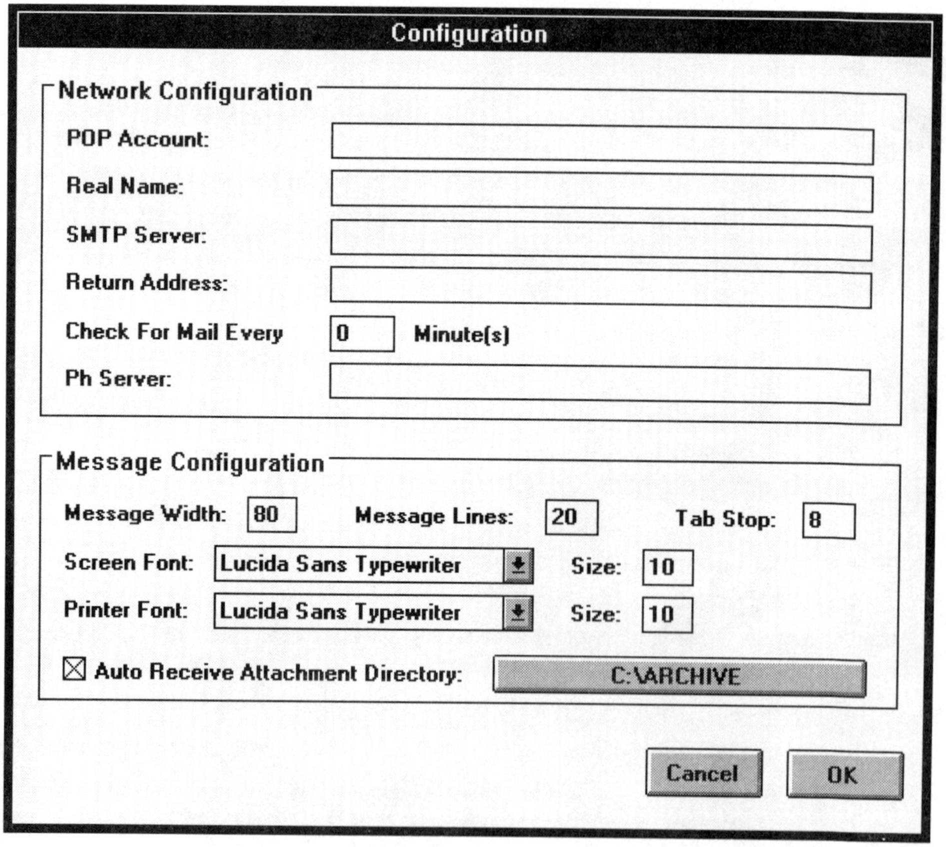

Figure 4-36: Eudora Configuration dialog box.

3. Enter your username in the POP Account: box in the format: user@domain.top-domain.

   - For example, my login name is mfraase and the name of the computer that provides my e-mail service is mr.net. I would enter **mfraase@mr.net** in the POP Account: box.

4. Enter your full name in the Real Name: box.
5. Enter the name of your mail server in the SMTP Server: box using the format: domain.top-domain.
6. Enter your e-mail address in the Return Address: box in the format: user@domain.top-domain. This will likely be the same domain name address you entered in the POP account box, but not necessarily.
7. Click the **OK** button. You've completed the basic configuration process for Eudora.

There are several other convenient features Eudora offers that you might want to take advantage of. Or, you can begin using Eudora to compose and end e-mail messages. If you want to begin using Eudora without configuring Eudora for your own personal preferences, you can skip the rest of this section and advance to "Using Eudora E-Mail" beginning on page 117.

Follow these steps to further customize Eudora to your own personal preferences.

1. Select the Configuration... command from the Special menu. The Configuration dialog box will be displayed, as shown in Figure 4-36.
2. Enter how often (in minutes) you want Eudora to look in your mailbox for new mail in the Check For Mail Every box. If you want to check for mail manually, leave this box empty.
3. Enter the name of your e-mail address lookup server in the Ph Server box. Leave this box empty if your mail server doesn't provide a Ph server. (For more information on the Ph protocol and Ph servers, see the Ph Servers sidebar on page 126.)
4. Enter the number of characters to display on each line of e-mail messages in the Message Width: box. Leave the box empty to use the default value of 80 characters.
5. Enter the number of lines of each message you want Eudora to display at a time in the Message Lines: box. Leave the box empty to use the default value of 20 lines.
6. Select a font to use to display e-mail messages from the Screen Font: pop-up menu.
7. Specify a font size to use to display e-mail messages in the Screen Font Size: box.

8. Select a font to use to print e-mail messages from the Printer Font: pop-up menu.
9. Specify a font size to use to print e-mail messages in the Printer Font Size: box.
10. Click the **Auto Receive Attachment Directory** check box if you want to save to a standard location any files that are attached to e-mail messages you receive.
11. Click the **Directory** button to specify a directory in which to save the attached files. A standard directory dialog box will appear, from which you can make your choice.
12. Click the **OK** button. You've completed the basic configuration process for Eudora.

A sample Eudora configuration is shown in Figure 4-37.

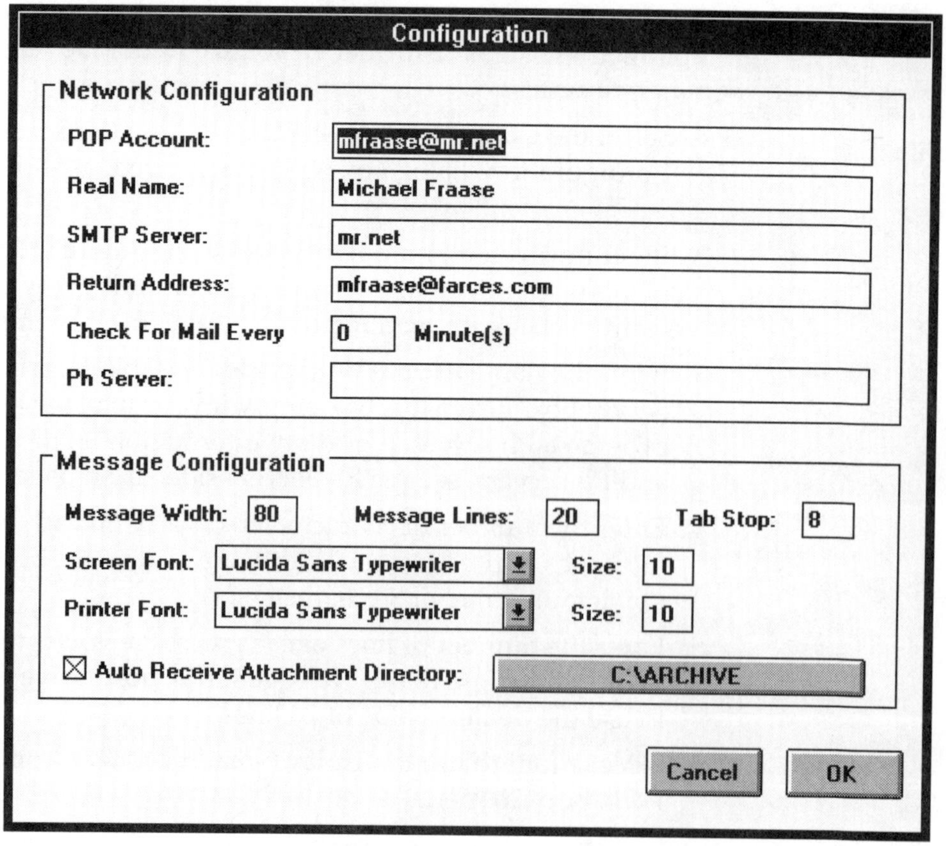

Figure 4-37: Completed Eudora Configuration dialog box.

At this point, you can further tweak Eudora's preferences to suit your individual needs, or you simply start using it. If you want to use Eudora without further configuration, skip the rest of this section and advance to "Using Eudora E-Mail" beginning on page 117.

The table below details the function of each option in the Switches dialog box. Use the information in the following table and execute these steps to finish configuring Eudora.

1. Select the Switches... command from the Special menu. The Switches dialog box will be displayed, as shown in Figure 4-38.

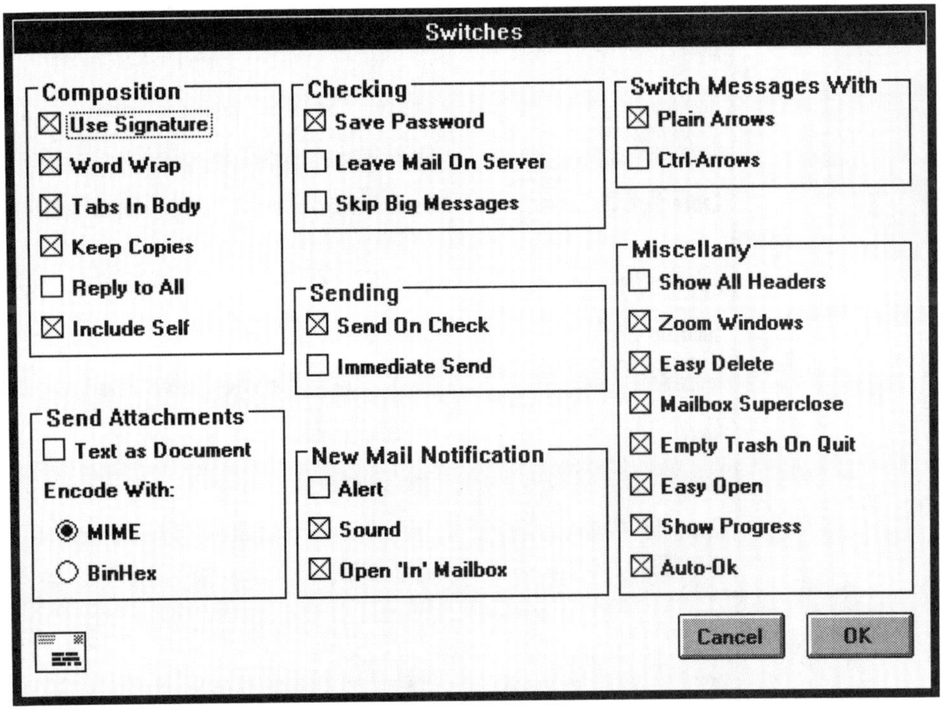

Figure 4-38: Eudora Switches dialog box.

2. Check or uncheck the available check boxes to suit your personal preferences, based on the information presented in Table 4-3.

Table 4-3: Eudora Switches settings.

Check Box	Function When Enabled
Use Signature	Signature file will be automatically attached to outgoing messages
Word Wrap	Automatically wraps line endings in outgoing messages
Tabs in Body	Inserts eight space characters each time Tab key is pressed
Keep Copies	Leaves copies of outgoing messages in Out mailbox
Reply to All	Reply message addressed to sender and all recipients
Include Self	Reply message includes your address
Text as Document	Sends attached text files as a separate document
MIME	Attached files will be encoded in MIME format
BinHex	Attached files will be encoded in BinHex format
Save Password	Saves login password between sessions
Leave Mail On Server	Retains copies of mail messages on mail server after they have been received
Skip Big Messages	Downloads only first few lines of very large messages
Send On Check	Sends any queued messages when checking for new mail
Immediate Send	Sends outgoing messages immediately, rather than queuing them
Alert	Uses dialog boxes to get attention
Sound	Uses sound to get attention
Open "In" Mailbox	Opens In mailbox when new e-mail is received
Plain Arrows	Arrow keys can be used to navigate messages
Ctrl-Arrows	Control-Arrow keys can be used to navigate messages
Show All Headers	Displays entire header, including routing information
Zoom Windows	New mailbox and message windows open to zoomed size
Easy Delete	Deletes messages without warning dialog box
Mailbox Superclose	Closing mailbox window also closes messages from that mailbox
Empty Trash On Quit	Empties trash mailbox when you quit Eudora
Easy Open	Deleting or transferring topmost message opens next message
Show Progress	Displays Progress window during network connections
Auto-Ok	Network problem dialog boxes are automatically dismissed

3. Click the **OK** button. The Switches settings will be saved.
4. From the Window menu, select the Signature command. An empty Signature window will be displayed.
5. Enter your *signature* in the Signature window.
   - A signature is a three- or four-line text file containing your contact information. An example is shown in Figure 4-39. (For more on signatures, see the Signatures sidebar.)

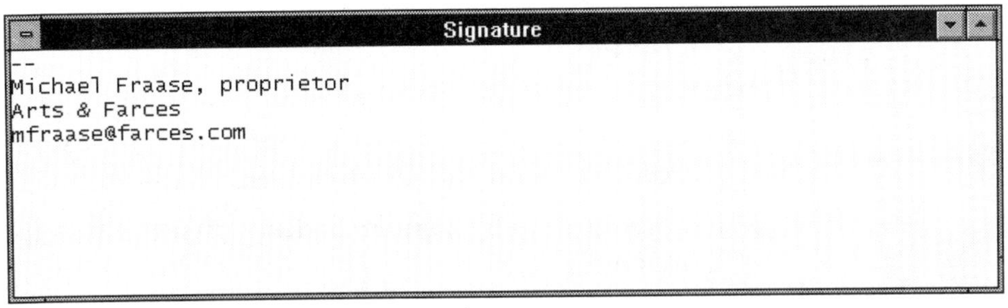

Figure 4-39: Example Eudora Signature window.

6. Double-click the Signature window's **Control** menu icon. You'll be asked if you want to save the changes you made to your signature.
7. Click the **Save** button.

You have now completely configured Eudora and are ready to use it to send and receive e-mail.

Using Eudora E-Mail

The freeware version of Eudora (discussed throughout this chapter) is a full-featured e-mail program comparable to many commercial products. In fact, Qualcomm Inc. also markets a commercial version of Eudora that adds support for filtering rules. You can always get the latest information about Eudora by sending e-mail to

eudora-info@qualcomm.com

The following sections provide instructions for using Eudora's basic features.

Retrieving & Reading E-Mail With Eudora

Use these steps to login to your mail server and automatically retrieve any waiting e-mail.

1. With Windows running and the Chameleon Sampler program group window open, double-click on the **Custom** icon. The Custom window appears, as shown in Figure 4-14.
   - Additionally, the Chameleon NEWT icon appears in the lower left corner of your monitor, indicating that the TCP/IP communications stack has been successfully loaded.
2. Click the **Connect** menu. Chameleon attempts to establish a connection using the configuration information you supplied in Chapter 2, and the Connect dialog box is displayed, as shown in Figure 4-15.
   - When the connection has been successfully established, the Connect dialog box is dismissed and the Custom program's Connect menu changes to a Disconnect menu.
3. Launch Eudora by double-clicking on its icon in the Program Manager.
   - If you have configured Eudora to automatically check for mail, the program will automatically login to the server and download any e-mail addressed to you. The rest of this section assumes that you will be checking for e-mail manually.
4. Select the Check Mail command from the File menu. The Password dialog box will be displayed.
5. Enter your e-mail password and click the **OK** button. The Progress window will be displayed at the top of your screen, providing feedback about the status of your e-mail retrieval.
   - If your password is rejected you'll have to reselect the Check Mail command from the File menu and then reenter your password in the Password dialog box.
   - If there is a problem connecting to the mail server, a dialog box will inform you of the problem. Try selecting the Check Mail command from the File menu again; if Eudora still has problems establishing a connection, see your network administrator.
   - If you have no e-mail waiting on the server, the Progress window will disappear, and Eudora will return to its previous state. If you have waiting e-mail, it will be downloaded and the status will be updated in the Progress window. When all your waiting e-mail has been retrieved, you will be notified (based

on the configuration settings you specified), and the In mailbox window will automatically be displayed. Your new messages will be listed as shown in Figure 4-40.

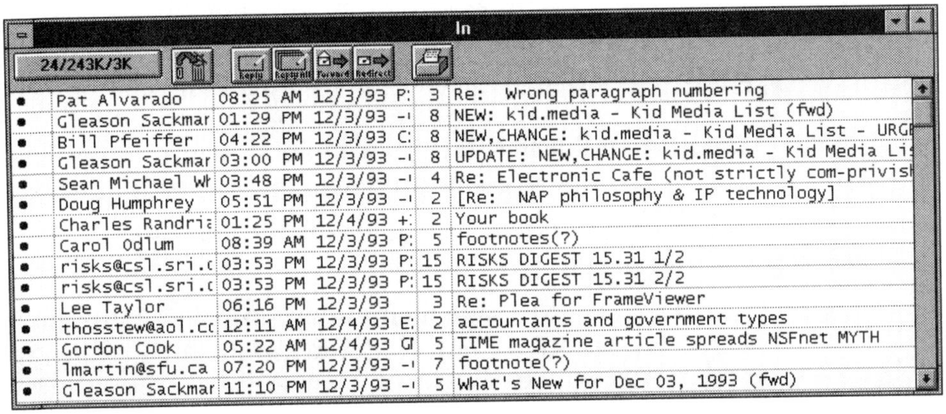

Figure 4-40: Eudora In mailbox window.

6. Double-click on the subject line of the message you want to read. The full message will be displayed, as shown in the example in Figure 4-41.

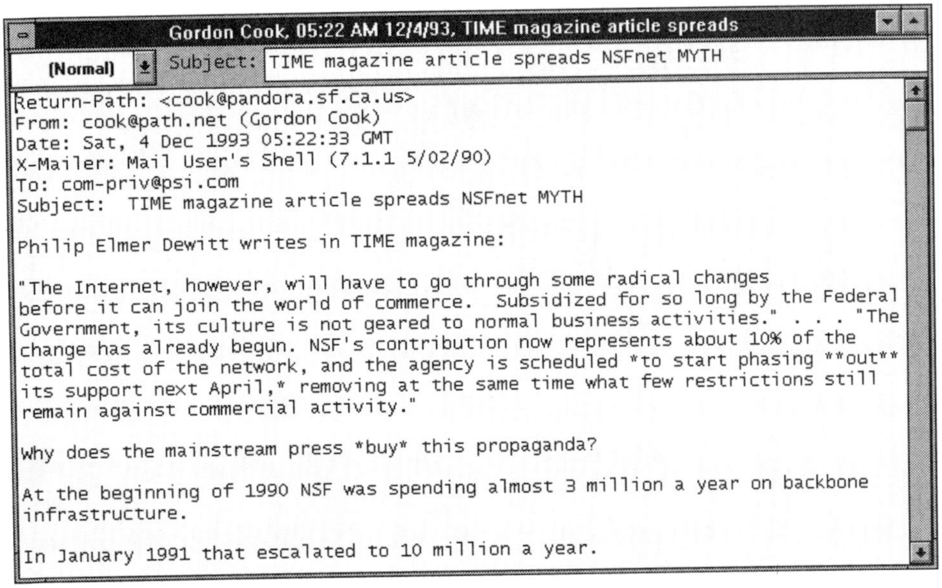

Figure 4-41: Eudora e-mail message.

7. Close the message window by double-clicking the Control menu icon.
8. Repeat steps 4–5 for each additional message you want to read.

E-mail messages are stored in the In mailbox until they are deleted or transferred to another mailbox. For more information, see "Managing E-Mail With Eudora" beginning on page 123.

Creating an E-Mail Message With Eudora

Use these steps to create an e-mail message with Eudora.

1. Launch Eudora by double-clicking on its icon in the Program Manager.
2. From the Message menu, select the New Message command. A new Message Composition window will be displayed, as shown in Figure 4-42.

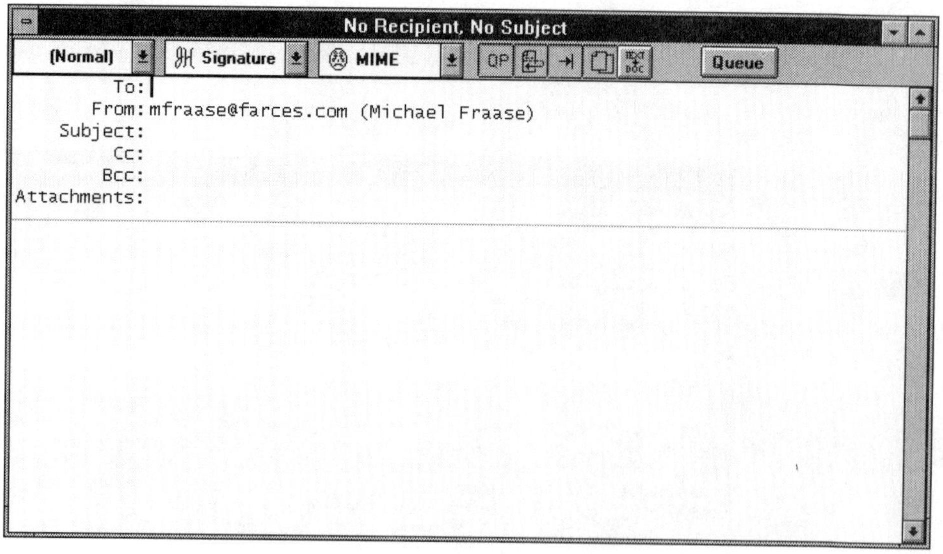

Figure 4-42: Eudora message composition window.

3. Enter the e-mail address of the recipient in the To: field and press the **Tab** key.
4. Enter a short subject for the message in the Subject: field and press the **Tab** key.
5. Enter the e-mail addresses of any recipients to whom you want to send a courtesy copy in the Cc: field and press the **Tab** key. Tab through the field if you don't want to include any courtesy copies.

- Courtesy copies are copies of your message sent to third parties *with* a notification to the addressee.

6. Enter the e-mail address of any recipients to which you want to send a blind courtesy copy in the Bcc: field and press the **Tab** key. Tab through the field if you don't want to include any blind courtesy copies.
   - Blind courtesy copies are copies of your message sent to third parties *without* a notification to the addressee. For more information, see the Blind Courtesy Copies sidebar.
7. Press the **Tab** key to advance through the Attachments: field.
8. Enter the body of your message. You can type or paste text into this field.
9. Click the **Queue** button. Your message will be stored on your hard drive and sent to the mail server when you select the Send Queued Messages command from the File menu.
   - If you have set Eudora's preferences to send mail immediately, there will be a Send button at the far right end of the icon bar instead of the Queue button.

Replying to E-Mail Messages With Eudora

Replying to an e-mail message is similar to creating a new message. Here's how to do it:

1. Double-click on the subject line of the message you want to read. The message will be displayed.
2. From the Message menu, select the Reply command. A new message composition window will be displayed with the original sender's e-mail address in the To: field. In addition, all of the text from the original message will also be included, with a ">" preceding each line, as shown in Figure 4-43.

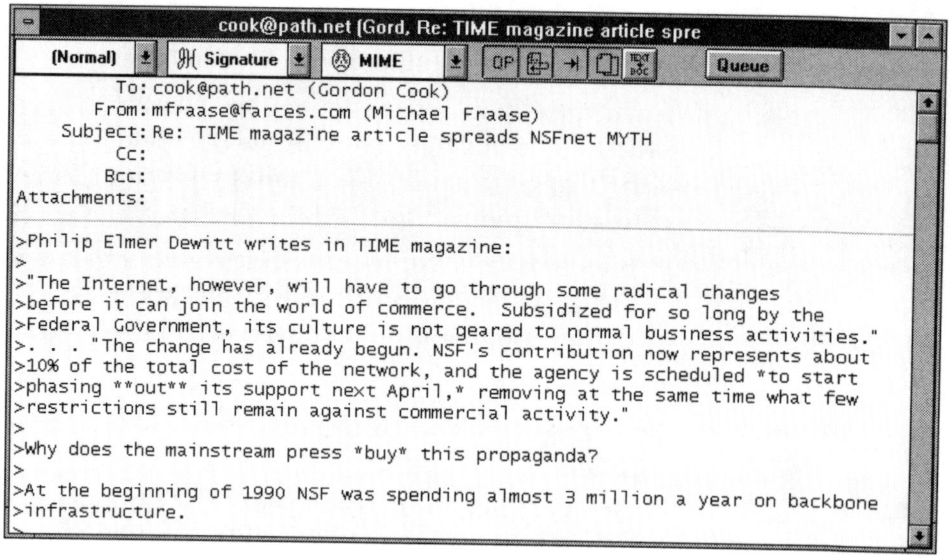

Figure 4-43: Replying to an e-mail message with Eudora.

- For more information about quoting messages, see the Internet Quoting Conventions sidebar.

3. Enter the body of your message. You can type or paste text into this area.
4. Click the **Queue** button. Your message will be stored on your hard drive and sent to the mail server when you select the Send Queued Messages command from the File menu.
   - If you have set Eudora's preferences to send mail immediately, there will be a Send button (instead of the Queue button) at the far right end of the icon bar.

Sending E-Mail Messages With Eudora

Based on how you've configured Eudora, you can either send messages immediately or queue them to your hard drive for batch sending when you connect to the mail server. In general, it's a more efficient use of network resources to queue your e-mail messages for batch sending unless you maintain a constant connection to the Internet.

To send your queued e-mail messages:

1. With Windows running and the Chameleon Sampler program group window open, double-click on the **Custom** icon. The Custom window appears, as shown in Figure 4-14.

- Additionally, the Chameleon NEWT icon appears in the lower left corner of your monitor, indicating that the TCP/IP communications stack has been successfully loaded.

2. Click the **Connect** menu. Chameleon attempts to establish a connection using the configuration information you supplied in Chapter 2, and the Connect dialog box is displayed, as shown in Figure 4-15.
   - When the connection has been successfully established, the Connect dialog box is dismissed and the Custom program's Connect menu changes to a Disconnect menu.
3. Launch Eudora by double-clicking on its icon in the Program Manager.
4. Select the Send Queued Messages command from the File menu. The Password dialog box will appear (unless you have configured Eudora to remember your password between sessions).
5. Enter your e-mail password and click the **OK** button. The Progress window will appear at the top of your screen, providing feedback about the status of your e-mail being sent.
   - If your password is rejected you'll have to reselect the Send Queued Messages command from the File menu and then reenter your password in the Password dialog box.
   - If there is a problem connecting to the mail server, a dialog box will inform you of the problem. Try selecting the Send Queued Messages command from the File menu again; if Eudora still has problems establishing a connection, see your network administrator.
   - When the last e-mail message has been sent to the mail server, the Progress window will disappear, and Eudora will return to its previous state.

Managing E-Mail With Eudora

Eudora lets you organize your incoming e-mail by creating new mailboxes for storing and moving messages.

To create new mailboxes:

1. Launch Eudora by double-clicking on its icon in the Program Manager.

2. From the Mailbox menu, select the New... command. The New Mailbox Dialog box will appear, as shown in Figure 4-44.

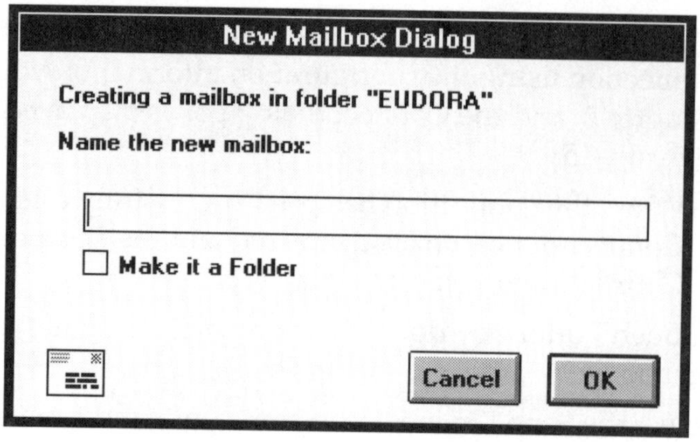

Figure 4-44: Eudora New Mailbox Dialog box.

3. Enter a name for the new mailbox.
4. Click the **OK** button. A new mailbox will be created with the name you specified in step 3.
   - Check the **Make it a Folder** check box if you want to create a new folder within an existing mailbox.
5. Repeat steps 2–4 to create any additional mailboxes you may need.
   - For more information on working with multiple mailboxes, see the Mailbox Strategies sidebar.

To move e-mail messages between your mailboxes:

1. Launch Eudora by double-clicking on its icon in the Program Manager.
2. Open the mailbox containing the message you want to move. You do this by selecting its entry from the lower portion of the Mailbox menu.
3. Select the subject line of the message you want to move. The subject line will be highlighted.
   - You can select a continuous range of messages by clicking on the first message and Shift-clicking on the last message. You can make multiple discontinuous selections by Control-clicking on the messages you want to select.
4. Select from the Transfer menu the new mailbox where you want to move the selected message, as shown in Figure 4-45.

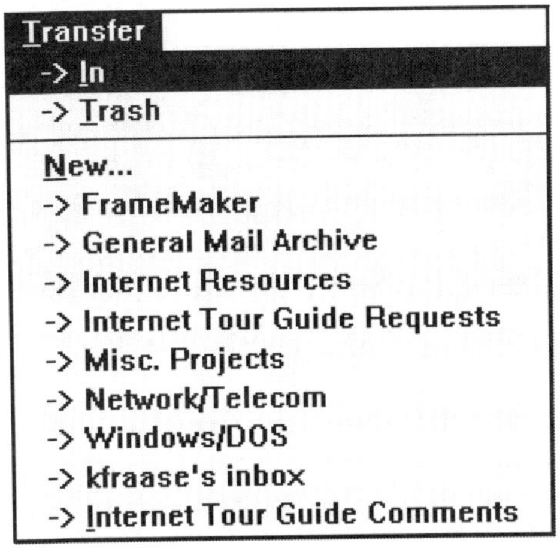

Figure 4-45: Eudora Transfer menu with custom mailboxes.

E-mail messages are stored in the In mailbox until they are deleted or transferred to another mailbox. To delete existing e-mail from any of your mailboxes:

1. Launch Eudora by double-clicking on its icon in the Program Manager.
2. Open the mailbox containing the message you want to delete. You do this by selecting its entry from the lower portion of the Mailbox menu.
3. Select the subject line of the message you want to delete. The subject line will be highlighted.
   - As with transferring messages, you can select a continuous range of messages by clicking on the first message and Shift-clicking on the last message. You can make multiple discontinuous selections by Control-clicking on the messages you want to select.
4. From the Message menu, select the Delete command.
   - "Deleted" messages aren't actually erased; they're simply moved to a special Trash mailbox. Any message that has been "deleted" can be recovered by moving it out of the Trash mailbox before the Empty Trash command is chosen.
5. From the Special menu, select the Empty Trash command. The messages you "deleted" in step 4 will be erased when you quit Eudora.

Finding Addresses

If you work within a large corporation or university, finding the e-mail addresses of your colleagues is usually simple enough because your site will probably have a Ph server. For more information on the Ph protocol and Ph servers, see the Ph Servers sidebar below. The problem is that the Ph server will probably only have addresses for people at your site or within your organization, which doesn't help you if you're trying to send e-mail to someone across the country or around the world.

The easiest way to find the e-mail address of someone is to call him or her on the telephone and ask for the e-mail address. It's a low-tech solution to a high-tech problem. Because of security and privacy concerns, and because there is no unifying standard for e-mail directories on disparate systems, there is no central directory for Internet e-mail addresses.

But even though no central Internet directory exists, there are a few tools you can use to try to find e-mail addresses.

Ph Servers.

The Ph protocol was developed by Steve Dorner—author of the Eudora e-mail program—while he was at the Urbana-Champaign campus of the University of Illinois. Ph provides a way to look up e-mail addresses for colleagues and associates, usually at a single location.

In order for you to use the Ph lookup capabilities of an e-mail program, your mail server must also have a Ph server installed and properly configured.

Unfortunately, Ph servers are provided only for single locations—a large corporate site or a university, for example. Ph is useful only if you know the organization with which the person you want to contact is affiliated.

There are other methods—some relatively simple, others mind-numbingly sophisticated—to find e-mail addresses, and a few are covered elsewhere in this book. But the easiest way to find out someone's e-mail address is to call him or her on the telephone and ask. Sometimes the simplest methods are the best.

Using Finger

Finger is a command that looks at the user login file on a UNIX system. Since most computers on the Internet run some variation of UNIX, Finger is probably the best place to start.

You can FTP (or transfer to your computer) a Windows version of Finger from sunsite.unc.edu in the /pub/micro/pc-stuff/ms-windows/winsock/apps/ directory. The current version as of December 1993 is 3.1; the filename is finger31.zip. For more information on using FTP to transfer files, see Chapter 6, "Transferring Files." Unfortunately, Finger requires you to know the name of the host machine where the person you are trying to locate has an account.

To use the Windows version of the Finger utility:

1. With Windows running and the Chameleon Sampler program group window open, double-click on the **Custom** icon. The Custom window appears, as shown in Figure 4-14.
   - Additionally, the Chameleon NEWT icon appears in the lower left corner of your monitor, indicating that the TCP/IP communications stack has been successfully loaded.
2. Click the **Connect** menu. Chameleon attempts to establish a connection using the configuration information you supplied in Chapter 2, and the Connect dialog box is displayed, as shown in Figure 4-15.
   - When the connection has been successfully established, the Connect dialog box is dismissed and the Custom program's Connect menu changes to a Disconnect menu.
3. Launch Finger by double-clicking on its icon in the Program Manager. The Finger window appears, as shown in Figure 4-46.

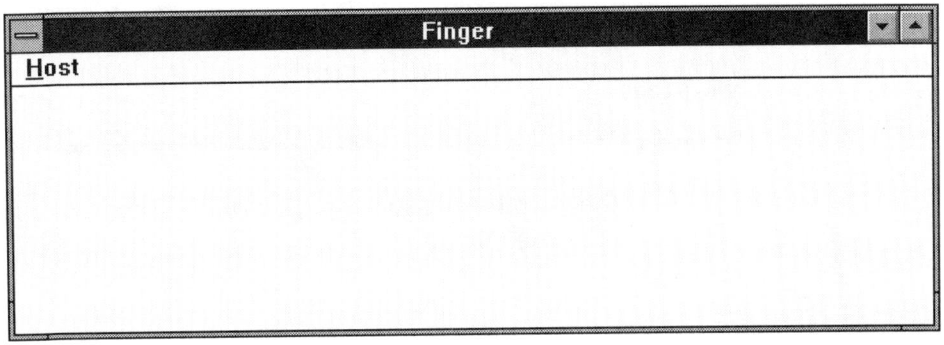

Figure 4-46: Finger window.

4. From the Host menu, select the Host... command. The Host window is displayed, as shown in Figure 4-47.

Figure 4-47: Finger Host window.

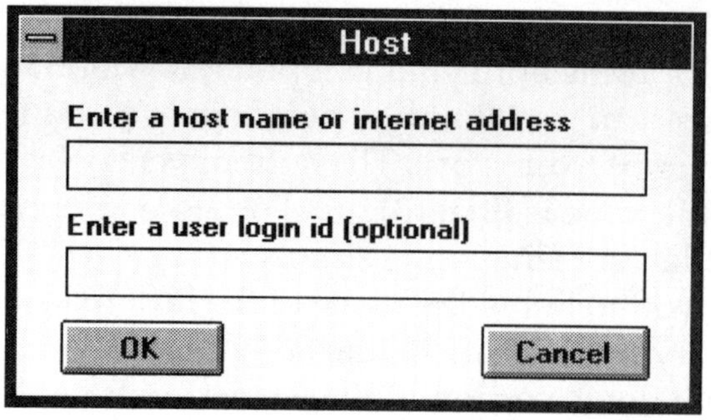

5. Enter a host name in the host name field, using the domain.top-domain format.
   - Alternatively, you can enter a valid IP address (the address that uses numbers instead of domain names) in the host name field.
6. Optionally, enter a username in the user login id field.
7. Click the **OK** button. The results will be displayed in a window like the example shown in Figure 4-48.

Figure 4-48: Finger Results window.

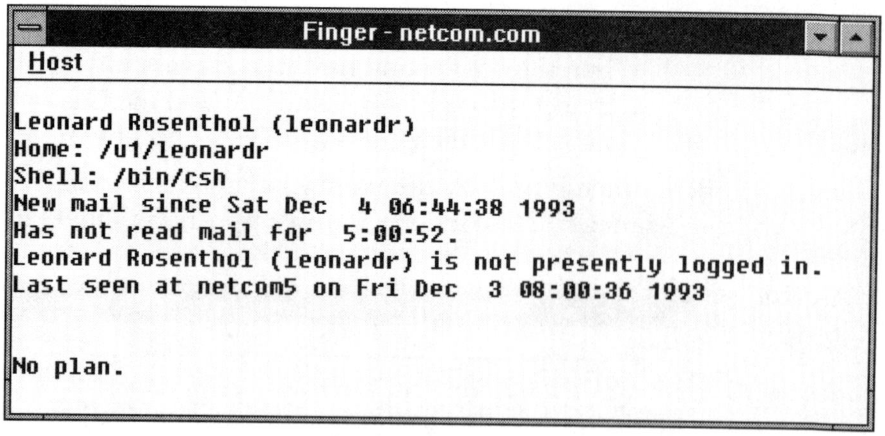

   - If the search is unsuccessful, a dialog box will appear, notifying you of the failure.

Qedit.
Qedit is a high-quality text editor that allows you to use the UNIX grep command to search for patterns of text across multiple files. The program is both powerful and easy to use and has become a mainstay on most MS-DOS users' computers. Qedit is so popular, it has its own directory at the largest MS-DOS file archive on the Internet. The program is available by FTP from oak.oakland.edu in the /pub/msdos/qedit/ directory.

Using MIT's USENET User List

If the person you are trying to locate has ever posted a message to any of the USENET news groups, you may be able to locate him or her by using a specialized mail server at the Massachusetts Institute of Technology (MIT). The MIT server constantly monitors incoming USENET postings and extracts each poster's name and e-mail address.

To use MIT's USENET User List service:

1. With Windows running and the Chameleon Sampler program group window open, double-click on the **Custom** icon. The Custom window appears, as shown in Figure 4-14.
   - Additionally, the Chameleon NEWT icon appears in the lower left corner of your monitor, indicating that the TCP/IP communications stack has been successfully loaded.
2. Click the **Connect** menu. Chameleon attempts to establish a connection using the configuration information you supplied in Chapter 2, and the Connect dialog box is displayed, as shown in Figure 4-15.
   - When the connection has been successfully established, the Connect dialog box is dismissed and the Custom program's Connect menu changes to a Disconnect menu.
3. Launch Chameleon Mail by double-clicking on the **Mail** icon in the Program Manager. The User Login dialog box appears, as shown in Figure 4-16.
4. Select your username from the Username menu, if necessary.
5. Enter your password in the Password: field.

6. Click the **OK** button. The main Mail window with Inbox folder open appears, as shown in Figure 4-17.
7. Click the **Create** button in the main Mail window. A New Mail window opens, as shown in Figure 4-22.
8. Create an e-mail message consisting only of the single line: send usenet-addresses/*name* where *name* is the name of the person you are trying to locate. For example, to search for my e-mail address, the line would be: **send usenet-address/fraase**.
9. Address the e-mail message to mail-server@pit-manager.mit.edu
10. Click the **Send** button. You'll soon receive a responding message from the MIT mail server that looks something like the one shown in Figure 4-49.

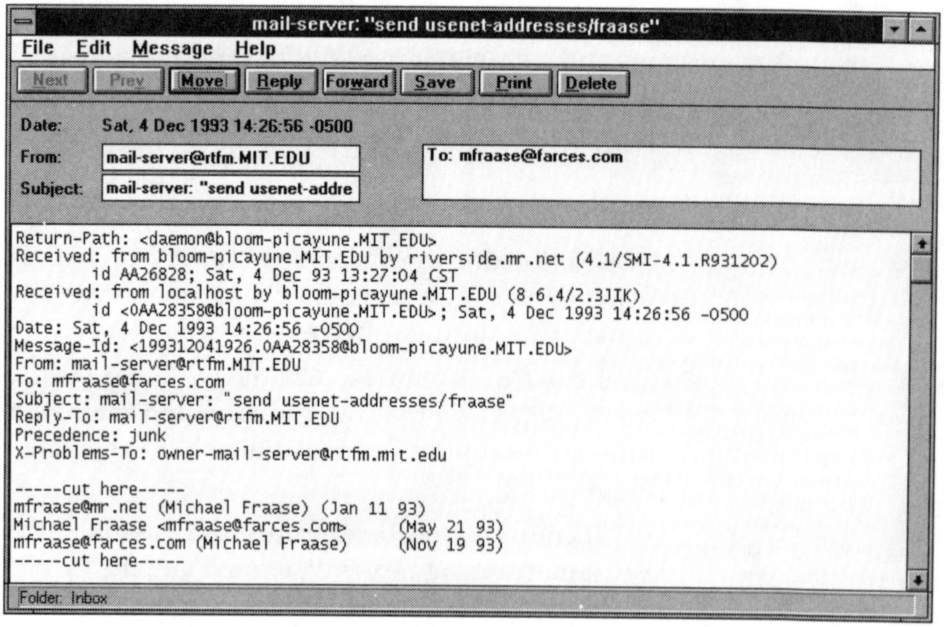

Figure 4-49: MIT USENET User List example.

Using WHOIS

WHOIS is a directory that is maintained by the DDN Network Information Center. Unfortunately it contains listings only for people who are responsible for the actual working of the Internet and is useless for most people in the real world.

The easiest way to access any available WHOIS server is by using Gopher. More information on using Gopher is provided in Chapter 7. You can download HGopher, an excellent Gopher client for Windows by FTP from lister.cc.ic.ac.uk in the /pub/wingopher/ directory.

Search for addresses using WHOIS in HGopher with these steps.

1. With Windows running and the Chameleon Sampler program group window open, double-click on the **Custom** icon. The Custom window appears, as shown in Figure 4-14.
   - Additionally, the Chameleon NEWT icon appears in the lower left corner of your monitor, indicating that the TCP/IP communications stack has been successfully loaded.
2. Click the **Connect** menu. Chameleon attempts to establish a connection using the configuration information you supplied in Chapter 2, and the Connect dialog box is displayed, as shown in Figure 4-15.
   - When the connection has been successfully established, the Connect dialog box is dismissed and the Custom program's Connect menu changes to a Disconnect menu.
3. Launch HGopher by double-clicking on its icon in the Program Manager. The Top Level Menu window of the "home" Gopher server you configured appears, as shown in the example in Figure 4-50.

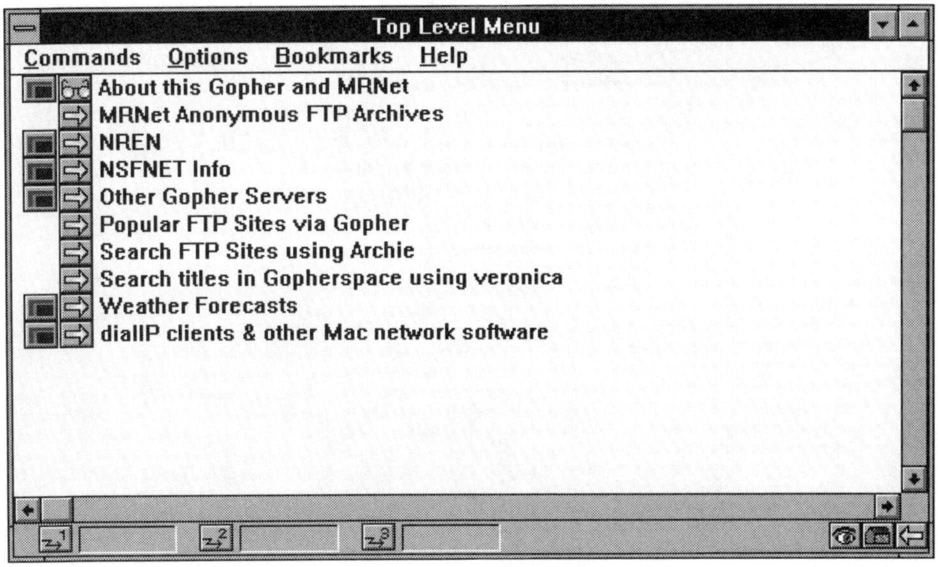

Figure 4-50: Sample HGopher Top Level Menu window.

4. Navigate to the Mother Gopher at gopher.tc.umn.edu. The main menu for the University of Minnesota Gopher server appears as shown in Figure 4-51.

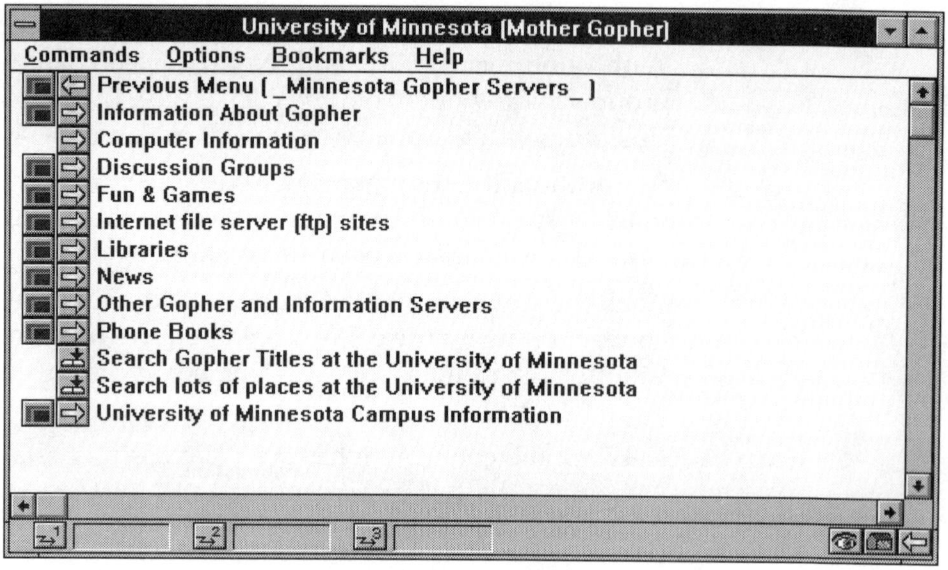

Figure 4-51: Sample HGopher main menu for the University of Minnesota Gopher server.

5. Double-click on the **Phone Books** menu item. The Phone Books menu is displayed, as shown in Figure 4-52.

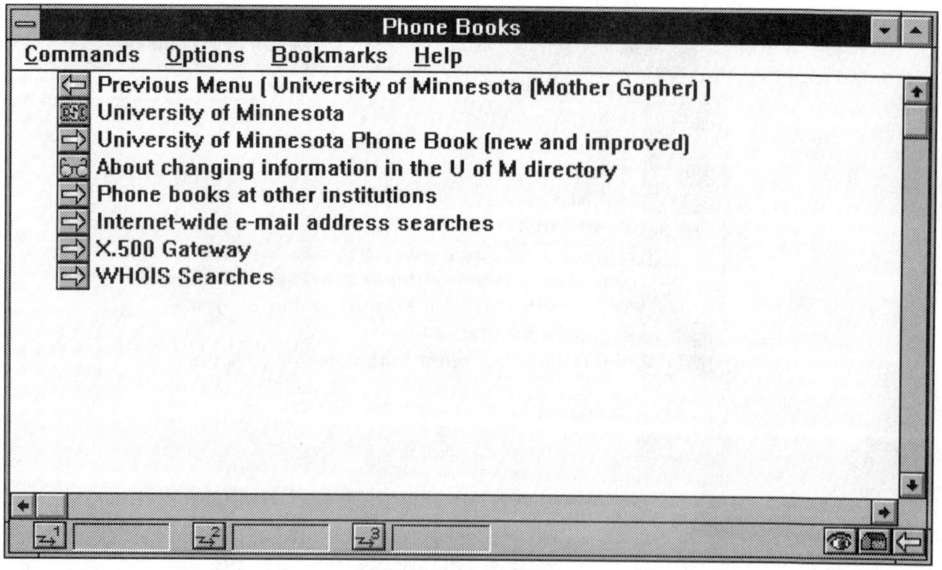

Figure 4-52: HGopher Phone Books menu.

6. Double-click on the **WHOIS Searches** menu item. A list of available WHOIS servers is displayed in a Gopher window, as shown in Figure 4-53.

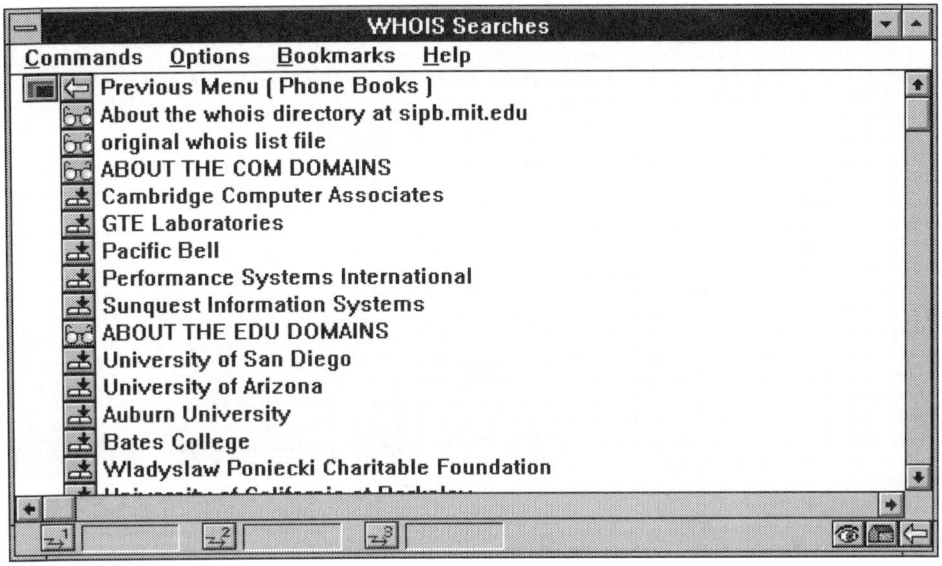

Figure 4-53: HGopher WHOIS servers menu.

7. Double-click on the WHOIS server you want to access from the list. An Index Search dialog box appears, as shown in Figure 4-54.

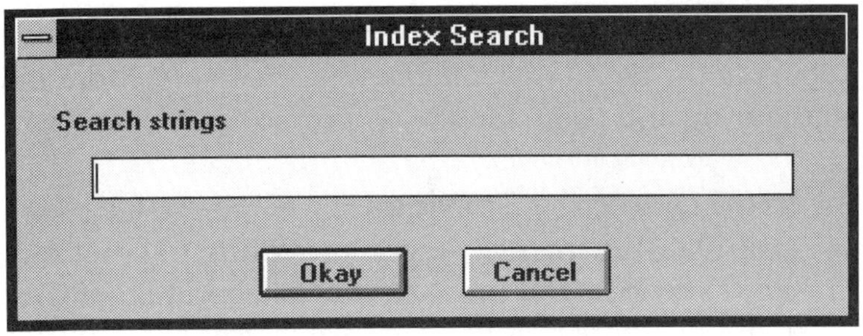

Figure 4-54: WHOIS server Search Index dialog box within HGopher.

8. Enter the last name of the person you want to search for in the Search strings field and press **Enter**. A menu will appear allowing you to read about the ramifications of the search or to commit to the search.
9. Double-click on the **Commit to search** item. The search will be initiated and the results will be displayed in a new window, as shown in Figure 4-55.

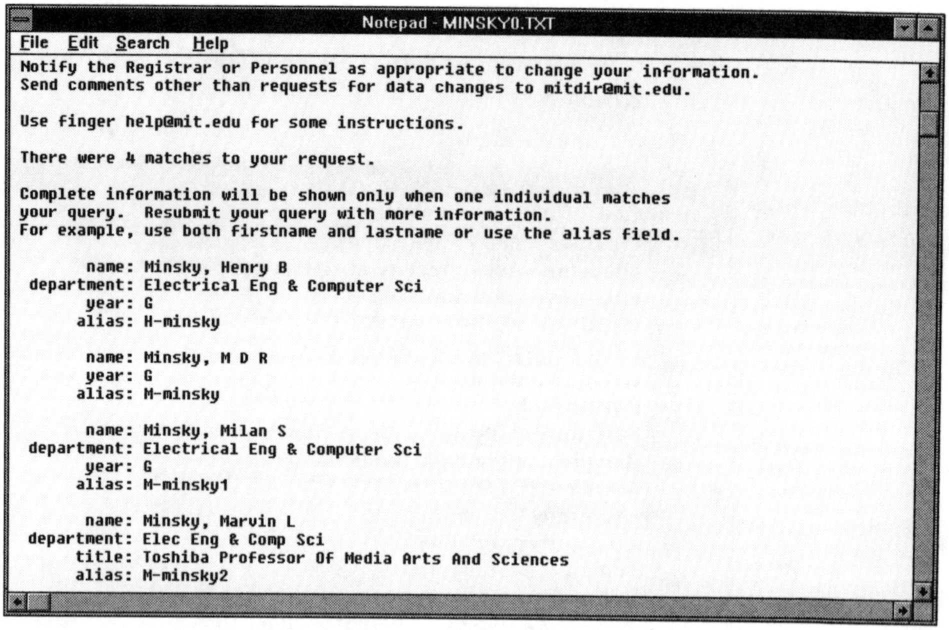

Figure 4-55: Results of a WHOIS search within HGopher.

Using the PSI White Pages

Performance Systems International (PSI)—an Internet service provider—offers a directory service that is accessible to Internet users. Unfortunately, most of the listings seem to be for PSI clients or employees.

The easiest way to access the PSI White Pages is by using Gopher as described in the previous section, "Using WHOIS." The PSI White Pages appear in the menu of available WHOIS servers. More information on configuring and using Gopher is provided in Chapter 7.

InterNIC Directory Services

In April 1993, the InterNIC began providing Internet registration and directory services. The InterNIC is a collaboration of General Atomics, AT&T and Network Solutions with a charter of simplifying the use of the Internet. The InterNIC's directory services are provided by AT&T, offering three core resources:

- Directory of Directories
- Directory Services
- Database Services

The InterNIC Directory Services are a sort of electronic White and Yellow Pages for registered Internet users. As of August 1993, the InterNIC had processed more than 100,000 requests for Internet registration information. If you're keeping score, that's more than one request every three minutes, 24-hours-a-day, since the service's inception.

There are various ways to access the InterNIC, but the easiest way to find someone's e-mail address is by using, yup, you guessed it—e-mail. Here's how:

1. With Windows running and the Chameleon Sampler program group window open, double-click on the **Custom** icon. The Custom window appears, as shown in Figure 4-14.
   - Additionally, the Chameleon NEWT icon appears in the lower left corner of your monitor, indicating that the TCP/IP communications stack has been successfully loaded.
2. Click the **Connect** menu. Chameleon attempts to establish a connection using the configuration information you supplied in Chapter 2, and the Connect dialog box is displayed, as shown in Figure 4-15.
   - When the connection has been successfully established, the Connect dialog box is dismissed and the Custom program's Connect menu changes to a Disconnect menu.
3. Launch Chameleon Mail by double-clicking on the **Mail** icon in the Program Manager. The User Login dialog box appears, as shown in Figure 4-16.
4. Select your username from the Username menu, if necessary.
5. Enter your password in the Password: field.
6. Click the **OK** button. The main Mail window with Inbox folder open appears, as shown in Figure 4-17.
7. Click the **Create** button in the main Mail window. A New Mail window opens, as shown in Figure 4-22.
8. Send an e-mail message consisting only of the single line: person *firstname lastname, organization, country*
   - *firstname* is the first name of the person you are trying to locate.
   - *lastname* is the last name of the person you are trying to locate.
   - *organization* is the name of the company or institution with which the person you are trying to locate is affiliated.

- *country* is the country in which the person you are trying to find is located.
- For example, to search for my e-mail address, the line would be person michael fraase, arts and farces, us

9. Address the e-mail message to mailserv@ds.internic.net
10. Send the e-mail message. You'll soon receive a responding message from the MIT mail server containing the e-mail address and other contact information for anyone matching the search criteria you entered.

The InterNIC also provides a wealth of other services for Internet users, and you can perform directory searches interactively. Look for more information on the InterNIC in Chapter 8, "Other Internet Resources," and in the electronic updates to this book.

E-Mail Address Starter Kit

Lots of PC-related companies and luminaries are accessible by Internet e-mail. A starter kit of some e-mail addresses is provided in Table 4-4.

Table 4-4: PC-related e-mail addresses.

Company/Person	E-Mail Address
PC WEEK	2393520@mcimail.com
Spencer the Katt	spencer@pcweek.ziff.com
John Perry Barlow	barlow@well.sf.ca.us
Jerry Berman	jberman@eff.org
InfoWorld	letters@infoworld.com
Stewart Brand	sbb@well.sf.ca.us
CPSR	cpsr-staff@csli.stanford.edu
Stewart Alsop	stewart_alsop@infoworld.com
Dan Farber	72511.124@compuserve.com
Bob Metcalfe	bob_metcalfe@infoworld.com
Rachel Parker	rachel_parker@infoworld.com
Tom Quinlan	tom_quinlan@infoworld.com
Mitch Kapor	mkapor@eff.org
University of MN SLIP	slip@boombox.micro.umn.edu
Howard Rheingold	hlr@well.sf.ca.us
Whole Earth Review	wer@well.sf.ca.us

And don't worry that you might be annoying these people by sending them mail—they've all published their e-mail addresses.

Electronic Mailing Lists

Electronic mailing lists have very little in common with their paper mail counterparts, even though they work in much the same manner.

- Electronic mailing lists actually serve a useful purpose.
- You have to specifically request to join an electronic mailing list.
- Electronic mailing lists don't overflow landfills.

Electronic mailing lists exist either as a forum for group discussions or as distribution lists. Currently there are close to 3,000 publicly accessible mailing lists on the Internet. They cover a wide variety of subjects, and the number grows daily. You can find a mailing list for just about any subject of interest. If not, you can always start your own.

You can join a mailing list by sending e-mail to the list administrator. Once your name has been added to the list, you'll begin receiving messages from other members of the list, and you can read and respond to any of those messages. Your responses will automatically be forwarded to all the other subscribers on the list.

The quality of mailing lists is generally higher than in USENET news groups because the "signal to noise ratio" is higher—there are generally more worthwhile messages in a day's mailing list message traffic than there are in a day's newsgroup message traffic. It's pretty rare to find an Ivy League freshman wanting to sell a microwave oven in a cyberpunk mailing list, but that's a pretty common happening in most any newsgroup (especially in the early autumn).

You can download a list of current mailing lists from ftp.nisc.sri.com in the directory /netinfo/interest-groups/. For more information on using the File Transfer Protocol (FTP) to download files, see "Downloading Files With Chameleon FTP" on page 199.

Subscribing to Mailing Lists

Most mailing lists are set up to automatically forward any message sent to the list to all members of the mailing list. You subscribe to an electronic mailing list by sending an e-mail request to the list's administrative address. The list's *administrative address* is almost always different from the list's *submission address*. Many mailing list administrative addresses can be recognized by the word "request" in the list address. Make sure you use the right address for the job.

In general, to subscribe to a mailing list you send a short message requesting a subscription to the mailing list's administrative address. Some mailing lists are automated and have specific subscription requirements.

For example, to subscribe to the automated New Mailing Lists mailing list:

1. With Windows running and the Chameleon Sampler program group window open, double-click on the **Custom** icon. The Custom window appears, as shown in Figure 4-14.
   - Additionally, the Chameleon NEWT icon appears in the lower left corner of your monitor, indicating that the TCP/IP communications stack has been successfully loaded.
2. Click the **Connect** menu. Chameleon attempts to establish a connection using the configuration information you supplied in Chapter 2, and the Connect dialog box is displayed, as shown in Figure 4-15.
   - When the connection has been successfully established, the Connect dialog box is dismissed and the Custom program's Connect menu changes to a Disconnect menu.
3. Launch Chameleon Mail by double-clicking on the **Mail** icon in the Program Manager. The User Login dialog box appears, as shown in Figure 4-16.
4. Select your username from the Username menu, if necessary.
5. Enter your password in the Password: field.
6. Click the **OK** button. The main Mail window with Inbox folder open appears, as shown in Figure 4-17.
7. Click the **Create** button in the main Mail window. A New Mail window opens, as shown in Figure 4-22.
8. Create an e-mail message consisting only of the single line: subscribe new-list *your name* where *your name* is your first and last name. For example, for my subscription, the line would be subscribe new-list michael fraase
9. Address the e-mail message to listserv@vm1.nodak.edu

10. Send the e-mail message. You'll receive a response introducing you to the mailing list and instructions on how to use it.

The New-List Digest is run by a *Listserv* automated mail server. A Listserv mail server is simply a computer program that accepts and responds to the commands you send it.

Use these steps to subscribe to a manual mailing list, like the Electronic Frontier Foundation's mailing list.

1. With Windows running and the Chameleon Sampler program group window open, double-click on the **Custom** icon. The Custom window appears, as shown in Figure 4-14.
   - Additionally, the Chameleon NEWT icon appears in the lower left corner of your monitor, indicating that the TCP/IP communications stack has been successfully loaded.
2. Click the **Connect** menu. Chameleon attempts to establish a connection using the configuration information you supplied in Chapter 2, and the Connect dialog box is displayed, as shown in Figure 4-15.
   - When the connection has been successfully established, the Connect dialog box is dismissed and the Custom program's Connect menu changes to a Disconnect menu.
3. Launch Chameleon Mail by double-clicking on the **Mail** icon in the Program Manager. The User Login dialog box appears, as shown in Figure 4-16.
4. Select your username from the Username menu, if necessary.
5. Enter your password in the Password: field.
6. Click the **OK** button. The main Mail window with Inbox folder open appears, as shown in Figure 4-17.
7. Click the **Create** button in the main Mail window. A New Mail window opens, as shown in Figure 4-22.
8. Send a brief message requesting to be added to the mailing list. Just a simple message like "please add me to the EFF mailing list, thanks" is enough.
9. Address the message to eff-request@eff.org
10. Send the e-mail message. You'll receive a response from the list owner or the person administrating the mailing list.

A general overview for some of the popular mailing lists is provided in Table 4-5.

Table 4-5: Electronic mailing list subscription information.

Mailing List	Administrative Address	Subscription Instructions	Submission Address
EFF	eff-request@eff.org	Send brief request	eff@eff.org
CPSR	listserv@gwuvm.gwu.edu	subscribe CPSR your name in message	cpsr@gwuvm.gwu.edu
New Mailing Lists	listserv@vm1.nodak.edu	subscribe new-list your name in message	new-list@vm1.nodak.edu
Grateful Dead	dead-flames-request@fuggles.acc.virginia.edu	Send brief request	dead-flames@fuggles.acc.virginia.edu
Computer Risks	risks-request@csl.sri.com	Send brief request	risks@csl.sri.com
NREN	nren-discuss-request@psi.com	Send brief request	nren-discuss@psi.com
Telecommunications	telecom-request@eecs.nwu.edu	Send brief request	telecom@eecs.nwu.edu
Computer Underground Digest	tk0jut2@mvs.cso.niu.edu	Send brief request	tk0jut2@mvs.cso.niu.edu
Chaos Corner	chaos-request@pelican.cit.cornell.edu	Send brief request	chaos@pelican.cit.cornell.edu

Canceling Subscriptions to Mailing Lists

In general, to cancel your subscription to a mailing list you send a short message requesting to be removed from the list to the mailing list's administrative address. Some mailing lists are automated and have specific subscription cancellation requirements.

For example, use these instructions to cancel your subscription to the automated New Mailing Lists mailing list.

1. With Windows running and the Chameleon Sampler program group window open, double-click on the **Custom** icon. The Custom window appears, as shown in Figure 4-14.
   - Additionally, the Chameleon NEWT icon appears in the lower left corner of your monitor, indicating that the TCP/IP communications stack has been successfully loaded.

2. Click the **Connect** menu. Chameleon attempts to establish a connection using the configuration information you supplied in Chapter 2, and the Connect dialog box is displayed, as shown in Figure 4-15.
   - When the connection has been successfully established, the Connect dialog box is dismissed and the Custom program's Connect menu changes to a Disconnect menu.
3. Launch Chameleon Mail by double-clicking on the **Mail** icon in the Program Manager. The User Login dialog box appears, as shown in Figure 4-16.
4. Select your username from the Username menu, if necessary.
5. Enter your password in the Password: field.
6. Click the **OK** button. The main Mail window with Inbox folder open appears, as shown in Figure 4-17.
7. Click the **Create** button in the main Mail window. A New Mail window opens, as shown in Figure 4-22.
8. Create an e-mail message consisting only of the single line: signoff new-list *your name* where *your name* is your first and last name. For example, for my subscription, the line would be signoff new-list michael fraase
9. Address the e-mail message to listserv@vm1.nodak.edu
10. Send the e-mail message. You'll receive a response acknowledging your subscription cancellation and removal from the mailing list.

Use these steps to cancel your subscription to a manual mailing list, like the Electronic Frontier Foundation's mailing list.

1. With Windows running and the Chameleon Sampler program group window open, double-click on the **Custom** icon. The Custom window appears, as shown in Figure 4-14.
   - Additionally, the Chameleon NEWT icon appears in the lower left corner of your monitor, indicating that the TCP/IP communications stack has been successfully loaded.

2. Click the **Connect** menu. Chameleon attempts to establish a connection using the configuration information you supplied in Chapter 2, and the Connect dialog box is displayed, as shown in Figure 4-15.
   - When the connection has been successfully established, the Connect dialog box is dismissed and the Custom program's Connect menu changes to a Disconnect menu.
3. Launch Chameleon Mail by double-clicking on the **Mail** icon in the Program Manager. The User Login dialog box appears, as shown in Figure 4-16.
4. Select your username from the Username menu, if necessary.
5. Enter your password in the Password: field.
6. Click the **OK** button. The main Mail window with Inbox folder open appears, as shown in Figure 4-17.
7. Click the **Create** button in the main Mail window. A New Mail window opens, as shown in Figure 4-22.
8. Send a brief message requesting to be removed from the mailing list. Just a simple message like "please remove me from the EFF mailing list, thanks" is enough.
9. Address the message to eff-request@eff.org
10. Send the e-mail message. You'll receive a response from the list owner or the person administrating the mailing list acknowledging your subscription cancellation and removal from the list.

E-Mail & Attached Files

In addition to sending *messages*, you can also use e-mail to send any sort of *file* through the Internet. Actually, most PC files first have to be converted to a text document before you can send them through the Internet, but the good news is that with the right tool, the process is automatic and transparent. While the freeware sampler version of Chameleon Mail is incapable of doing this, Eudora is just such a tool, and it automatically converts any PC file for transmission over the Net.

Sending Files in E-Mail Messages

To attach a file to an e-mail message in Eudora:

1. Create an e-mail message as you ordinarily would (following steps 1–8 in "Creating an E-Mail Message With Eudora" beginning on page 120).
2. Select the BinHex option from the Enclosures menu in the Message window.
3. From the Message menu, select the Attach Document... command. The Attach Document dialog box appears, as shown in Figure 4-56.

Figure 4-56: Eudora Attach Document dialog box.

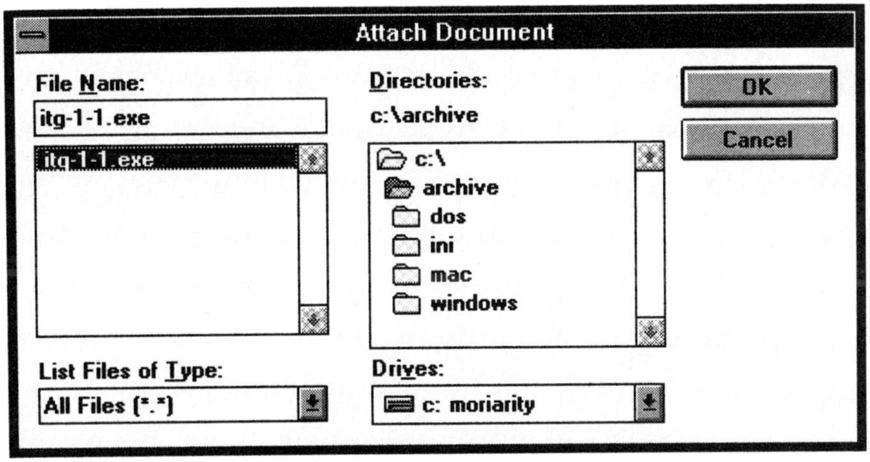

4. Navigate to the file you want to attach and click the **OK** button. The Attachments: line of your Message window screen will be updated to reflect the pathname of the file attachment, as shown in Figure 4-57.

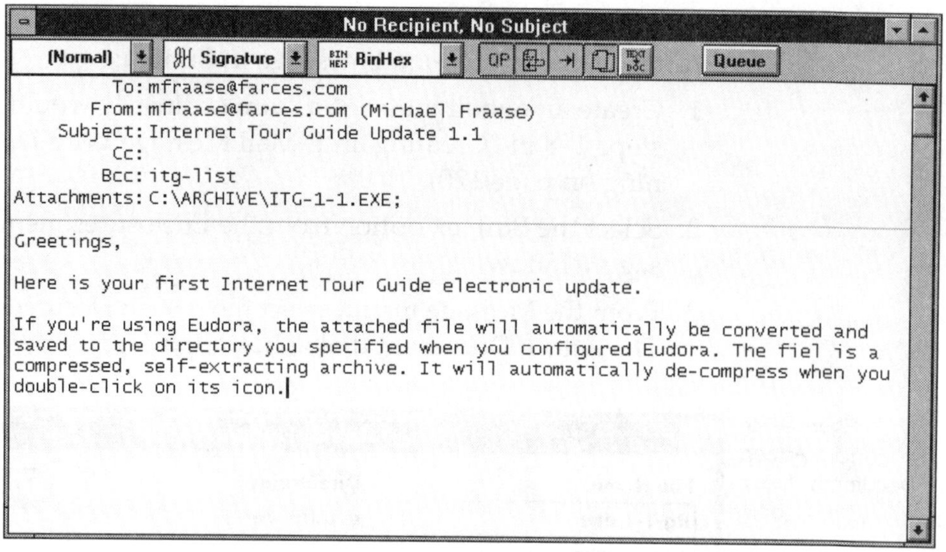

Figure 4-57: Eudora message window with pathname of file enclosure.

5. Repeat steps 3–4 if you want to attach additional files.
6. Click the **Queue** button. Your message will be stored on your hard drive and sent to the mail server when you select the Send Queued Messages command from the File menu.
   - If you have set Eudora's preferences to send mail immediately, there will be a **Send** button at the far right end of the Icon Bar instead of the **Queue** button.

Receiving Files in E-Mail Messages

Receiving files enclosed in e-mail messages is automatic in Eudora. The attached files of any e-mail message are automatically converted and saved in the folder you specified for received files when you configured the program. Receiving enclosed files with other e-mail programs may require that the file be processed or decoded after it's received. Refer to the documentation that came with your e-mail program if you have any questions. Note that the freeware sampler version of Chameleon Mail is incapable of receiving e-mail messages with file attachments.

Note that many files you receive in e-mail are likely to be compressed. You'll need to use the appropriate file decompression utility to extract the file(s) from the compressed archive. For more information on decompressing files you receive in e-mail, see Chapter 6, "Transferring Files."

Files in E-Mail Caveats

From time to time you may receive non-PC files by e-mail. One of the hottest trends in cross-platform software is something called "binary compatibility." That's a software program that runs on different kinds of computer hardware and saves its documents in a format that is common to all the different kinds of computers. FrameMaker documents, for example, are binary compatible regardless of the kind of computer used to create them. I can open NeXT, Macintosh or UNIX FrameMaker files on my PC without converting them.

But since people often compress binary files before sending them, and there are different compression utilities for each kind of computer, you can imagine the problems that can arise. What do you do with UNIX files you receive that have been "tarred and compressed?" Or what about those goofy Mac files that have been "stuffed?" This dilemma is covered in "A Primer on File Types" on page 186.

Be careful with the size of the files you send by e-mail. Most of the e-mail gateways provided by the commercial information services like CompuServe and America Online have severe file-size limitations, as indicated in Table 4-1.

Moving On

This chapter has given you a thorough overview of electronic mail, from the nuts and bolts of how to send and receive it to the subtleties of e-mail courtesy and etiquette. Look for more in-depth information about using e-mail (plus evaluations of new e-mail products) in this book's electronic updates.

E-mail is most useful for communicating with individuals or small groups of people. But what if you want to exchange information with large groups of people, all over the world? That's what Network News is for, the topic of the next chapter. So let's stop the tour bus at that newsstand just ahead and take a break to learn about reading and posting USENET news articles.

CHAPTER 5

NETWORK NEWS & NEWSGROUPS

Broadsheets of the Broadband

As our tour through the Internet continues, it's easy to become overwhelmed with the size and scope of all that it offers. But one of the most important resources on the Net is easy to overlook: people. Network news and newsgroups are valuable because of the insights and information that people bring to them.

For instance, wouldn't it be great if you could poll all the most knowledgeable folks on the Internet for answers to technical questions, or advice on everything from buying the best VCR to cooking the perfect pot roast? While electronic mail is useful for communicating with another individual or small workgroup, you can't send e-mail to thousands of people you don't know, asking questions about topics that don't interest them. (Well, I suppose you *could*, but it probably wouldn't be very productive. And if you think it sounds like it might be a good idea, put this book down and go outside for a walk. A long walk.) But with network news, there's a better way.

What Is Network News & What Are Newsgroups?

Think of network news as a worldwide collection of automatically updated electronic bulletin boards. Except these aren't bulletin boards like the single-line systems set up by thousands of hobbyists in small towns across America. Network news messages are seen by millions of people who generate as much as 40mb of network news information every day.

Electronic bulletin boards are like the cork bulletin boards you see at your local grocery store. You know, where you can find a great deal on a 1955 Buick or a litter of prize poodle puppies. Network news on the Internet is the same concept, only it's all electronic and much more extensive. Imagine the electronic equivalent of 4,000 different grocery store cork bulletin boards, and you've got a pretty good grasp of the thousands of newsgroups that make up network news.

If you've used CompuServe or America Online you're probably familiar with the concept of forums or bulletin boards. Each newsgroup is roughly equivalent to a message area on America Online or CompuServe, except that network news newsgroups are seen by many more people, and on the Internet, highly specialized newsgroups are available for just about any topic.

Freeware SLIP software.

The programmers at the University of Minnesota have created and released a freeware SLIP driver for MS-DOS computers. SLIP software allows you to login to the Internet (via a SLIP server) using a high-speed modem and ordinary telephone lines. It works quite well and is part of the UMSLIP distribution package. Windows users may find it useful because it can be configured to support Windows-specific Internet client software. The current version of the software is available by anonymous FTP at boombox.micro.umn.edu in the /pub/pc/slip/ directory.

You'll see everything from announcements for new software products to in-depth technical discussions to candid—and sometimes heated—conversations. These super-heated discussions are called *flame wars*; each individual message in a flame war is called a *flame*. Flames are considered to be in bad taste (except in newsgroups set up just for flames), and starting a flame war will win you lots of enemies with long memories. Each message within an individual newsgroup is called a *post* or an *article*. Articles can be cross-posted to several newsgroups, but this practice is considered to be bad form unless the article is especially relevant to several newsgroups.

Articles within each newsgroup are arranged in *topics*. Topics within a newsgroup about laptop computers, for instance, may include battery conservation tips, problems with a specific model's keyboard, or comparisons between different available configurations. Initial queries or informational articles will likely generate several responses. This patchwork of queries and responses form a *message thread* within a specific topic. The software you use to read network news will automatically piece together the various queries and responses in logical order. The original article will appear first, followed by any available *followup* (response) articles in the message thread.

E-mail blind courtesy copies that aren't.

There is a troublesome fluke with most mail servers on the Internet that could prove to be embarrassing for you. If you send an e-mail message to a group of people, with each recipient sent a blind courtesy copy, make sure you also e-mail a copy to at least one address in the To: field. If you send an e-mail message with the To: field empty, most mail servers will insert "Apparently-To:" addresses, neatly listing every recipient of your blind courtesy copy.

Network news is actually not even part of the Internet—although, to the uninitiated, it is probably perceived as being the most easily recognizable part of the Internet. Network news is transmitted on USENET, a network of about 3 million people (mostly UNIX users). USENET is even more disjointed and anarchic than the Internet. Just about the only thing USENET sites have in common is that they communicate using the UNIX-to-UNIX Copy Protocol (UUCP). Some USENET sites have connections to the Internet, which is how network news—and other USENET traffic—gets to the Internet.

Internet sites that provide a network news server use the Network News Transfer Protocol (NNTP) to provide a database for local news clients and to transfer news between servers. In order to read network news on the Internet, you must use NNTP client software (like the kind we'll discuss in this chapter) or use the archaic UNIX commands for navigating and reading newsgroups.

Network news is divided into *newsgroups*. Each newsgroup is devoted to a single topic (at least hypothetically; most newsgroups sort of cross-pollinate one another). Each newsgroup article is received and stored on each participating USENET computer. Unlike e-mail, where the messages are actually sent to your computer and stored on your own hard drive, newsgroup articles are stored on a *news server*, at the site that services your account. The newsgroup articles you read are stored on the news server, not on your own computer.

The network news—or USENET—newsgroups are organized in a hierarchy. Each newsgroup has a name with periods in it similar to the Internet domain name system. The periods (read as "dots") separate the various hierarchical levels. For example, comp.sys.ibm.pc.digest is read as "comp-dot-sys-dot-ibm-dot-pc-dot-digest" or "comp-sys-ibm-pc-digest" and reflects the hierarchy shown in Figure 5-1.

Figure 5-1: Network news newsgroups hierarchy.

comp.sys.ibm.pc.digest

translates in the newsgroup hierarchy to:

Computers

Systems

IBM

PC

Digest

There are several top-level newsgroup categories in the hierarchy, as shown in Table 5-1.

Table 5-1: Network news newsgroups top-level categories.

Category	Topic Explanation
alt	Alternative discussions; not carried by all sites. The newsgroups found here range from the bizarre to the useful. The most useful "alt" newsgroups were created in this top-level hierarchy to avoid going through the bureaucratic hassle of forming a certified newsgroup.
bionet	Biology discussions.
bit	Discussions that originate from Bitnet Listserv mailing lists.
biz	Business discussions. Commercial articles are permitted only in this top-level hierarchy.
comp	Computer discussions.
misc	Miscellaneous discussions—topics that don't fit in any of the other top-level hierarchies.
news	Discussions related to network news and the software used to transmit, read and create articles.
rec	Recreation discussions and topics related to the arts.
sci	"Hard" science discussions.
soc	Discussions related to social issues.
talk	Argumentative discussions.

An Overview of Newsgroups

There are more than 4,000 active newsgroups covering virtually every conceivable topic. Some network-savvy observers in mainstream media hypothesize that the Internet will eventually replace most sources of news. It simply won't happen, at least not for another 10 years or so. Computer news and Grateful Dead concert dates travel faster on the Net than they do through other channels, but that's about it.

There was one case of "pseudo-news" on the Internet. In April 1992, an area developed on IRC (Internet Relay Chat—similar to a wide-open international conference call using keyboards instead of phones) carried news relays of the Los Angeles riots following the first Rodney King verdict. Of course, most of the information came from people who were simply relaying what they had received from local television coverage.

You can always find a regularly updated list of all available newsgroups by reading the news.list newsgroup.

Interesting Newsgroups

Interesting newsgroups exist for just about any topic you can think of. A listing of some is provided in Table 5-2.

Table 5-2: Interesting newsgroup descriptions.

Newsgroup	Description
comp.archives	Listings and descriptions of public-access archives (moderated)[1]
comp.dcom.isdn	Discussions related to the Integrated Services Digital Network (ISDN)
comp.dcom.telcom	Telecommunications digest (moderated)
comp.infosystems.gopher	Discussions related to Gopher
comp.newprod	Computer product announcements (moderated)
comp.org.acm	Discussions related to the Association for Computing Machinery (ACM)
comp.org.eff.news	Electronic Frontier Foundation (EFF) news (moderated)
comp.org.eff.talk	Discussions related to the Electronic Frontier Foundation (EFF)
comp.risks	Discussions related to the risks of computers (moderated)
comp.society.cu-digest	Computer Underground Digest (moderated)
comp.society.privacy	Discussions related to computers and privacy in society (moderated)
comp.text.desktop	Discussions related to desktop publishing
misc.consumers	Discussions related to consumer interest
misc.entrepreneurs	Discussions related to running a business
misc.invest	Discussions related to investing
misc.jobs.contract	Postings of work-for-hire contract availability
misc.jobs.offered	Listings of positions available
misc.jobs.offered.entry	Listings of entry-level positions available

Newsgroup	Description
misc.jobs.resumes	Listings of resumes and position queries
news.announce.important	Announcements of general interest (moderated)
news.announce.newgroups	Announcements of new newsgroups (moderated)
news.announce.newusers	Important announcements for new users (moderated)
news.newusers.questions	Questions and answers for new users
rec.arts.movies	Discussions related to film
rec.arts.movies.reviews	Movie reviews (moderated)
rec.mag	Discussions related to magazines
rec.music.bluenote	Discussions related to jazz and blues
rec.music.dylan	Discussions related to Bob Dylan's music
rec.music.gdead	Dead-head discussions
rec.music.reggae	Discussions related to reggae music
rec.sport.baseball	Discussions related to baseball
soc.culture.japan	Discussions related to Japan and Japanese culture
soc.politics	Political discussions (moderated)
soc.rights.human	Discussions related to human rights and activism

1. Moderated newsgroups are best described as read-only newsgroups. Don't send articles directly to the newsgroup; instead follow the instructions available in each moderated newsgroup. In general, you send articles to the group's moderator, who posts them as appropriate.

Remember, this is just a tiny sample of the thousands of newsgroups you can access via the Internet.

IBM PC, MS-DOS & Windows Newsgroups

Several newsgroups cater specifically to the PC community. A listing of these newsgroups is provided in Table 5-3.

Figure 5-3: PC newsgroups descriptions.

Newsgroup	Description
comp.os.msdos.4dos	Discussions related to the 4DOS operating system
comp.os.msdos.apps	Discussions related to MS-DOS software programs
comp.os.msdos.desqview	Discussions related to Desqview
comp.os.msdos.mail-news	Discussions related to MS-DOS e-mail and news programs
comp.os.msdos.misc	Discussions related to miscellaneous MS-DOS issues
comp.os.msdos.pcgeos	Discussions related to the Geos operating system
comp.os.msdos.programmer	Discussions related to programming for MS-DOS
comp.os.msdos.programmer.turbovision	Discussions related to programming for MS-DOS Turbovision
comp.os.ms-windows.advocacy	Discussions related to the relative merits of Microsoft Windows
comp.os.ms-windows.announce	Announcements related to Microsoft Windows and associated products
comp.os.ms-windows.apps	Discussions related to Microsoft Windows-specific software programs
comp.os.ms-windows.misc	Discussions related to miscellaneous Microsoft Windows issues
comp.os.ms-windows.setup	Discussions related to installing and configuring Microsoft Windows
comp.sys.ibm.pc.demos	Discussions related to PC demonstration software
comp.sys.ibm.pc.digest	Discussions related to general PC use; includes listings ofadditions to major archive sites (moderated)
comp.sys.ibm.pc.games	Discussions related to general PC games
comp.sys.ibm.pc.games.action	Discussions related to arcade and action style PC games
comp.sys.ibm.pc.games.adventure	Discussions related to adventure style PC games
comp.sys.ibm.pc.games.announce	Announcements related to general PC games (moderated)
comp.sys.ibm.pc.games.flight-sim	Discussions related to flight simulator style PC games
comp.sys.ibm.pc.games.misc	Discussions related to miscellaneous PC games
comp.sys.ibm.pc.games.rpg	Discussions related to role playing PC games
comp.sys.ibm.pc.games.strategic	Discussions related to strategy style PC games

Newsgroup	Description
comp.sys.ibm.pc.hardware	Discussions related to PC hardware
comp.sys.ibm.pc.hardware.cd-rom	Discussions related to using CD-ROMs with PCs
comp.sys.ibm.pc.hardware.chips	Discussions related to various chipsets used in PCs
comp.sys.ibm.pc.hardware.comm	Discussions related to PC-specific telecommunications hardware issues
comp.sys.ibm.pc.hardware.misc	Discussions related to miscellaneous PC hardware issues
comp.sys.ibm.pc.hardware.networking	Discussions related to PC networking issues
comp.sys.ibm.pc.hardware.storage	Discussions related to PC hard drives and other storage mechanisms
comp.sys.ibm.pc.hardware.systems	Discussions related to various PC systems and their configuration
comp.sys.ibm.pc.hardware.video	Discussions related to PC-specific video display hardware products
comp.sys.ibm.pc.misc	Discussions of miscellaneous PC topics
comp.sys.ibm.pc.rt	Discussions related to the RT workstation
comp.sys.ibm.pc.soundcard	Discussions related to various audio and sound hardware for PCs
comp.sys.ibm.ps2.hardware	Discussions related to IBM PS2 systems

A Primer on Newsgroup Etiquette

The USENET news system is a remarkable beast. By nature, it is a wide open terrain with absolutely no restraints on freedom of expression. Each author assumes the responsibility for his or her articles, and the uncensored environment of network news is widely appreciated.

News article posting etiquette is based pretty much on the kind of behavior you'd expect in a college dormitory: don't hit anyone, and clean up your own messes. The sole overriding principle is that just about anything is allowed, as long as it does not put the network itself in jeopardy. While you're pondering what that really means, here are a few tips to get you started.

- I remember asking one of my teachers how long an essay I had been assigned should be; her response simultaneously answered my question and taught me about metaphor. She told me the essay should be like a woman's skirt: short enough to be interesting but long enough to cover the subject. Her advice is appropriate for news articles as well.
- Lots of people on the Internet read hundreds of messages each day. You can't reasonably expect someone to remember what has been said in every previous message. Include appropriate background material that will help the reader understand the context of your message.
- By the same token, you don't need to provide 50 lines of background about a message if you're only responding to a small part of it. Don't, for example, quote a 1,000-line article only to add "I agree!"

Evangelizing the Internet.

Paul Jacoby is a consultant with David Mitchell & Associates on assignment with 3M. He's been working long and hard to introduce 3M employees to the Internet:

"I've been in the process of evangelizing the Internet to the folks I work with here at 3M. The main response I get from people who begin to delve into the depths of the Internet is 'Wow, I had no idea this existed!' Followed closely by 'You mean it's *free*?'

"People are continually amazed at the concepts of software archives ('... filled with *free* software?') and the near instantaneous access to points across the globe. Most are tickled to death to find associates with Internet addresses, exchanging e-mail with turn-around time in the sub-minute range.

"In presenting a summary of the Internet and trying to describe how it works, I boiled all the technical stuff down to one important phrase: It's *automagic*, i.e., don't worry, be happy, use and learn without worrying about the fine points. Most people are quite happy to operate this way :-)"

- Limit your lines to lengths of 80 characters or less.
- Don't use long, rambling signatures or include ASCII graphics—keep it to four lines or less.
- Don't post "me too!" follow-up articles unless you have a worthwhile comment to add.

- Use the right newsgroup for the job. Some newsgroups are intended for discussions while others are intended for announcements. Don't engage in discussions on newsgroups intended for announcements.
- Newsgroups are called newsgroups, not bulletin boards, boards or bboards.
- Don't post private e-mail correspondence in a network news article without the permission of the author. While it may be technically legal to do so, it's rude and could be a copyright violation in some circumstances. (Besides, would you want someone plastering your private e-mail on a network where 10 million people could read it?)
- Don't ask what ":-)" means (tilt your head ninety degrees to the left and see "Smiley Gallery " on page 160).
- Don't post flames outside a newsgroup labeled specifically for flames. (See "Flames, Flame-Bait & Flaming" on page 159).
- Don't end your post with a snooty comment like "Please send e-mail, because I don't read this newsgroup." If you don't read a newsgroup, why would you be posting messages there?
- Don't use excessive CAPITALIZATION & Punctuation!!!!!!!!!!!!
- Don't cross-post to multiple newsgroups unless it's completely relevant and absolutely necessary.
- If you ask for help with a software program, make sure you state what kind of computer you're using. Not everyone uses a PC. (There are tons of UNIX and Mac users on the Internet too.) Also, include specific details like what brand and model PC you have, how much RAM you have, what version of DOS you're using, what kind of monitor you have, any special cards you've installed or any other particulars about your unique PC configuration.
- Keep a sense of humor. There's little room for self-righteous stuffed shirts in the world of network news.
- Don't post articles about what kind of computer is better. Similarly, don't respond to articles arguing the issue.
- Before posting a question in a newsgroup, read its Frequently Asked Questions (FAQ) file. These files contain answers to—you guessed it—the most frequently asked questions. Most news-

groups post the FAQ file to the newsgroup on a regular basis. The FAQ files for most newsgroups are available by FTP from pit-manager.mit.edu

- Understand that you're going to make mistakes, and as sure as grits is groceries, some jerk's going to let you know about it when you do. Try to keep a thick skin about it. See "My First Network News Mistake" for an example.

My First Network News Mistake.

Just less than a month after I started using the Internet, I asked a stupid question in a newsgroup. I had accumulated quite a few PostScript files—mostly documentation—some of them very large.

I didn't want to waste paper by printing these files out if I could view them on the screen. My assumption was that if there were all these wonderful Internet software tools, there was probably a PostScript viewer somewhere. I had checked every archive I knew about, but I couldn't find one.

Timidity is not usually one of my more defining personality qualities, but I timidly—*yes timidly*—posted a very short query on comp.sys.mac.misc. Something on the order of "Does anyone know where I can find a PostScript viewer for the Mac? This is for multi-page, raw PostScript files, not EPS documents."

Within hours I received 10 e-mail responses. The more polite of the bunch were to the effect of "You ignorant *?!)&$. Why don't you read the *$?)#!* FAQ??!! I didn't have the slightest idea what a FAQ was, and I sure wasn't going to ask.

A day or so later the comp.sys.mac.misc FAQ was posted and, of course, my question was answered:

IS THERE A UTILITY TO VIEW POSTSCRIPT FILES ON THE MAC? (11.1)

Net godhood awaits the first person to write a shareware or freeware solution to this problem. The payware products Canvas 3.0 and TScript allow viewing PostScript files on the Mac, but both are large packages with other purposes and cost over $50 each.

I drew some strange consolation that the FAQ file is at least partially wrong. I've never heard of TScript, but Canvas can't deal with multi-page, raw PostScript files.

What continues to confound me is that every one of the pinheads that responded to my original question at length could have saved themselves a lot of trouble with a simple, two-letter, one-word response: NO.

I think it's either a network culture thing ("let's jump the newbie") or these guys have canned messages that they automatically send out as one of their few means of entertainment.

Since then, a PostScript viewer—GhostScript—has been released. It's available in the Oakland University archive if you're interested, but it's useless for multi-page documents.

Flames, Flame-Bait & Flaming

You'll hear a lot about *flames* while reading network news. A flame is an inflammatory message usually posted for no other reason than to start an argument. It's pretty common for someone to login to one of the comp.sys.ibm.pc newsgroups (a stronghold of PC advocates) and post a message with a title like "PCs suck, buy a Mac!" The best response to this sort of wasted bandwidth is to ignore it. Unfortunately, the message always gets answered and a *flame war* erupts with vile epithets hurled in all directions.

Emotion is hard to communicate on the network. Irony and sarcasm are easily misinterpreted without verbal cues or body language. Similarly, terseness can come across as rudeness. And until we can add italics and bold type to our messages, things are even worse—we're limited to ASCII text as the lowest common denominator.

In general, use of capital letters is considered shouting, so be careful how you use them. You can show emphasis by setting off a word or phrase with asterisks: That's *not* what I said. This is considered more polite and respectful than: That's NOT what I said.

Another result of the difficulty of communicating with only ASCII text is the *smiley*. Tilt your head 90 degrees counterclockwise and look at this:

:-)

Remember those yellow "Have a Nice Day" smiley faces? Well, a smiley, like the one shown above, is the electronic equivalent. Smileys are used to convey emotion within an electronic message, and you'll find them widely used throughout the Internet. I hate them, and I almost never use them (in fact, I can't think of a single time I've used one), but they are everywhere, and you'd better learn to decode them. For more information, see the"Smiley Gallery " located below.

Smiley Gallery.
Here are a few of the more common smileys you're likely to encounter.

Smiley	Meaning
:-)	basic smiley; connotes cheer or a grin, sometimes tongue-in-cheek sarcasm
;-)	wink; connotes light sarcasm
:-I	indifference
:->	devilish grin; connotes heavy sarcasm
:-(	frown; connotes anger or displeasure
@:-)	curly hair
8-)	eye-glasses
:-D	shock or surprise
:-/	perplexed
:-7	tongue sticking out

Now that you know a little about the politics and etiquette of using network news, you can start reading and posting on your own. But first, you'll need a first-class utility for navigating newsgroups and composing and posting articles.

Selecting a News Reader

A news reader is a Windows software program that runs on your PC that simplifies the process of navigating and reading network news articles. You use this program to select which newsgroups you want to monitor on a regular basis and which articles you want to read. You also use the news reader to post new articles or reply to existing ones. It's important that you choose a news reader that you can live with—one that lets you navigate quickly through the thousands of pages of articles available—to target the information you need.

Abbreviation Mysteries.

There is a set of abbreviations that are commonly used as shorthand in network communications. Don't worry too much about decoding abbreviations you see. You'll find that they're pretty self-explanatory in context; sort of like reading real-estate listings or personal ads in the newspaper. Here are some of the abbreviations in widest use.

Abbreviation	Meaning
IMHO	in my humble opinion (it very rarely is)
BTW	by the way
ROTFL	rolling on the floor laughing
TNSTAAFL	there's no such thing as a free lunch
OBO	or best offer
RTFM	read the funny manual
FYI	for your information

There are several good news readers available for Windows, and new ones under development. One of the most popular Windows news readers is Peter Tattam's Trumpet. Trumpet is distributed as *shareware*. You can evaluate the program for 30 days, but if you continue to use it beyond the evaluation period, you must pay the $40 shareware fee.

If you don't already have a news reader and you want to get your hands on a great one, you can use FTP (the Internet's File Transfer Protocol) to download the most recent version of Trumpet. You'll find it in the /pc/trumpet/wintrump/ directory at ftp.utas.edu.au (the filename is wtwsk10a.zip). The Trumpet newsreader is also available in the Visitors Center. If you'd like to get a copy of Trumpet but you're unfamiliar with how to download files, "Downloading Files With Chameleon FTP" beginning on page 199, gives you complete instructions on how to download files anywhere on the Net.

In this chapter, we'll walk through the steps for configuring and using Trumpet for reading network news.

Configuring Trumpet

You can always find the latest version of Trumpet (and the other major freeware and shareware programs covered in this book) in *The Windows Internet Tour Guide*'s "Visitors Center," at ftp.farces.com. Check the /pub/visitors-center/software/windows/network-news/ directory for Trumpet and other interesting items. You can also always download the latest version of Trumpet (and related software and documentation) from the FTP site at ftp.utas.edu.au in the /pc/trumpet/wintrump/ directory. As of mid-December 1993, the current version of Trumpet is 1.0 Revision A.

To configure Trumpet for use with your news server.

1. With Windows running and the Chameleon Sampler program group window open, double-click on the **Custom** icon. The Custom window appears, as shown in Figure 5-2.

Figure 5-2: Chameleon Custom window.

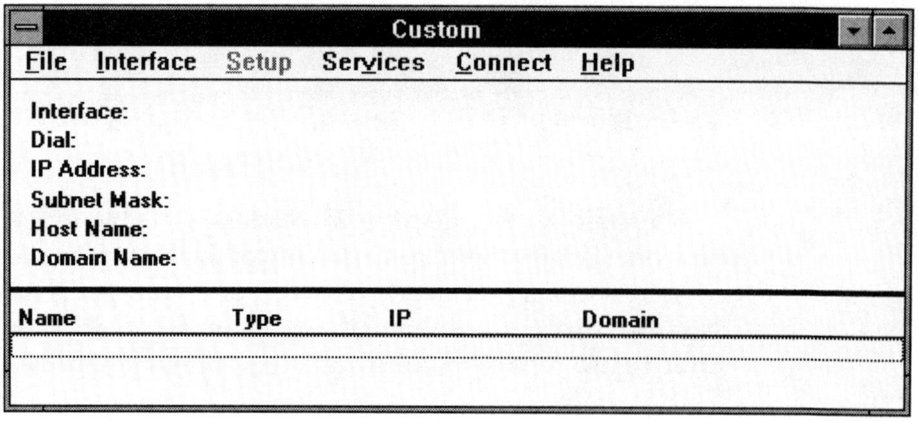

- Additionally, the Chameleon NEWT icon appears in the lower left corner of your monitor, indicating that the TCP/IP communications stack has been successfully loaded.

2. Click the **Connect** menu item. The Connect dialog box appears, and your SLIP or PPP connection will be automatically established.

- If you have trouble establishing your connection, select the Log... command from the Setup menu. This opens a window in which you can monitor and debug your connection activity.

3. Launch Trumpet by double-clicking its icon in the Program Manager. The Trumpet Setup window appears, as shown in Figure 5-3.

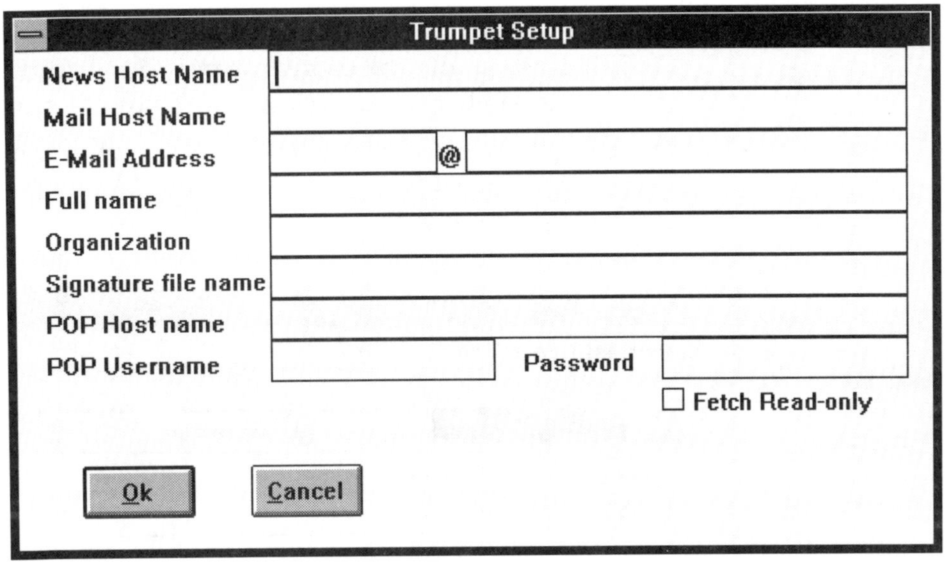

Figure 5-3: Trumpet Setup window.

4. Enter the domain name address of your network news server—using the domain.top-domain format—in the News Host Name field.
5. Enter the domain name of your SMTP mail server—using the domain.top-domain format—in the Mail Host Name field.
6. Enter the username portion of your e-mail address (the part to the left of the "@" symbol) in the first box of the E-Mail Address field.
7. Enter the domain name part of your e-mail address—using the domain.top-domain format—in the second box of the E-Mail Address field.
8. Enter your first and last name in the Full name field.
9. Optionally, enter the name of your company, department or organization in the Organization field.
10. Enter the filename of your signature file in the Signature file name field. A signature is a three- or four-line text file containing your contact information. For more information about signatures, see the "Internet Signatures" sidebar on page 169.

- If the file is in a directory other than the Trumpet directory, enter the full pathname of the file.

11. Enter the domain name of your POP mail server—using the domain.top-domain format—in the POP Host name field.
12. Enter your username on the POP mail server in the POP Username field. This is usually the username portion of your e-mail address (the part to the left of the "@" symbol), but not always.
13. Enter your password for the POP mail server in the Password field. The Trumpet Setup window should look similar to the example in Figure 5-4.

Figure 5-4: Trumpet Setup window with example settings.

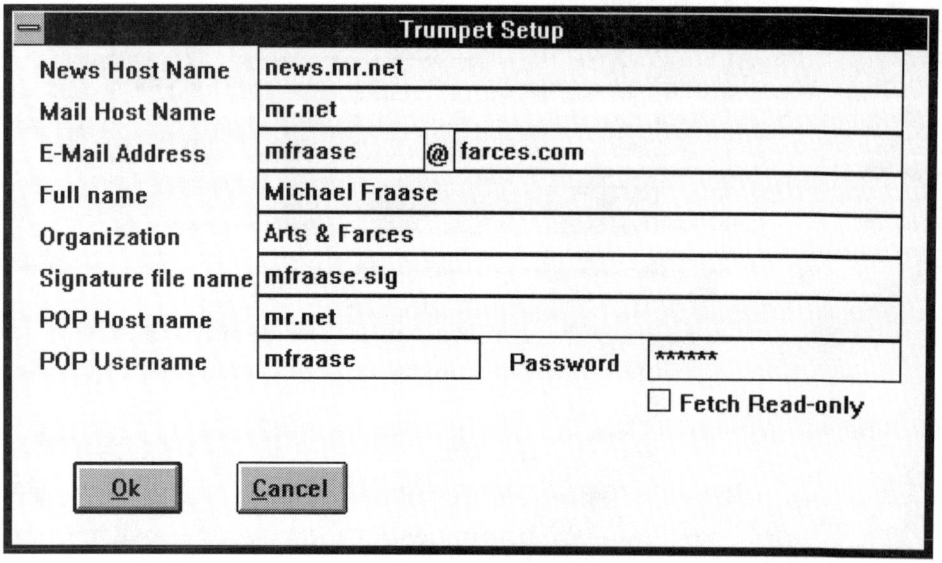

14. Click the **OK** button. Trumpet will save your configuration settings to disk and connect to the NNTP server you specified.
    - Trumpet will retrieve and build a list of all available newsgroups on your news server. This may take a while. This process occurs only the first time you configure your subscribed newsgroups and whenever you choose the Subscribe command from the Group menu.

The first time you use Trumpet to connect to your network news server it will create a list of available newsgroups for you and the Subscribe to News Groups window is displayed, as shown in Figure 5-5.

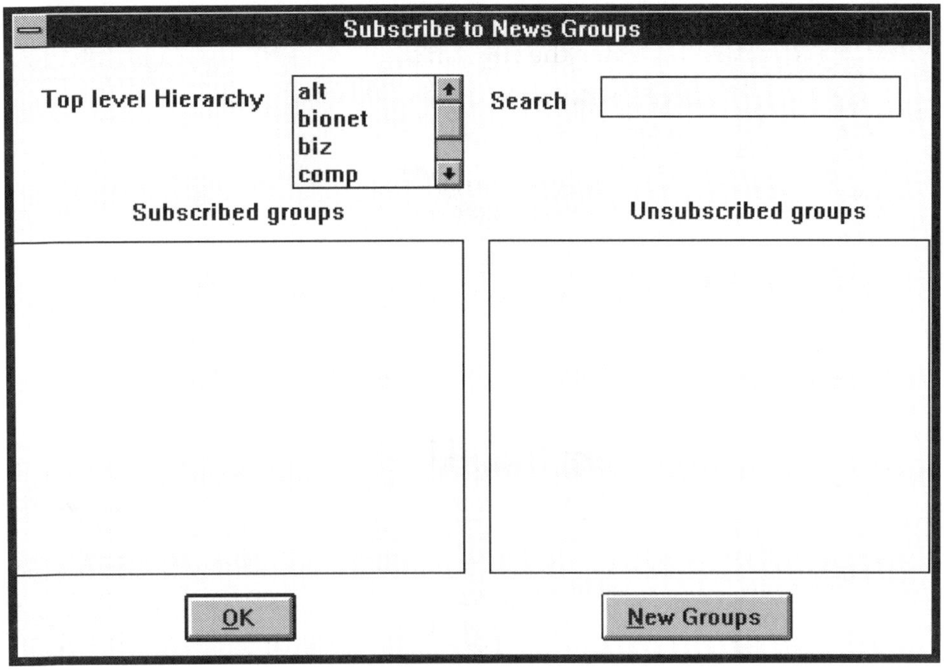

Figure 5-5: Trumpet Subscribe to News Groups window.

Use these steps to select the newsgroups that interest you.

1. Select the top level hierarchy item that contains the first newsgroup to which you want to subscribe. A list of available newsgroups appears in the Unsubscribed groups list, as shown in Figure 5-6.

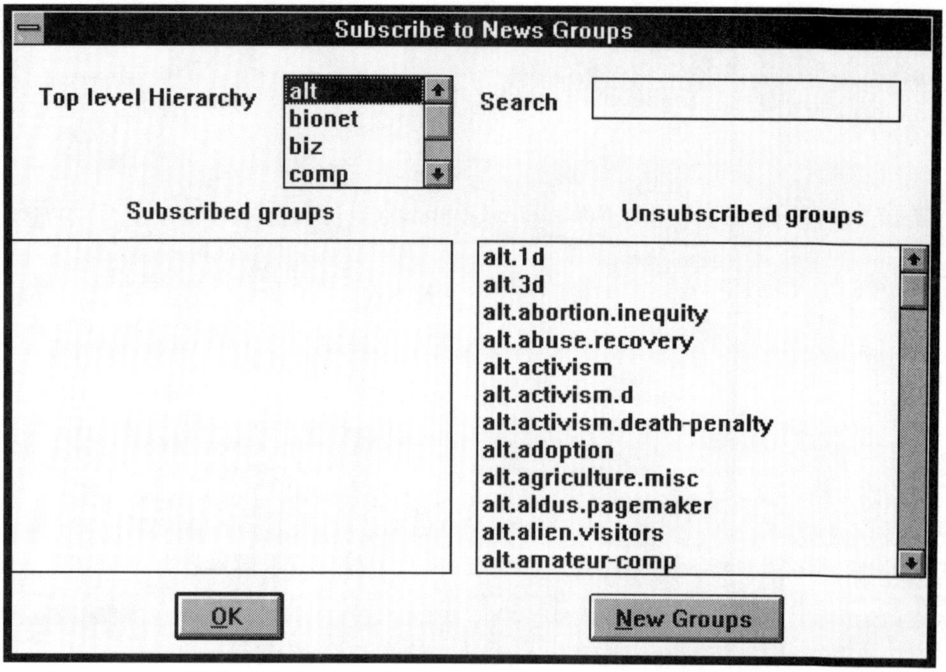

Figure 5-6: Trumpet Subscribe to News Groups window with Unsubscribed groups list.

2. Click on the newsgroup to which you want to subscribe. The newsgroup will be added to the Subscribed groups list, as shown in Figure 5-7.

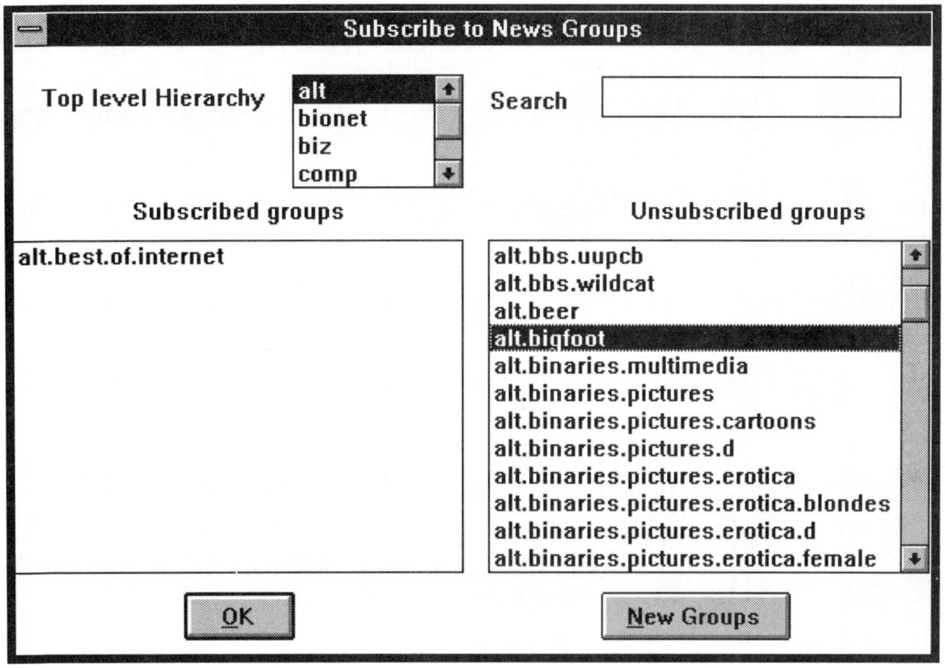

Figure 5-7: Trumpet Subscribe to News Groups window with Subscribed groups list.

- If you select a newsgroup by mistake, click on its name in the Subscribed groups list. The newsgroup will be returned to the Unsubscribed groups list.

3. Repeat steps 1–3 for each additional newsgroup to which you want to subscribe.

   - You can also search for the name of a newsgroup by entering enough of the group's name in the Search field until the newsgroup appears in the list.

4. When you're finished selecting newsgroups, click the **OK** button in the Subscribe to News Groups window. Your subscribed newsgroups will appear in the Trumpet News Reader window, as shown in the example in Figure 5-8.

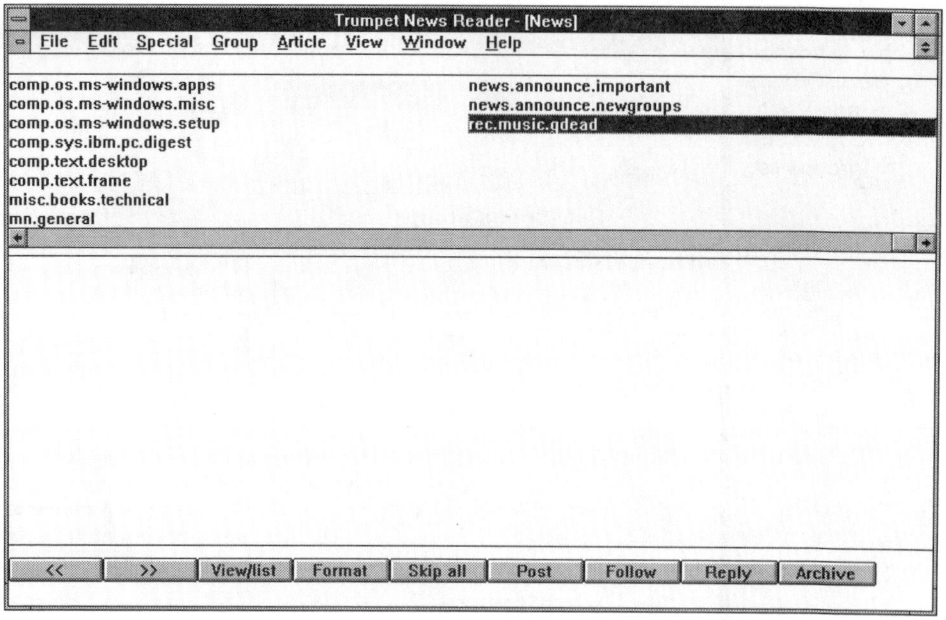

Figure 5-8: Trumpet News Reader window with subscribed newsgroups.

Meckler Publishing.
Meckler Publishing (Westport, CT) is aggressively developing Internet guides for librarians, researchers and information professionals. Contact meckler@jvnc.net for notification of upcoming books on Internet basics, electronic scholarship, Internet directories, WAIS and Gopher servers, citation of electronic sources, Internet/NREN policy, etc. Meckler's quarterly *Electronic Networking* will now be *Internet Research: Electronic Networking, Applications, and Policy.*

Managing network news and newsgroups can quickly become an overwhelming task. A good approach is to begin by selecting only those newsgroups you are especially interested in. Later, if you find you have enough time to read more articles, you can create additional lists or add more newsgroups to existing lists. It's much easier to add newsgroups later than to wade through massive amounts of information you may not be interested in.

You can add newsgroups to your subscription list at any time (select the Subscribe command from the Groups menu). But now that you've got at least a few newsgroups lined up for reading, we'll learn how to read news articles with Trumpet.

Internet Signatures.

Electronic communications—both e-mail and network news postings—are usually much less formal than the typical business letter. Formal salutations are rarely called for and are generally considered something of a waste of bandwidth.

Similarly, formal closings are almost never seen. Instead, most networkers end their messages with a *signature.* A signature is a short—four lines or less—identification tag that includes your full name, organization and contact information.

Signatures range in style from the strictly functional to almost rococo-like. The function of a signature is to provide identification and contact information in case the address header is incorrect or incomplete.

The best signatures usually include a quote that tells you something about the person writing the message. Quotes are fine, but should be kept short and pithy.

In creating a signature, remember that ASCII text is still the lowest common denominator for Internet communications. Use a monospaced font and keep the length of each line under 80 characters.

Here's the signature I use:

```
—
Michael Fraase,        | "Nothing to tell, let the words be
 proprietor            | yours. I am done with mine...."
Arts & Farces          | Weir/Barlow
Saint Paul, MN USA     |____________________
mfraase@farces.com     | Writing and document design
```

You can gather a lot of interesting information from a person's signature. From mine you could assume that I'm self-employed (the top-level domain is a commercial account and the domain name matches part of my company name); I live in Minnesota; and I like the Grateful Dead more than just a little (and you can draw your own conclusions from that).

Sometimes, signatures carry a disclaimer stating that the comments represent the views of the individual posting the message but not necessarily the views of that person's employer, company or organization. Sometimes these disclaimer lines are even written with a sense of humor:

```
Opinions this ludicrous are mine. Reasonable opinions will
cost you.
```

More

Here are some of the better signature tag lines I've come across lately:

I need some indication that all of this is real now.

Slipping into madness is good for the sake of comparison.

"Tens of thousands of messages, hundreds of points of view. It was not called the Net of a Million Lies for nothing." -Vernor Vinge

Spread peanut butter, not AIDS.

Fear is a little darkroom where negatives are developed.

Stop yawning. Start yearning.

Bandwidth expands to fit the waste available.

Practice random kindness and senseless acts of beauty.

"I stand behind all of my misstatements." – Dan Quayle

How to Read, Post & Reply to Articles

In a graphical environment like Trumpet, each news article is represented individually. You read an article by selecting it. You can reply to an article by selecting the range of text to which you want to respond and using your news reader's Reply command. Sometimes you'll want to create a completely new topic within a newsgroup. To do this, simply create a new message using the appropriate Create New Message command in your news reader. This section shows you how to read, post and reply to network news articles using the news reader module in Trumpet.

Using Trumpet

Trumpet is one of the most popular news readers in the Windows community, probably because it's inexpensive, performs well and offers an intuitive interface. Subscribed newsgroups appear in the upper portion of the Trumpet News Reader window, with a list of available messages in the current newsgroup in the lower portion of the window.

Reading News With Trumpet

Use the following steps to read network news articles with Trumpet. This section assumes that you have already properly configured Trumpet and selected the newsgroups you want to monitor. The examples provided here use only a few newsgroups, but Trumpet works the same for all available newsgroups.

1. With Windows running and the Chameleon Sampler program group window open, double-click on the **Custom** icon. The Custom window appears, as shown in Figure 5-2.
   - Additionally, the Chameleon NEWT icon appears in the lower left corner of your monitor, indicating that the TCP/IP communications stack has been successfully loaded.
2. Click the **Connect** menu item. The Connect dialog box appears, and your SLIP or PPP connection will be automatically established.
   - If you have trouble establishing your connection, select the Log... command from the Setup menu. This opens a window in which you can monitor and debug your connection activity.
3. Launch Trumpet by double-clicking its icon in the Program Manager. The Trumpet News Reader window appears, as shown in Figure 5-9.

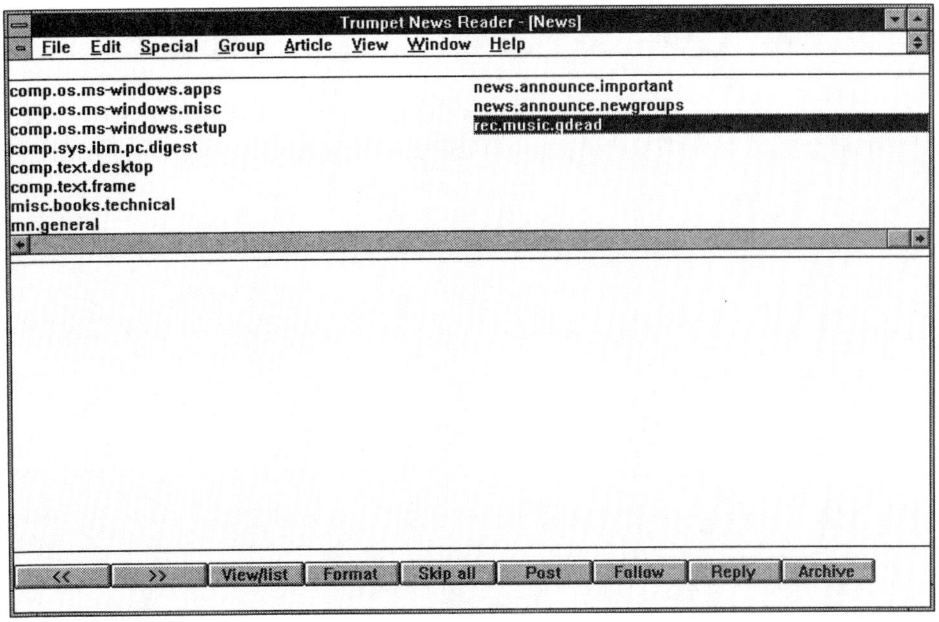

Figure 5-9: Trumpet News Reader window with subscribed newsgroups.

4. Double-click on the newsgroup containing articles you want to read. The bottom panel of the window displays a list of available articles in the selected newsgroup, as shown in Figure 5-10.

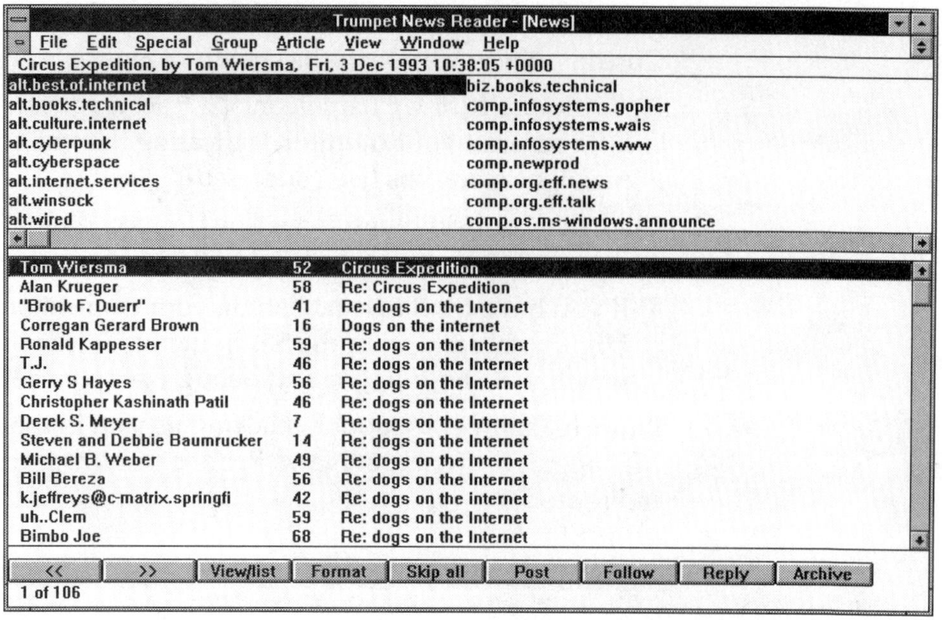

Figure 5-10: Trumpet News Reader window with selected newsgroup and available articles.

5. Double-click on the title in the list of the article you want to read. The article will be displayed, as shown in Figure 5-11.

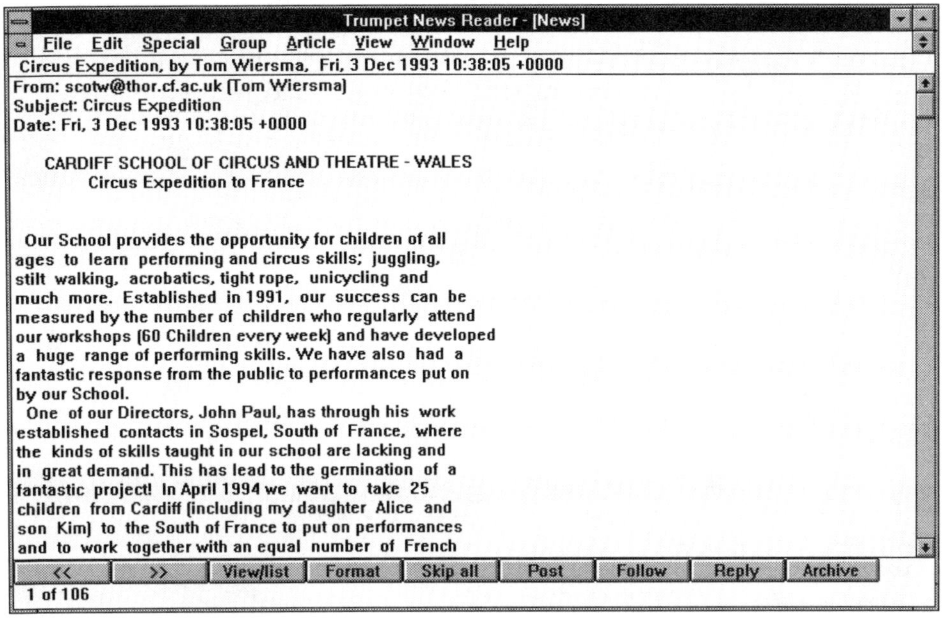

Figure 5-11: Trumpet News Reader with article.

- Alternatively, you can use the **Arrow** keys to navigate the list of available articles, and press **Enter** when the article you want to read is selected.

6. Click the **View/List** button to re-display the list of articles available in the selected newsgroup.
   - Alternatively, click the << or >> buttons to browse through the text of the available articles.
7. Alternatively, click the **Archive** button to save the article as a text file on your disk.
8. Repeat steps 4–7 for each additional newsgroup you want to read.

Posting a News Article With Trumpet

Reading news articles is only half the point of participating in newsgroups. To get the most out of your time with network news, you also have to know how to post original articles and responses to existing articles. To post a news article with Trumpet:

1. With Windows running and the Chameleon Sampler program group window open, double-click on the **Custom** icon. The Custom window appears, as shown in Figure 5-2.

- Additionally, the Chameleon NEWT icon appears in the lower left corner of your monitor, indicating that the TCP/IP communications stack has been successfully loaded.

2. Click the **Connect** menu item. The Connect dialog box appears, and your SLIP or PPP connection will be automatically established.
   - If you have trouble establishing your connection, select the Log... command from the Setup menu. This opens a window in which you can monitor and debug your connection activity.
3. Launch Trumpet by double-clicking its icon in the Program Manager. The Trumpet News Reader window appears, as shown in Figure 5-12.

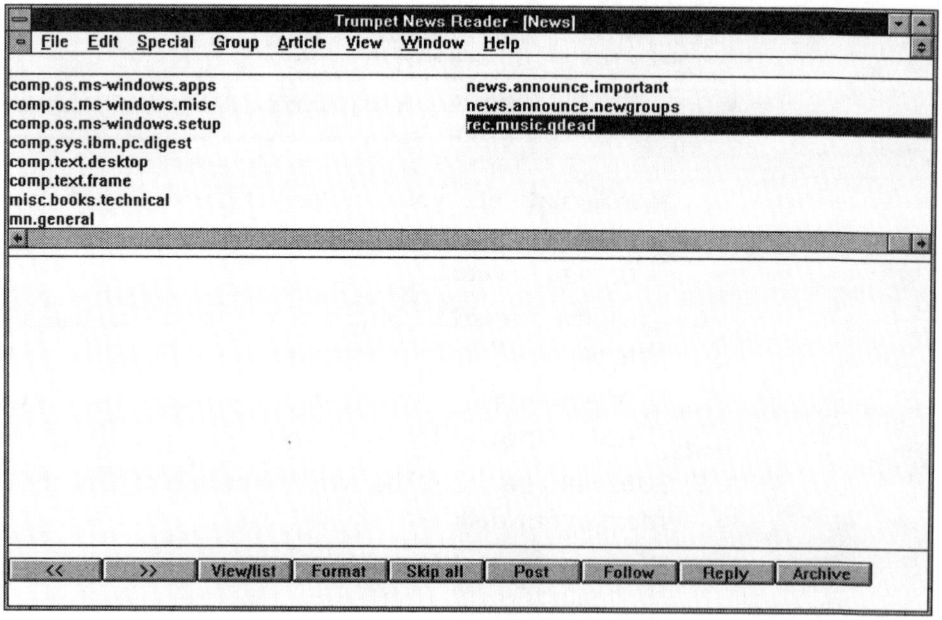

Figure 5-12: Trumpet News Reader window with subscribed newsgroups.

4. Double-click on the newsgroup containing articles related to the topic about which you want to post an article. The bottom panel of the window displays a list of available articles in the selected newsgroup, as shown in Figure 5-13.

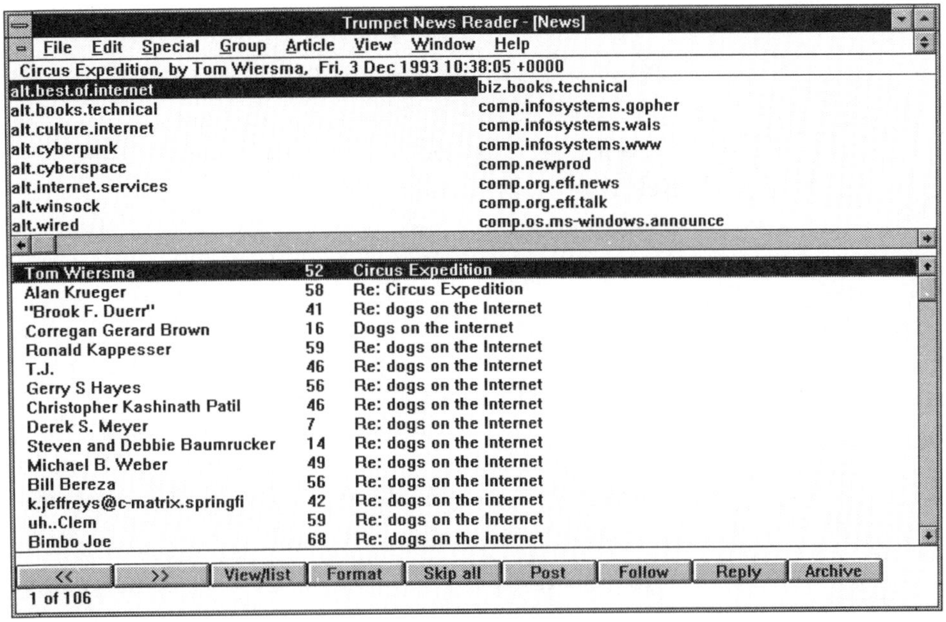

Figure 5-13: Trumpet News Reader window with selected newsgroup and available articles.

5. Click the **Post** button. The Post Article window is displayed, as shown in Figure 5-14.

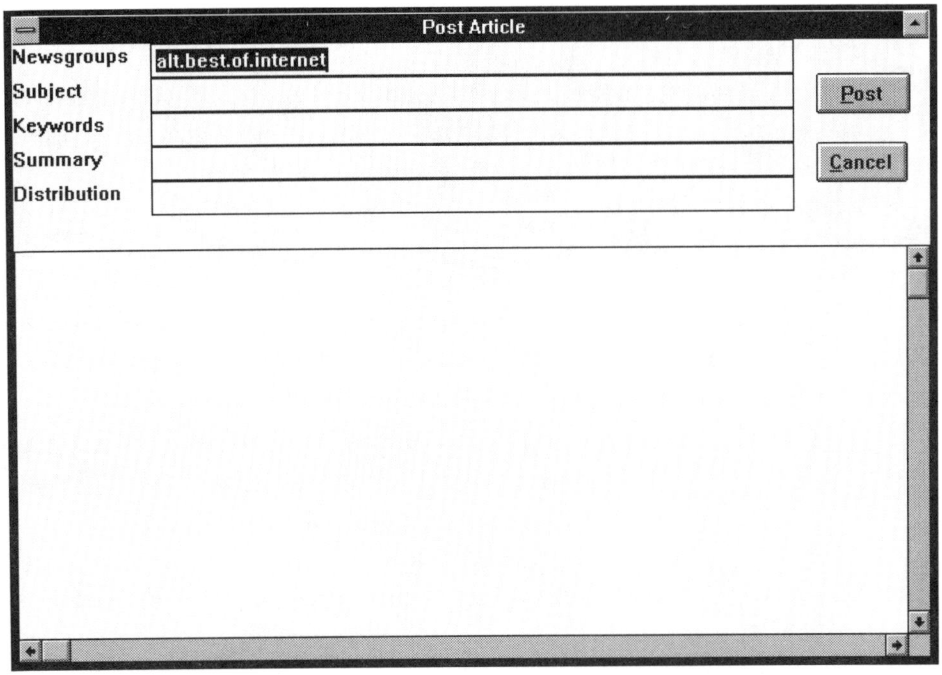

Figure 5-14: Trumpet Post Article window.

6. Enter a subject or title for your news article in the Subject field.
7. Optionally, enter the appropriate key words for your article in the Keywords field.
8. Optionally, enter a brief summary for your article in the Summary field.
9. Enter a level of distribution for the article—World, North America, US, State, City or Local, for example—in the Distribution field.
   - This determines how widely your article is distributed, and you should set it with some caution. If you're posting an article that has little or no interest outside your geographic location, specify a narrower level of distribution. If you're selling a large monitor, for example, you may want to limit the distribution of your article to your local area.
10. Enter the body text of your news article. You can type or paste text into the article.
11. Click the **Post** button. Your news article will be posted to the currently active newsgroup.

MOOGopher

MOOGopher is an object-oriented, multi-user dimension that uses an integrated Gopher client. Objects in the environment can contain Gopher items, and you navigate the Gopherspace as if you're exploring a game. You can try it by pointing your Gopher program at theory.cs.mankato.msus.edu port 1709. (For more on Gopher, see Chapter 7.)

Many times you'll want to respond to something you read in a network news article. Use these steps to reply to a news article with Trumpet.

1. Use the steps outlined in the "Reading News With Trumpet" section, beginning on page 170, to read the available news articles in the newsgroups to which you have subscribed.
2. With the article to which you want to respond open, select the range of specific text to which you want to respond. If you want to respond to the entire article, there's no need to select any text.

3. Click the **Follow** button. The original message (or the range of text you selected) will be opened in the Post Article window, with a ">" preceding each line, as shown in Figure 5-15.

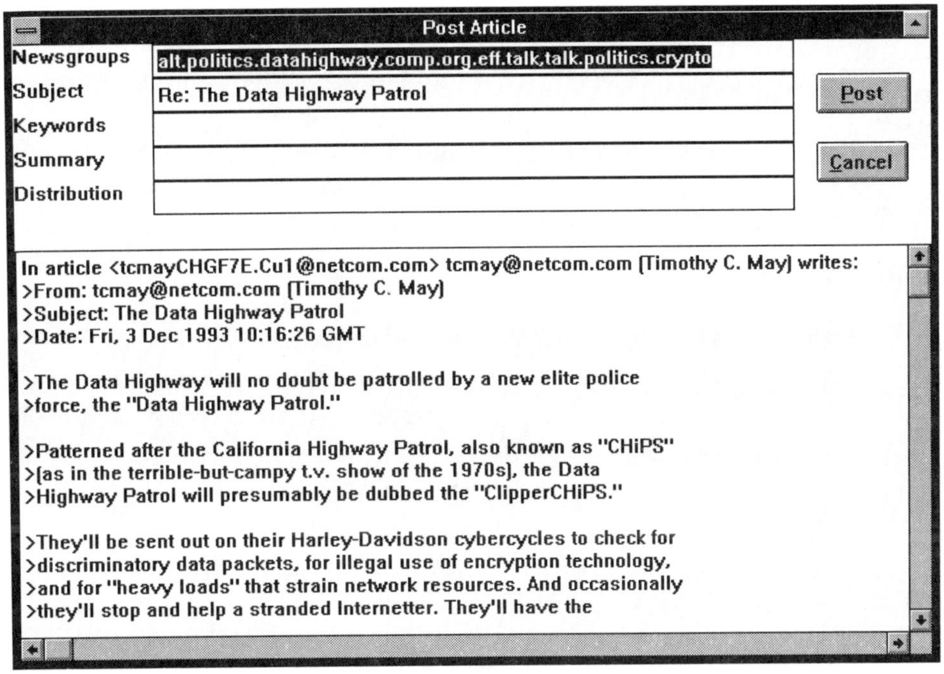

Figure 5-15: Trumpet Post Article window with reply to news article.

- Note that the Subject field is automatically filled as a response ("re:") to the original article subject.

4. Optionally, enter the appropriate key words for your article in the Keywords field.
5. Optionally, enter a brief summary for your article in the Summary field.
6. Enter a level of distribution for the article—World, North America, US, State, City or Local, for example—in the Distribution field.
   - This determines how widely your article is distributed, and you should set it with some caution. If you're posting an article that has little or no interest outside your geographic location, specify a narrower level of distribution. If you're selling a large monitor, for example, you may want to limit the distribution of your article to your local area.

7. Enter the body text of your response article. You can type or paste text into the article.
8. Click the **Post** button. Your news article will be posted to the currently active newsgroup.

How Fast Can UFOs Go?

There are all sorts of strange newsgroups available on the Internet. Here's a sample exchange—the message title is "How fast can UFOs go?"—from the alt.alien.visitors newsgroup.

[Original post]"Putting aside the energy requirements for accelerating to c, how far is 'far into space?' Assuming that their solar system is constructed similarly to ours, and the time spent in 'hyper-space' is effectively none, that would imply a 3.5 hour trip to the jump point on each side of the hyper-flight. I vaguely recall my high school astronomy teacher telling me that Pluto is 5 lighthours from the sun. So in order to reach a point at which the light speed drive can be used, our insystem drive needs to reach 1.4c? I'm available to these guys as an efficiency consultant."

[Follow-up post]"When I think of the problem of needing to get some distance from a gravitational source—Earth, Moon, Sun, whatever—I would not head towards Pluto. I would head straight up the Y-axis. Cartoon analogy: When a truck is headed towards Daffy Duck, he runs away down the road instead of going left or right to get off the road. The solar system is sort of flat, the universe is not."

Alternatively, you can reply to an article's author privately, via e-mail, with these steps.

1. Use the steps outlined in the "Reading News With Trumpet" section, beginning on page 170, to read the available news articles in the newsgroups to which you have subscribed.
2. With the article to which you want to respond open, select the range of specific text to which you want to respond. If you want to respond to the entire article, there's no need to select any text.
3. Click the **Reply** button. The original message (or the range of text you selected) will be opened in the Mail Article window, with a ">" preceding each line, as shown in Figure 5-16.

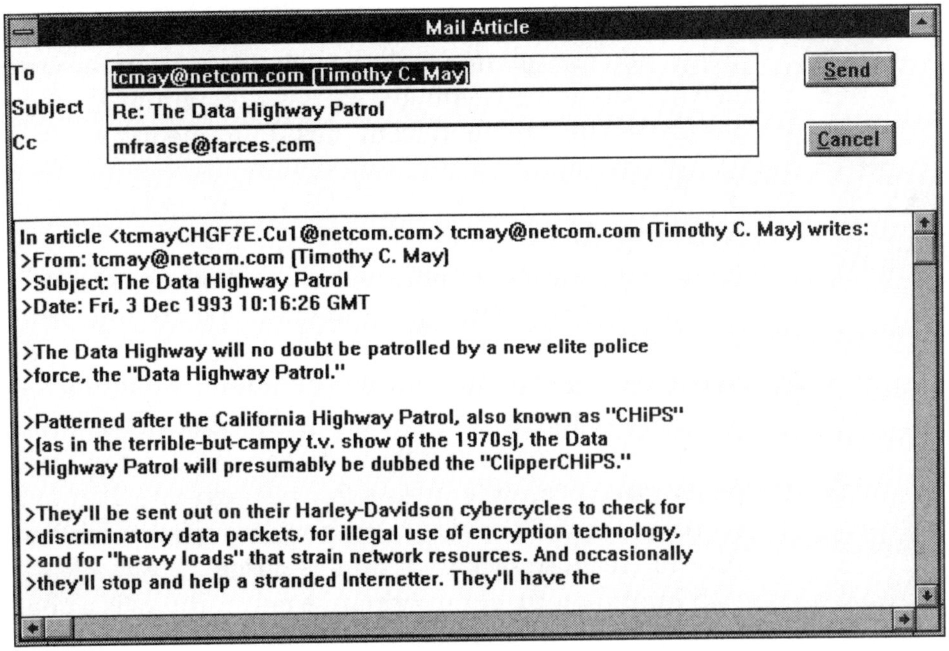

Figure 5-16: Trumpet Mail Article window with reply to news article.

- Note that the Subject field is automatically filled as a response ("re:") to the original article subject.

4. Enter the body text of your response. You can type or paste text into the article.
5. Click the **Send** button. Your reply will be sent to the author of the original article.

Managing Network News With Trumpet

Keeping up with even a handful of newsgroups can be burdensome at times, especially when you're out of town. Even if you unsubscribe from some newsgroups while you're gone, there will likely be more articles than you can deal with when you return. Although network news articles aren't stored on the news server indefinitely, it's not uncommon for most news servers to have more than 100mb of news articles on any given day.

Here's a shortcut to avoid having to wade through the process of re-subscribing to the newsgroups you're interested in. You can easily eliminate all news articles in the currently active newsgroup and advance to the next newsgroup to which you've subscribed by clicking the **Skip all** button in the Trumpet News Reader window. Alternatively, you can eliminate all the news articles in the currently active newsgroup while keeping your position within Trumpet by selecting the Catch Up command from the Group menu.

Moving On

Now you're ready to venture into the thousands of newsgroups on the Internet. But be careful, you can waste a lot of time trolling through network news looking for nuggets of useful information. Unfortunately, there are no proven secrets to tracking down worthwhile articles. I've found that the best information tends to cluster within the smaller newsgroups and those that are moderated. Also, it's usually a better idea to carefully read a few newsgroups than to try to skim scores of them. There are more newsgroups available than anyone can possibly read, so pick your targets wisely.

If hunting for truly informative newsgroups is a challenge, then finding great files is a cakewalk. As our tour bus cruises through the next chapter, you'll learn how to effectively use the Internet's File Transfer Protocol (FTP) and the FTP client built into Chameleon to mine these information-rich resources.

CHAPTER 6

TRANSFERRING FILES

The Mother Downlode

Part of the fun of visiting any distant place is taking snapshots and collecting souvenirs to take back home. Our tour through the Internet is no exception. There are plenty of strange and wondrous curios—as well as practical items you'll use every day—nestled throughout the Net. And you don't have to hop a steamer or board a plane to collect them all. Thanks to the Internet's File Transfer Protocol (FTP), it takes only a few commands to download a shareware program or text file from a computer halfway around the world. But perhaps the most satisfying thing about using the Internet's FTP to download files is that you get exactly the information you want without wading through a lot of stuff you don't want.

Depending on how relevant it is to you as an individual, information has a level of density. E-mail is usually information-dense on one level because it is of unique concern to you. Network news, on the other hand, is comparatively information-sparse, because there are a lot of useless messages you must plow through to get to the information that's important to you. Files that you download and use on your PC are information-dense, perhaps more than anything else you will encounter on the Internet.

In this chapter, we'll cover the basics of the File Transfer Protocol itself, and we'll also go over the details of using a popular software program (Chameleon's FTP module) that lets you transfer files across the Internet. So sit back, get your cameras ready and fish out those traveler's checks—we're going souvenir hunting.

What Is FTP?

FTP is an acronym for File Transfer Protocol, but nobody says File Transfer Protocol; everyone says FTP, as in "you can FTP that file from the CICA archive" or "that file is available by FTP from the Minnesota archive."

People use FTP as a noun when they refer to the actual File Transfer Protocol, but they also use it as a verb when describing the process of transferring files on the Internet. Technically, FTP is a full-fledged data-transfer protocol like Z-Modem or Kermit. It allows files to be transferred between different kinds of computers, without regard to the operating system used by the computers or even how they are connected.

Why Would You Want to Transfer Files?

You can use Windows applications (like Chameleon) that employ FTP to send and receive files between your PC and any other computer on the Internet that supports FTP. There is a wealth of software available through the Internet by *anonymous FTP*. Anonymous FTP is an Internet service that allows anyone to enter publicly accessible file archives, practically anywhere in the world, without having an account on that archive. If an FTP server accepts anonymous logins (and there are thousands that do), you login with the username *anonymous* and any text as a password. It is a generally accepted convention that anonymous FTP users should enter their complete e-mail address—in the username@domain.top-domain format—as their password.

Hot News on the Net.

Savvy folks in public relations and publicity departments know that news travels fast along the Net. That's why you can count on the Internet to be one of the first places to offer news releases from all kinds of sources, ranging from the White House to Microsoft. In short, you can see it on the Net today, or read about it in the paper tomorrow.

"INTERNET WORLD '93 and DOCUMENT DELIVERY WORLD '93

"Conference and Exhibition Dealing with the Commercial and Non-Commercial Utilization of these Services and the Impact they Have on Information Providers and Users

"December 6–9, 1993, Jacob Javits Convention Center, New York City

"Sponsored by Internet World Magazine and Document Delivery World Magazine

"Travel into the future of the Internet and electronic Document Delivery and much more. Over 100 speakers and 100 exhibitors present ideas, applications, and products that will enable you to take advantage of these important information technology delivery systems.

"Meckler has created workshops and seminars designed for professionals and end-users in several interest categories. You decide which workshops or seminars are right for you. There are 8 pre-conference workshops, 41 seminars and 4 post-conference workshops that address your specific needs. INTERNET WORLD '93 is unequaled in the industry. It is the only program built around the concept of the delivery of information on the Internet.

"Over 100 exhibitors will be showcasing a universe of the latest products, programs and services related to Internet utilization and electronic Document Delivery. You can explore the world of Internet by testing the "super electronic highway" at numerous hook-ups in our exhibit hall. INTERNET WORLD is the trade show for information and technology related to Internet services. Register now and begin your successful competition in the 'information world' of tomorrow."

Resources available from anonymous FTP archives include fully functional software programs (spreadsheets, text editors, telecommunications programs, databases, graphics programs, utilities and more) as well as graphic images, sounds, animations and texts ranging from President Bill Clinton's speeches to *Macbeth*. Some of the most valuable software resources available on the Internet are updaters and bug fixes for commercially distributed software. Software companies distribute the updaters to the general public via the Internet and various online services. People who own a program that may not be compatible with a new hardware or software release can download the updater and run it on their outdated program to upgrade it to the newest version. It's a classic win-win situation: users get quick updates and the vendor gets inexpensive distribution and loads of goodwill within the community while at the same time keeping its installed base of users current and up-to-date.

Other valuable resources—information resources—are available by FTP. Developer notes, technical reports, technical support documents, electronic magazines, journals, templates and tutorials are all available. And then there are the thousands of "miscellaneous" resources that seem to find their way to FTP sites: things like musical notation and lyric sheets for just about any piece of music from the last 30 years, and full-text copies of classic literature ranging from *Alice in Wonderland* and *Peter Pan* to the complete works of Shakespeare.

A Primer on Software Resources

For the time being, there are three general types of software resources you can find on the Internet: information resources, software programs and program-specific files for use with those software programs (templates and samples). Information resources—documents that were distributed as ink (or toner) on paper in the past—are widely available from numerous sources on the Internet. Software programs and files for use with those programs are generally less widely available, but plentiful nonetheless.

Dial "S" for Software.

Just about the only kind of software resource you won't find on the Internet is commercially distributed software. And even that may change in the relatively near future. Imagine the benefit MondoCorp can reap if it can distribute within seconds a new version of its MondoWriter software to anyone on the Internet. Users could simply type in a credit card number and instantly download the software and documentation right to their hard drives. Look for this to happen soon, and look to see who the initial players are. Chances are the first companies to distribute their software across the Internet will be the most forward-thinking in the industry.

In broadest terms, there are three classifications for the software resources you will find on the Internet: public domain, freeware and shareware. Let's take a look at the differences between these three distribution methods.

Public Domain

Public domain resources are those that carry no copyright. The author or developer has created the resource for the good of the community and has released it for any and every use. There is no limit on redistribution or sale of public domain resources, and it can be modified or transformed by anyone.

Freeware

Freeware resources are those that carry the author's copyright. The author retains copyright, but allows you to use the resource free of charge. There are generally some restrictions on freeware resources, most often regarding distribution and modification. The usual case with freeware is that you can give it away, but you can't sell it, and the author retains copyright.

Shareware

Shareware resources are those that are distributed on a "try-before-you-buy" basis. The author retains copyright and allows you to use the resource on a trial basis for a short evaluation period. At the end of the evaluation period you must either pay the author for the resource or destroy all the copies of the resource in your possession. You are encouraged to make copies for your friends, but you can't charge for them. Shareware resources carry a relatively low price because the author doesn't have to pay distribution or advertising costs. The author cuts out the middlemen like distributors and resellers, dealing with you—the user—directly.

Trumpet—the network news reader used as an example in this book—is an example of shareware.

Freeware PPP software.

PPP software allows you to login to the Internet using a high-speed modem and ordinary telephone lines. SLIP is currently more common than PPP, but PPP will probably surpass SLIP in the near future because it offers more features and better throughput during interactive sessions where small bits of information are passed in both directions. EtherPPP, for MS-DOS computers, is available by anonymous FTP at merit.edu in the /pub/ppp/ directory.

Making Shareware Work

If shareware is to remain a viable way to distribute and sell software, people who use it must pay the shareware authors. If you regularly use a piece of shareware, it's in your own best interest to pay the shareware fee.

A Primer on File Types

Files on the Internet are usually going to have names that are pretty much the same as what you're used to seeing. Most PC files that you find will be listed in this filename format:

filename.ext.

The "ext" part of a file's name represents the compression tool used to create the file. The most common options are: zip, lha and zoo. (For more information on what these extensions mean, see Table 6-1.) The "exe" or "doc" extension indicates that the file has been placed on the FTP server in its native file format and need not be processed after it's downloaded. An "hqx" extension is rare in the PC world, but indicates that the file has been placed on the FTP server in BinHex format. BinHex is a standard format that allows files to be accessed by virtually any computer, regardless of the hardware or software it uses.

You'll also probably find a lot of files that end with a "txt" or "ps" extension. These are ASCII text and PostScript files respectively and are intended for use on all kinds of computers. ASCII text can be read by any word processor and PostScript files can be printed—fully formatted—by any PostScript-capable output device.

Chameleon's FTP module will use the transfer mode you specify—ASCII or Binary—to download files on the Net.

PKWARE's PKUNZIP utility will automatically decompress files created with PKZIP, the most widely used PC compression program. You can find the current version of PKUNZIP in the Visitors Center (FTP to ftp.farces.com and look in the /pub/visitors-center/software/ms-dos/compression/ directory) and most major software archives on the Net. To use PKUNZIP, simply type **pkunzip filename.ext** (where filename.ext is the name and extension of the file you want to decompress) at the DOS command prompt. Of course, the PKZIP family of compression products offers a wealth of other options for compressing and decompressing files, but that's the basic command. For more information, see the PKZIP documentation.

If you're a sensitive new-age sort of Windows user who doesn't like to sully yourself with DOS commands, a solution is available. Nico Mak Computing Inc.'s shareware WinZip provides a Windows front-end to the major PC file compression utilities and has PKZIP compatibility for both compressing and decompressing files built-in. You can download the current version of WinZip by FTP from ftp.farces.com in the /pub/visitors-center/software/windows/compression/ directory or from ftp.cica.indiana.edu in the pub/pc/win3/util/ directory.

Information about the file extensions and file types used on the Internet is provided in Table 6-1.

Table 6-1: Archived file type extensions.

Ext.	Compression Program Used
exe, doc	Native file formats created by various software programs (these files aren't processed by PKZIP); note that filenames with an .exe extension may be self-extracting archive files; to decompress them, simply type the filename at the command prompt
hqx	BinHex 4.0
zip	PKZIP
arj	ARJ
lha	LHA
zoo	ZOO
arc	ARC

If you stick to the major PC FTP servers, you'll probably never see any other filename extensions. But then you'd be missing out on most of the software resources available on the Internet. (For a list of the most popular PC FTP sites on the Internet, see "Famous PC FTP Archives" on page 208.)

If you download files almost exclusively from the most popular PC archives, you'll probably be able to decompress them with the free PKUNZIP utility. But if you're planning to wander the Net, sampling files from all over, you'll need several compression utilities; there is no "Swiss army knife" compression utility for PCs. PKZIP is the most widely used, however, and is available as shareware from PKWARE Inc., 9025 North Deerwood Drive, Brown Deer, WI 53223; 414/354-8699; 414/354-8559 (Fax).

Nice Pictures.
Lview is a freeware multi-format graphics image viewer. It's a simple, no-nonsense viewer that offers a very clean interface and outstanding performance. It requires at least an 80386 processor for best performance and is available by FTP from ftp.cica.indiana.edu in the pub/pc/win3/desktop/ directory. The filename is lview31.zip

A SCAN Utility for Viruses

If you're going to download files from any FTP archive on the Internet, you run the risk of having your system infected with a *virus*. A virus (and similar files like trojan horses or worms) is actually a computer program imbedded within another file you download. It "infects" your computer in one of a number of different ways. Some viruses are merely annoying, but others can cause severe damage by erasing files on your hard disk, scrambling your disk's file catalog or a number of other malicious tricks.

Your computer can't get infected by a text file, only by binary files, but it's generally a good policy to consider any file you download to be a potential source of viruses. While viruses are relatively rare, the Internet is a fertile breeding ground for them. So many files are uploaded and transferred every day, it's impossible to check them all, especially since there's no single system in place for checking for viruses.

The best way to protect yourself is to download the current version of McAfee Associates' SCAN anti-virus program. You can always find the latest version of SCAN at oak.oakland.edu in the /pub/msdos/virus/ directory as the filename scanvxxx.zip (where xxx is the current version number). SCAN is a DOS program, but you can configure WinZip to use SCAN to automatically check files you download for viruses from within Windows.

University of North Carolina's Winsock archive.
The Winsock archive maintained by the University of North Carolina is one of the most popular archives on the Internet. Just about any public domain, freeware or shareware software for Winsock-specific networking is available here. It's accessible with Gopher (as well as the traditional methods). Point your Gopher at gopher.unc.edu port 70.

Alternatively, all files are available by anonymous FTP at sunsite.unc.edu. You can download an index of descriptions of all available files in the /pub/micro/pc-stuff/ms-windows/winsock/ directory.

Using SCAN

SCAN is probably the most frequently updated and widely used anti-virus utility for the PC. With it, you can periodically check your hard drive and local area network for viruses and eradicate most any viruses you might find. The easiest way to use SCAN is to configure WinZip to automatically check for viruses in files you've downloaded when you unzip them.

To scan your hard drive for any known virus and repair the drive if a virus is found:

1. Navigate to the directory that contains the SCAN program.
2. At the prompt, enter **SCAN** and press **Enter**. The SCAN instructions will be displayed, as shown in Figure 6-1.

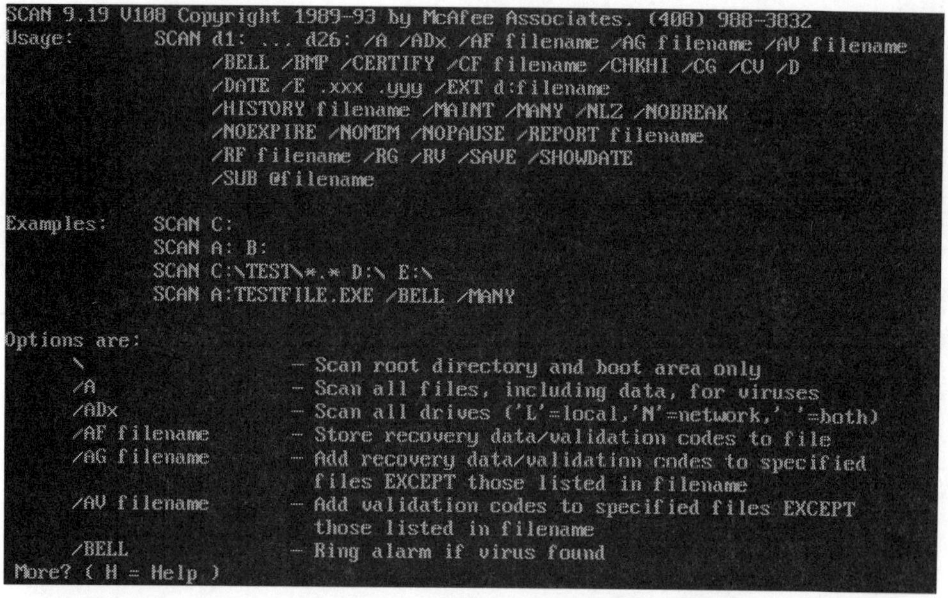

Figure 6-1: SCAN instructions.

3. At the prompt, enter **SCAN X:** where x is the logical drive location for your hard drive.
   - For example, if the logical location for your hard drive is C, you would enter **SCAN C:** at the prompt. The contents of your computer's memory and hard drive will be scanned for viruses and the results of the scan appear, as shown in Figure 6-2.

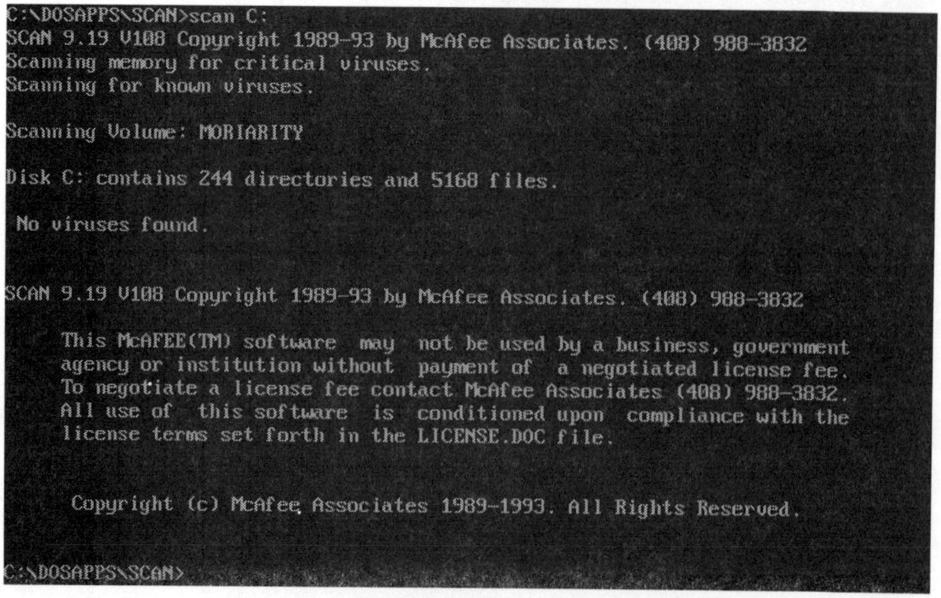

Figure 6-2: SCAN results.

The SCAN distribution package contains extensive documentation. Refer to the documentation for further instructions on using SCAN, including the licensing information.

All About Winsock.

Windows Sockets, commonly known by the name "Winsock," is a 1991 specification intended to address the problem of supporting the plethora of network adapters encountered by TCP/IP vendors. The idea behind the specification is to ensure compatibility between any TCP/IP products that are Winsock-compliant.

The specification itself is implemented as a DLL file: WINSOCK.DLL offers 16-bit support and is most common, while WSOCK32.DLL provides 32-bit support.

Microsoft has announced that Windows, Windows for Workgroups and Windows NT will all support Windows Sockets, and all major TCP/IP vendors have announced support for Windows Sockets.

You can get a freeware version of the WINSOCK.DLL by anonymous FTP at ftp.utas.edu.au in the /pc/trumpet/winsock/ directory (the filename is winsock.zip).

Even better, the Chameleon WINSOCK.DLL is included on *The Windows Internet Tour Guide Companion Disk.*

Using FTP to Transfer Files

The Chameleon Sampler, included on *The Windows Internet Tour Guide Companion Disk,* contains a complete File Transfer Protocol (FTP) module written by a team of programmers at NetManage Inc. With Chameleon FTP, you can quickly and easily download (get) files from or upload (put) files to a remote host on the Internet. The file transfer speed will vary based on the type of Internet connection you have. I use a Serial Line Internet Protocol (SLIP) connection and a V.32bis modem with error correction and data compression. I almost always get throughput of about 1,300 characters-per-second on compressed data files and significantly faster results on text files. Using a V.32bis modem with error correction and data compression, you can expect to download a 500k file in about five or six minutes. Of course, if you're fortunate enough to enjoy a direct connection to the Internet, you can transfer a 500k file in a few seconds (just a little bit longer than it takes to transfer the same amount of data from your local file server).

Chameleon FTP is an excellent, full-featured FTP program—in fact, it's the Windows FTP tool I use most often. It is simple to use, providing an intuitive directory-tree interface for the FTP process. It automatically translates standard file conventions into the required FTP commands.

Shocking Growth.
Counting the number of nodes on the Internet is sort of like counting the number of stars in the sky. OK, not exactly, but you get the idea.

Vinton Cerf, widely acknowledged to be the "father" of the Internet, made the following observations in September 1993:

June 1991 was the fulcrum point in the commercialization of the Internet. In that month commercial use of the Net exceeded academic use.

As of September 1993, the NSFNet backbone was carrying about 7 terabytes of traffic each month.

As of fall 1993, the Internet is growing at a rate of 12% per month.

By the end of 1993, the Internet will be comprised of more than 2 million hosts on 46,000 registered IP networks within 22,000 registered domains in 91 countries.

Configuring Chameleon FTP

Note: this section assumes that you have installed the Chameleon Sampler software as part of the installation process outlined in Chapter 2.

You may want to configure a few of your favorite FTP servers before you begin to transfer files with Chameleon FTP. Chapter 7 of this book describes how to use HGopher to browse information resources on the Net. This section shows you how to configure Chameleon FTP for use with the FTP server on which the HGopher program originates.

To configure remote hosts for use with Chameleon FTP:

1. With Windows running and the Chameleon Sampler program group window open, double-click on the **FTP** icon. The FTP window is displayed, as shown in Figure 6-3.

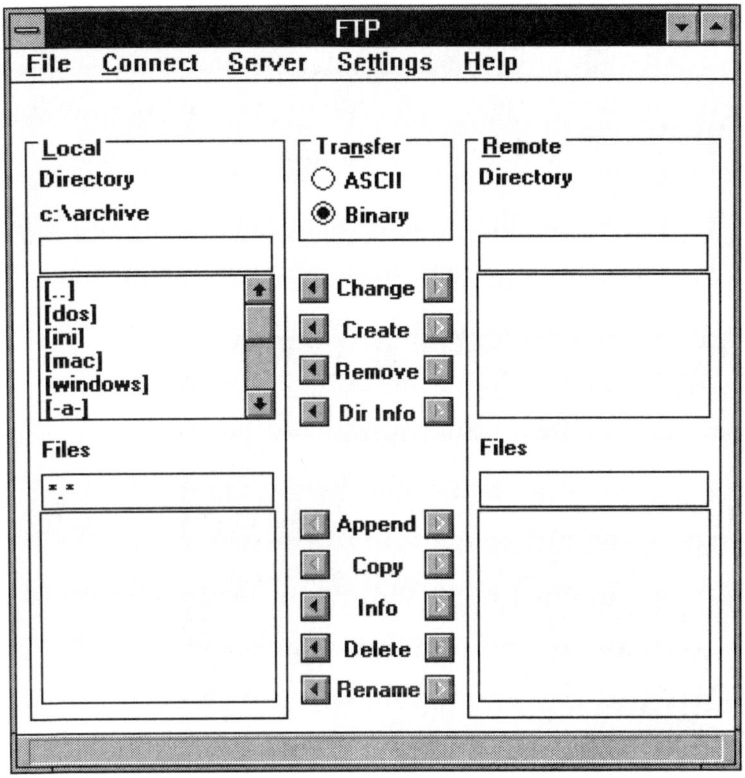

Figure 6-3: Chameleon FTP window.

- Additionally, the Chameleon NEWT icon appears in the lower left corner of your monitor, indicating that the TCP/IP communications stack has been successfully loaded.

2. From the Settings menu, select the Preferences... command. The Preferences dialog box appears, as shown in Figure 6-4.

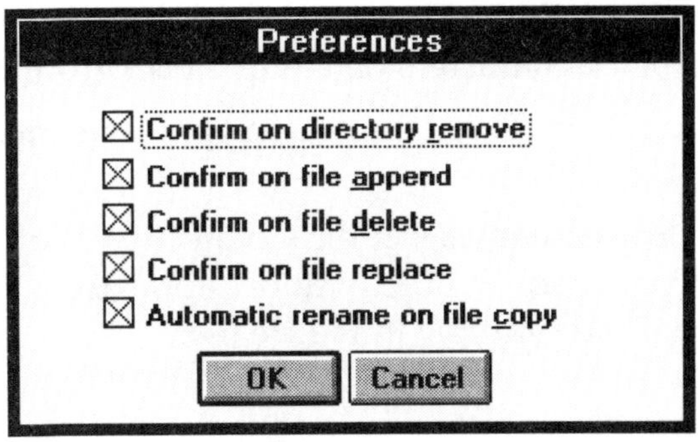

Figure 6-4: Chameleon FTP Preferences dialog box.

3. Set the file management preferences to suit your needs.
   - In most cases, leaving all of the check boxes checked is the best option at least until you've used the program for a while.
4. Click the **OK** button. Your preference settings will be saved to disk.
5. From the Settings menu, select the Colors... command. The Color dialog box is displayed, as shown in Figure 6-5.

Figure 6-5: Chameleon FTP Color dialog box.

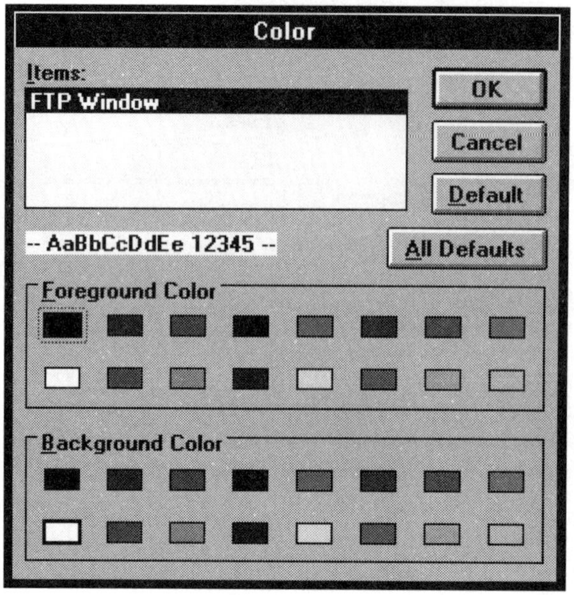

6. Change the foreground and background colors for the FTP window to suit your taste.
   - Alternatively, click the **Default** button to return the color scheme to black characters on a white background.
7. Click the **OK** button. The color settings you specified will be saved to disk.
8. From the Settings menu, select the Connection Profile... command. The Connection Profile window appears, as shown in the already configured example in Figure 6-6.

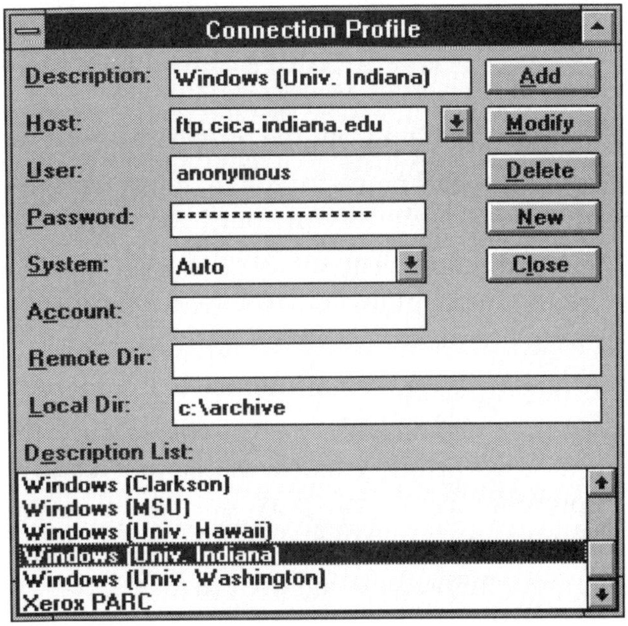

Figure 6-6: Chameleon FTP Connection Profile window.

9. Click the **New** button.
10. Enter the addressing and account information for the archives you regularly visit. Here are the settings for Imperial College's FTP server in London, the home of HGopher:
    - Enter a name or description for the archive in the Description: field. For this example, enter **HGopher/Imperial College (London)** or something similar to remind you about the FTP archive.
    - Enter the domain name of the host computer—in the domain.top-domain format—in the Host: field. For this example, enter **lister.cc.ic.ac.uk**
    - Enter your username—*on the remote host computer*, not your e-mail or "home" account username—in the User: field. If you don't have an account on the remote host, enter **anonymous** in the field.
    - Enter your password—on the remote host computer, not your e-mail or "home" account password—in the Password: field. If you don't have an account on the remote host, enter your e-mail address in the username@domain.top-domain format

field. Note that it is common Internet convention and courtesy to use your full e-mail address as your password when you login to an FTP server as an anonymous user.

- Select the Auto item from the System: pop-up menu.
- Enter the full pathname for the directory where you want to save files you download on your hard drive.

11. Click the **Add** button. The remote host you specified will be added to the Description List and the configuration information will be saved to disk.
12. Repeat steps 9–10 for each additional FTP archive you want to add.
13. When you're finished adding FTP archives, click the **Close** button. The Connection Profile window is dismissed and the configuration information is saved to disk.

Congratulations, the user—called the *client*—side of Chameleon FTP is now configured. Before you venture out on the Net trawling for files, though, take a quick look at the next section about configuring the host side of Chameleon FTP.

To configure Chameleon FTP for use as an FTP server:

1. With Windows running and the Chameleon Sampler program group window open, double-click on the **FTP** icon. The FTP window is displayed, as shown in Figure 6-3.
   - Additionally, the Chameleon NEWT icon appears in the lower left corner of your monitor, indicating that the TCP/IP communications stack has been successfully loaded.
2. From the Server menu, select the Settings... command. The Server Settings dialog box is displayed, as shown in Figure 6-7.

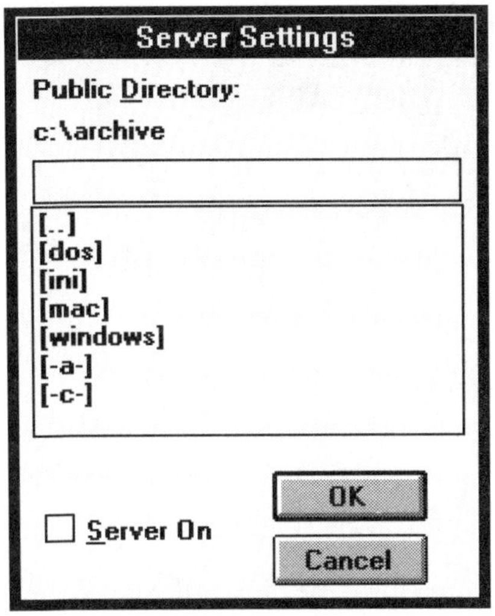

Figure 6-7: Chameleon FTP Server Settings dialog box.

3. From the scrolling list, select the directory on your disk to which you want to allow anonymous access.

   - *Be very careful with this setting*. The contents of the directory you select will be available to anyone on the Internet who accesses your FTP server.

4. Check the **Server On** check box.

   - If you want to only use the client side of Chameleon FTP, disallowing all access to your computer over the Net, uncheck the **Server On** check box and move on to the next section.

5. Click the **OK** button. The Server Settings dialog box disappears and your settings are saved to disk.

6. From the Server menu, select the Users... command. The Users dialog box appears, as shown in Figure 6-8.

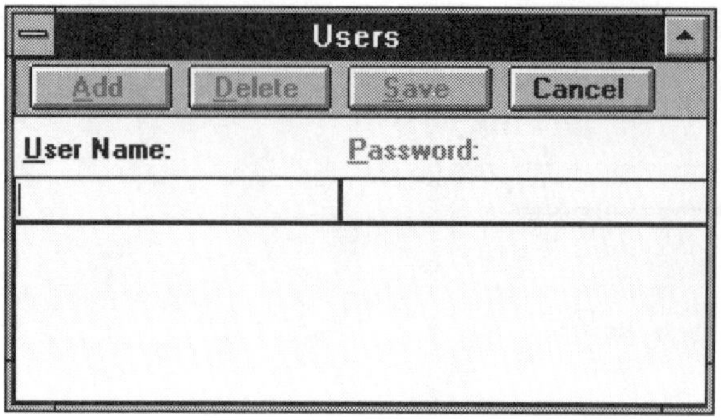

Figure 6-8: Chameleon FTP Users dialog box.

7. Enter the username of the person to whom you want to grant access to your FTP server in the User Name: field.
8. Enter the password of the person to whom you want to grant access to your FTP server in the Password: field.
   - Remember that passwords should never be someone's first name, and a good password includes both numbers and letters and mixes of both upper- and lowercase letters.
9. Click the **Add** button.
10. Repeat steps 7–9 for each additional person to whom you want to grant access to your computer.
11. Click the **Save** button. The Users dialog box disappears, and the usernames and passwords of people who can access your computer over the Internet via FTP are saved to disk.

Etiquette for Uploaders.

Here's a quick check-list of things to keep in mind when you upload files to remote FTP sites:

Make sure you include all relevant documents.

Compress your files using either PKZIP or as a self-extracting archive (these are the two "standard" file compression utilities in the PC community).

Check your files for viruses before uploading them.

Upload your file to the appropriate directory.

Provide a brief, but accurate, description for your uploaded file.

Downloading Files With Chameleon FTP

An important information-browsing tool—HGopher—is discussed in the next chapter. HGopher brings a simple but very powerful interface to the Internet, and it's a program every Windows Internet user should have. You can use Chameleon FTP to download the HGopher application files.

1. With Windows running and the Chameleon Sampler program group window open, double-click on the **Custom** icon. The Custom window appears, as shown in Figure 6-9.

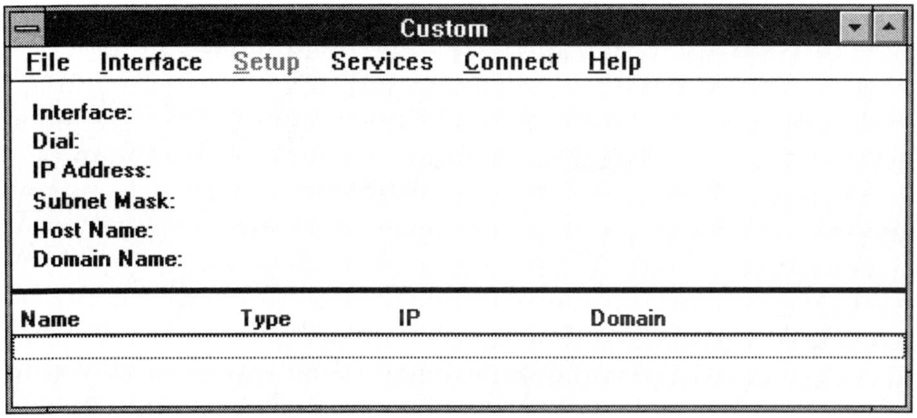

Figure 6-9: Chameleon Custom window.

   - Additionally, the Chameleon NEWT icon appears in the lower left corner of your monitor, indicating that the TCP/IP communications stack has been successfully loaded.

2. Click the **Connect** menu item. The Connect dialog box appears, and your SLIP or PPP connection will be automatically established.

   - If you have trouble establishing your connection, select the Log... command from the Setup menu. This opens a window in which you can monitor and debug your connection activity.

3. Launch Chameleon FTP by double-clicking its icon in the Program Manager. The FTP window is displayed, as shown in Figure 6-3.
4. Click the **Connect** menu item in the Chameleon FTP menu. The Connect dialog box is displayed, as shown in Figure 6-10.

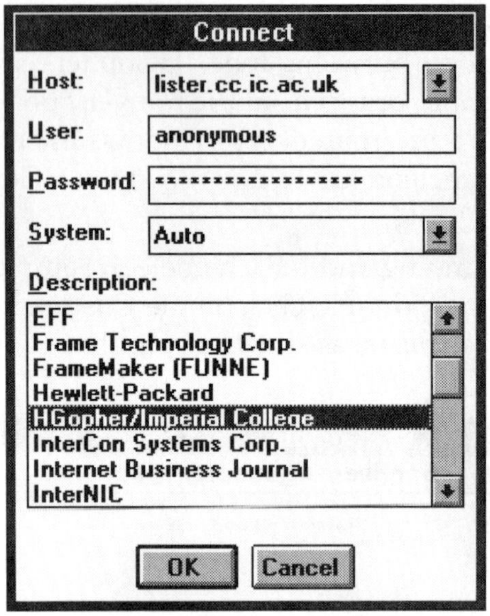

Figure 6-10: Chameleon FTP Connect dialog box.

5. Select the HGopher/Imperial College item from the list. The Connect dialog box should look like the example in Figure 6-10.
   - Note that this step assumes that you added the Imperial College FTP server to your Chameleon FTP configuration, as explained in the previous section. If you skipped that section, enter **lister.cc.ic.ac.uk** in the Host field, enter **anonymous** in the User: field and enter your full e-mail address in the Password: field.

Locating FTP servers.

Can't get enough of downloading files via FTP? Don't worry, it's not likely you'll run out of files or FTP sites.

A list of publicly accessible FTP sites is available by FTP from pilot.njin.net in the /pub/ftp-list/ directory.

Any FTP site listed allows anonymous logins. It's Internet courtesy to supply your e-mail address—in the username@domain.top-domain format—as your login password.

6. Click the **OK** button. Chameleon FTP will establish an FTP connection with Imperial College's FTP server, log you in as an anonymous user and update the Remote Directory browser in the FTP window to reflect the current directory.
   - In this case, the directory you login to is the *root* directory (called the root directory because it is the lowest level directory), as shown in Figure 6-11.

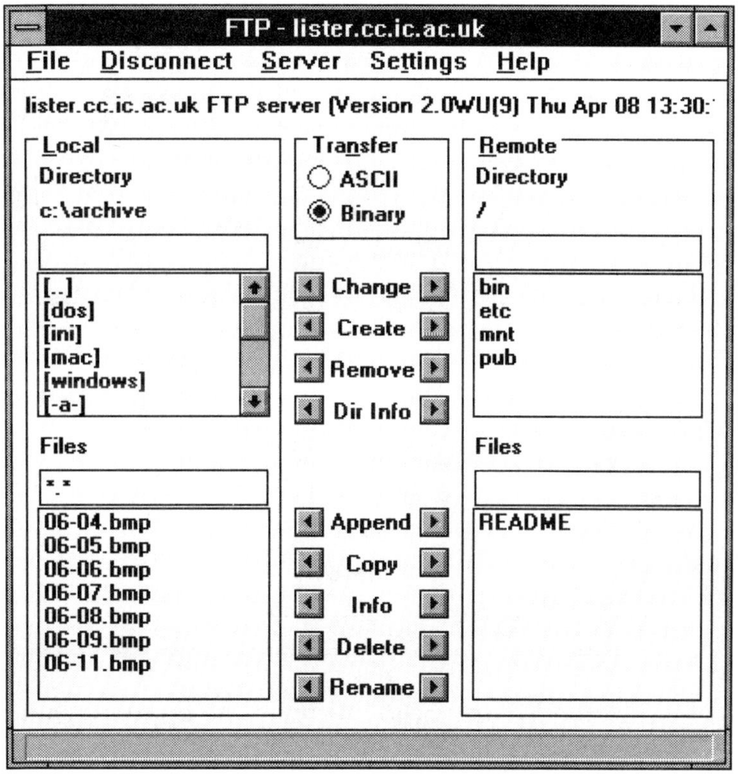

Figure 6-11: Chameleon FTP Window with Remote Directory browser for Imperial College.

7. Navigate through the directory hierarchy on the remote FTP server by double-clicking on the appropriate icons in the Remote Directory list in the upper right panel of the FTP window.
   - In this example, double-click on the pub directory and then double-click on the wingopher directory. This hierarchy of directories is known as a *pathname* and is written like this: /pub/wingopher/. The root directory is indicated by the first backslash (/).

8. Locate the most recent version of the HGopher file.
   - As of mid-December 1993, the current version was 2.3, and the complete pathname is /pub/wingopher/hgopher2.3.zip. The FTP window should look like the example shown in Figure 6-12.

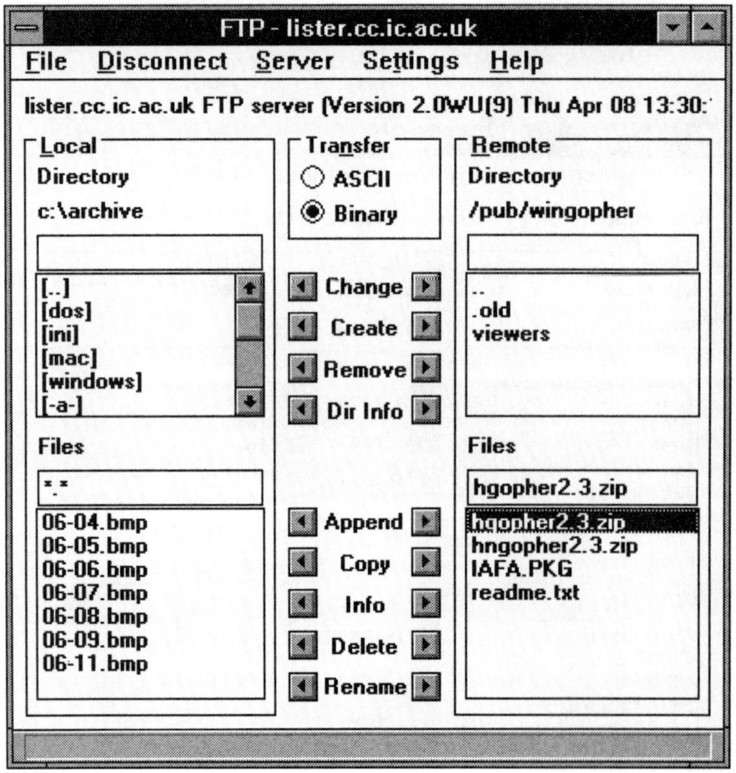

Figure 6-12: Chameleon FTP Window with HGopher file selected.

9. Click the **Binary** radio button in the upper portion of the FTP window.
   - If the file you wanted to download was a text file, a BinHex file or a PostScript file, you would click the **ASCII** radio button.
10. Click the **Left Copy** button. The file transfer will begin, and its progress will be reported in the File Transfer dialog box, as shown in Figure 6-13.

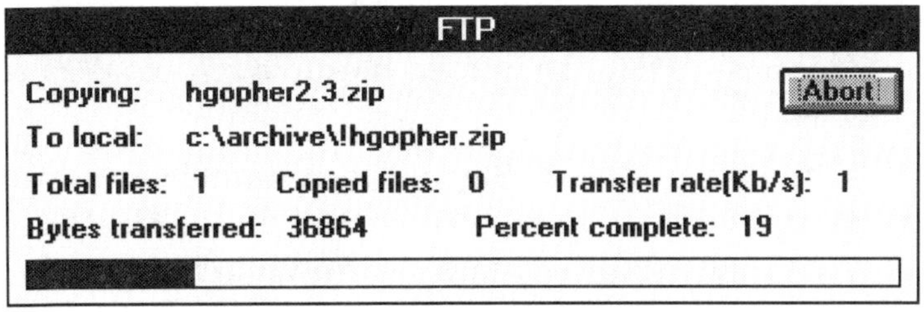

Figure 6-13: Chameleon FTP dialog box.

11. When the file transfer is complete, you can download additional files from the same FTP server by repeating steps 7–10 for each file. Feel free to browse the files available at this site and download any that interest you.
12. When you are finished transferring files, click the **Disconnect** menu item in the FTP window. The Disconnect dialog box is displayed, as shown in Figure 6-14.

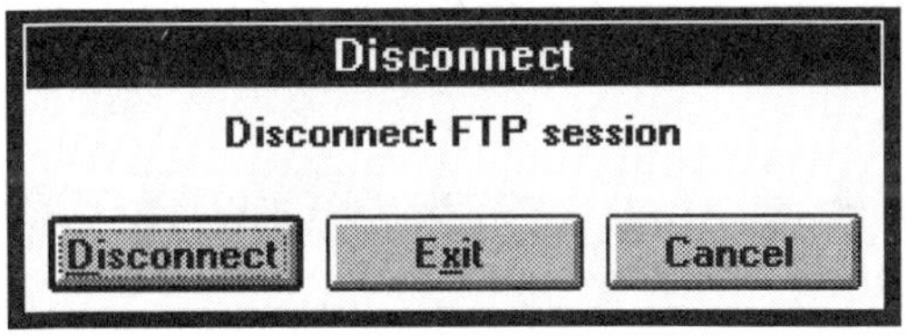

Figure 6-14: Chameleon FTP Disconnect dialog box.

13. Click the **Disconnect** button. Your connection to the remote FTP server will be severed.

Commercial software updates.
The Oakland University archive offers updater programs for various commercial software programs on its FTP server. Updater programs for AfterDark, Canvas, FileMaker Pro, CrossTalk and ProComm are only a few of those you can download and use completely free. They're available by FTP from oak.oakland.edu in the appropriate directories.

Uploading Files With FTP

Downloading files is just one side of the file transfer coin. You can also *upload*, or send files, to a remote FTP server using Chameleon FTP. If you have a file that you want to share with the rest of the world, consider uploading it (as long as there are no restrictions on its distribution) to your favorite FTP site. To upload files to a remote FTP server with Chameleon FTP:

1. With Windows running and the Chameleon Sampler program group window open, double-click on the **Custom** icon. The Custom window appears, as shown in Figure 6-9.
   - Additionally, the Chameleon NEWT icon appears in the lower left corner of your monitor, indicating that the TCP/IP communications stack has been successfully loaded.
2. Click the **Connect** menu item. The Connect dialog box appears, and your SLIP or PPP connection will be automatically established.
   - If you have trouble establishing your connection, select the Log... command from the Setup menu. This opens a window in which you can monitor and debug your connection activity.
3. Launch Chameleon FTP by double-clicking its icon in the Program Manager. The FTP window is displayed, as shown in Figure 6-15.

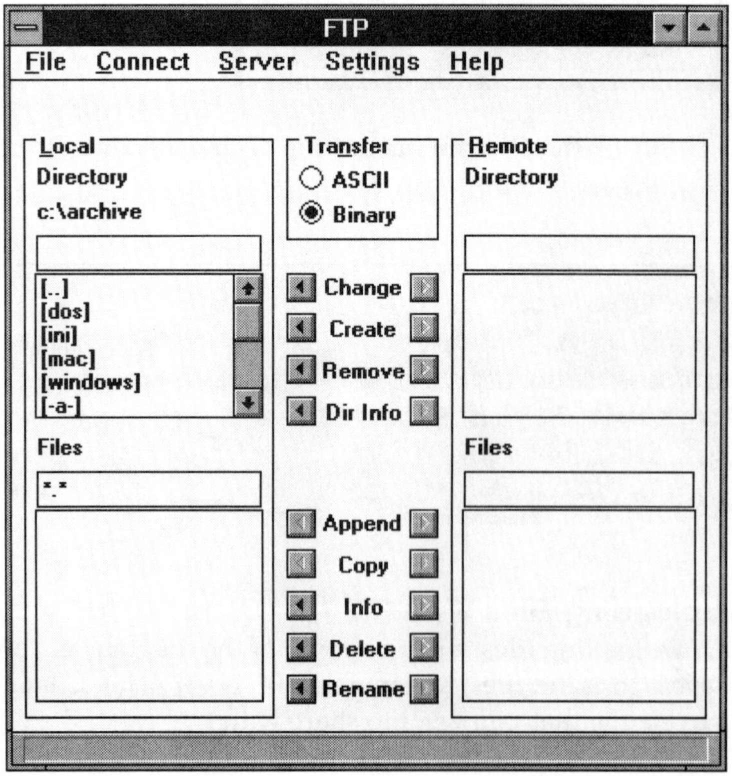

Figure 6-15: Chameleon FTP window.

4. Click the **Connect** menu item in the Chameleon FTP menu. The Connect dialog box is displayed, as shown in Figure 6-16.

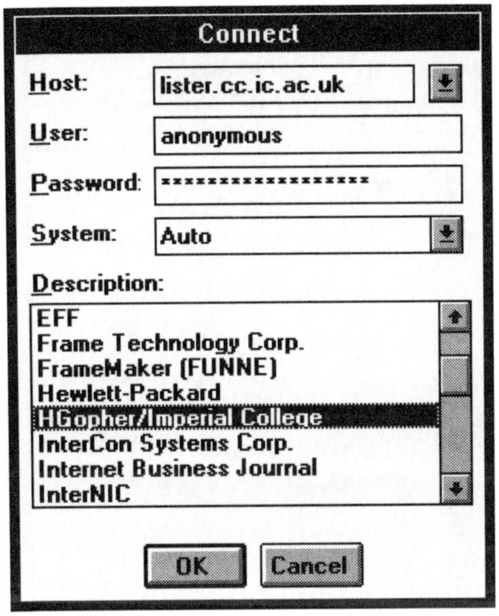

Figure 6-16: Chameleon FTP Connect dialog box.

5. Select the FTP server to which you want to upload a file from the list. The Connect dialog box will be updated to reflect your selection.
6. Click the **OK** button. Chameleon FTP will establish an FTP connection with the FTP server, log you in and update the Remote Directory browser in the FTP window to reflect the current directory as shown in the example in Figure 6-17.

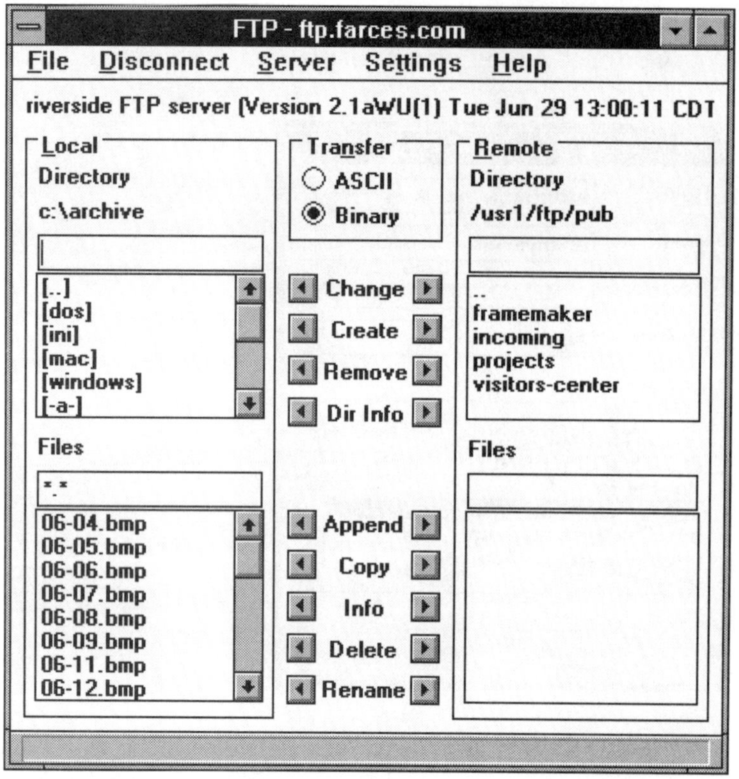

Figure 6-17: Chameleon FTP window with updated Remote Directory browser.

File Extensions.

Every file you download from the Internet will probably have at least one—and perhaps several—*filename extensions*. This is a method used to identify the types of files (and the software program used to create the files). Filename extensions have become a veritable alphabet soup, and often end up confusing people more than they inform.

The filename extension will give you a clue about which transfer mode (ASCII or Binary) to use in your FTP program. The good news is, if you're using Chameleon all this is automatically handled for you.

If you're using another FTP program, files that end with hqx, txt or ps extensions are the *only* files that can be downloaded in ASCII mode. All other types of files *must* be downloaded in Binary (also called Image) mode. Chances are that if you get errors during file decompression indicating that your file is corrupt, it's because you used ASCII mode when you should have used Binary mode.

For more information, see "A Primer on File Types" beginning on page 186.

- In most cases, the directory you login to is the *root* directory.

7. Navigate through the directory hierarchy on the remote FTP server by double-clicking on the appropriate icons in the Remote Directory list in the upper right panel of the FTP window.
8. Create a new directory on the remote FTP server, if necessary, by entering a valid name for the directory in the Remote Directory field and clicking the **Right Create** button.
   - Note that you must have the appropriate permissions on the remote FTP server in order to create a new directory. It's generally not a good idea to try creating new directories at remote FTP sites without clearing it first with that site's network administrator.
   - Note also that your new directory will be created as a subdirectory within the current directory on the remote FTP server.
9. Navigate through the directory hierarchy on your PC by double-clicking on the appropriate icons in the Local Directory list in the upper left panel of the FTP window.
10. Select the file you want to upload in the Local Files list.
11. Click the **Binary** radio button in the upper portion of the FTP window.
    - If the file you want to upload is a text file, a BinHex file or a PostScript file, click the **ASCII** radio button.
12. Click the **Right Copy** button. The file transfer will begin, and its progress will be reported in the File Transfer dialog box, as shown in Figure 6-13.
13. When you are finished transferring files, click the **Disconnect** menu item in the FTP window. The Disconnect dialog box is displayed, as shown in Figure 6-14.
14. Click the **Disconnect** button. Your connection to the remote FTP server will be severed.

Famous PC FTP Archives.

Here are the most popular PC-specific FTP sites. All accept anonymous logins, but be sure to use your full e-mail address—in the username@domain.top-domain format—as a password.

Domain Name	Directory
oak.oakland.edu	/pub/msdos/
archive.umich.edu	/msdos/
ftp.microsoft.com	/pub/
microlib.cc.utexas.edu	/microlib/pc/
ftp.funet.fi	/pub/pc/
ftp.lu.se	/pub/pc/
boombox.micro.umn.edu	/pub/pc/
lister.cc.ic.ac.uk	/pub/wingopher/
ftp.msen.com	/pub/winsock/
ftp.ncsa.uiuc.edu	/pc/
ftp.qualcomm.com	/pceudora/windows/
sunsite.unc.edu	/pub/micro/pc-stuff/
ftp.utas.edu.au	/pc/
ftp.cica.indiana.edu	/pub/pc/win3/

A mirror site is an exact copy of another site. They are designed to relieve the heavy traffic in the major FTP sites. If you find that you can't login to one of the sites in the above listing, try one of these mirror sites.

Domain Name	Directory
archie.au	/micros/msdos/
ftp.lth.se	/msdos/
minnehaha.rhrk.uni-kl.de	/pub/pc/
utsun.s.u-tokyo.ac.jp	/msdos/
wuarchive.wustl.edu	/mirrors/msdos/
shark.mel.dit.csiro.au	/pc/

More information on these and other FTP sites is provided in Chapter 8, "Other Internet Resources," and the electronic updates for this book.

Moving On

There are huge repositories of very interesting files scattered throughout the thousands of FTP servers available on the Internet. With a little perseverance—and more important, knowing where to look—you can use FTP to find files on just about any topic. There is an important Internet resource that can help you navigate many of the available FTP servers—its name is Archie, and you'll learn about it in Chapter 8, "Other Internet Resources." Of course, the electronic updates to this book are another important resource available to you.

One of the best ways to navigate quickly and effectively through the Internet is the University of Minnesota's Gopher, covered in the next chapter. When it comes to touring the Net, Gopher is a knowing native, helpful concierge and savvy travel agent, all rolled into one.

CHAPTER 7

USING GOPHER
Burrowing for Information

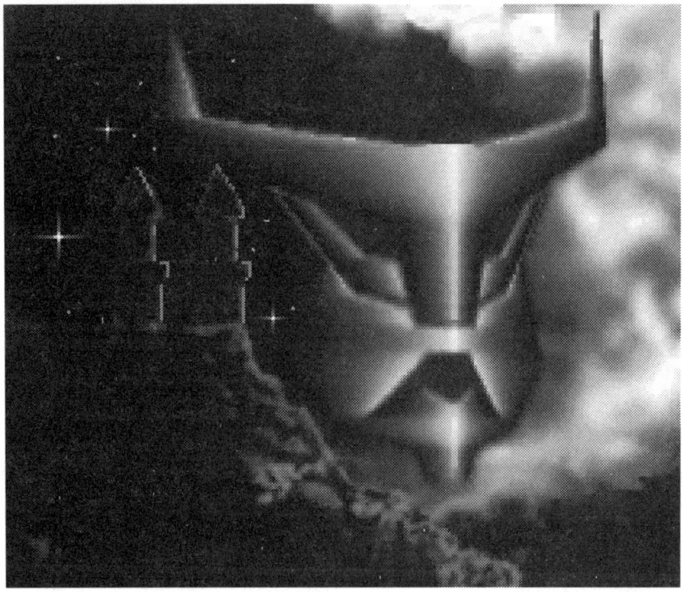

So far, our tour has covered the many strange languages and customs of the Internet, but we've barely scratched the surface of the vast resources the Net has to offer. And when navigating unexplored territories, even pioneers need all the help they can get. It's always a relief to find an amicable cab driver or savvy concierge who can clue you in to those great out-of-the-way spots where most tourists never venture. In this chapter we'll explore how to use Gopher—the Internet's most sociable, well-connected pathfinder—to browse aimlessly or search specifically for everything from Russian poetry to local weather reports.

What Is Gopher?

Network news, e-mail, and FTP are great tools for specific tasks. As you've seen, it's simple enough to use Chameleon Mail to dash off an e-mail message to someone, and it's a snap to use the Trumpet news reader to look for PC-specific information in some place like the comp.os.msdos newsgroups. Even finding and downloading a specific file from an FTP archive is a cinch if you're using Chameleon FTP. These programs and Internet resources are all specific tools for specific jobs.

But what if you don't know exactly what you're looking for, or only have a broad idea about a topic of interest? What if you just want to surf through the oceans of information available on the Internet? That's where Gopher comes in.

Gopher is one of the most powerful resources available to Internet users, and Martyn Hampson's HGopher is one of the easiest to use and fastest implementations of the Gopher protocol. Written by Hampson at London's Imperial College, HGopher puts a menu-based interface on many of the Internet's resources, making moving from spot to spot on the Net as easy as picking options from a list—and often easier.

Whole Earth 'Lectronic Link (WELL) Gopher.
The Whole Earth folks have put some of the best articles from the *Whole Earth Review* in a Gopher server. You'll find articles by Bruce Sterling, Stewart Brand and many others. This is one of the best information resources on the Internet. You can access it by pointing your Gopher program at nkosi.well.sf.ca.us port 70.

If Gopher had been developed in California, instead of on the far edge of Minnesota, it might have been called Surfer. Its name comes from the University of Minnesota's mascot, the Golden Gopher. Information servers on the Internet that support access with the Gopher software are always called *Gopher sites*, *Gopher servers* or *Gopher holes*. The software's actual communication and database protocol is also referred to as *Gopher*. The software you run on your PC to browse through Gopher holes is also called *Gopher*.

What Can I Use Gopher For?

Gopher (the protocol) lets you burrow through information resources using a series of easy-to-navigate menus that appear as lists. Gopher (the program) lets you navigate through Gopher information resources using standard menus and submenus. You can use HGopher for Windows to navigate huge "dataspaces" by simply double-clicking the left mouse button.

Gopher is best used as a browsing tool. It doesn't matter where an information resource you find with Gopher is physically located. As long as it is compatible with Gopher, it simply appears as another menu item in the hierarchy. You don't have to worry about IP addresses or even domain names with Gopher—when you find a resource you want to browse, just select it from the menu.

Extensions to the Gopher protocol allow you to browse through different kinds of information resources—pictures, sounds, video, computer files, as well as text. Instead of groping around blindly through a series of interconnected servers, connecting and disconnecting with each one in turn, you can use Gopher to wander aimlessly without worrying about the process of connecting and disconnecting. This chapter also explains how you can wander around through *Gopherspaces* (those areas that support the Gopher protocol) purposefully, as if you had a well-trained research librarian helping out.

Why Should I Use Gopher Instead of FTP?

Gopher is a *stateless* software program, making the most efficient possible use of network resources. Instead of keeping a connection to a remote site continuously open, Gopher opens a connection to initiate your request, closes the connection, and then reopens a connection to receive the host's response. By comparison, FTP maintains a continuous connection while you are browsing directories and transferring files. Many of the best archive sites restrict FTP access, while allowing unrestricted Gopher access. You can be a good Internet citizen by using Gopher whenever you can. Most of the major FTP archives also support Gopher access, and more Gopher servers are continually being added. Some sites support only FTP access, though, so it's important that you use the right tool for the job.

Using HGopher

The elegant simplicity of Gopher is that its developers didn't reinvent the wheel. They configured Gopher, and the HGopher software you use from your PC, to take advantage of existing network conventions. When you use the HGopher application to login to a Gopher server and select a network resource, Gopher automatically determines the right tool for the job. If you're accessing a computer file, it's sent to you using FTP. If you select a login resource, Gopher automatically opens a TELNET session. It's all handled transparently and automatically.

Configuring HGopher

The latest version of the HGopher software is available from a number of FTP sites throughout the Internet. Complete instructions for downloading the program are provided in Chapter 6, "Transferring Files," beginning with the section "Downloading Files With Chameleon FTP" on page 199.

To configure HGopher:

1. With Windows running and the Chameleon Sampler program group window open, double-click on the **Custom** icon. The Custom window appears, as shown in Figure 7-1.

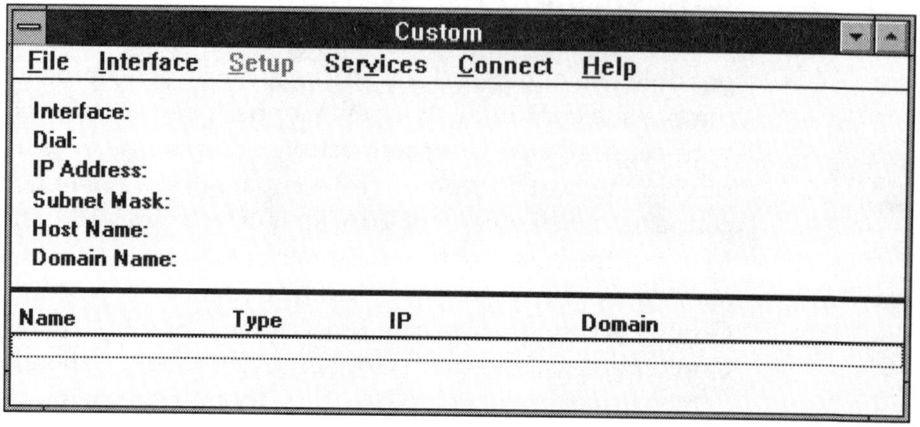

Figure 7-1: Chameleon Custom window.

   - Additionally, the Chameleon NEWT icon appears in the lower left corner of your monitor, indicating that the TCP/IP communications stack has been successfully loaded.

2. Click the **Connect** menu item. The Connect dialog box appears, and your SLIP or PPP connection will be automatically established.
   - If you have trouble establishing your connection, select the Log... command from the Setup menu. This opens a window in which you can monitor and debug your connection activity.
3. Launch HGopher by double-clicking its icon in the Program Manager. The default Book Marks window is displayed, as shown in Figure 7-2.

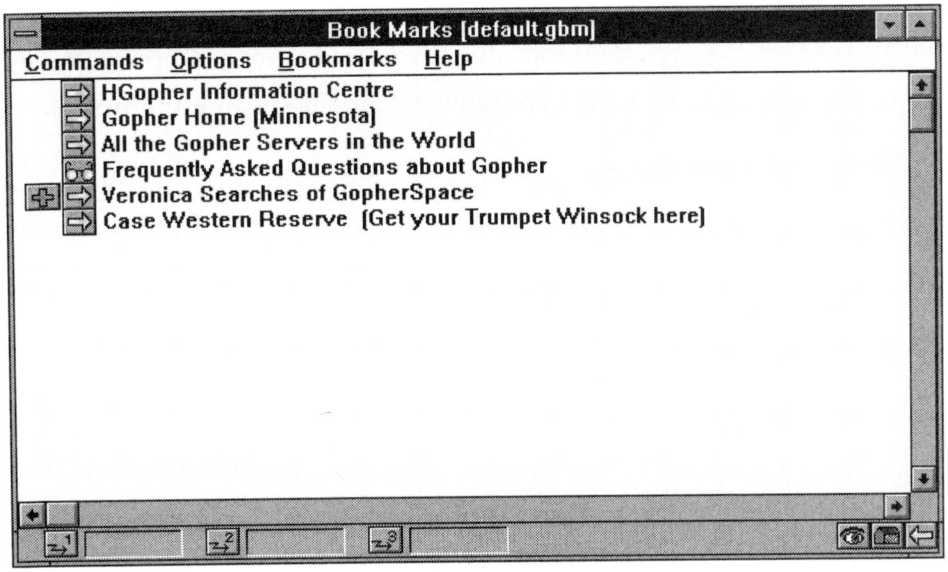

Figure 7-2: HGopher default Book Marks window.

4. From the Options menu, select the Gopher Set Up... command. The Gopher Set Up Options window appears, as in Figure 7-3.

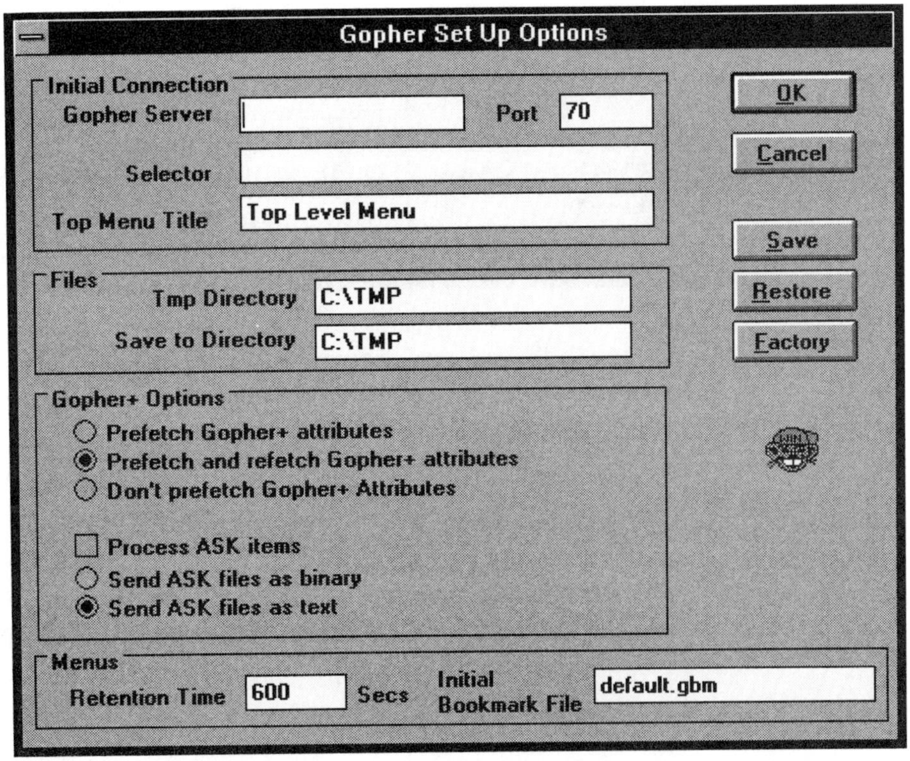

Figure 7-3: HGopher Gopher Set Up Options window.

5. Enter the domain name of your Home Gopher server—using the domain.top-domain format—in the Gopher Server field.
6. Enter the complete pathname of a temporary directory in the Tmp Directory field.
   - This can be any valid directory on your drive, but it's usually a directory that you've explicitly set up for scratch files. I always use C:\. This lets me easily delete orphaned files in the event of a system crash.
7. Enter the complete pathname of the directory in which you want to save files you download using HGopher.
8. Click the **OK** button. The Gopher Set Up Options window is dismissed and your settings will be saved in the HGOPHER.INI file.
9. From the Options menu, select the Network Set Up... command. The Network Setup window appears, as shown in Figure 7-4.

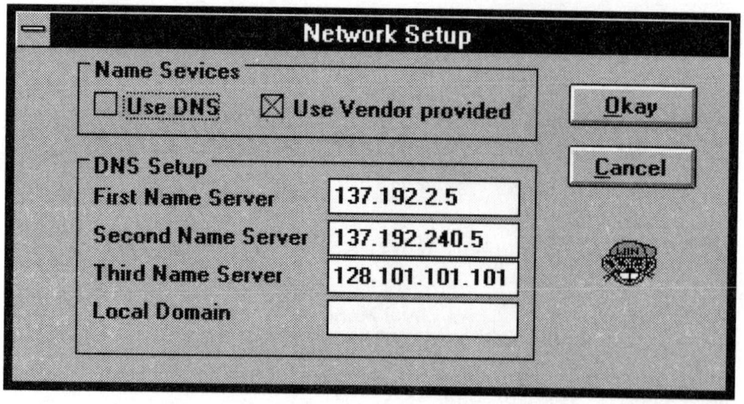

Figure 7-4: HGopher Network Setup window.

10. Check the **Use Vendor provided** check box to use the domain name servers you specified when you installed and configured the Chameleon Sampler software.
    - The **Use DNS** check box configures HGopher to use its domain name server method of accessing name services on the Net, and is not of use when using the Winsock version of HGopher.
11. Click the **Okay** button. The Network Setup window is dismissed and your settings will be saved in the HGOPHER.INI file.
12. From the Commands menu, select the Exit command.

You've configured HGopher for use with your Home Gopher server. There are other aspects of HGopher that you can configure, but the previous sequence takes care of the main configuration. If you're interested in fine-tuning the types of documents HGopher can display, and other fine points of the program's operation, refer to HGopher's excellent online help.

International technical support in a flash.

North Americans take technical support for granted because the vast majority of software developers are located in the United States and Canada. International users are faced with a host of problems when they have technical questions. Many use the Internet as their sole avenue of support. Zviki Cohen of Israel is a good example:

"I'm from Israel, and I work and study at the Technion—Israel Institute of Technology. I use the Internet as an important tool to get support. Last month I was interested in buying some products. In America or Europe you can pick [up] a phone, dial a toll-free number and hear all about it, but here, when you are interested in a product the local salesman hasn't heard of (and there are plenty...) you can forget about it.

"Well, not with the Internet. A few e-mails to the companies sorted out the problem and I got a few suggestions for the products I needed. When I found a serious bug in a software program I bought, I didn't wait until the Tech Support people here get [sic] me the answer from across the sea. I got it myself the next day from the companies headquarters in the USA."

Browsing Information With HGopher

If you know how to use the standard File Manager in Windows, you already know how to use HGopher. Navigate Gopherspace—that is, browse through those resources accessible via the Gopher protocol—by double-clicking on anything that looks interesting. It's as simple as that. Really!

- Double-clicking on a title associated with a directory **Arrow** icon opens that directory and displays its contents. The **Right Arrow** icon represents a Gopher directory; the **Left Arrow** icon represents the previous Gopher directory.
- Double-clicking on a title associated with a text file's **Glasses** icon displays the text of the document on your screen. If the file is

larger than what can be held in memory, you'll be prompted to save the file to disk.

- Double-clicking on a title associated with a **Binary** icon downloads that software resource to your PC; you'll be prompted to save the file to disk.
- Double-clicking on a title associated with the **Music Note** icon plays the sound resource associated with that Gopher item.
- Double-clicking on a title associated with the **CSO** icon connects to a CSO server.
- Double-clicking on a title associated with the **Camera** icon displays the image associated with that Gopher item.
- Double-clicking on a title associated with the **Book Pointer** icon accesses an index Gopher item.
- Double-clicking on a title associated with the **Film** icon displays the video associated with that Gopher item.
- Double-clicking on a title associated with the **H** icon displays the associated HTML hypertext document.
- Double-clicking on the **IBM Terminal** icon causes HGopher to open a TN3270 session.
- Double-clicking on a **Terminal** icon causes HGopher to open a TELNET session.
    - Regardless of the type of Gopher resource you access, be sure to *double-click on the title associated with the icon, not the icon itself.*

Use these steps to browse vast stretches of Gopherspace.

1. With Windows running and the Chameleon Sampler program group window open, double-click on the **Custom** icon. The Custom window appears, as shown in Figure 7-1.
    - Additionally, the Chameleon NEWT icon appears in the lower left corner of your monitor, indicating that the TCP/IP communications stack has been successfully loaded.
2. Click the **Connect** menu item. The Connect dialog box appears, and your SLIP or PPP connection will be automatically established.

- If you have trouble establishing your connection, select the Log... command from the Setup menu. This opens a window in which you can monitor and debug your connection activity.

3. Launch HGopher by double-clicking its icon in the Program Manager. HGopher will automatically login to your home Gopher server and display its Top Level menu, like the example shown in Figure 7-5.

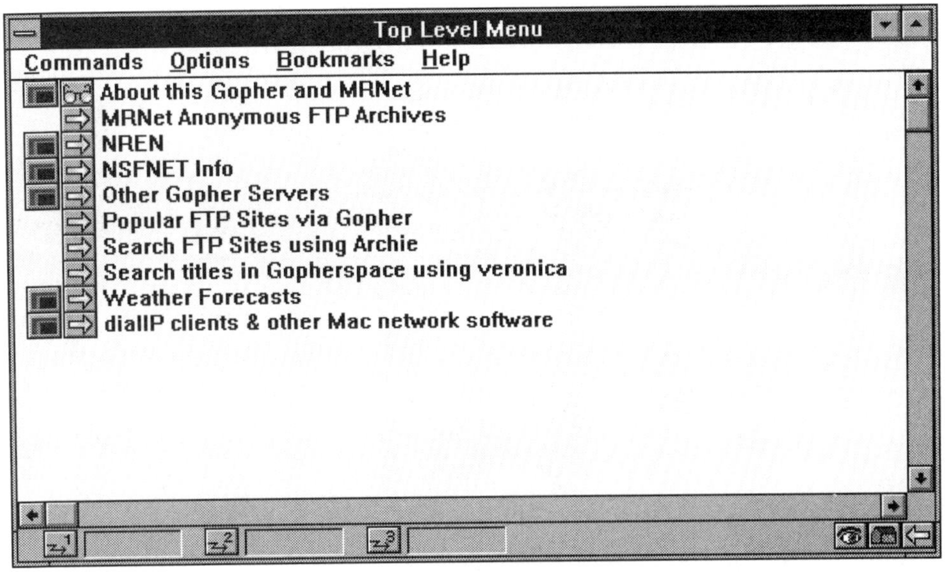

Figure 7-5: Sample HGopher window with Top Level Menu for example home Gopher server.

- Note that most Gopher servers provide an item named "Other Gopher Servers" or something similar. From within this item you can usually find an item named "All the Gopher Servers in the World," which contains alphabetical and geographic listings of every available Gopher Server, as shown in Figure 7-6.

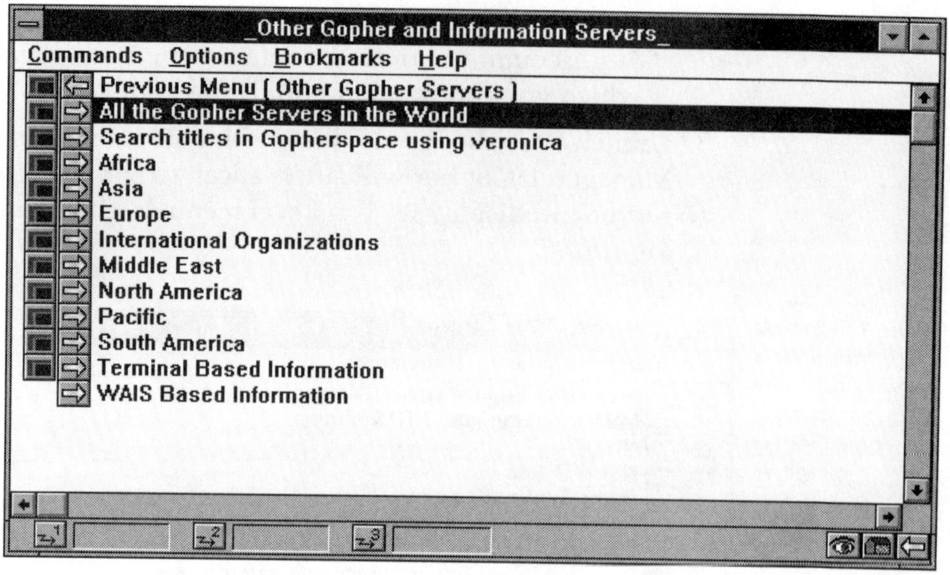

Figure 7-6: HGopher window with All the Gopher Servers in the World item selected.

4. Continue to navigate your way through the available Gopher servers, double-clicking on any item that interests you.

Eventually you'll find that you've followed the Gopher too deep into one of the many Gopher holes on the Internet. Here's how to backtrack your way out of a Gopher hole.

1. With your Internet connection established and the HGopher window active, double-click on the **Previous Menu** item.
   - Note that the Previous Menu item is usually the first item in the list within any HGopher window except the Top Level menu of your home Gopher server.
   - You can also backtrack one level by clicking the **Left Arrow** icon in the bottom right corner of the HGopher window.
2. Repeat step 1 for each level of the Gopherspace hierarchy you want to backtrack through.

Congratulations! You've mastered the mechanics of navigating any Gopherspace on the Internet.

The Politics of Gopher.

As the Internet changes from a network of networks dominated by research and education institutions to one populated by a mixture of commercial and academic users, the Internet community itself is experiencing great stress.

Nowhere has this stress been more apparent recently than with Gopher and the University of Minnesota's Gopher development team.

Gopher, like most other Net resources, had always been made available for use by anyone, free of charge. In March 1993, however, the Gopher team decided it was time to recover some of their expenses and issued a policy statement that requires commercial sites to pay an annual license fee for any Gopher servers they operate.

Under the initial policy, the Gopher team was charging a first-year license fee of $5,000 per server ($2,500 license fee for succeeding years) to any commercial site accessible from the Internet that offers only free information. For commercial sites that sell their information or charge a fee for access, an additional license fee of 7.5 percent of receipts was required.

Needless to say, a firestorm erupted in the comp.infosystems.gopher newsgroup—the spot on the Net where users discuss Gopher-related issues. Charges of "greed killing Gopher" were fired off by angry Gopher users. People who had contributed to the development of Gopher publicly wondered how they would be compensated for their work. Others wondered how a tax-payer-supported university could attempt to turn a profit on something they had already been compensated for. A few days later, the University of Minnesota's Gopher development team posted an article stating that the Gopher server license fees would be "negotiable."

Within a month, a freeware Gopher-compliant server (software that would allow administrators to set up their own Gopher servers without using the University of Minnesota's software) was available on the Internet, with no license fee for commercial use. It was reportedly somewhat buggy, but it was available. The new software was provided by a consortium of programmers, in the spirit of the free-flow of information that characterizes the Internet.

Should the University of Minnesota be able to charge license fees for what they used to give away free of charge? Sure. Gopher is theirs to do with as they please. That doesn't prohibit someone else from developing a competing product and giving it away. And in fact that's what happened.

A few months later, the University of Minnesota announced a modified fee structure for the use of Gopher servers. Organizations that do not charge for access to their Gopher server and do not offer products or services for sale are required to pay $100 per year per server.

Organizations with less than $3.5 million gross income (from the Gopher server alone) per year who use a Gopher server to offer products or services for sale (but do not charge for access to the server) are required to pay the University of Minnesota $500 per year per server.

More

For organizations with less than $3.5 million gross income per year (from the Gopher server alone) who use a Gopher server to offer products or services for sale and charge access fees on the server, the license fee is the greater of $500 per server or 2.5% of the amount charged for access to the server each year.

Organizations with more than $3.5 million gross income per year (from the Gopher server alone) who use a Gopher server to offer products or services for sale and charge access fees on the server are required to pay the greater of $2,500 per server or 2.5% of the amount charged for access to the server each year.

This problem of fee structures isn't going to go away and the commercialization of the Internet is something the researchers and academics are going to want to accept.

Now that you know the basics of how to navigate through Gopherspace (double-click on anything that interests you; use the **Left Arrow** icon to backtrack), let's take a look at using Gopher to actually retrieve useful information.

1. With Windows running and the Chameleon Sampler program group window open, double-click on the **Custom** icon. The Custom window appears, as shown in Figure 7-1.
   - Additionally, the Chameleon NEWT icon appears in the lower left corner of your monitor, indicating that the TCP/IP communications stack has been successfully loaded.
2. Click the **Connect** menu item. The Connect dialog box appears, and your SLIP or PPP connection will be automatically established.
   - If you have trouble establishing your connection, select the Log... command from the Setup menu. This opens a window in which you can monitor and debug your connection activity.
3. Launch HGopher by double-clicking its icon in the Program Manager. HGopher will automatically login to your home Gopher server and display its Top Level menu, like the example shown in Figure 7-5.
4. Navigate to the University of North Carolina's SUNsite Gopher server.
   - The actual procedure for navigating to a particular server will vary, based on your home Gopher server. From within the

"Other Gopher Servers" (or similar) menu item, double-click the "North America," "United States," "North Carolina," "University of North Carolina at Chapel Hill (Ogphre/ SUNsite)" directory items in succession. When you get there, your Gopher window should look similar to the one shown in Figure 7-7.

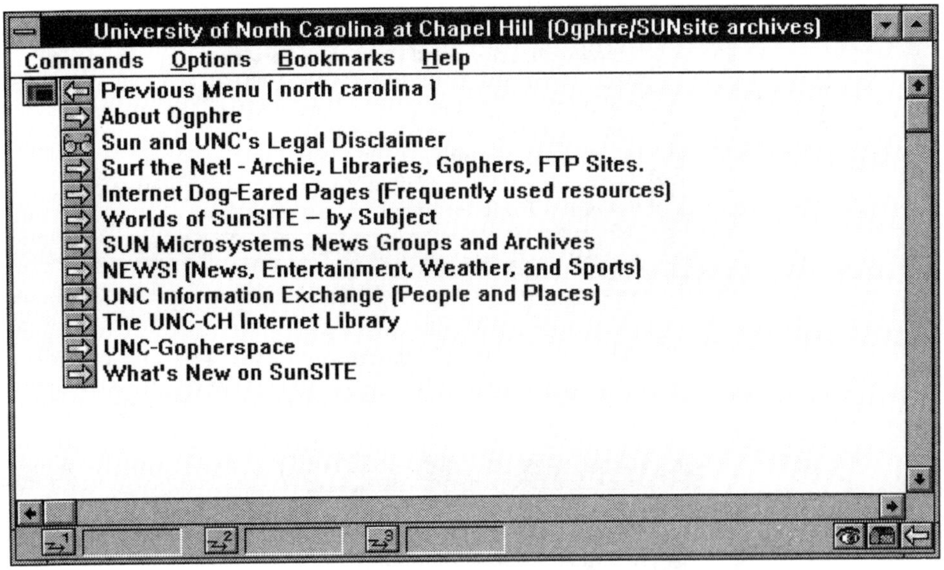

Figure 7-7: HGopher window for the University of North Carolina's SUNsite Gopher server.

5. Double-click the **Dog-Eared Pages** directory icon to open that directory, as shown in Figure 7-8.

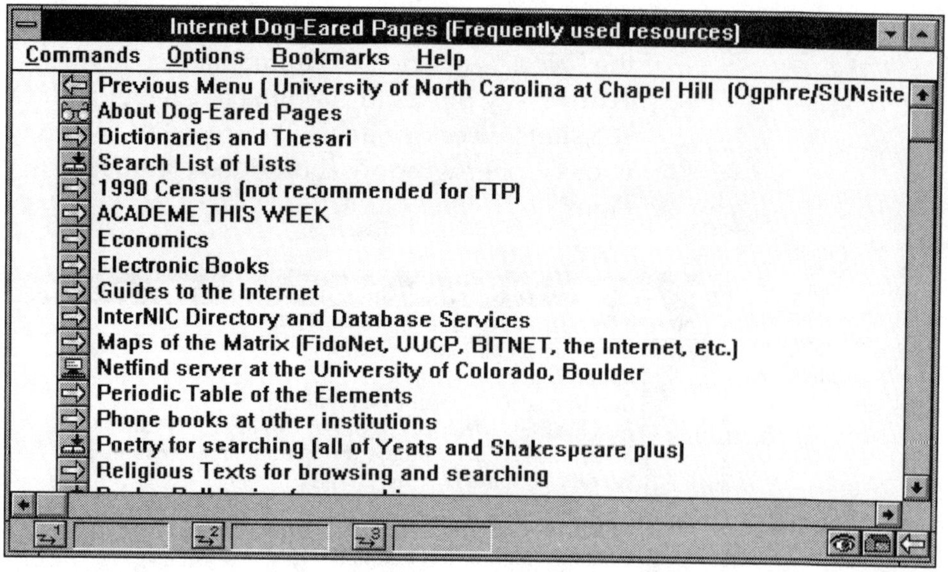

Figure 7-8: HGopher window with SUNsite's Internet Dog-Eared Pages directory.

6. Double-click the **Dictionaries and Thesari** directory icon to open that directory, as shown in Figure 7-9.

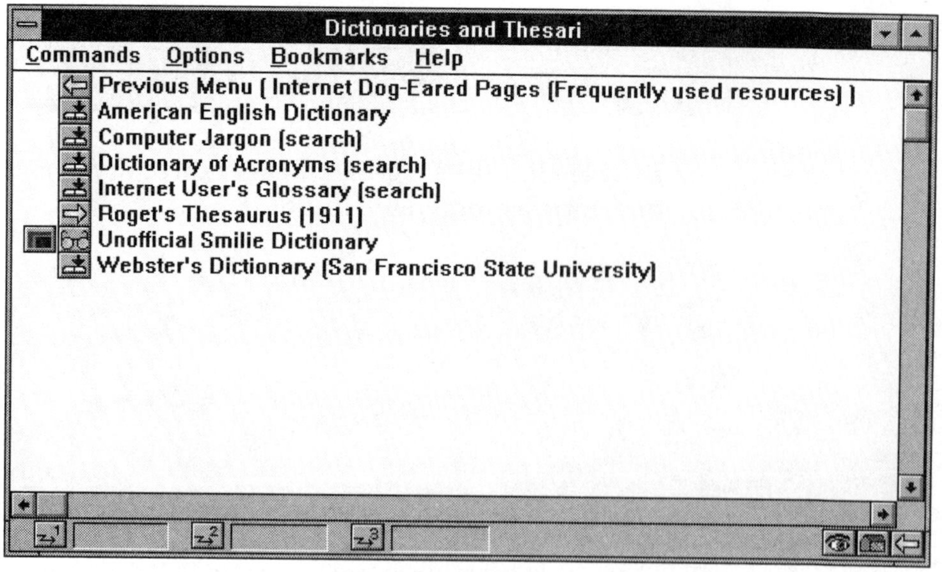

Figure 7-9: HGopher window with SUNsite's Dictionaries and Thesari directory.

7. Double-click the Webster's Dictionary **book pointer** icon. An Index Search dialog box appears, as shown in Figure 7-10.

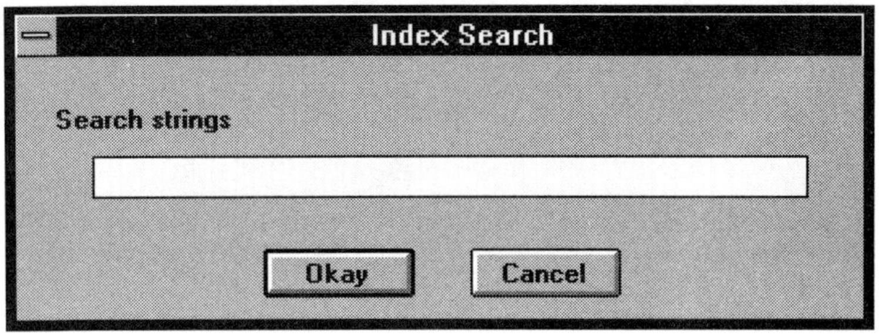

Figure 7-10: HGopher Index Search dialog box.

8. Enter the word you want to search for in the Search strings field and press **Enter**. This example uses the word "intrepid" as the search item. A menu of matched items appears, as shown in Figure 7-11.

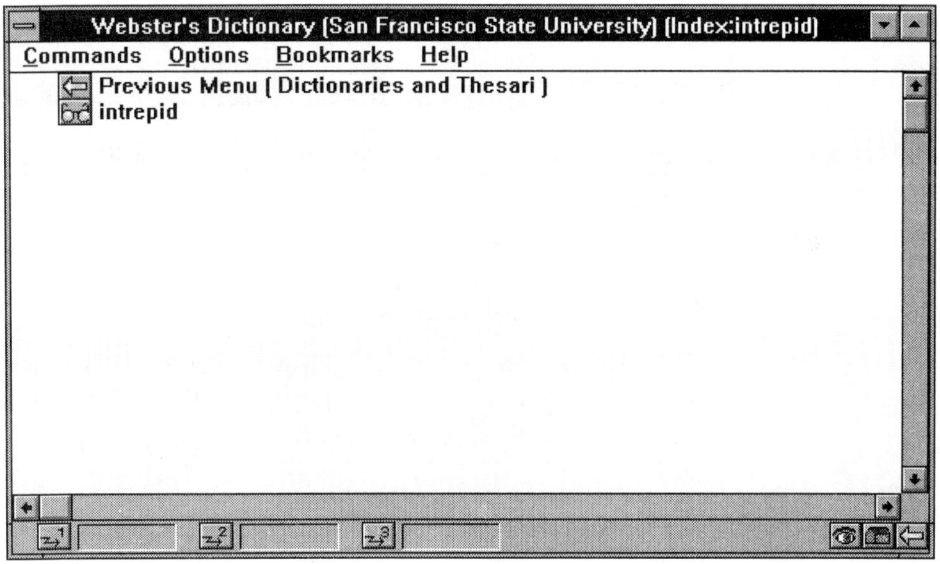

Figure 7-11: HGopher list of matched items.

9. Double-click on the appropriate matched item. The results of the search appear in a new Notepad window, as shown in Figure 7-12.

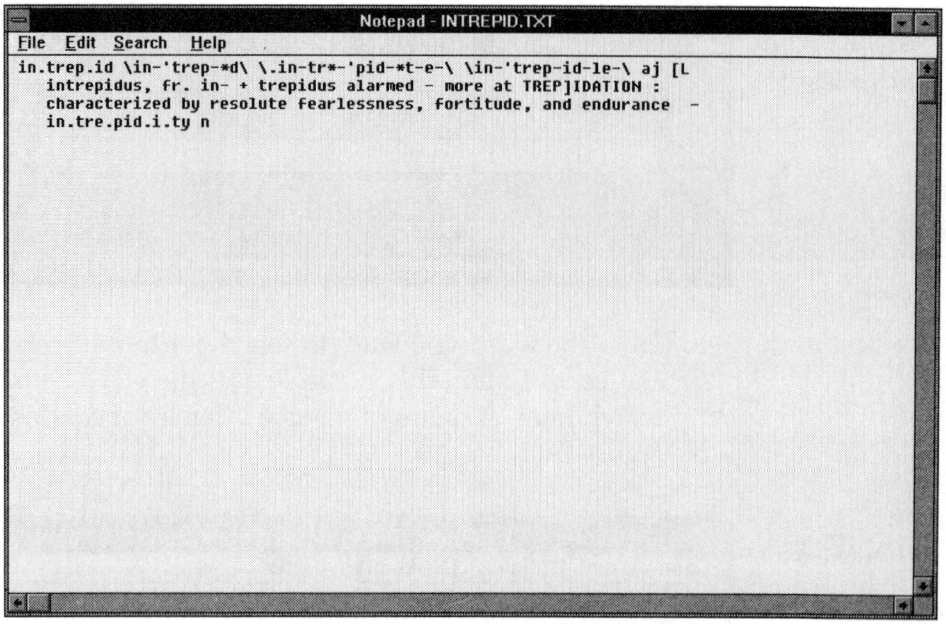

Figure 7-12: Notepad window with results of HGopher search.

10. Close the Notepad window by double-clicking its **Control** menu icon.
11. Click the **Left Arrow** icon in the bottom right corner of the HGopher window to backtrack through the Gopherspace directory hierarchy as necessary.
    - Alternatively, click the **Home** icon in the lower portion of the HGopher window to return directly to the Top Level menu of your home Gopher server.

NCSA Mosaic.
Developed by the University of Illinois National Center for Supercomputing Applications, Mosaic, like HGopher, is a wonderful tool for browsing and grazing through vast information spaces, looking for bits that might tickle your interest. Mosaic is described briefly in the following section, "Downloading Files With HGopher." For complete information on configuring and using this powerful new Internet tool, or to order additional copies, see ordering information in the back of this book.

Barney the Dinosaur.

I don't know about you, but I just don't understand this Barney the Dinosaur phenomenon. At the April Fools Day 1993 Grateful Dead concert, Barney appeared on stage. Everyone there except the kids thought it was bassist Phil Lesh in a purple suit. The kids knew it was Barney.

But lately, there's been a kind of strange, grass-roots Barney backlash. Kids across America are singing macabre songs defaming Barney's name and mocking his message of caring and sharing. Two Texas youths even attacked an unsuspecting Barney—pummeling him and trying to rip his head off—during his visit to a shopping mall. (Whether it was the real Barney or one of Barney's many look-alike "helpers" we still don't know.)

And on the Internet there are dozens of savvy adults, wise to Barney's global conspiracy to brainwash kids into spewing a mindless doctrine of vapid grins and hyperkinetic world-glee. In fact, one guy even started a newsgroup, alt.barney.dinosaur.die.die.die, to help rally opposition against the "Great Evil Purple One."

Downloading Files With HGopher

Some of the most popular FTP sites (especially archives rich with DOS and Windows software) on the Internet offer access to their files via Gopher. This means you can use Gopher instead of another program to download files from those sites, conserving network resources.

To download files with Gopher:

1. With Windows running and the Chameleon Sampler program group window open, double-click on the **Custom** icon. The Custom window appears, as shown in Figure 7-1.
   - Additionally, the Chameleon NEWT icon appears in the lower left corner of your monitor, indicating that the TCP/IP communications stack has been successfully loaded.
2. Click the **Connect** menu item. The Connect dialog box appears, and your SLIP or PPP connection will be automatically established.
   - If you have trouble establishing your connection, select the Log... command from the Setup menu. This opens a window in which you can monitor and debug your connection activity.
3. Launch HGopher by double-clicking its icon in the Program Manager. HGopher will automatically login to your home Gopher server and display its Top Level menu, like the example shown in Figure 7-5.

- Mosaic is an indispensable Windows Internet program that provides a Windows front-end interface to the World Wide Web. You can browse all sorts of information with Mosaic and it's quickly becoming one of the most widely used programs on the Internet. Mosaic is available at many FTP archives on the Internet (it originated at ftp.ncsa.uiuc.edu), and this section will show you how to use Gopher to download the program from the Washington University mirror archive.

4. Navigate to Washington University's archive.

   - The actual procedure for navigating to a particular server will vary, based on your home Gopher server. From within the "Other Gopher Servers" (or similar) menu item, double-click the "North America," "United States," "Missouri," "Washington University—St. Louis," "Washington University FTP Archives" directory items in succession. When you get there, your Gopher window should look similar to the one shown in Figure 7-13.

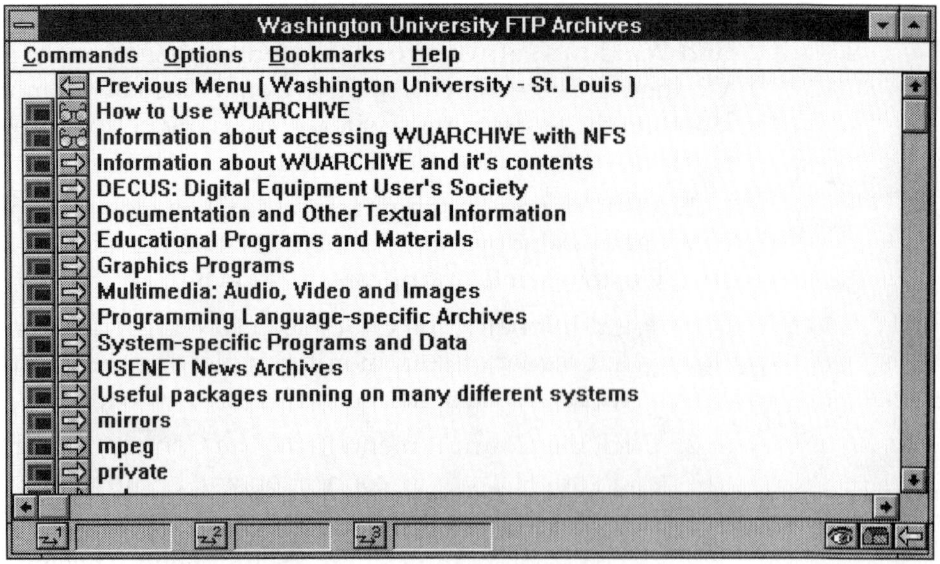

Figure 7-13: HGopher window for Washington University's FTP archives.

5. Double-click the **mirrors** directory item. The HGopher window will be updated to reflect the new directory, as in Figure 7-14.

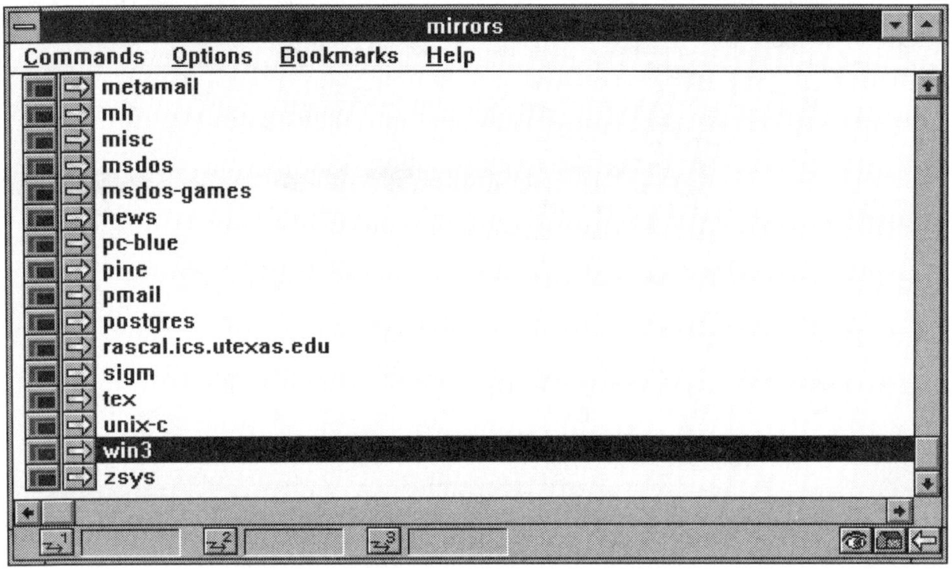

Figure 7-14: HGopher window for Washington University's mirrors archives.

6. Double-click the **win3** directory item. The HGopher window updates to reflect the new directory, as shown in Figure 7-15.

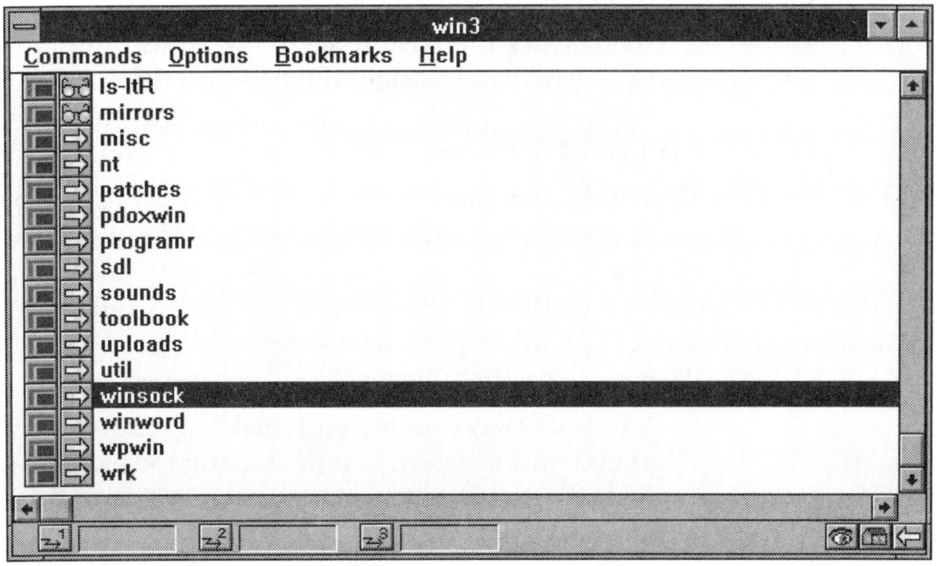

Figure 7-15: HGopher window for Washington University's mirror of Indiana University's CICA Windows archive.

7. Double-click the **winsock** directory item. The HGopher window updates to reflect the new directory, as shown in Figure 7-16.

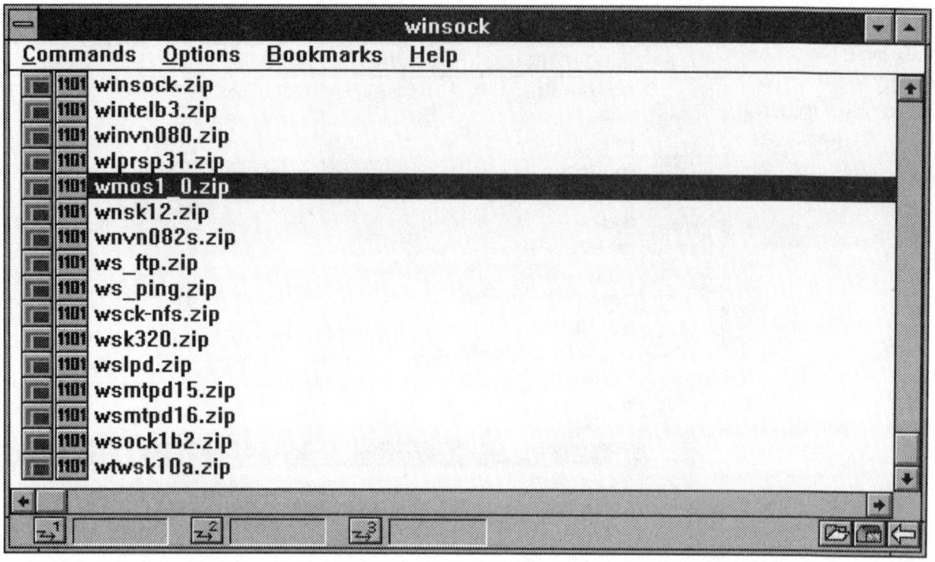

Figure 7-16: HGopher window for CICA winsock directory.

8. Click the **Eye** icon in the bottom portion of the HGopher window twice. The icon will change to the **Open Folder** icon, signifying that you wish to retrieve items on which you double-click to your local hard drive.
9. Double-click the **wmos1_0.zip** item (this is the Mosaic file). The file will be downloaded to the directory you specified when you configured HGopher and the status of the file transfer will be updated in the lower left portion of the HGopher window.

Sometimes you just want to browse through a Gopher server looking for interesting files and documents. This is a great way to keep up with what's happening on the Net. One of the most interesting Gopher holes on the Internet is the Whole Earth 'Lectronic Link (WELL) Gopher server.

To browse through the WELL Gopher server:

1. With Windows running and the Chameleon Sampler program group window open, double-click on the **Custom** icon. The Custom window appears, as shown in Figure 7-1.
   - Additionally, the Chameleon NEWT icon appears in the lower left corner of your monitor, indicating that the TCP/IP communications stack has been successfully loaded.
2. Click the **Connect** menu item. The Connect dialog box appears, and your SLIP or PPP connection will be automatically established.

- If you have trouble establishing your connection, select the Log... command from the Setup menu. This opens a window in which you can monitor and debug your connection activity.

3. Launch HGopher by double-clicking its icon in the Program Manager. HGopher will automatically login to your home Gopher server and display its Top Level menu, like the example shown in Figure 7-5.
4. Navigate to the WELL's Gopherspace.

- The actual procedure for navigating to a particular server will vary, based on your home Gopher server. From within the "Other Gopher Servers" (or similar) menu item, double-click the "North America," "United States," "California," "The WELLgopher—The Whole Earth 'Lectronic Link's Gopherspace" directory items in succession. When you get there, your Gopher window should look similar to the one shown in Figure 7-17.

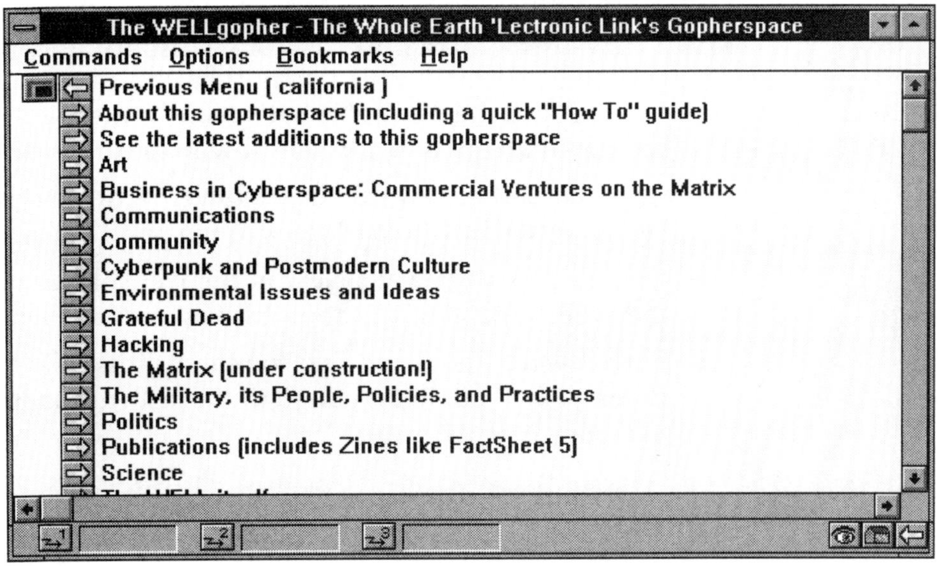

Figure 7-17: HGopher window for the WELL's Gopher server.

- The WELL's Gopher server is a very fertile information resource. You can browse around on your own, or you can come along on the guided tour. We'll begin the tour by taking a look at what's new at the WELL.

5. Double-click the **See the latest additions to this gopherspace** directory item to open that directory, as shown in Figure 7-18.

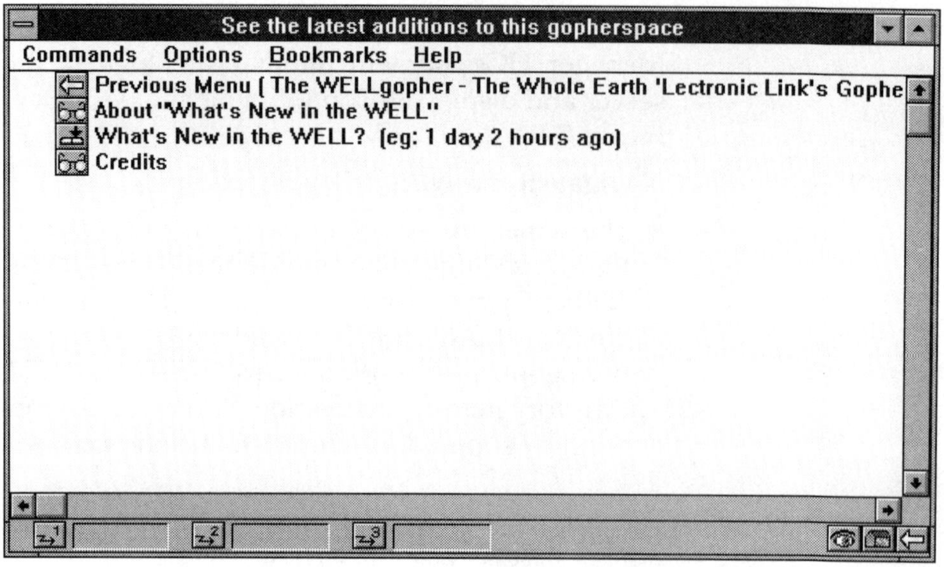

Figure 7-18: HGopher latest additions to the WELL directory.

6. Double-click the **About "What's New in the WELL"** item. A text file explaining how to retrieve new information appears.
7. Click the **Left Arrow** icon in the lower right portion of the HGopher window to backtrack to the previous directory.
8. Double-click the **What's New in the WELL?** book pointer icon. An Index Search dialog box appears, as shown in Figure 7-10.
9. Enter **1 week ago** in the Text to Search strings field and press **Enter**. A menu of items added in the last week appears, as shown in Figure 7-19.

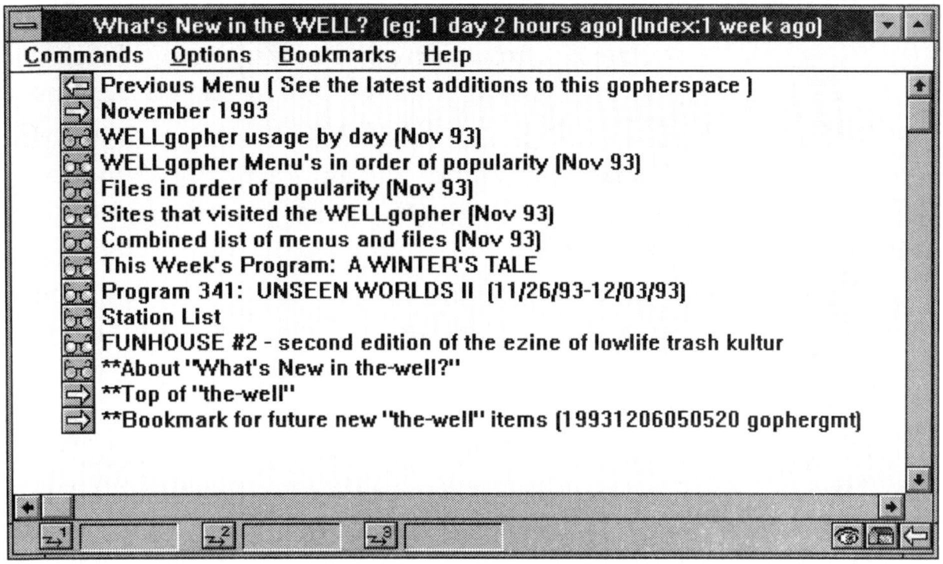

Figure 7-19: HGopher menu of new items added in the last week.

10. Double-click an item that interests you.
    - Alternatively, double-click the **Top of "the-well"** item to return to the WELL's top directory.

Using HGopher Bookmarks

Gopher is great for browsing through lots of different kinds of information resources on the Internet. As you gain more experience prowling these resources, you'll probably start wishing for a way to leave a crumb trail to your favorite Gopher servers so you can easily find your way to them again. Gopher's Bookmark feature lets you define a trail to your favorite Gopher servers. This allows you to quickly and easily login to your favorite Gopher servers by selecting a single menu item.

To set Bookmarks within HGopher:

1. With Windows running and the Chameleon Sampler program group window open, double-click on the **Custom** icon. The Custom window appears, as shown in Figure 7-1.
    - Additionally, the Chameleon NEWT icon appears in the lower left corner of your monitor, indicating that the TCP/IP communications stack has been successfully loaded.
2. Click the **Connect** menu item. The Connect dialog box appears, and your SLIP or PPP connection will be automatically established.

- If you have trouble establishing your connection, select the Log... command from the Setup menu. This opens a window in which you can monitor and debug your connection activity.

3. Launch HGopher by double-clicking its icon in the Program Manager. HGopher will automatically login to your home Gopher server and display its Top Level menu, like the example shown in Figure 7-5.
4. Navigate through Gopherspace by double-clicking on items until you reach the resource for which you want to create a Bookmark.
5. With the resource selected, select the Mark Item command from the Bookmarks menu. The resource will be added as the last item in your Bookmark file.
6. Repeat steps 4–5 for each additional Bookmark you want to add.

Use these steps to use the Bookmarks you have created.

1. With Windows running and the Chameleon Sampler program group window open, double-click on the **Custom** icon. The Custom window appears, as shown in Figure 7-1.
   - Additionally, the Chameleon NEWT icon appears in the lower left corner of your monitor, indicating that the TCP/IP communications stack has been successfully loaded.
2. Click the **Connect** menu item. The Connect dialog box appears, and your SLIP or PPP connection will be automatically established.
   - If you have trouble establishing your connection, select the Log... command from the Setup menu. This opens a window in which you can monitor and debug your connection activity.
3. Launch HGopher by double-clicking its icon in the Program Manager. HGopher will automatically login to your home Gopher server and display its Top Level menu, like the example shown in Figure 7-5.
4. From the Bookmarks menu, select the Show Bookmarks command. Your Bookmarks file will be loaded and will appear in the HGopher window, as shown in Figure 7-20.

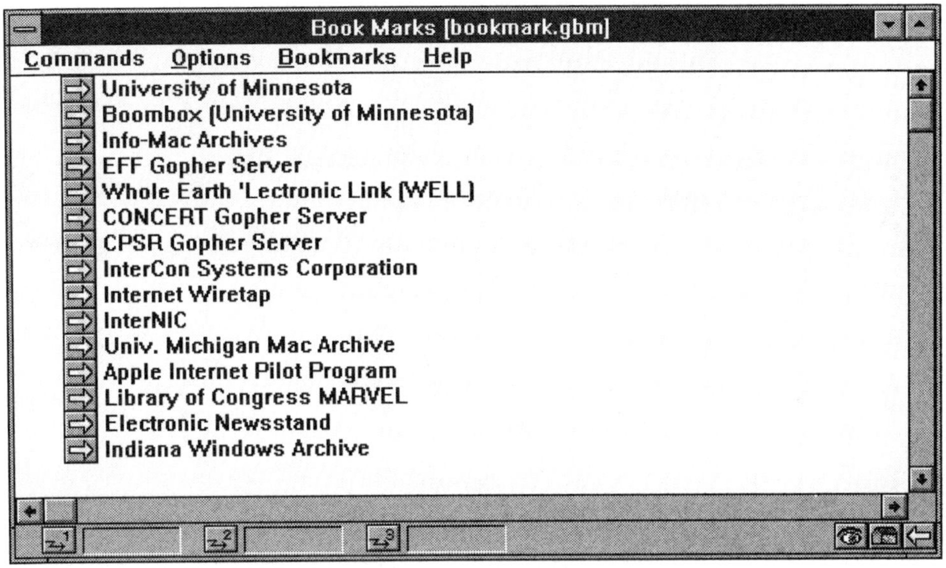

Figure 7-20: HGopher Book Marks window.

5. Double-click the Bookmark you want to use. The Gopher resource represented by the Bookmark will be activated.
   - If the Bookmark you selected is a directory item, you will be logged into that Gopher server.
   - If the Bookmark you selected is a file item, the file will be displayed (if it's a text file) or downloaded to your hard drive (if it's a binary file).
   - If the Bookmark you selected is an index item, the Index Search dialog box will be displayed.
   - If the Bookmark you selected is a TELNET menu item, the login process will be initiated on the remote computer.

You can delete any Bookmark by selecting it and selecting the Remove Bookmark command from the Bookmarks menu.

You can set Bookmarks for any resource within Gopherspace. For instance, if you're constantly downloading telecommunications software from the /msdos/communications/ directory of the Merit software archives, you can set a Bookmark specifically for the communications directory. Double-clicking the communications Bookmark will cause Gopher to immediately login to the Merit archive's /msdos/communications/ directory, rather than forcing you to navigate through the directory hierarchy. You don't even have to be logged into the Merit Gopher server for this to work. Double-clicking the communications Bookmark will automatically login to the Merit server and navigate instantly to the /msdos/communications/ directory.

Locating e-mail addresses.

You can locate the e-mail address of anyone who has posted a network news article by sending this message to mail-server@pit-manager.mit.edu

send usenet-addresses/*name*

where *name* is the name of the person for whom you want an e-mail address.

Remote Login With HGopher

HGopher can be used to login remotely to distant computers on the Internet using the TELNET protocol and the Chameleon TELNET module. Of course, you can use a terminal emulation program to login to remote computers, but Gopher provides you with a way of browsing terminal-based information in the same manner as any other information resource that is accessible with Gopher. Terminal emulation programs provide the advantage of complex emulations for various hardware terminals. HGopher's implementation is very simple and will not work with some Internet resources accessible by remote login, but HGopher offers the advantage of ease of use—you don't have to know or remember machine addresses; just select the resource you want to use from the Gopher menu.

Use these steps to login to remote computers with HGopher.

1. With Windows running and the Chameleon Sampler program group window open, double-click on the **Custom** icon. The Custom window appears, as shown in Figure 7-1.
   - Additionally, the Chameleon NEWT icon appears in the lower left corner of your monitor, indicating that the TCP/IP communications stack has been successfully loaded.
2. Click the **Connect** menu item. The Connect dialog box appears, and your SLIP or PPP connection will be automatically established.
   - If you have trouble establishing your connection, select the Log... command from the Setup menu. This opens a window in which you can monitor and debug your connection activity.

3. Launch HGopher by double-clicking its icon in the Program Manager. HGopher will automatically login to your home Gopher server and display its Top Level menu, like the example shown in Figure 7-5.
4. Navigate to the remote login resource you want to access.
   - Remote login resources appear as **Terminal** or IBM **Terminal** icons in Gopher directories.
   - This section will use the University of Colorado, Boulder's CUline as an example. The actual procedure for navigating to this resource will vary, based on your home Gopher server. From within the "Other Gopher Servers" (or similar) menu item, double-click the "Terminal Based Information" menu item. When you get there, your Gopher window should look similar to the one shown in Figure 7-21.

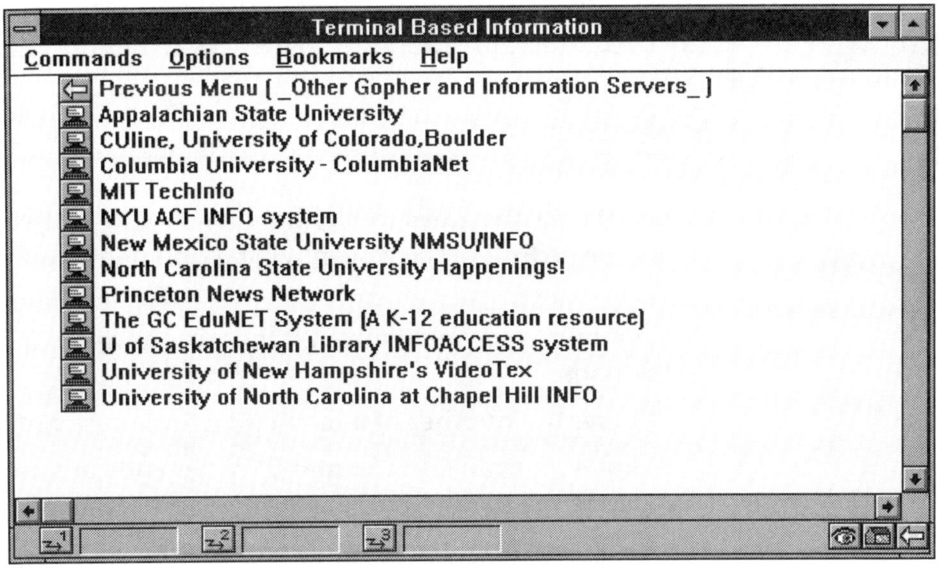

Figure 7-21: HGopher window for Terminal Based Information resources.

5. Double-click the CUline, University of Colorado, Boulder Terminal item. You will be logged into the CUline system as a remote user and a Chameleon TELNET window will be opened, as shown in Figure 7-22.

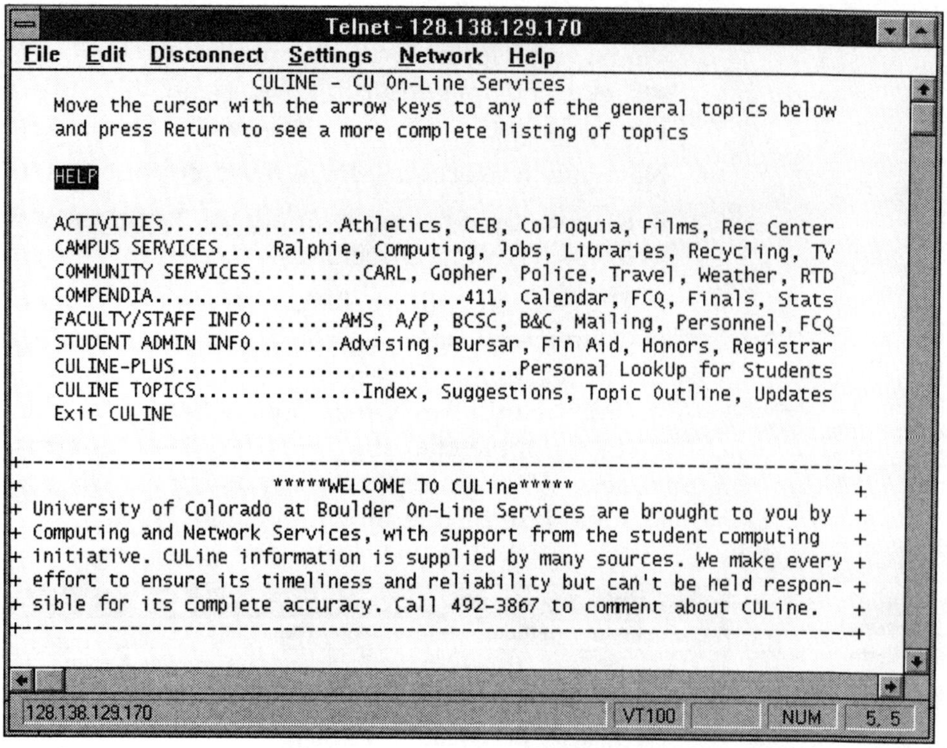

Figure 7-22: Chameleon Telnet window opened within a Gopher session.

6. Use the **Arrow Keys** to highlight a menu item that interests you and press **Enter**. The screen will be updated to reflect your selection.
7. Continue to navigate through the various menu items using these methods:
   - Enter the **number** of a menu item and press **Enter**.
   - Enter an available **command** (commands are usually displayed along the bottom of the window) and press **Enter**.
8. Disconnect from the remote computer by clicking the **Disconnect** menu item and closing the Chameleon TELNET window when you are finished browsing the available resources. The connection to the remote computer will be broken and the last Gopher menu you used will be displayed.
   - Note that only the network connection to the remote computer is broken; your connection to the Internet is still live.

Gopher Servers

There are a number of unique and information-rich sites throughout the Internet that support the Gopher protocol. A listing of just a few of the more interesting Gopher servers available on the Internet is provided in Table 7-1.

Table 7-1: Gopher servers.

Domain Address	Comments
boombox.micro.umn.edu	Gopher distribution archive
gopher.uis.itd.umich.edu	University of Michigan archive
ashpool.micro.umn.edu	Washington University (St. Louis) archive
wx.atmos.uiuc.edu	Weather maps
gopher.eff.org	Electronic Frontier Foundation archive
ashpool.micro.umn.edu	Supreme Court rulings
gopher.well.sf.ca.us	Whole Earth 'Lectronic Link (WELL) archive
gopher.bu.edu	Boston metropolitan guide
gopher.concert.net	University of North Carolina archives
wiretap.spies.com	White House press release service
siggraph.org	Conference proceedings and materials from the graphics special interest group (SIGGRAPH)of the Association for Computing Machinery
ashpool.micro.umn.edu	Internet Resource Guide
hunter.cs.unr.edu	Search Gopherspace using Veronica
wcni.cis.umn.edu	Academic Position Network
gopher.cpsr.org	Computer Professionals for Social Responsibility archive
gopher.msen.com	Search for individuals on the Internet
akasha.tic.com	Sample issues of John Quarterman's *Matrix News* Internet newsletter
internic.net	Internet directory services

The Gopher of the Future.

Although the original Gopher protocol is frozen, a forward-compatible protocol (called Gopher +) is currently in development by the Gopher Team at the University of Minnesota.

Gopher is currently the tenth-most-used protocol in terms of number of connections and the ninth-most-often-used protocol in terms of the number of bytes transferred.

Gopher + will support multiple views of a document, allowing information providers to include Microsoft Word, PostScript, RTF and ASCII text versions of a single document, for example.

Support for forms is also planned for inclusion in Gopher +. This will allow an interface to database back-ends as well as user information ranking, user-created items and directories, and conferencing systems.

Authentication support will be included in Gopher +. This will allow a finer control of information access on Gopher servers. Although it's not designed to replace public-key encryption or Kerberos, Gopher + authentication will allow access to particular information to be granted on an individual basis. Interestingly, the password is never sent across the network, so security will also be enhanced.

Moving On

Gopher is the best way to navigate parts of the Internet you aren't familiar with, because it sports a familiar interface of directories and subdirectories. And because Gopher is a *stateless* software program, it makes the most efficient possible use of network resources.

While previous chapters of this book have focused on the most widely used programs and most frequently visited spots on the Internet, the next chapter will take a look at the dozens of other small but important Internet resources. You'll learn about TELNET, another software program widely used to access Internet resources, and we'll visit a few of the more secluded cul-de-sacs on the Net.

Our tour bus is making only one more excursion before our trip is over. If there's a program, resource, organization or site on the Internet that you're still wondering about, odds are we'll be visiting it in the next chapter. So now would be a good time to stock up on provisions and get a little rest, because the final leg of our tour promises to be the most exciting one yet.

CHAPTER 8

OTHER INTERNET RESOURCES

Geez, what is all this stuff?

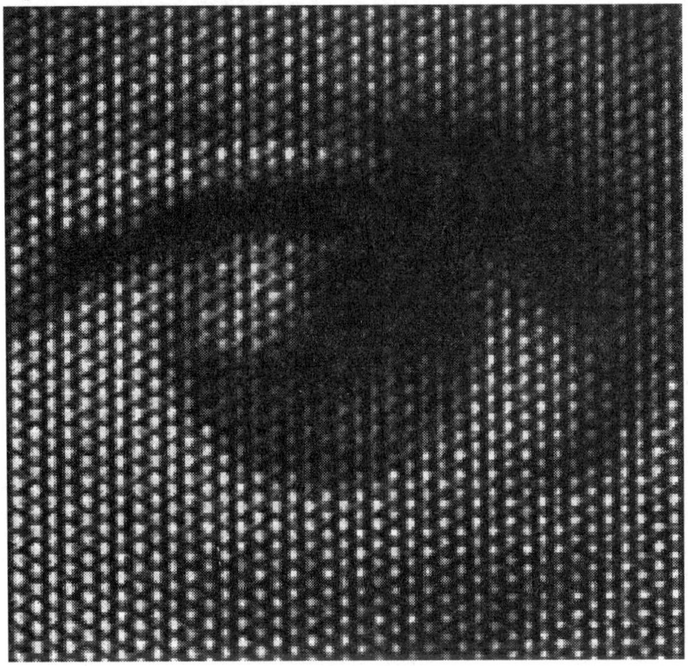

By this point in our tour, you're an old pro at cruising the Internet. You've learned the terrain of the network, the language and customs of its inhabitants and the quickest routes to the information you need. Yet there are still dozens of helpful but lesser-known resources that can make your time online more productive and enjoyable. For this last leg of our tour, we're loading up the bus for a final loop around the outer fringe of the Net. We'll be moving pretty fast, so climb aboard and hang on.

For those who use PCs on the Internet, electronic mail, network news, FTP and Gopher are four of the most widely used resources. TELNET is also a commonly used Internet resource. Specialized, task-specific software programs keep appearing that make TELNET less necessary on the Internet. But some applications will probably always require the use of TELNET. This chapter offers a look at TELNET, as well as some of the many organizations and resources available via the Internet. We'll also cover some of the less commonly used software tools available for use on the Net.

What Is TELNET?

Using TELNET, you can login to other computers on the Internet in an interactive, command-line mode. You use TELNET to access experimental services, library card catalogs, weather reports and various other specialized databases. If you have a UNIX account on another computer on the Internet, you use TELNET to login remotely to your account on that computer.

In the early days of the Internet, TELNET was one of the few tools available to the infonaut. Today, many of the services available by TELNET also provide an alternative method of access, like WAIS or WWW or Gopher (covered in detail in Chapter 7, "Using Gopher"). Although more and more TELNET services are becoming accessible via other methods, some Internet services still require a TELNET connection.

The Chameleon TELNET and TN3270 modules provided on *The Windows Internet Tour Guide Companion Disk* are complete implementations for logging into remote computers on the Internet. NCSA TELNET is a freeware application program for Windows that also lets you take full advantage of the TELNET protocol. It is available by anonymous FTP from ftp.ncsa.uiuc.edu in the /pc/ directory. Extensive documentation is also available in the same directory.

Using TELNET

You use TELNET to login remotely across the Internet to virtually any computer that offers public access or on which you have an account. While there are more powerful implementations of TELNET available, Chameleon will meet the needs of most users, and this section focuses on the fundamental aspects of using TELNET effectively.

Note that Chameleon TELNET and Chameleon TN3270 both operate the same. The only difference is in the terminal emulations each tool provides. Chameleon TELNET offers DEC VT100 emulation while Chameleon TN3270 offers IBM 3270 terminal emulation. As in all things, use the right tool for the job. The instructions provided in this section can be applied to either Chameleon TELNET or Chameleon TN3270, and I'll use TELNET to refer to both tools generically.

To open a TELNET session with Chameleon:

1. With Windows running and the Chameleon Sampler program group window open, double-click on the **Custom** icon. The Custom window appears, as shown in Figure 8-1.

Figure 8-1: Chameleon Custom window.

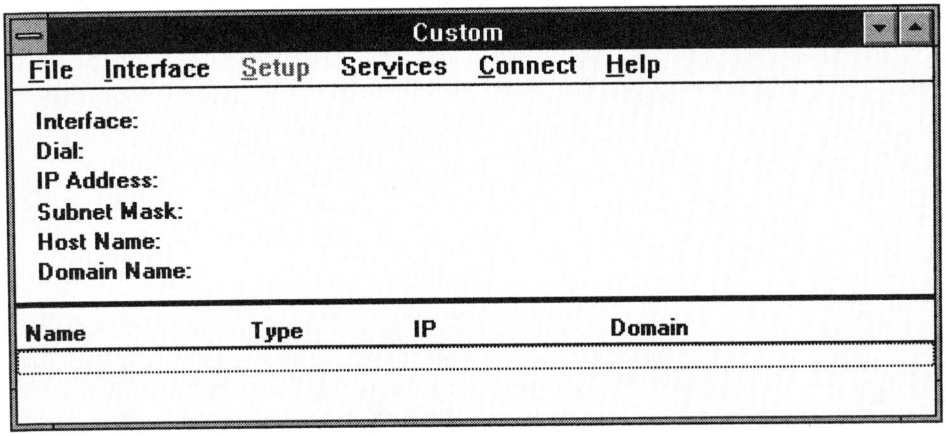

   - Additionally, the Chameleon NEWT icon appears in the lower left corner of your monitor, indicating that the TCP/IP communications stack has been successfully loaded.

2. Click the **Connect** menu item. The Connect dialog box appears, and your SLIP or PPP connection will be automatically established.

   - If you have trouble establishing your connection, select the Log... command from the Setup menu. This opens a window in which you can monitor and debug your connection activity.

3. Launch TELNET by double-clicking its icon in the Program Manager. The Telnet window is displayed, as shown in Figure 8-2.

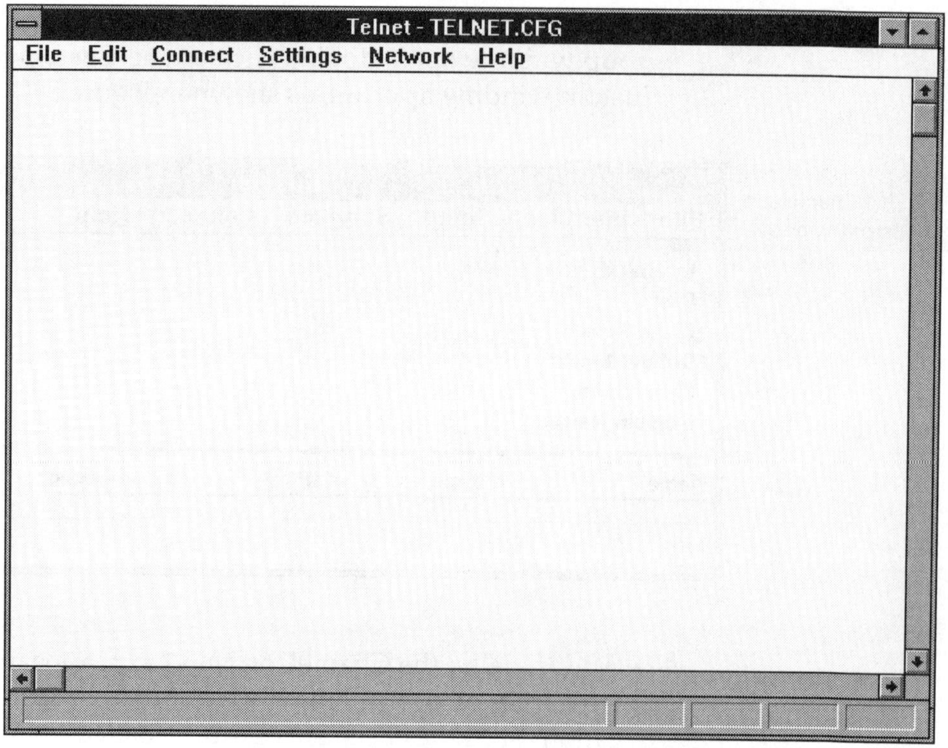

Figure 8-2: Chameleon Telnet window.

4. Click the **Connect** menu item. The Connect To dialog box appears, as shown in Figure 8-3.

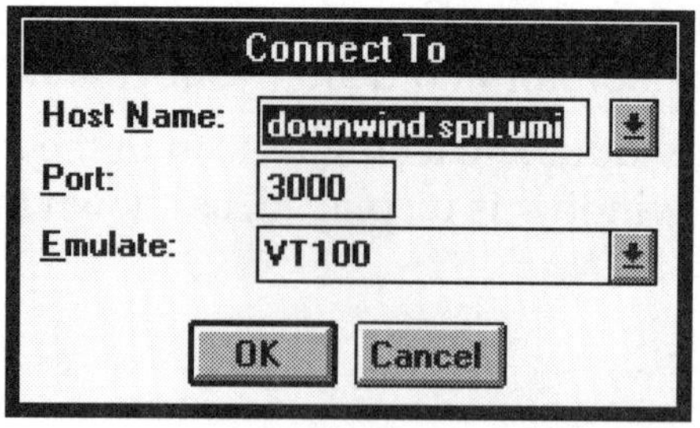

Figure 8-3: Chameleon TELNET Connect To dialog box.

5. Select the host to which you want to login from the Host Name: pop-up menu.
   - You can add hosts you login to regularly in the Chameleon Custom program.
   - Alternatively, enter the domain name—in the domain.top-domain format—for the host to which you want to login in the Host Name: field.

- This exercise will use the weather information available from the University of Michigan's Weather Underground as an example, so if you're following along, enter **downwind.sprl.umich.edu** in the Host Name: field and enter **3000** in the Port: field. Alternatively, several other TELNET resources—including online library card catalogs, Supreme Court rulings and major league baseball schedules—are mentioned later in this chapter.

6. Press **Enter**. Chameleon TELNET will establish a connection to the host you specified, and a Telnet window will be opened, as shown in Figure 8-4.

Figure 8-4: Chameleon Telnet window showing login to the University of Michigan Weather Underground.

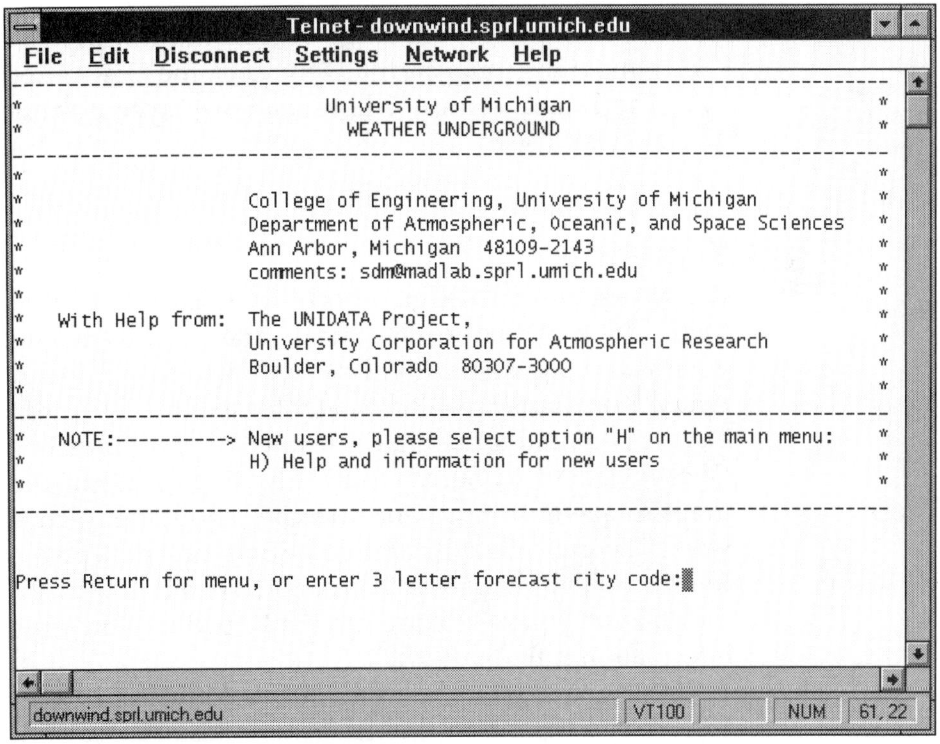

- Note that some hosts may prompt you for a terminal type (The University of Michigan's Weather Underground service doesn't). Sometimes there is a menu selection available, but many times there is simply a TERMINAL: prompt. Chameleon TELNET emulates a VT102 terminal, so you can enter **VT100** (or **VT102**) at the prompt. Almost every host will support a VT102 terminal.

- Note that if you are logging into a remote host on which you have an account, you may have to set the terminal type yourself. For a UNIX host, using the C shell, enter **set term=vt100;tset** at the command prompt. For a VAX/VMS host, enter **set term /inq** at the command prompt.

7. You can navigate through the choices and information on the host by entering commands and menu selections at the command prompt.

   - Menu selections are usually self-explanatory. The commands available to you vary from host to host; refer to each specific host's documentation for an explanation of the commands that may be available.

8. Enter **exit** or **logout** at the command prompt to logout, ending the remote session. Alternatively, click the **Disconnect** menu item. The Telnet window will remain displayed even when the connection is closed.

Knowbots

Knowbots are knowledge robots—or at least that's the theory behind them. Think of them as electronic librarians that can help you find what you're looking for when you don't know where to look. Currently, Knowbots are used mostly for looking up Internet addresses, but the potential for using Knowbots for other uses is very exciting. (Vice President Al Gore is fond of touting the possibilities of knowbots in his frequent writings and speeches about the electronic superhighway.) Theoretically, you should be able to send a Knowbot into the Internet with a set of search criteria. When it finds sources for the information you're looking for, the Knowbot would return with the information it finds.

Unfortunately, I've never been able to login to a site where the Knowbots live, and the general consensus of those on the Net is that Knowbots aren't quite ready for prime time. Look for more information about Knowbots in one of the electronic updates to this book.

Kermit.
Kermit is a complete implementation of the Kermit file transfer protocol for Windows. Both host and client modes are supported, as are script files for automated use. Various versions of the program and companion utilities are available by FTP from ftp.cica.indiana.edu in the /pub/pc/win3/util/ directory.

Netfind

Netfind is a program that searches certain databases to help you find an e-mail address. It's not very easy to use and requires that you login remotely using TELNET, but Netfind can be useful when other options prove fruitless.

To use Netfind to locate someone's e-mail address:

1. Use Chameleon TELNET or Chameleon TN3270 to login to bruno.cs.colorado.edu.
2. At the login: prompt enter **netfind** and press **Enter**.
3. Select the Search item from the menu.
4. At the prompt enter the name and general location (called "keys") for the person you're looking for.
   - For example, let's say you're trying to find the e-mail address of your pal, Wanda Caldwell, at the University of Georgia. You think she might have "wanda" as part of her address, but it's a pretty good bet that she'll have "caldwell" in her address, so you would enter **caldwell uga edu** at the prompt. A list of people named Caldwell at the University of Georgia will be displayed, and you can select the entry that matches the person you're looking for.
5. Select the Exit item from the menu.

The key to working with Netfind is to learn how to conduct searches that are neither too vague nor too specific. If you enter a search that is too vague—like Caldwell Georgia—the search will return too many possible choices. Conversely, if you enter a search that is too specific—like Caldwell peachnet uga edu—the search will yield no results.

Finger

Finger is a useful program for searching the user log on a computer connected to the Internet. This allows you to find someone's e-mail address provided you know the name of the computer he or she uses.

The word "Finger"—like many of the other Internet terms including "FTP" and "TELNET"—is used as both a noun and a verb. You use the word "Finger" to refer to the program you use to "Finger" (the process of obtaining information with the Finger program) a person or resource on the Net.

Making the world a smaller place.

Sheldon Smith forwarded news of a project undertaken by his wife's 5–6 grade class in San Luis Obispo, California.

"This is an example of how the Internet brings the world into the classroom. We, as educators, cannot take the kids out into the world, but Internet can bring the world to the kids.

"About the time when Ross Perot re-announced his candidacy, an American ship accidentally shot a Turkish ship during a NATO exercise, killing the Captain and three crew members. Because of the Presidential election, there was not much about it in the news.

"My wife's students heard about the accident and felt the U.S. should apologize. The kids wrote notes of apology which was compiled into a class letter.

"I sent their letter to the Turkish newsgroup, and I also forwarded it to my sister, who moderates a Middle Eastern conference on PeaceNet. She works for AWAIR which is a non-profit group that produces curriculum materials on the Middle East. In any case, after posting their letter my wife and I received about 30 replies over a two week period."

Here are excerpts from two students' letters:

"Hi my name is Jesse Cutburth. I do not understand why we shot your ship I think we should apologize and this is what I am doing. I don't understand how we shot your ship on accident I think we should replace your ship with one of ours but we can't replace four people."

"Hi, my name is Brianne Reimer. As an American, I am very sorry about what we did. I don't know what we were doing there. But I am only a child. Someday, I hope I will go to Turkey. And if I do go I will surely apologize to you face to face. Sorry."

Although Finger is most commonly used to find someone's e-mail address or to get a list of everyone currently logged into a computer, it can also be used for some other, sometimes unusual, things. You can use Finger as a sort of general information server. Finger has the ability to display a text file (named .plan if you're curious) to any Finger query. You can find all sorts of interesting information on the Internet by using Finger. If you're interested in baseball, for example, Finger jtchern@ocf.berkeley.edu for a list of today's scores.

A freeware Finger program is available by anonymous FTP at ftp.cica.indiana.edu in the /pub/pc/win3/winsock/ directory.

If you Finger buckmr@rpi.edu, a list of this week's top popular U.S. music recordings will be displayed.

Perhaps the strangest Finger resources are the cold-drink vending machines that some universities have connected to the Internet. When Fingered, these machines report which bins in the vending machine are empty and which bins hold the coldest drinks, as shown in Figure 8-5.

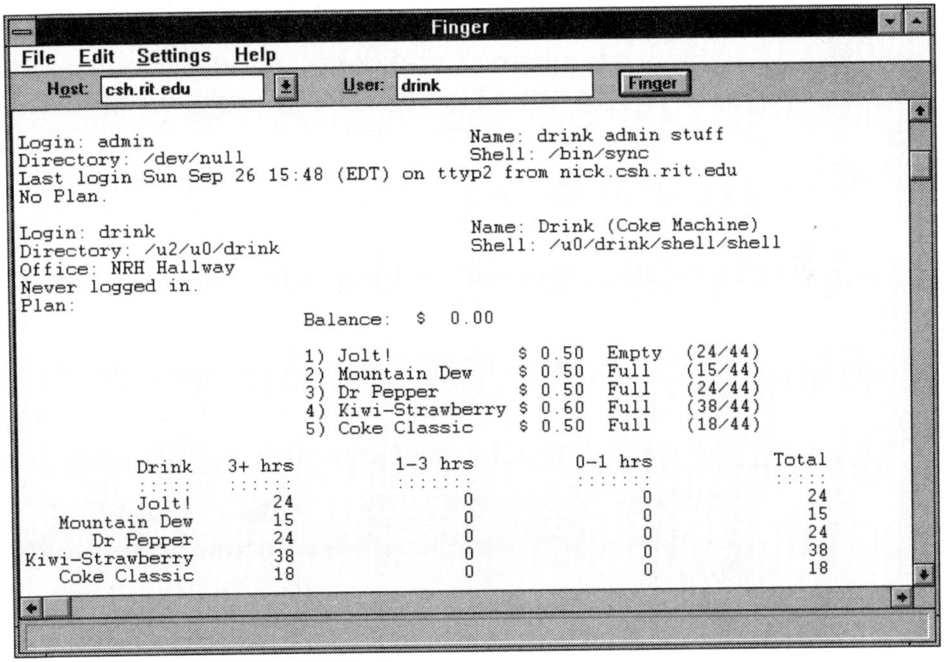

Figure 8-5: Finger cold-drink vending machine.

Since I'm sure you're going to ask for it later if I don't include it now, here's a list of vending machines attached to the Internet.

coke@cs.wisc.edu
@coke.elab.cs.cmu.edu
mnm@coke.elab.cs.cmu.edu
bargraph@coke.elab.cs.cmu.edu
drink@csh.rit.edu

LHA.

LHA is a popular (though not as popular as PKZIP) file compression utility for IBM PCs and compatibles. With LHA, you can create self-extracting archive files, and in some cases the program's archiving capabilities are quicker than those of PKZIP. LHA is available by FTP from oak.oakland.edu in the /msdos/archivers/ directory. Don't let the .exe file extension scare you; it's distributed as a self-extracting archive.

Archie

Archie is an Internet service, originally developed at McGill University, that allows you to search indexes of available files on publicly accessible FTP servers. In other words, you can ask Archie if a certain file exists on the Internet, and if so, where is it? Archie can be helpful in a number of circumstances. You can use it to search for files when you know their names. You can enter just part of a file's name, like "zip," to search for the popular program.

You search Archie's indexes by specifying a string of characters. Archie returns a list of filenames that match your search criteria and the name of the FTP servers where they're located.

As a Windows user, you have two options for using Archie:

- You can TELNET to an Archie server and muddle through a command-line interface.
- You can use Gopher to search the Archie database.

A list of Archie servers is available in Table 8-1.

Table 8-1: Archie servers.

Archie Server	Geographic Area
archie.ans.net	ANS Network sites
archie.internic.net	United States
archie.au	Australia and Pacific Basin
archie.doc.ic.ac.uk	United Kingdom and Ireland
archie.funet.fi	Europe
archie.mcgill.ca	Canada
archie.rutgers.edu	Northeastern United States
archie.sura.net	Southeastern United States
archie.unl.edu	Western United States

Try to use the Archie server that is geographically closest to you. This will help balance network traffic.

Using the Gopher Archie Client

The Gopher Archie client is extremely easy to use.

1. With Windows running and the Chameleon Sampler program group window open, double-click on the **Custom** icon. The Custom window appears, as shown in Figure 8-1.
   - Additionally, the Chameleon NEWT icon appears in the lower left corner of your monitor, indicating that the TCP/IP communications stack has been successfully loaded.
2. Click the **Connect** menu item. The Connect dialog box appears, and your SLIP or PPP connection will be automatically established.
   - If you have trouble establishing your connection, select the Log... command from the Setup menu. This opens a window in which you can monitor and debug your connection activity.
3. Launch HGopher by double-clicking its icon in the Program Manager. HGopher will automatically login to your home Gopher server and display its Top Level menu, like the example shown in Figure 8-6.

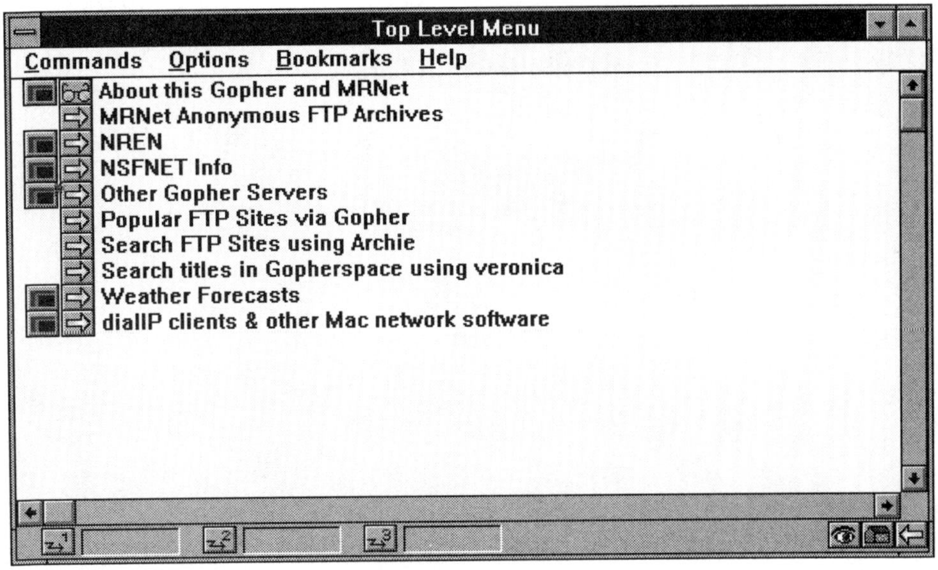

Figure 8-6: HGopher window with Top Level Menu for example home Gopher server.

4. Navigate to the Search FTP Sites using Archie menu item.
   - If you're using the University of Minnesota's "mother" Gopher as your Home Gopher server, it's located inside the Internet file server (ftp) sites directory, as shown in Figure 8-7.

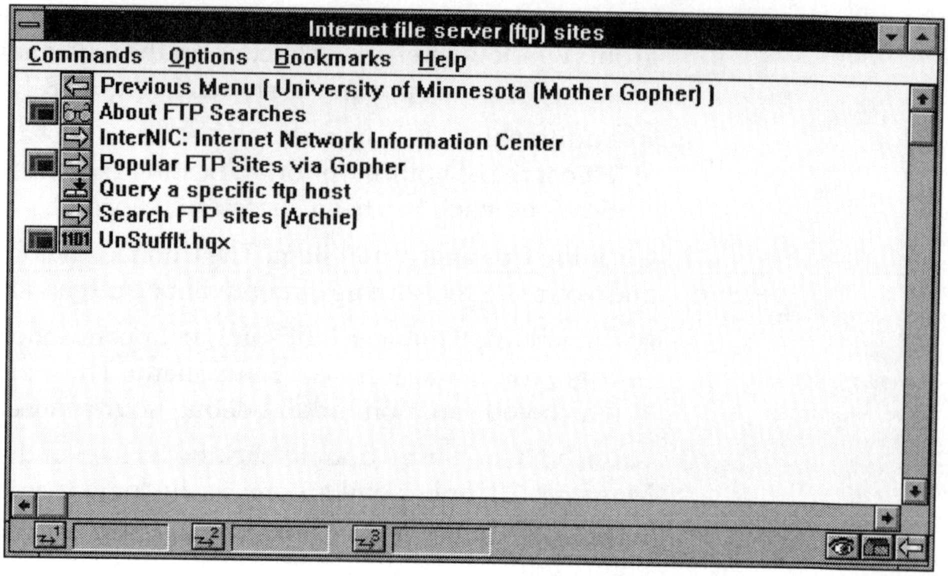

Figure 8-7: HGopher Archie Internet file server (ftp) sites directory.

5. Double-click the Search FTP sites (Archie) directory item. The directory will be opened displaying two **book pointer** index items, as shown in Figure 8-8.

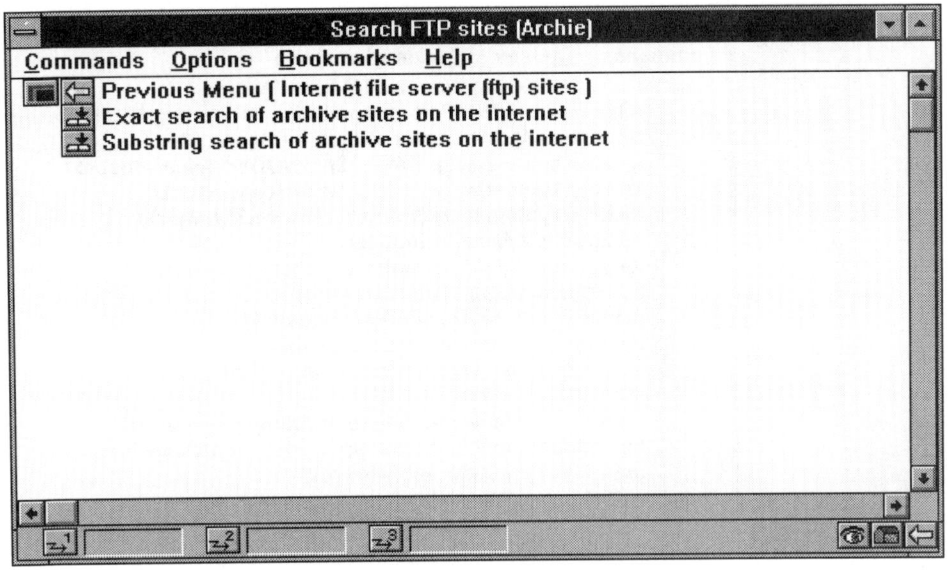

Figure 8-8: HGopher Archie search directory.

6. Double-click the Exact search **book pointer** index item. An Index Search dialog box appears, as shown in Figure 8-9.

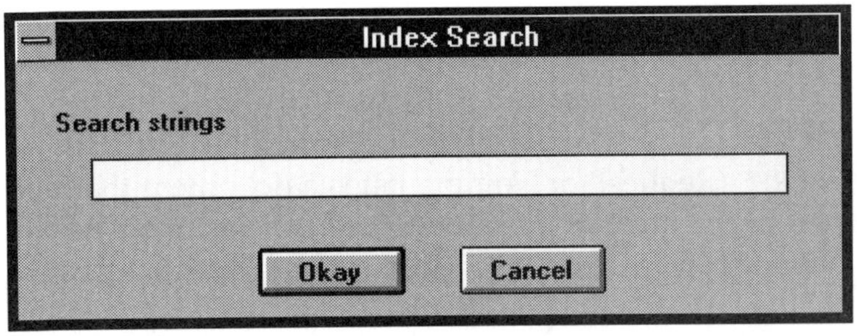

Figure 8-9: HGopher Index Search dialog box.

7. Enter a word or series of words contained in the document or filename you wish to download and press **Enter**.

   - HGopher will search within the Archie database for documents and filenames matching the search words you specified. A new Gopher directory will appear, showing a list of the documents and files matching your search words, like the example search results for "winsock" shown in Figure 8-10.

Figure 8-10: HGopher Archie search results.

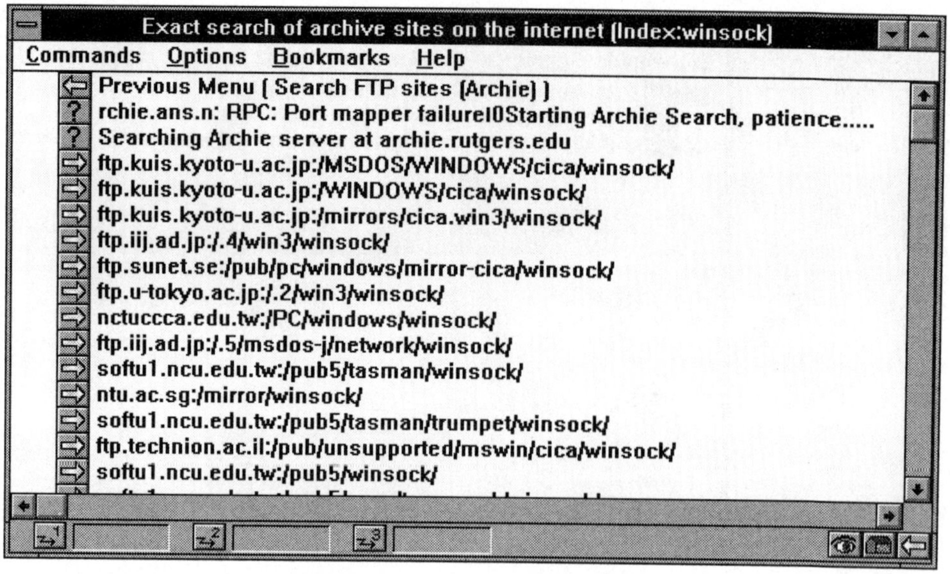

An advantage of using Gopher for Archie searches is that the search results window contains "live" Internet resources. You can simply double-click any item in the search results window to automatically login to an anonymous FTP archive or download a file.

RFCs

An RFC (Request for Comments) is a document that defines a specific part of the Internet itself. Because of the anarchic nature of the Internet, anyone can write an RFC. Most are highly technical and relate to topics that are of little interest to the average user. Some RFCs, however, are veritable goldmines of useful information for real people. RFCs are always referred to by their number and may be available in either text or PostScript formats (text versions have a .txt suffix; PostScript versions have a .ps suffix).

RFCs are available from many FTP archives, including the "official" depositories shown in Table 8-2.

Table 8-2: Official RFC depositories.

FTP Site	Directory
nic.ddn.mil	/rfc/
nis.jvnc.net	/rfc/
nisc.sri.com	/rfc/
wuarchive.wustl.edu	/doc/rfc/
nnsc.nsf.net	/rfc/
src.doc.ic.ac.uk	/rfc/

Because all RFCs are available only by RFC number, it's a good idea to first download the index of RFC files (rfc-index.txt). This file contains a complete index of all currently available RFCs.

You can also obtain RFCs by e-mail with these steps:

1. Launch your e-mail program.
2. Create a new message to the address mail-server@nisc.sri.com
3. Enter a one-line message consisting of send rfcxxx.txt (where xxx is the number of the RFC you want to receive.
   - To receive the index, enter a one-line message consisting of send rfc-index.txt
4. Send your e-mail message.

A list of some of the RFCs that are useful for average users is provided in Table 8-3.

Figure 8-3: Useful RFCs.

RFC	Title
1432	Recent Internet books
1402	There's Gold in them thar Networks! or Searching for Treasure in all the Wrong Places
1392	Internet Users' Glossary
1359	Connecting to the Internet: What connecting institutions should anticipate
1325	FYI on questions and answers: Answers to commonly asked "new Internet user" questions
1296	Internet Growth (1981-1991)
1259	Building the open road: The NREN as test-bed for the national public network
1244	Site Security Handbook
1208	Glossary of networking terms
1207	FYI on Questions and Answers: Answers to commonly asked "experienced Internet user" questions
1192	Commercialization of the Internet summary report
1180	TCP/IP tutorial
1178	Choosing a name for your computer
1175	FYI on where to start: A bibliography of internetworking information
1167	Thoughts on the National Research and Education Network
1118	Hitchhikers guide to the Internet

FAQs

A FAQ (Frequently Asked Question) is a collection of questions (and their answers) most often asked by new Internet users. FAQs exist for all network news newsgroups and most mailing lists. Until you get your Internet legs, read the FAQ for the newsgroups you frequent. You can save yourself a lot of embarrassment by skimming FAQ files.

Most FAQs are posted to their related newsgroups on a monthly basis. In addition, FAQs for all the newsgroups are consolidated and posted to the news.answers newsgroup. You can also obtain FAQs by FTP from pit-manager.mit.edu in the /pub/usenet/ directory.

Internet Organizations

As the Internet has evolved from a project researching ways to ensure communications in the event of a nuclear attack into a research and business tool used by millions of individuals, a number of diverse and vital organizations have sprung up. The actions of two of these organizations—the Internet Society and the Electronic Frontier Foundation—have repercussions for every Internet user.

WinQVT/Net.
WinQVT/Net is a fully integrated Windows program for navigating the Internet. E-mail, network news, FTP, and TELNET tools are all included in a single application with a unified interface. The program is available by anonymous FTP from biochemistry.bioc.cwru.edu in the /pub/qvtnet/ directory.

Electronic Frontier Foundation

On July 10, 1990, two unlikely cohorts announced they were forming a foundation to "address social and legal issues arising from the impact on society of the increasing pervasive use of computers as a means of communication and information distribution." Mitch Kapor is best known as the founder of Lotus Development Corporation, the publisher of the Lotus 1-2-3 spreadsheet program. John Perry Barlow is a sometimes lyricist for the Grateful Dead, one-time Congressional candidate and Wyoming rancher.

A number of factions are battling for control and influence over cyberspace, and the Electronic Frontier Foundation (EFF) is entrenched in the front lines of the battlefield. On one side of the battle lines are a number of government agencies, corporations and other entities that want to limit access to information and dictate what people can do in cyberspace. On the other side, there are those—like the members of the EFF—who want to widen (and deepen) everyone's access to information, and extend the rights most Americans enjoy in physical reality to cyberspace.

Kapor and Barlow came together when both were questioned by the FBI following an incident at Apple Computer where a group calling itself the NuPrometheus League had distributed the Color QuickDraw source code to members of the computer press and luminaries in the computer industry.

John Perry Barlow was amazed at the level of computer ignorance exhibited by the FBI agent who visited him in May 1990. Barlow had been a longtime member of the Internet-connected Whole Earth 'Lectronic Link (WELL) and describes himself as a "techno-crank." From the agent, Barlow learned that computer hackers—*all* computer hackers—were under suspicion as Evil Criminals. He also learned that the FBI was tracing anyone who had visited the Hackers Conference, an invitation-only affair begun in 1984 that drew attendees from the top levels of the computer industry, including executives, consultants, pundits and journalists.

It's important to draw the distinction between hackers (those who like to explore systems for the sake of learning something about those systems) and crackers (those who are out to wreak havoc by breaking into systems, deleting files and reaping financial gain illegally).

Barlow, alarmed at the implications of computer ignorance within the FBI (and the possibility of a high-tech witch hunt), sounded the alarm on the WELL. One of the many WELL inhabitants who took note of Barlow's outcry was Mitch Kapor, who had already endured being fingerprinted by the FBI.

Kapor flew to Barlow's Wyoming ranch in June 1990 to lay the groundwork for the EFF, and Barlow wrote "Crime and Puzzlement," an article announcing the pair's intention of forming a political organization intent on extending Constitutional rights to cyberspace.

The response from the computing community was astounding. Original funding for EFF was provided by Kapor and Apple co-founder Steve Wozniak. John Gilmore (one of the founders of Sun Microsystems) contributed, and others quickly followed.

The Electronic Frontier Foundation continues to fight for a careful balance of freedom, access and privacy throughout the networks, and they've even won a few battles.

You can download a wealth of information from the EFF's FTP or Gopher server at ftp.eff.org and gopher.eff.org respectively. Here's a sampling:

- Back issues of *EFFector Online*, the electronic newsletter of the EFF.
- Testimony of EFF staff and board members.
- Papers and articles by EFF staff and board members.

- EFF Newsnotes and informational postings.
- Papers and articles about cyberspace from luminaries including Bruce Sterling, John Perry Barlow and Dorothy Denning.
- Information about various legal issues affecting the Internet.
- Text of various laws and proposed laws relevant to the electronic frontier.

Electronic Frontier Foundation
666 Pennsylvania Avenue, SE
Suite 303
Washington, DC 20003
202/544-9237
202/547-5481 (Fax)
617/576-4510 (Legal hotline)
eff@eff.org

Internet Society

The Internet Society exists to encourage cooperation among the various networks that comprise the Internet, fostering a global communications infrastructure. The organization focuses on the future of the Internet and the emerging and established technologies that impact the Net. The Internet Society appoints a small group of members to the Internet Architecture Board—the closest thing the Internet has to a board of governors, although it's more accurate to think of the body as a group of tribal elders.

The Internet Architecture Board (IAB) is responsible for the technical management of the Internet. It adopts proposed standards and allocates addresses. The Internet Architecture Board also oversees two groups:

- The Internet Engineering Task Force (IETF), which is responsible for the technical operation of the Internet.
- The Internet Research Task Force (IRTF), which is responsible for research and development issues surrounding the Internet.

The Internet Society sponsors an annual conference, publishes a quarterly newsletter and supports an electronic mail distribution list.

Internet Society
1895 Preston White Drive
Suite 100
Reston, VA 22091
703/620-8990
isoc@nri.reston.va.us

Neat Stuff

New information resources are added to the Internet every minute. It's impossible to keep up with everything on the Net—about the best you can do is seek out those things that specifically interest you. Keep in close touch with your friends and associates, tipping them off to new files, sites and resources that they might be interested in—and ask them to do the same for you. When you find something worth sharing, e-mail pointers (a "trail" through the Net) to each other. Exchange Gopher bookmarks.

The electronic updates that come with this book are another great way to keep up with what's new and worthwhile on the Internet. For more details, see "Electronic Updates & Visitors Center" beginning on page 309.

As your tour guide, it's impossible for me to show you *all* of the Internet. (That's like trying to ride every ride at Disneyworld in just one day!) Because the Net is constantly changing, any collection of Internet resources is only a snapshot of what's interesting *right now* (Winter 1993). Of course, what's interesting to me may not be interesting to you at all, so I'm providing pointers of general interest.

Besides, who would want to ride *every* ride at Disneyworld? There are always lemons—disappointing resources (or amusement park rides)—that don't deliver what they promise. So rather than bury you under mountains of untested, untried programs, sites or resources, you'll only find the most stable, useful and widely acclaimed resources listed in this chapter. For information on a wide variety of interesting Net items, be sure to check *The Windows Internet Tour Guide* electronic updates.

Naturally, many of you will wonder why your favorite site or resource isn't listed with those that follow. The most likely answer is space limitations, but you should still e-mail your favorite Internet finds to me for inclusion in future editions and electronic updates.

Send your useful, bizarre and otherwise enticing resources to me at: mfraase@farces.com.

Here's how the resource entries that follow are organized:

- The **Type**: field tells you what software tool or protocol you need to use to access the resource.
- The **Address**: field tells you the domain name address for the resource.
- The **Pathname**: field tells you the pathname for the directory or file of the resource.
- The **Summary**: field provides a brief description of the resource and any necessary login information.

Acronyms by E-Mail

Type: E-mail
Address: freetext@iruccvax.ucc.ie
Summary: The Irish have always had a way with the language, and the University of Cork offers an e-mail based Acronym Server.

Send an e-mail message with the word "help" (without the quotes) in the body of the message to get instructions on using the server.

Alex

Type: FTP
Address: alex.sp.cs.cmu.edu
Pathname: /doc/README/
Summary: Alex provides a way to transparently read remote files at anonymous FTP sites.

Almanac

Type: Finger
Address: copi@oddjob.uchicago.edu
Summary: Provides a list of notable birthdays, events in history and planetary occurrences for each day, as shown in the example in Figure 8-11.

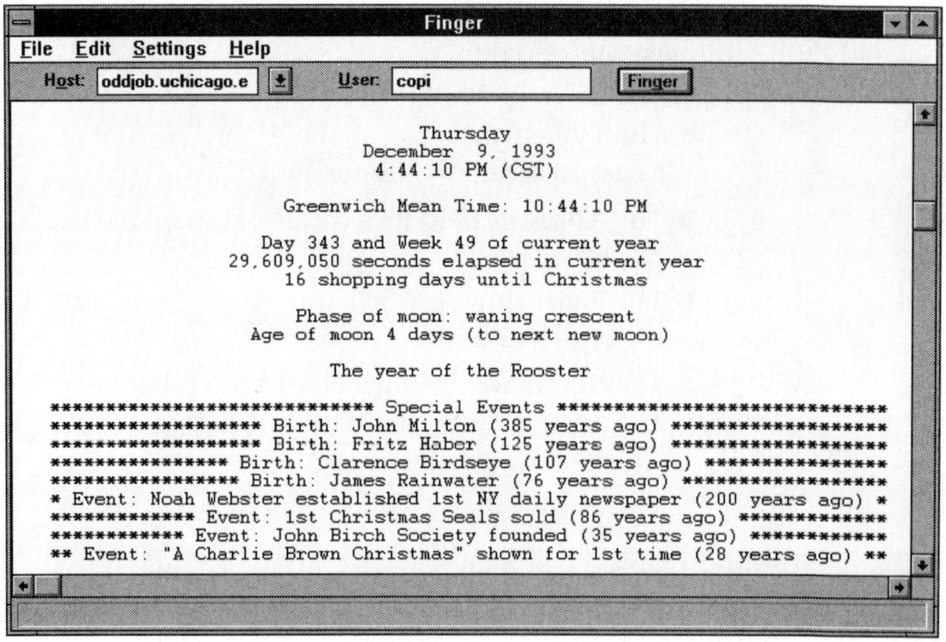

Figure 8-11: Finger Almanac results.

AskERIC

Type: Gopher (also available via TELNET)
Address: ericir.syr.edu
Login: gopher (TELNET only)
Summary: Electronic library access (also available via Gopher) for querying education-related questions.

Aspen Gopher

Type: Gopher
Address: aspen.com
Summary: A Gopher hole devoted to topics of relevance to Aspen, Colorado.
Contact: aspen@aspen.com

Bookstore (University of California, San Diego)

Type: TELNET
Address: ucsdbkst.ucsd.edu (132.239.83.66)
Summary: Provides information about titles in stock as well as titles on-order and the *New York Times* bestseller lists. An example of the menu system is shown in Figure 8-12.

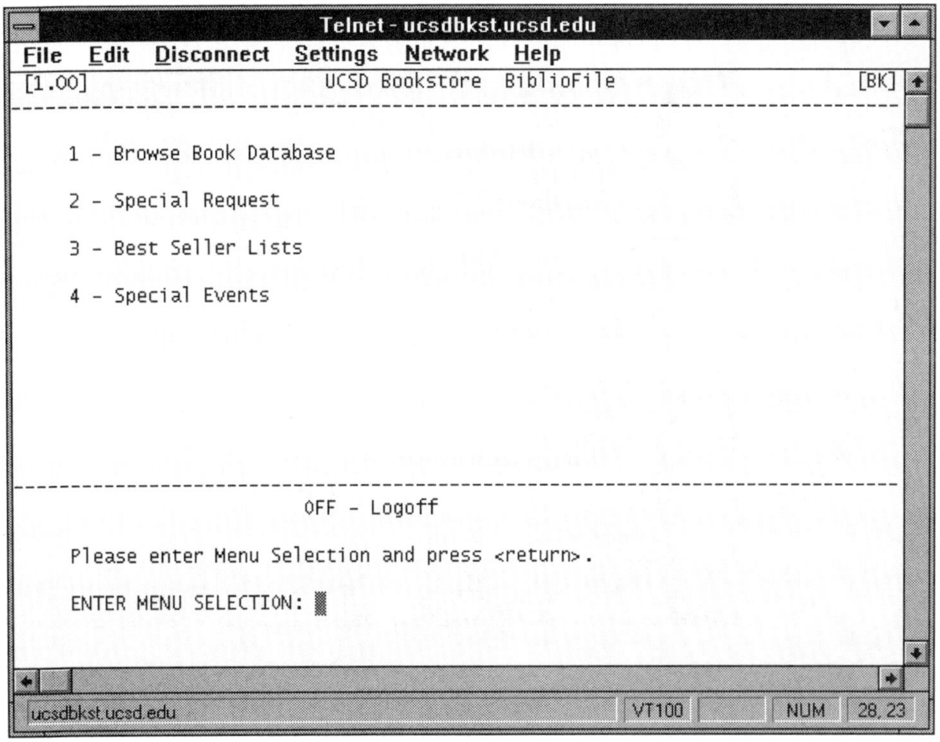

Figure 8-12: TELNET example of UCSD Bookstore menu system.

California Common Cause Political Contributors Report

Type: FTP
Address: synnyside.com
Pathname: /ccause/
Summary: An electronic version of California Common Cause's report on the top ten political contributors in 1991–1992.

Carnegie Mellon University English Server

Type: Gopher
Address: english-server.hss.cmu.edu
Summary: A Gopher server developed by the graduate students in the English department of Carnegie Mellon University designed to freely distribute documents and information on a wide range of subject matter. This is truly one of the most comprehensive information resources on the Net. The top-level menu is shown in Figure 8-13.

Figure 8-13: Top-level menu of CMU English Server.

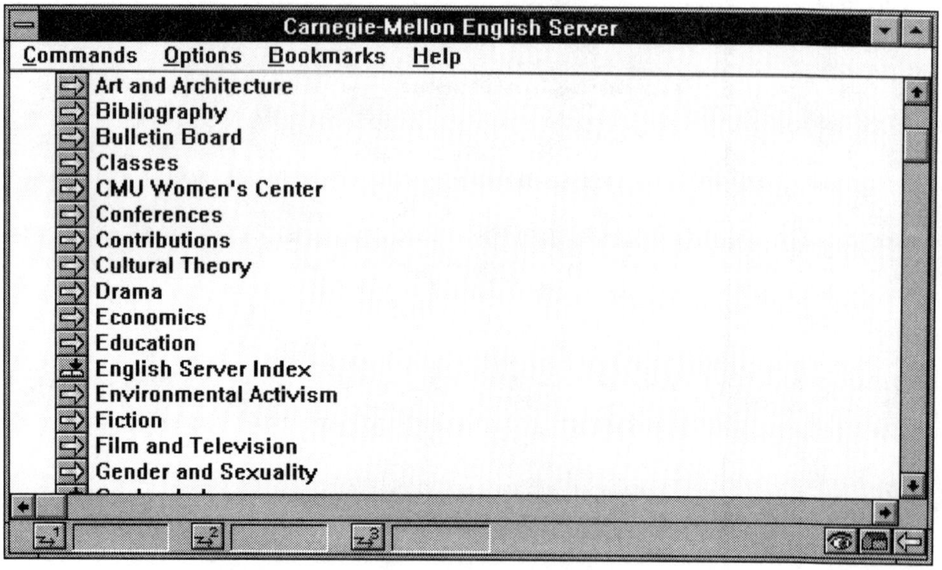

Chess Server

Type: TELNET
Address: 128.2.209.147 5000 or 130.225.16.162 5000 (in Europe)
Summary: Observe or play chess matches against human opponents in real-time.

Clearinghouse for Networked Information Discovery and Retrieval (CNIDR)

Type: FTP
Address: cnidr.org
Summary: The Clearinghouse for Networked Information Discovery and Retrieval is an organization dedicated to aiding Internet citizens in their searches for information throughout the network. CNIDR works with a number of other organizations to make information more accessible and standardized across the Internet.

Colorado Alliance of Research Libraries (CARL)

Type: TELNET
Address: pac.carl.org
Summary: The Colorado Alliance of Research Libraries provides access to a number of different academic and public library online catalogs, current article indexes, the Internet Resource Guide and the Academic American Encyclopedia. CARL also offers a service through which you can request (for a small fee charged to your credit card) a fax copy of any journal article in its catalog, as well as access to other services, such as Journal Graphics, which offers transcripts of popular news and public affairs television programs. A gateway to other library systems is also offered. The public access database menu is shown in Figure 8-14.

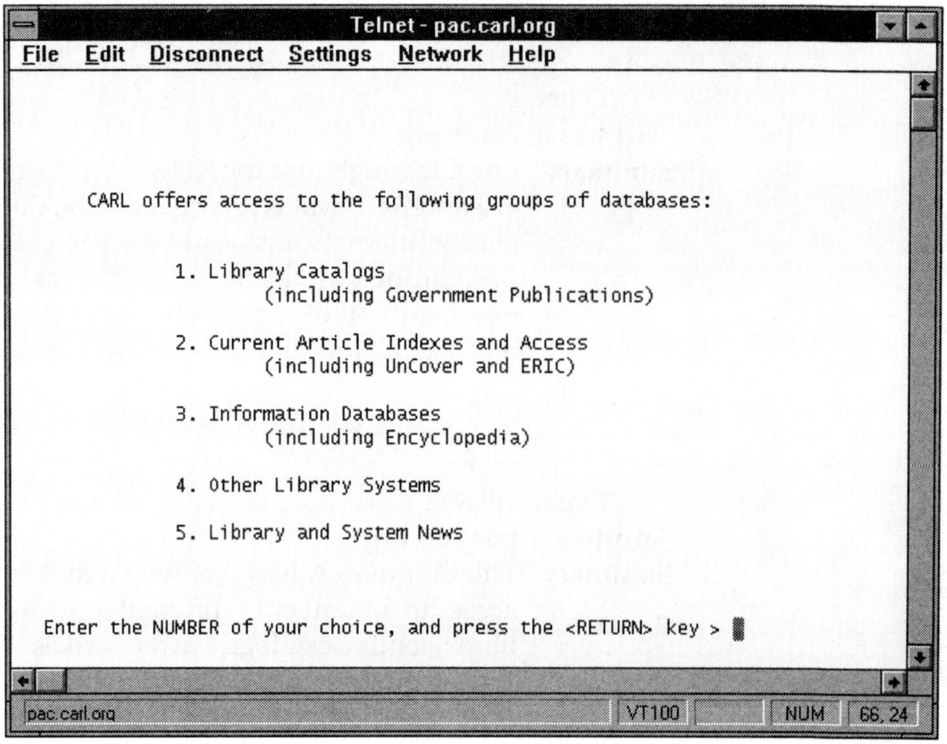

Figure 8-14: CARL public access database menu.

Commerce Business Daily

Type: Gopher
Address: cscns.com
Summary: CNS, one of the regional service providers in the United States, is offering free Gopher access to the *Commerce Business Daily*. The service is updated each evening with information for the next day.
Contact: info@cscns.com or 800/748-1200.

Community Computer Networks: Building Electronic Greenbelts

Type: FTP
Address: ftp.apple.com
Pathname: /alug/communet/
Summary: Steve Cisler's excellent overview of community networks examining what kinds of information and

services can be found on these systems, what groups are running community networks and cost aspects. The essay discusses current models for community networks and the impact these networks have on their local (physical) environment.

Contact: Steve Cisler
Apple Library
4 Infinite Loop
MS 304-2A
Cupertino, CA 95014
408/974-3258
sac@apple.com

Computer-Mediated Communication

Type: FTP
Address: ftp.rpi.edu
Pathname: /pub/communications/internet-cmc
Summary: John December's compiled list of resources describing the Internet, computer networks and computer-mediated communication.

Computer Professionals for Social Responsibility (CPSR) Mailing List

Type: Mailing List
Address: listserv@gwuvm.gwu.edu
Summary: Send a one-line message in e-mail:
subscribe CPSR *your name*
where *your name* is your full name (not your e-mail address).

Computer Professionals for Social Responsibility is a professional organization that concerns itself with the social and political aspects of computing. Mailing list subscribers will receive updates on CPSR's current Freedom of Information Act (FOIA) requests, position statements and news releases on topics including privacy and cryptography.

Consumers Access Service

Type: TELNET
Address: columbia.ilc.com (38.145.77.221)
Login: cas
Summary: Browse listings and place online orders for audio CDs, videotapes and computer software.

Cookie Server

Type: TELNET
Address: astro.temple.edu 12345 (129.32.1.100)
Summary: Displays a quote whenever you TELNET in to this address.

Current Cites

Type: TELNET
Address: melvyl.ucop.edu
Summary: Provides a bibliography of current journal articles related to computers and information technology. Enter **SHOW CURRENT CITES** at command prompt.
Contact: drobinson@library.berkeley.edu

Dictionary Server

Type: TELNET
Address: cs.indiana.edu 2627
Summary: Provides access to an online Webster's Ninth Collegiate Dictionary.
Login as webster
Enter **HELP** for online help system.

E-Mail Address Locator

Type: E-mail
Address: mail-server@pit-manager.mit.edu
Summary: In body of letter enter:
send usenet-addresses/*name*
where *name* is the name of the person you want to locate.

The service will return the e-mail address of the person in the username@domain.top-domain format.

This service works only if the person you are looking for has posted an article to one of the USENET newsgroups.

Earthquake Information

Type: Finger
Address: quake@geophys.washington.edu
Summary: Reports recent earthquake information including location, magnitude and time of occurrence.

Electronic Frontier Foundation (EFF) Mailing List

Type: Mailing List
Address: eff-request@eff.org
Summary: Send a brief e-mail message requesting to be added to the mailing list. The Electronic Frontier Foundation is a professional organization concerned with the legal, social and political aspects of civilizing cyberspace. If you subscribe to the EFF mailing list, you'll receive copies of the *EFFector Online* electronic newsletter and news releases.

Electronic Journal on Virtual Culture

Type: FTP
Address: byrd.mu.wvnet.edu
Pathname: /pub/ejvc/
Summary: Very interesting and well-written journal of virtual community and the Internet. Each issue contains three or four feature articles, non-refereed opinion columns and essays, and the Cyberspace Monitor (a listing of important happenings, publications, products and services related to cyberspace and the Net).

Electronic Newsstand

Type: Gopher
Address: gopher.netsys.com port 70 (also available via TELNET: gopher.netsys.com login: enews)

Summary: The New Republic Inc. of Washington, D.C. and The Internet Company of Hudson, Mass., created the Electronic Newsstand Inc. on July 25, 1993, to provide a marketing vehicle for magazine publishers on the Internet.

According to Jeffrey Dearth, president of *The New Republic* magazine and founder and CEO of Electronic Newsstand, "The estimated 10 to 15 million Internet users can browse the table of contents and selected articles from publications on our newsstand 24 hours a day, seven days a week, and send orders to us electronically."

Publications available on the Electronic Newsstand are *The New Yorker, The Economist, The New Republic, Foreign Affairs, National Review, Technology Review, Eating Well, Outside, The Journal of NIH Research, The Source* and *New Age Journal*.

The marketing concept behind the Electronic Newsstand, according to Robert Raisch, president of The Internet Company and COO of Electronic Newsstand is that "the more people are exposed to a magazine's editorial content, the more likely they are to be interested in subscribing to a hard copy, or in purchasing a single issue." An example is shown in Figure 8-15.

Contact: Paul Vizza
202/331-7494
info@enews.com
staff@enews.com
Rob Raisch
raisch@netsys.com

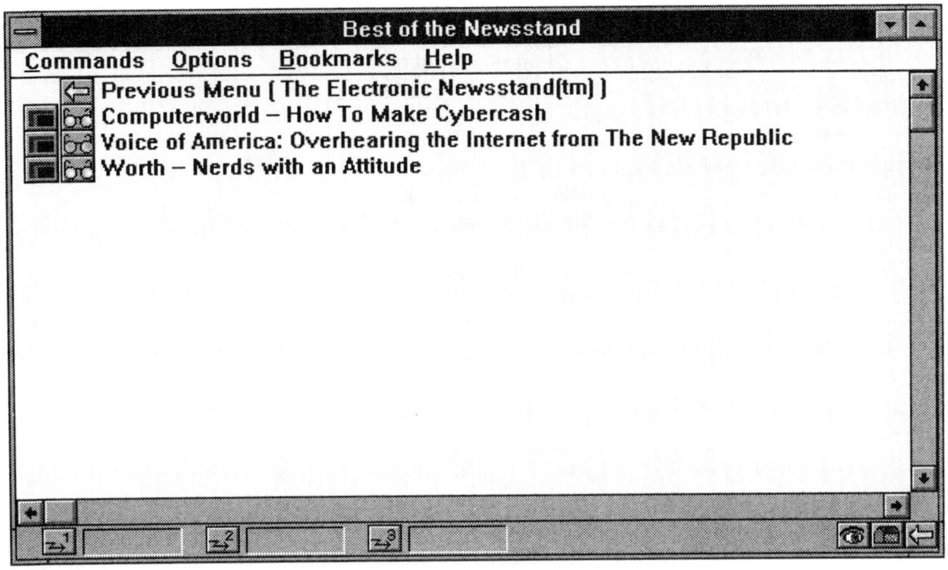

Figure 8-15: Electronic Newsstand sample material.

Electronic Publications

Type: Gopher

Address: gopher.cic.net

Summary: CICNet is probably the biggest archive available for electronic publications. Publications are organized by both alphabetical order and subject matter. An example directory of just a single section is shown in Figure 8-16.

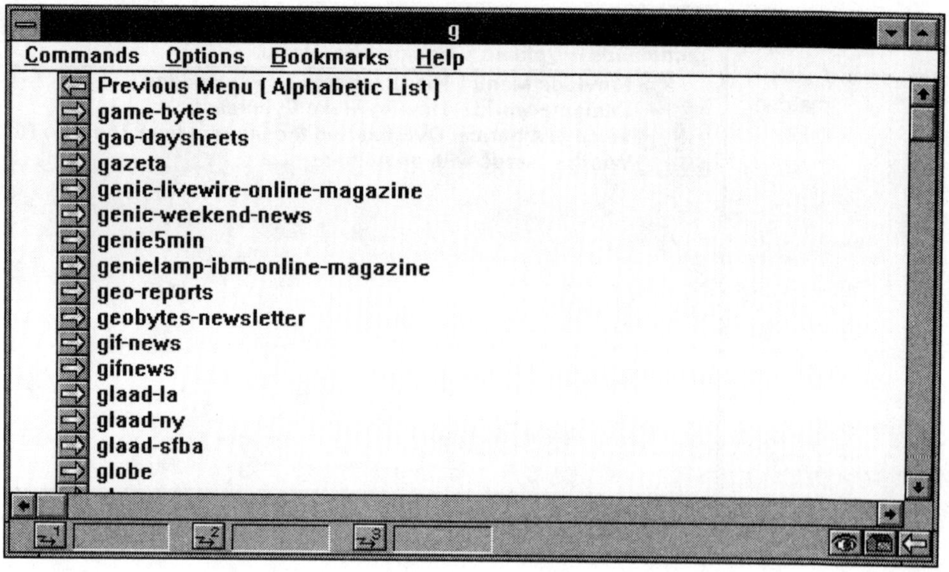

Figure 8-16: Directory of a single section of the electronic publications available on the CICNet Gopher server.

Electronic Serials List

Type: E-Mail
Address: listserv@uottawa.bitnet
Summary: An automated distribution server of a comprehensive list of electronic serials on various topics including computers, science, politics, literature, etc.

Send the following lines in an e-mail message:
GET EJOURNL1 DIRECTORY
GET EJOURNL2 DIRECTORY

EPA Gopher Server

Type: Gopher
Address: gopher.epa.gov
Summary: The Environmental Protection Agency has established a Gopher server to provide information about the agency's work on futures research. Pointers to all other Gopher servers operated by the federal government are also available.
Contact: Dave Rejeski
Head, Future Studies Unit
EPA
202/260-6523
rejeski.dave@epamail.epa.gov

Fax (Remote Printing) Experiment

Type: E-mail
Address: tpc-faq@town.hall.org
Summary: Based on the notion that sending packets of data across the Internet is significantly less expensive than placing long-distance telephone calls, a group of researchers began an experiment in providing fax services on the Internet during July 1993. To use the fax system, based on remote printing services available on the Internet, you send an e-mail message with the destination fax telephone number in the address field. MIME is supported, allowing you to include styled text and graphic images in your message. The e-mail message is automatically routed to an Internet site that has agreed to serve a local geographic "cell" for delivery of the fax message.

Participating regions, as of July 1993, include all of Japan, Australia, the Netherlands and Ireland. In addition, metropolitan Washington D.C., Silicon Valley and parts of the San Francisco Bay area are also participating in the experiment.

For more information on the service, send an e-mail message (the subject and message content are ignored) to tpc-faq@town.hall.org

FTP Sites List

Type: FTP
Address: pilot.njin.net
Pathname: /pub/ftp-list/ directory (download the file ftp.list).
Summary: Provides a list of publicly accessible FTP sites.

Geographic Server

Type: TELNET
Address: martini.eecs.umich.edu 3000
Summary: Provides geographic information including population, elevation, latitude, longitude and more by city or area code. You navigate the information with onscreen menus.

Government Policy Statements re: Internet

Acceptable Use Policies

Type: FTP
Address: nic.merit.edu
Pathname: /acceptable.use.policies/*.txt
Summary: Acceptable Use Policies for several networks that are part of the Internet. Policies are available for CICnet, CREN, JVNCnet, MICHnet, NorthWestNet, NSFnet, OARnet and SURAnet.

Cable-Telco Local Exchange Competition Bill

Type: FTP
Address: ftp.eff.org
Pathname: /pub/EFF/legislation/infra-act-s1086*
Summary: The full text of the Senate bill, introduced during Summer 1993, lifting the ban on cable television and telephone companies from entering the local exchange market. At the bill's first hearing, almost no support was heard, but the committee chair, Inouye, and ranking minority member, Danforth, seemed determined to enter the bill for consideration.

Economic Case for Public Subsidy of the Internet

Type: FTP
Address: ssugopher.sonoma.edu
Pathname: /pub/schickele.txt (or schickele.ps for PostScript version)
Summary: Sandra Schickele's economic analysis of a publicly funded Internet.

FEDLINE

Type: FTP
Address: ftp.nwnet.net
Pathname: /user-docs/government/fedline*
Summary: Not just politicians are interested in the electronic distribution of government information. "FEDLINE: A Feasibility Study of Establishment and Operation of FedWorld, A Government-Wide Information Locator

System at NTIS," is a document that outlines a governmental study on electronic distribution of information our tax dollars have already paid for. ASCII-text, WordPerfect 5.1 and PostScript versions of the study are available on the NorthWestNet FTP server.

High Performance Computing Act (HPCA)

Type: FTP
Address: nic.merit.edu
Pathname: /nren/hpca.1991/nrenbill.txt
Summary: The House-Senate final version of S. 272 (passed House on Nov. 20, 1991; passed Senate on Nov. 22, 1991; signed by President Bush on Dec. 9, 1991), forming the National Research and Education Network (NREN). The bill was originally authored by then-senator Al Gore.

Information Infrastructure and Technology Act (IITA)

Type: FTP
Address: nic.merit.edu
Pathname: /nren/iita.1992/gorebill.1992.txt
Summary: The press release, summary and draft text of then-senator Al Gore's Information Infrastructure and Technology Act of 1992.

National Research and Education Network (NREN)

Type: FTP
Address: nic.merit.edu
Pathname: /nren/nrencongr.txt (or nrencongr.ps for PostScript version)
Summary: The Director of the Office of Science and Technology's report to Congress on the National Research and Education Network (NREN).

OMB Circular A-130

Type: FTP
Address: nic.merit.edu
Pathname: /omb/omb.a130.rev2

Summary: The Office of Management and Budget's report on Management of Federal Information Resources. This report specifies how federal information is to be made publicly accessible in electronic form.

Health Security Act

Type: WWW, FTP, Gopher, WAIS
Address: sunsite.unc.edu
URL: http://sunsite.unc.edu/nhs/NHS-T-O-C
Summary: The Clinton administration's Health Security Act is available on the University of North Carolina's sunsite. The full text of the report and the full text of the legislation are available by FTP, Gopher, WAIS and WWW. A full hypertext version of the legislation for access via WWW clients was under development as of early November 1993.
FTP: sunsite.unc.edu in the /pub/academic/political-science/Health-Security-Act/ directory
Gopher: sunsite.unc.edu (select item 13 from the menu)
WAIS: sunsite.unc.edu port 210 in the Health-Security-Act database

Hot off the Tree (HOTT)

Type: TELNET
Address: melvyl.ucop.edu
Summary: Provides excerpts and abstracts of information technology articles from trade journals and online news services. HOTT is updated every week by the Technology Watch Information Group at the University of California at San Diego. Only two issues at a time are available online, so check this resource regularly if it's of interest to you.

Enter command **SHOW HOTT** at the command prompt. A menu of items will appear; enter your selection at the prompt. An example is shown in Figure 8-17.

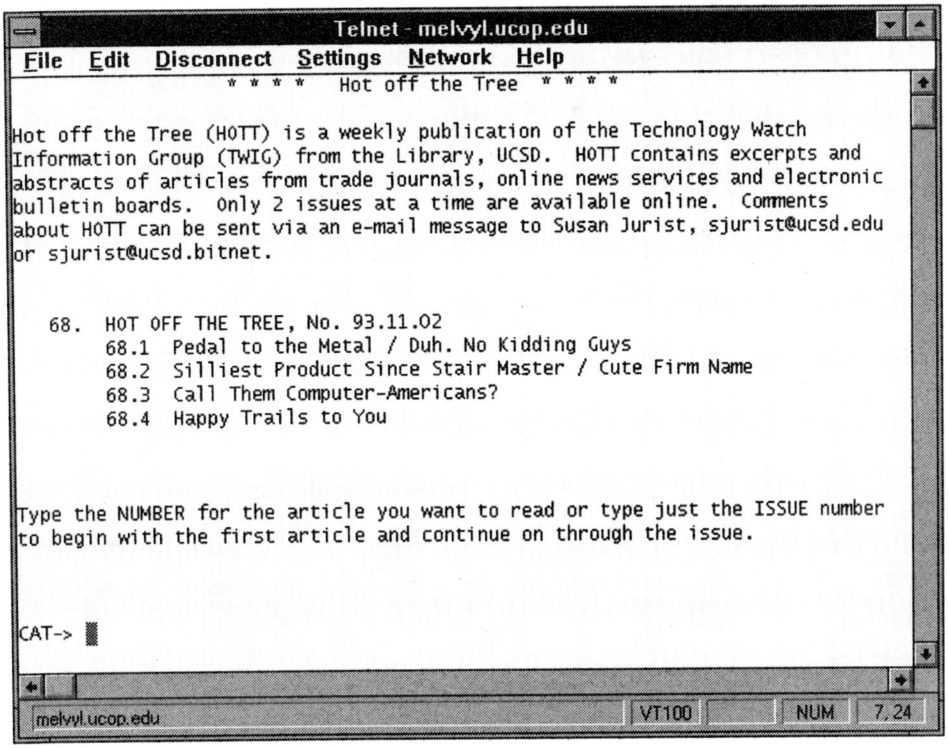

Figure 8-17: HOTT example session.

HPCwire

Type: TELNET
Address: hpcwire.ans.net
Summary: Provides menu-driven information searches related to high-performance computing and information services. Information about everything from workstations to supercomputers is available. Login as hpcwire. An example is shown in Figure 8-18.

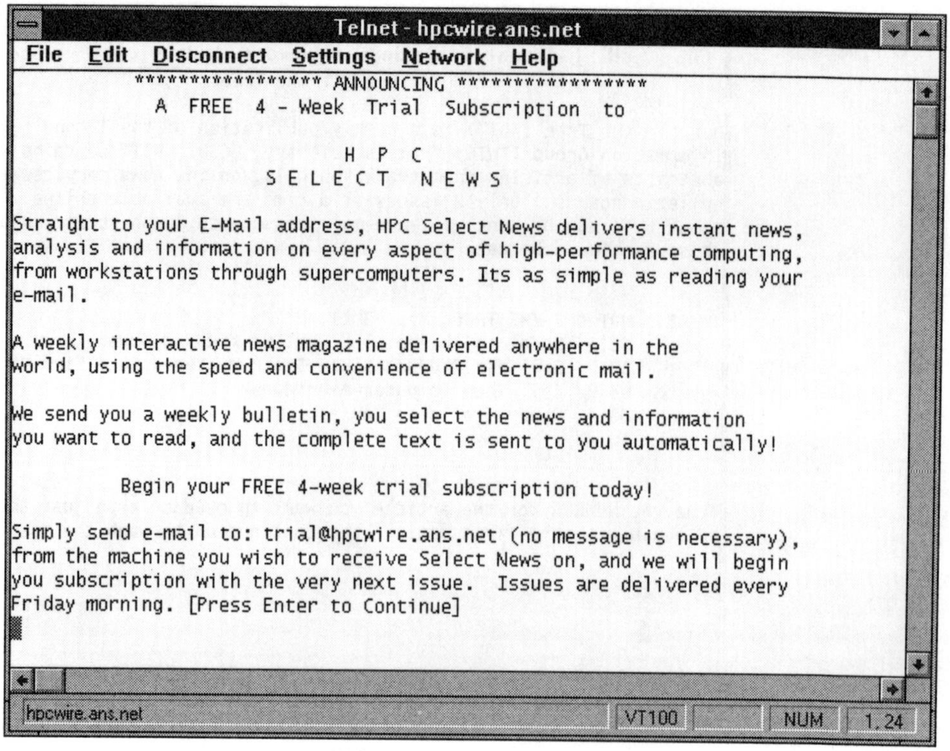

Figure 8-18: HPCwire example session.

Hytelnet Documentation

Type: FTP

Address: access.usask.ca

Pathname: /pub/hytelnet/README/

Summary: Access TELNET resources using a hypertext browser. Hytelnet is Peter Scott's implementation of a hypertext database of publicly accessible Internet sites. More than 1,300 sites are currently listed, including libraries, campus-wide information systems, Gopher, WAIS and WWW servers. The Hytelnet software for the Macintosh is currently implemented as a HyperCard stack. Hopefully, a stand-alone application will evolve for the Macintosh (after all, the original versions of Gopher for the Mac were implemented as HyperCard stacks).

You can use the UNIX version of Hytelnet with a terminal emulator:

Type: TELNET
Address: access.usask.ca
Login: hytelnet
A Hytelnet mailing list is also available:
Type: E-mail
Address: listserv@kentvm.kent.edu
Summary: Send a one-line mail message:
subscribe hytel-l *your name*
where *your name* is your first and last name (not your e-mail address).

Hytelnet Server

Type: TELNET
Address: access.usask.ca
Summary: Provides access to several university and library card catalogs. This is a useful way to search for books and journal articles on a specific topic, but you will not be able to access the full text of these resources via a remote Internet login.
Login as hytelnet

IEEE Document Vending Machine

Type: E-mail
Address: info.new.technology@ieee.org
Summary: If you have problems navigating the Internet, information vending machines offer an answer. Right now most of these vending machines are free, but expect to pay for the information they dispense in the future. These vending machines work by responding to e-mail messages.

Send a message—the contents of the message or the subject line don't matter. You'll receive an e-mail message containing an index of available files. Here are some of the more interesting files available as of Summer 1993:

- info.new.tech.bt@ieee.org (Broadcast Technology Society)
- info.new.tech.ce@ieee.org (Consumer Electronics Society)

- info.new.tech.e@ieee.org (Education Society)
- info.new.tech.it@ieee.org (Information Theory Society)
- info.new.tech.pc@ieee.org (Professional Communication Society)
- info.new.tech.sit@ieee.org (Society on Social Implications of Technology)

Incomplete Guide to the Internet

Type: FTP
Address: ftp.ncsa.uiuc.edu
Pathname: /misc/ directory
Summary: An excellent guide to the Internet written by the NCSA Education Group. Contains coverage of SLIP connections and the use of various freeware and shareware Net utilities.

Internet Company E-Mail Forwarding Service

Type: E-mail
Address: messenger@internet.com
Summary: In mid-August 1993, the Internet Company announced a service that allows Internet users to receive e-mail sent to addresses within their domains, even if they have only a single account on a commercial service. Called Messenger, the new service is designed to provide domain name type services for individuals and small businesses that do not enjoy full Internet connectivity. For example, a user with an MCI Mail account can use the Messenger service to establish a sort of pseudo domain name. Instead of an address like joeuser@mcimail.com, for instance, a series of addresses—joeuser@company.com, support@company.com, info@company.com, etc.—can all be created with all e-mail routed to the original e-mail address (joeuser@mcimail.com).

Three levels of Messenger service are available:

- **Personal Messenger** routes all mail sent to any username within a registered domain to one or more e-mail accounts, anywhere on the Internet.

- **Corporate Messenger** allows specific addresses within the domain to forward mail to several e-mail accounts. This permits "virtual organizations" to be designed, where e-mail addressed to joeuser@company.com is routed differently than that addressed to jilluser@company.com.
- **Organization Messenger** allows large organizations to offer distinct e-mail addresses within their domain.

Internet Information Mailing List

Type: E-mail
Address: tristan@gibbs.oit.unc.edu
Summary: A general information distribution list related to services, programs, guides and frequently asked questions (FAQs) about the Internet and various services offered on it.

To subscribe:

Send a brief message requesting to be added to the distribution list to tristan@gibbs.oit.unc.edu

Internet Maps

Type: FTP
Address: ftp.merit.edu
Pathname: /maps/ directory
Summary: A collection of PostScript-format maps of the Internet. You must have a PostScript-capable printer to be able to print and view these maps.

Internet Monthly report

Type: FTP
Address: nis.nsf.net
Pathname: /internet/newsletters/internet.monthly.report/ directory
Summary: Monthly Internet usage reports. The reports contain information from the Internet Research Group concerning the accomplishments and problems of the participating organizations. Each report usually con-

tains an article from the Internet Architecture Board and a few Internet Engineering reports. Brief articles are also submitted by the various regional networks, and a calendar of upcoming events is included.

Internet Relay Chat (IRC) Documentation

Type: FTP
Address: cs.bu.edu
Pathname: /irc/support/tutorial*
Summary: Documentation and tutorial for using IRC for real-time discussions divided into separate channels on the Internet.

Internet Society Archive

Type: FTP
Address: nnsc.nsf.net
Pathname: /internet-society/ directory
Summary: Contains a collection of Internet Society materials, including status reports, position statements, etc.

Internet Talk Radio Archives

Type: FTP
Address: ftp.uu.net
Pathname: /usenet/news.answers/internet-talk-radio/anonymous-ftp-list.z
Summary: A listing of FTP archive sites that make the Internet Talk Radio sound files available via anonymous FTP. Current FTP archive sites in the United States include (*make sure to use the site that's geographically closest to your physical location*):

Address	**Pathname**
ftp.nau.edu (134.114.64.70)	/talk-radio/
csn.org (128.138.213.21)	/pub/internet-talk-radio/
ftp.cic.net (192.131.22.2)	/pub/talk-radio/
sunsite.unc.edu (152.2.22.81)	/pub/talk-radio/
ftp.sterling.com (192.124.9.1)	/talk-radio/
ftp.acsu.buffalo.edu (128.205.7.9)	/pub/talk-radio/

Address	Pathname
ftp.uoregon.edu (128.223.32.35)	/pub/internet-talk-radio/
ftp.utexas.edu (128.83.185.16)	/pub/itr/
ecosys.drdr.virginia.edu (128.143.86.233)	/pub/talk-radio/
radio.ans-core.com (192.77.167.77)	/pub/radio/

Internet World

As of September 1993, *Internet World* is no longer a newsletter and is now an advertiser-supported magazine. *Internet World* is published by Meckler Corp. and appears bi-monthly. Subscriptions are available for $30 per year. The first magazine issue includes articles by Mike Godwin (EFF), Peter Deutsch (Archie), Jane Smith (CNIDR), Mike Barrow (Boston Computer Society), Mary Reindeau (The World) and others. The first magazine issue was available at the Interop/Fall 1993 show (August 23–27, 1993) in San Francisco.

Contact: Meckler Corporation
11 Ferry Lane West
Westport, CT 06880
800/632-5537
203/454-7269 (Fax)
meckler@jvnc.net

Daniel Dern, Editor
Internet World
P.O. Box 309
Newton Center, MA 02159
617/969-7947
617/969-7949 (Fax)
ddern@world.std.com

InterNIC

Type: Organization
Address: info@ls.internic.net
Summary: A set of three organizations funded in part by the National Science Foundation dedicated to serving the needs of the Internet community. The InterNIC specializes in helping new users and in compiling registration, directory and database information. You can call their hotline at 800/444-4345 for more details.

Interpersonal Computing and Technology Electronic Journal

Type: E-mail
Address: listserv@guvm.georgetown.edu
Summary: *Interpersonal Computing and Technology* (IPCT: An Electronic Journal for the 21st Century) is a peer-reviewed electronic journal focusing on topics including the use of electronic networks in the classroom, electronic publishing, library applications, professional relationships and the general use of electronic communication. The IPCT-J distribution list will carry only abstracts and a table of contents for each issue.

To subscribe:
send a one line e-mail message:
subscribe ipct-j *your name*
where *your name* is your first and last names (not your login name).

A general discussion list (IPCT-L) for the same range of topics is also available.

To subscribe:
send a one line e-mail message:
subscribe ipct-l *your name*
where *your name* is your first and last names (not your login name).

Articles can be submitted to Gerald Phillips, editor-in-chief: gmp3@psuvm.psu.edu

Introduction to TCP/IP

Type: FTP
Address: topaz.rutgers.edu
Pathname: /tcp-ip-docs/ directory
Summary: An excellent guide to TCP/IP. This is the best and most clearly written reference available for installing, configuring and administering a TCP/IP connection.

IP Address Resolver

Type: Directory Service
Address: resolve@cs.widener.edu
Summary: In body of e-mail message, enter:
site *address*
where *address* is the name of the site in the domain.top-domain format.
The service will return the IP address of the site.

Law Library

Type: TELNET
Address: liberty.uc.wlu.edu
Summary: Provides law libraries and legal research. Information on law library archives, White House electronic access, the United Nations, gay rights, adoption laws, privacy rights, copyright and much more is available.
Login as lawlib. An example session is shown in Figure 8-19.

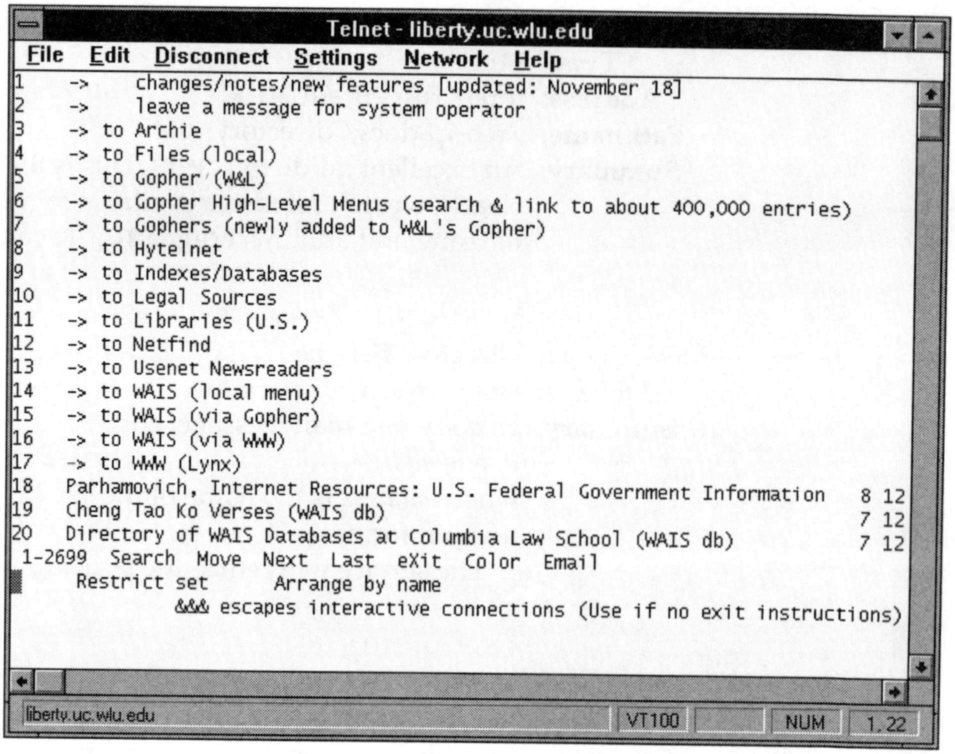

Figure 8-19: Law Library example session.

LawNet

Type: TELNET

Address: dessert.law.columbia.edu or lawnet.law.columbia.edu

Summary: Offers legal information and card catalog access. Columbia University's Law School library card catalog, information server, academic services and career services are all accessible.

Login as lawnet. An example session screen is shown in Figure 8-20.

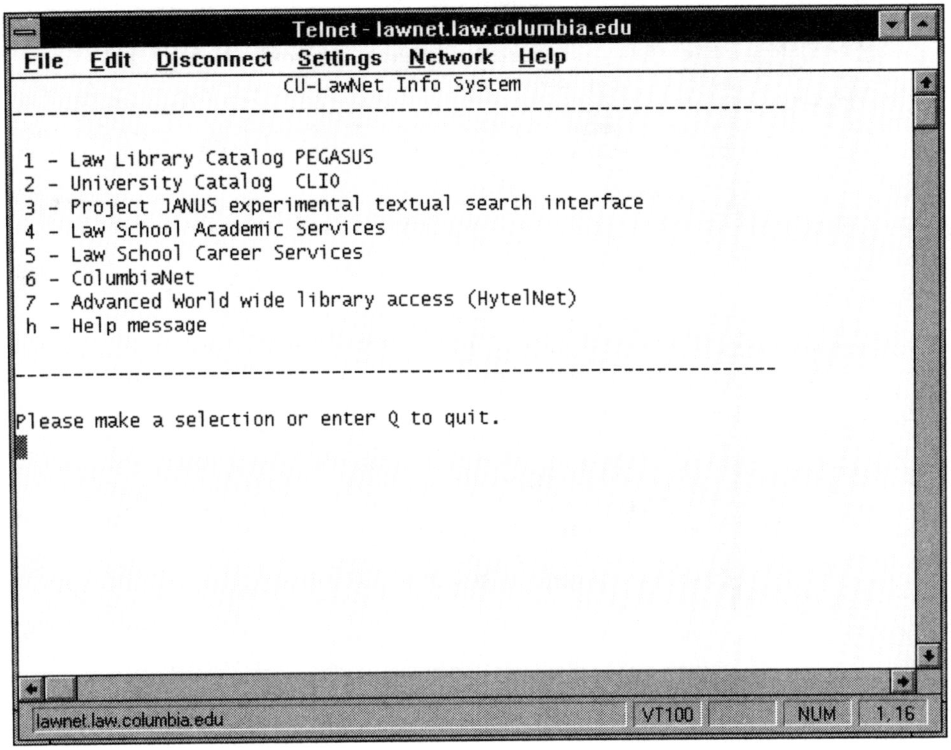

Figure 8-20: Lawnet example session.

Library of Congress

Type: TELNET

Address: dra.com

Summary: Provides access to the catalog of the Library of Congress. Again, you won't be able to access the full text of the library's holdings, but this is a very useful resource when simply compiling a list of possible sources for a topic of research. Various methods of searching are available, as shown in Figure 8-21.

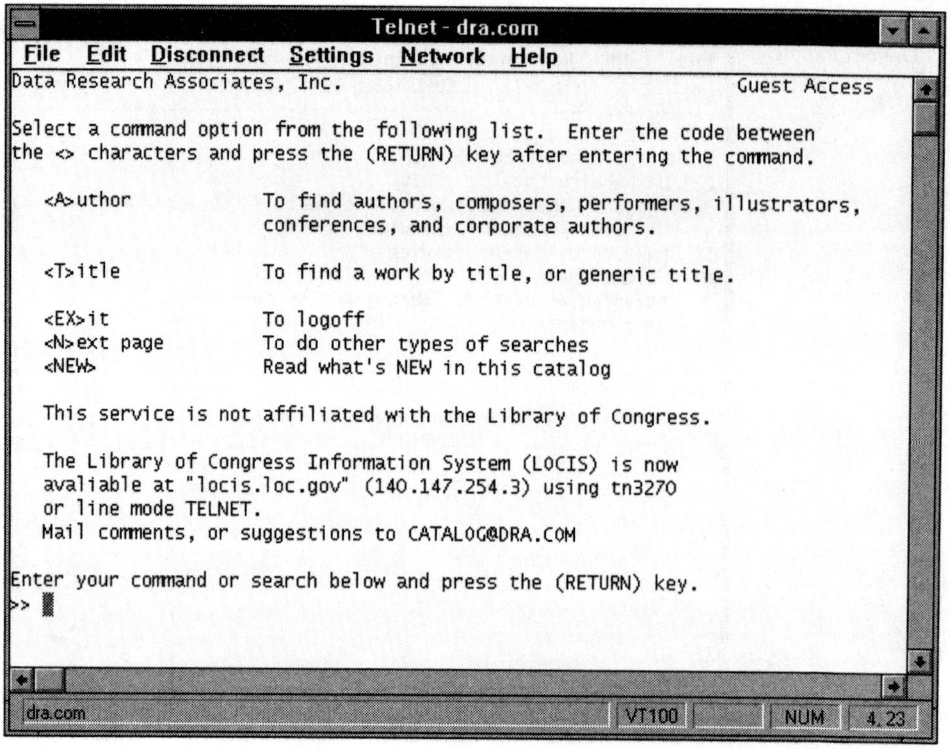

Figure 8-21: Library of Congress searching methods.

Library of Congress Information System (LOCIS) Quick Search Guide

Type: FTP
Address: seq1.loc.gov
Pathname: /pub/LC-On.line/
Summary: A guide to using the Library of Congress Information System (LOCIS). Available in both ASCII and Microsoft Word formats. Note that the ASCII format version is not properly formatted for an 80-character per line display.

LIBS

Type: TELNET
Address: nessie.cc.wwu.edu
Summary: Provides gateway access to many TELNET services. Library card catalogs in various countries are accessible, as are several campus-wide information systems.

This service is referred to as a gateway because you can access other services through this portal.

Login as LIBS. An example session is shown in Figure 8-22.

Figure 8-22: LIBS example session.

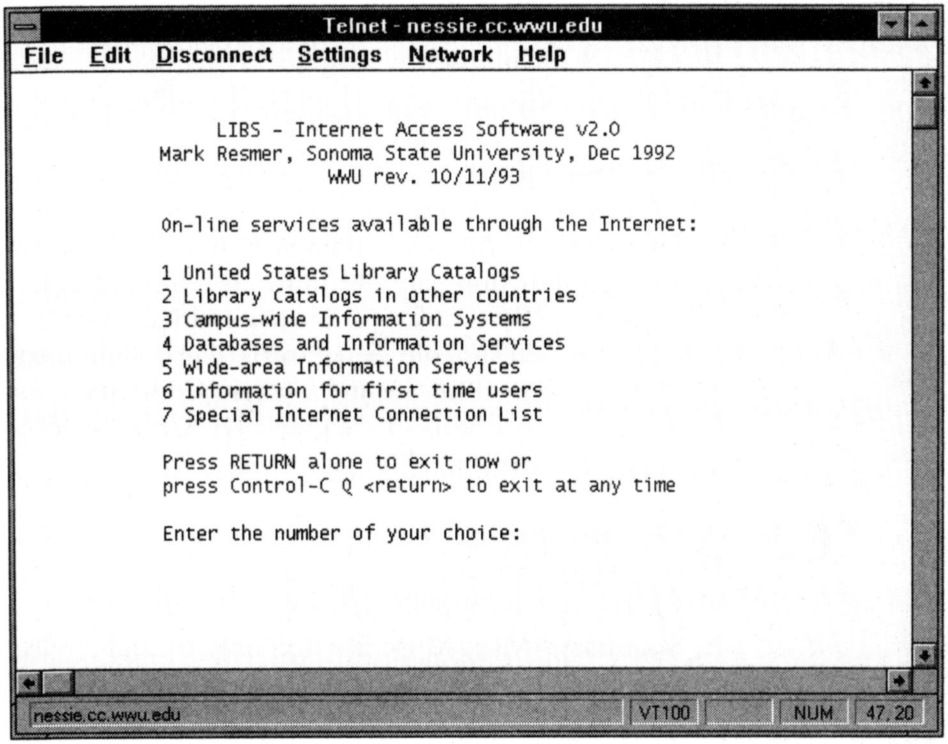

Mailing Lists List

Type: E-mail

Address: listserv@vm1.nodak.edu

Summary: An automated distribution server of a comprehensive list of e-mail mailing lists. For more information on mailing lists, see "Electronic Mailing Lists" beginning on page 137.

Send the following lines in an e-mail message:

LIST GLOBAL

Mbone FAQ

Type: FTP
Address: venera.isi.edu
Pathname: /mbone/faq.txt
Summary: The Mbone provides live audio and video multicasting across a virtual network that lives on top of the Internet.

MELVYL

Type: TELNET
Address: melvyl.ucop.edu
Summary: The MELVYL database contains the entire catalog of the University of California's monographs and periodicals. Several California state universities' holdings are accessible via MELVYL. The system also provides access to MEDLINE and Current Contents. Other systems are accessible by a gateway. Access to some resources is restricted by password.

MicroMuse

Type: TELNET
Address: michael.ai.mit.edu
Summary: MicroMuse is a text-only virtual environment under development at MIT. It's like the old-style text adventure games, with a politically correct spin. Education, cooperation and concern for the environment are stressed in this game-like environment. MicroMuse is something easier experienced than explained; try it.

Login as guest. An example session screen is shown in Figure 8-23.

Figure 8-23: MicroMuse example session.

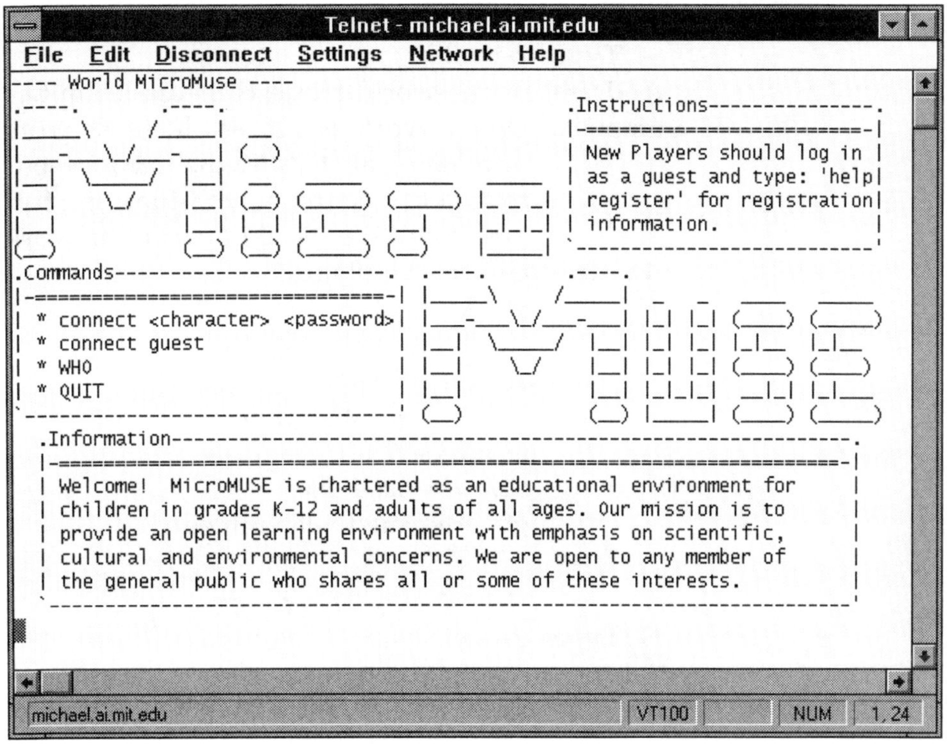

Mining the Internet

Type: FTP
Address: ucdavis.edu
Pathname: /ucd.netdocs/mining/ directory
Summary: This text file offers a good overview of the information resources offered on the Internet, using a mining metaphor.

MIT Media Lab ACCESS Service

Type: FTP
Address: media-lab.media.mit.edu
Pathname: /access/
Summary: MIT's Media Lab has established an anonymous FTP server to provide information about current projects, publications and sponsors.

MIT Media Lab Online World

Type: E-mail

Address: online-world-request@media-lab.mit.edu

Summary: Online World is a low-volume electronic mailing list originating at MIT's Media Lab focused on discussions related to electronic publishing, the future of news media and the social impact of networks.

Contact: Gilberte Houbard
MIT Media Lab
Room E15-430
20 Ames Street
Cambridge, MA 02139
617/253-9787
617/258-6264 (Fax)
gilberte@media-lab.mit.edu

Movie Database

Type: E-mail

Address: movie@ibmpcug.co.uk

Summary: Provides a database of movies, actors and directors via e-mail. Send an e-mail message with the single line "help" (without quotes) to receive complete instructions on using the database.

Command	**Returns**
TITLE	information about the movie specified
DIRCT	information about the director specified
ACTOR	information abut the actor specified
COMPO	information about the composer specified
WRITE	information about the writer specified
CINEM	information about the cinematographer specified
MOVIE	full list for movie plus lists of all other movies by cast and crew

For example:

MOVIE O Lucky Man
DIRECTOR Kubrick, Stanley
ACTOR McDowell, Malcolm

Would return full information on the movie *O Lucky Man*, the director Stanley Kubrick and the actor Malcolm McDowell.

MTV Hits the Net

Type: FTP, Finger and Gopher
Address: mtv.com
Pathname: /various/
Summary: MTV vee-jay Adam Curry has registered the mtv.com domain name and has begun to provide popular-music-related information accessible via Gopher and FTP. Curry is also publishing a shareware electronic newsletter focusing on the popular music scene. Eventually graphic images, lyrics and audio files will be available. The top-level menu of the MTV Gopher server is shown in Figure 8-24.

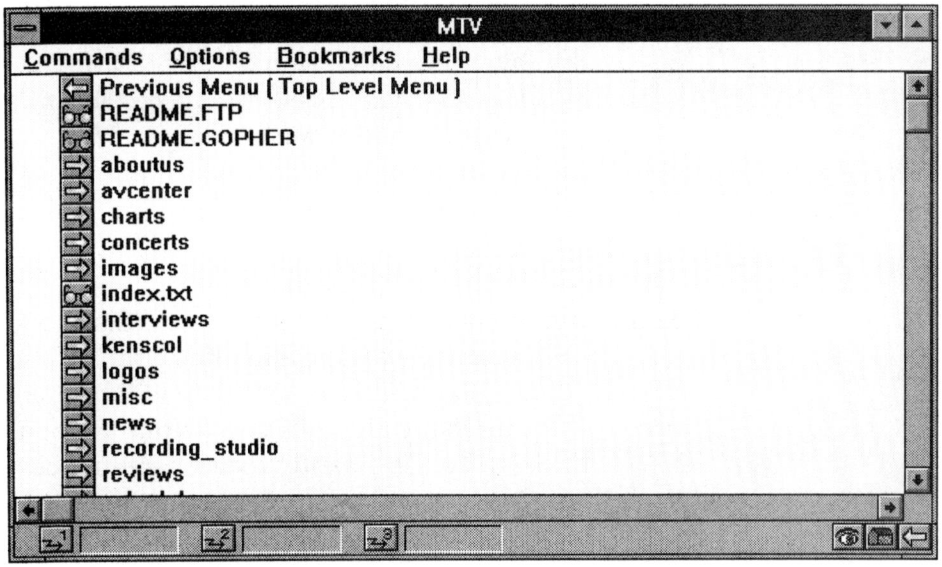

Figure 8-24: Top-level menu of MTV Gopher server.

MUD FAQ

Type: FTP
Address: ftp.math.okstate.edu
Pathname: /pub/muds/misc/mud-faq/part*
Summary: MUD is an acronym for Multi-User Dimensions (or Dungeons). A MUD is a real-time interaction that is usually based upon some sort of social role-playing.

Music Server

Type: FTP
Address: ftp.uwp.edu
Pathname: /pub/lyrics/ directory
Summary: This site is popular with college students. It provides lyrics, pictures, guitar chords and tablature for a wide array of popular music.

Nasdaq Financial Executive Journal

Type: WWW
Address: http://fatty.law.cornell.edu:80/usr2/wwwtext/nasdaq/nasdtoc.html
Summary: The Nasdaq Stock Market and the Legal Information Institute at Cornell Law School have made available a hypermedia version of the *Nasdaq Financial Executive Journal* (NFEJ). The NFEJ is accessible via the World Wide Web in HTML format.

Network News Mailing List

Type: Mailing List
Address: listserv@vm1.nodak.edu
Summary: A collection of Internet resources and facts. Since this resource exists as a mailing list, you can expect fairly regular updates—and they will be mailed to you automatically until you revoke your subscription to the list. This is a handy tool for staying current with the Net's resources.

Send a one-line message in e-mail:
subscribe nnews *your name*

where *your name* is your full name (not your e-mail Address).

New Users' Guide

Type: FTP
Address: nysernet.org
Pathname: /pub/resources/guides/ directory
Summary: New User's Guide to Unique and Interesting Resources on the Internet is authored by the New York State Education and Research Network (NYSERNet). It

covers about 50 Internet resources in more than 145 pages.

NorthWestNet User Services Guide

Type: FTP
Address: ftphost.nwnet.net
Pathname: /nic/nwnet/user-guide/ directory
Summary: NorthWestNet User Services Internet Resource Guide (about 300 pages) covers electronic mail, FTP, remote login, supercomputer access and online library catalogs.

NREN Information

Type: FTP
Address: nis.nsf.net
Pathname: /nren/ directory
Summary: Collection of information on the National Research and Education Network (NREN).

The Online World

Type: FTP
Address: oak.oakland.edu
Pathname: /pub/msdos/info/online10.zip
Summary: Norwegian author Odd de Presno has released his book, *The Online World*, as shareware. *The Online World* was previously published in Norwegian as a 275-page hardcover (ISBN: 82-90628-67-6) and is still available in bookstores. The work covers the practical side of using the global networks and provides examples ranging from databases to entertainment. The FTP-accessible file is in ASCII text format and can be read with any text editor or word processing program.
Contact: opresno@extern.uio.no

PGP v2.2 Encryption Utility

Type: FTP
Address: soda.berkeley.edu
Summary: PGP 2.2 is a data encryption utility that uses the IDEA cipher patented in Switzerland. This utility is of special

interest because it has not been sanctioned for general use by the National Security Agency (NSA), which governs issues of coding and encryption in the United States. (This means that data encoded with PGP is probably safer from prying eyes than it would be if you used a "government-approved" encryption method.)

Anonymous public key server sites:
pgp-public-keys@junkbox.cc.iastate.edu
tbird.cc.iastate.edu [/usr/explorer/public-keys.pgp]
pgp-public-keys@toxicwaste.mit.edu
toxicwaste.mit.edu [/pub/keys/public-keys.pgp]
pgp-public-keys@phil.utmb.edu
phil.utmb.edu [/pub/pgp/public-keys.pgp]

Project Gutenberg

Type: FTP
Address: mrcnext.cso.uiuc.edu
Pathname: /etext/ directory
Summary: Project Gutenberg was formed to encourage the creation and distribution of electronic text, hoping to have one trillion volumes available by the end of 2001. Texts currently available include *Alice in Wonderland*, *Peter Pan*, Shakespeare's complete works, and Milton's *Paradise Lost*.

Prospero Documentation

Type: FTP
Address: prospero.isi.edu
Pathname: /pub/prospero/doc/README-prospero-documents
Summary: Prospero provides a user-centered view of remote files on FTP servers.

Public Network News Servers

Type: Network News
Address: various, see Summary
Summary: These publicly accessible network news servers are sites where you can login to read (and in some places, respond to) network news articles.

cc.usu.edu (read only)
etl.go.jp (read/post)
europa.eng.gtefsd.com (read only)
fconvx.ncifcrf.gov (read only)
gaia.ucs.orst.edu (read only)
hermes.chpc.utexas.edu (read only)
mailer.cc.fsu.edu (read only)
munnari.oz.au (read/post)
netnews.cc.lehigh.edu (read only)
news.funet.fi (read only)
news.unomaha.edu (read only)
news.yale.edu (read only)
news.ysu.edu (read only)
newshub.nosc.mil (read only)
newsserver.jvnc.net (read only)
quip.eecs.umich.edu (read/post)
sbcs.sunysb.edu (read/post)
sol.ctr.columbia.edu (read/post)
suntan.ec.usf.edu (read/post)
uicvm.uic.edu (read only)
umd5.umd.edu (read only)
usenet.coe.montana.edu (read only)
uunet.ca (read/post)
uwec.edu (read/post)
vax1.mankato.msus.edu (read only)
vaxc.cc.monash.edu.au (read/post)
willis1.cis.uab.edu (read only)

SIGGRAPH Publications

Type: FTP
Address: siggraph.org
Pathname: /ftp/publications/May_93_online

Summary: The Association of Computing Machinery's (ACM) special interest group for graphics (SIGGRAPH) publications for May 1993.

Special Internet Connections

Type: FTP
Address: csd4.csd.uwm.edu
Pathname: /pub/inet.services.txt
Summary: Scott Yanoff's excellent guide to Internet services.

Also available by mailing list by sending a subscription request to yanoff@csd4.csd.uwm.edu. The list is also posted regularly to several USENET newsgroups including biz.comp.services and alt.internet.services.

Sports Schedules

Type: TELNET
Address: culine.colorado.edu
Summary: Provides daily schedules for a wide array of professional sporting events, including hockey, basketball and football.

TELNET to the specified port for the sport schedule you want:

NBA: culine.colorado.edu 859
NHL: culine.colorado.edu 860
MLB: culine.colorado.edu 862
NFL: culine.colorado.edu 863

Enter **HELP** for online help.

After login, press **Enter** for today's schedules.

Terminal Compromise

Type: FTP
Address: ftp.netsys.com or soda.berkeley.edu
Pathname: /pub/novel/
Summary: The first novel distributed on the Internet, Winn Schwartau's *Terminal Compromise* is a high-tech thriller about the invasion of the United States by computer terrorists. The novel was first published in print (ISBN: 0-962-87000-5) by INTER.PACT Press. *Terminal Compro-*

mise is being distributed electronically, on the Internet, as shareware.

Travel Agency on the Net

Type: E-mail
Address: fly@hpcwire.ans.net
Summary: This is a travel agency connected to the Internet. For a price quote on air fare, send a request for a quote, including the departure city, departure date, destination and return date. They'll either call you or send you e-mail with the best fare they can find.

Travel Information

Type: FTP
Address: ccu.umanitoba.ca
Pathname: /pub/rec-travel/ directory
Summary: Provides worldwide travel information including travel guides and FAQs. Here's a brief excerpt from Gary Fischman's entry for St. Maarten:

There isn't much in the way of tourist sights in St. Maarten/St. Martin. There is the old ruins of the fort in Marigot. It's up on a small hill next to the Marigot waterfront. The fort itself isn't much to see, but there is a great view of the northwest corner of the island.

University of North Carolina LaUNChpad

Type: TELNET
Address: launchpad.unc.edu
Summary: Provides access to a wide variety of Campus Wide Information Servers (CWIS). From LaUNChpad, you can also use a menu-driven interface to access a number of other Internet resources, including WAIS searches, Gopher servers, Supreme Court ruling databases, CARL and many of the other resources listed here. The advantage is that, as when working with Gopher, LaUNChpad automatically logs you in and out of each site—you don't have to memorize domain addresses and login passwords.

Login as launch

At the main menu, select item 3, "On-line Information Systems (LIBTEL)." An example login to the University of Minnesota Lumina system is shown in Figure 8-25.

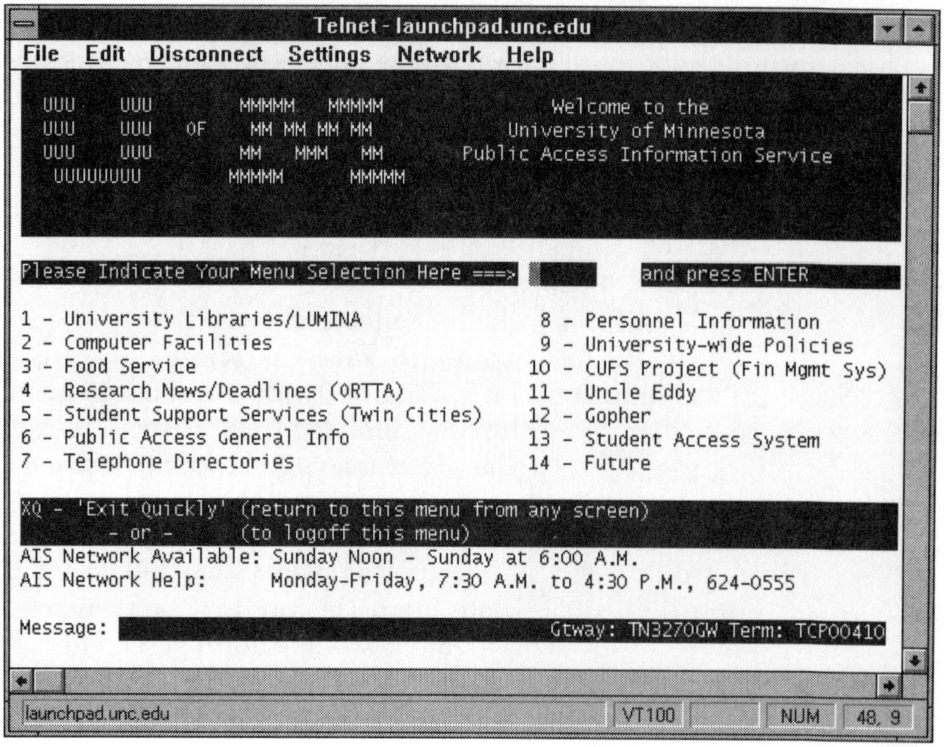

Figure 8-25: LaUNChpad login to the University of Minnesota Lumina system.

U.S. State Department Travel Advisories

Type: FTP

Address: world.std.com

Pathname: /obi/US.StateDept/Travel/ directory

Summary: Foreign travel advisories provided by the U.S. State Department. The advisories are stored by country name, and each new advisory is appended to the end of the file.

VAX Manual

Type: FTP
Address: decoy.uoregon.edu
Pathname: /pub/vaxbook/vms.ps (make sure you also get the errata files that are updated on a regular basis).
Summary: Joe St. Sauver's excellent guide to the University of Oregon's VAX8000 system. At more than 300 pages, the guide provides information that is useful for general network users, not just VAX users.

Veronica FAQ

Type: FTP
Address: veronica.scs.unr.edu
Pathname: /veronica/veronica-faq
Summary: Veronica is used to search for title keywords of Gopher items.

Voices from the Net

Type: E-mail
Address: swilbur@andy.bgsu.edu or mgardbe@andy.bgsu.edu
Summary: *Voices from the Net* is an electronic publication that focuses on providing an "outlet for the expression of views on and about the 'Net.'" These views will include interviews, essays and other expository forms. The first issue was released in early August 1993 and included an interview with Tom Maddox, an essay by Andy Hawks and comments from others. The second issue (released in September) included interviews with Adam Curry and Billy Idol.

To subscribe:
send a one line e-mail message with the word:
Subscribe
with the Subject line:
Voices From the Net

Washington University Gateway

Type: TELNET
Address: library.wustl.edu
Summary: Provides gateway access to many TELNET services.
Login as services
An example of the services provided is shown in Figure 8-26.

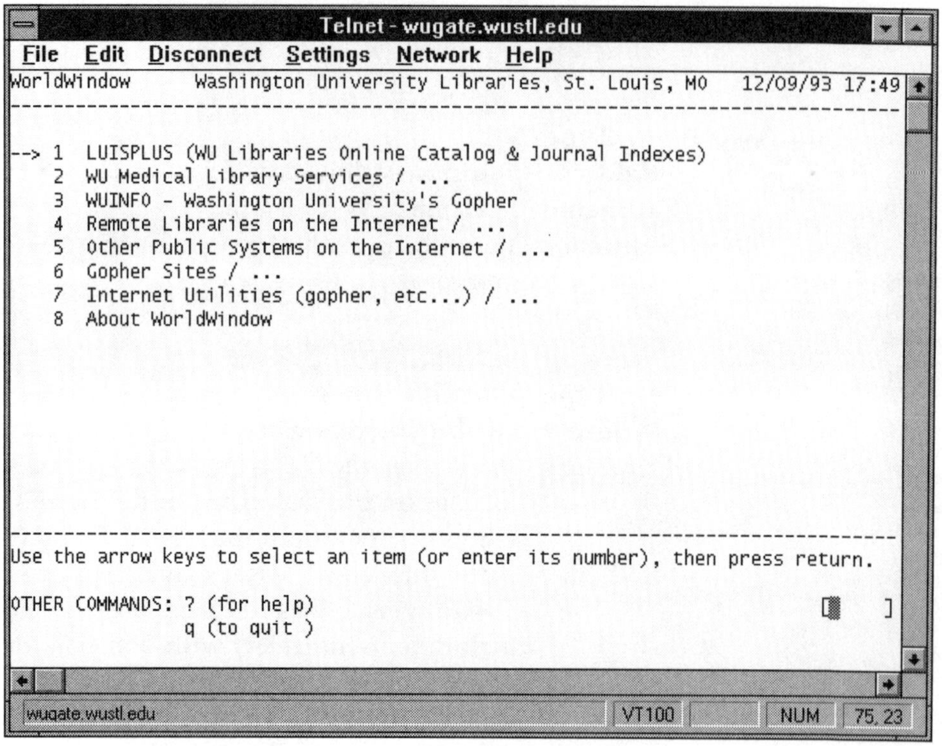

Figure 8-26: Washington University Telnet gateway services.

Weather Maps

Type: FTP
Address: vmd.cso.uiuc.edu
Pathname: /pub/wx/ directory
Summary: Provides current infrared weather maps and surface analysis.

Weather Service

Type: TELNET
Address: downwind.sprl.umich.edu 3000
Summary: Provides complete weather forecasts as well as other related information, such as earthquake reports, ski conditions and more.

White House Almanac Information Server

Type: E-mail
Address: almanac@esusda.gov
Summary: E-mail accessible documents from the White House concerning press briefings, Executive Orders, photo opportunities and other information. Gopher, WAIS and Mosaic access is also available.

To request a specific document, send an e-mail message to:

almanac@esusda.gov

and in the body of the message:

send white-house *nn*

where *nn* is the number of the document you wish to receive.

To receive a guide to other documents available from the USDA Extension Service Almanac, in the body of the message:

send catalog

To receive instructions for using Almanac, in the body of the message:

send guide

Contact: wh-admin@esusda.gov

White House E-Mail

Type: E-mail
Address: president@whitehouse.gov and vice.president@whitehouse.gov
Summary: Send e-mail to the president and vice president of the United States.

White House Press Releases

Type: E-mail
Address: clinton-info@campaign92.org
Summary: This e-mail server is not designed to answer e-mail letters, comments or requests for specific information. It is designed solely to distribute press releases.

The e-mail server works by reading the subject line of your message and taking an appropriate action based on that subject line.

Subject: RECEIVE HELP
Help file for the e-mail server.

Subject: RECEIVE ECONOMIC POLICY
Press releases related to the economy including budget news, technology policy reviews, etc.

Subject: RECEIVE FOREIGN POLICY
Press releases related to foreign policy.

Subject: RECEIVE SOCIAL POLICY
Press releases related to social issues.

Subject: RECEIVE SPEECHES
All speeches made by the president and the most important speeches made by other administration officials.

Subject: RECEIVE NEWS
Transcripts of White House Communications office press conferences.

Subject: RECEIVE ALL
All releases from all subject areas.

(More) White House Press Releases

Type: FTP
Address: sunsite.unc.edu
Pathname: /home3/wais/white-house-papers/ directory
Summary: News and press releases related to economic policy, foreign policy, social policy, press conferences and speeches.

Conclusion

So now you're a pro at practically all things Internet. What's that? You feel like we've just gone around the world in 80 days (or perhaps only eight)? You're still overwhelmed with all the things you can do, people you can meet and places you can visit? The secret to finding your way around the Internet is to forget about where you're going and just go. Explore. Take a sidetrip. Have fun.

The good news is, you're not on your own. There are plenty of friendly people all over the Net who can offer you help whenever you need it. And just by buying this book, you'll get two electronic updates free. (For more details on taking advantage of the electronic updates, see "Electronic Updates & Visitors Center" beginning on page 309.)

But for now, you might want to get back out into the Net to check out a few of the resources listed in this chapter. And don't forget to drop me a line if you spot something extraordinary.

Electronic Updates & Visitors Center

Appendix A

Electronic Updates & Visitors Center

New services are added to the Internet on a daily—sometimes hourly—basis. It's impossible for one person to keep up with everything that's happening on the Net.

I grew up in the 1960s, and I was constantly told by my elders that there was no such thing as a free lunch. I think the saying originated with signs that used to hang in taverns offering free lunches.

I've got good news for you: there is a free lunch. (OK, you had to buy this book to get the free updates, but you had to buy a drink or two to get a free lunch in the taverns of my youth.)

Because the Internet is in a constant state of flux, Ventana Press and Arts & Farces are offering you two free electronic updates to this book. The updates will include: reviews of the latest Internet client software releases, summaries of new information resources, tips and tricks for finding your way around the Net, news about trends and industry developments, and much more.

Updates Are Just a Postcard Away

It's easy to make sure you receive your exclusive electronic updates, which are available only to owners of the *Tour Guide*. Updates will be distributed via e-mail. This way, they'll be sent directly to your electronic mailbox. To receive your free updates:

- Fill out the response card bound into the back of the book. Make sure you've completed every portion of the card. (Incomplete cards will not be acknowledged and will not qualify for the two free updates.)

- Make certain you've included your Internet-accessible e-mail address in the standard format: username@domain.top-domain. (Addresses in any other format will not be acknowledged and will not qualify for the two free electronic updates.)
- If you'd like to receive occasional informational mailings about other books and materials about the Internet and the PC, simply check the appropriate box on the card.
- Note that the updates may be larger than can fit through the e-mail gateways of some of the commercial information services like CompuServe and America Online. These updates will be sent to you in multiple segments.

The Electronic Visitors Center

It's always nice to have a "home base" when traveling in strange and foreign territory. The Visitors Center is a place where *Tour Guide* owners can stop and rest on their ramblings through the Net. And better still, it's also where you'll find the latest versions of all the great freeware and shareware software discussed in the *Tour Guide*, as well as the latest updates, news, tips, tricks and other hot information.

Access *The Windows Internet Tour Guide* Visitors Center by FTP at ftp.farces.com, using Gopher at gopher.farces.com, and using Mosaic at www.farces.com.

Current versions of interesting Windows programs for use on the Internet are available via anonymous FTP. Special Read Me files and other goodies are available there. The Visitors Center is open to anyone, not just *Tour Guide* readers, so spread the word.

Also in the Visitors Center you'll find the latest versions of the programs discussed and demonstrated throughout the *Tour Guide*.

How to Subscribe to a Full Year of Updates

The Windows Internet Tour Guide electronic updates will be published and distributed on a quarterly basis. As a purchaser of this book, you'll receive the first two updates free of charge. If you want to subscribe to additional quarterly updates, the current subscription rate is $25 per year (4 issues).

To receive a full year of updates, simply send a check for $25 (U.S. funds only) payable to Arts & Farces to:

Arts & Farces
2285 Stewart Avenue
Suite 1315
Saint Paul, MN 55116

For more information on subscribing to future updates, send e-mail to: tour-guide-request@farces.com

A Note About Privacy

The Internet is a place where privacy has to be balanced against the free flow of information. The real world is no different. You'll notice there's a good deal of information you're providing on *The Windows Internet Tour Guide* electronic update request postcards. But how that information is used is up to you. If, like many Internet and PC enthusiasts, you like to stay informed about the latest publications and related materials that are relevant to your interests, simply check the appropriate box on the card. Otherwise, the information you provide is for use by Arts & Farces only. I don't sell, lend or rent our mailing list. The transactional information you provide is between the two of us, and is no one's business but our own.

Quick-Reference Page

Use this page and its reverse side to keep track of important information about your Internet account. The information will always be close at hand, even when you aren't logged in to the Internet. You can also copy this page and fax or mail it to vendors and software developers to aid them in their technical suppport efforts.

Your Internet Account Information

User Name ______________________________

Computer Name ______________________________

Domain Name ______________________________

E-mail Address ______________________________

IP Address of Your Computer ______________________________

IP Subnet Mask of Your Computer ______________________________

IP Address of Domain Name Server ______________________________

IP Address of Local Gateway ______________________________

SLIP/PPP Access Number ______________________________

Address of News Server ______________________________

Address of Mail Server ______________________________

Network Administrator E-mail ______________________________

Frequently Used E-mail Addresses ______________________________

Frequently Accessed Resources ______________________________

Frequently Accessed Resources ______________________________

Frequently Accessed Resources ______________________________

Technical Support

Software/Service	E-mail	Phone
Network Administrator	____________	____________
Connection Problems	____________	____________
Network Service Problems	____________	____________
Chameleon	support@netmanage.com	408/973-7171
Eudora	eudora-info@qualcomm.com	N/A
HGopher	m.hampson@ic.ac.uk	N/A
Trumpet	peter@psychnet.psychol.utas.edu.au	N/A

Windows FTP Sites

Archive Site	Domain Address
Indiana University CICA	ftp.cica.Indiana.edu
University of Michigan	archive.umich.edu
University of Minnesota	boombox.micro.umn.edu
Washington University (mirrors)	wuarchive.wustl.edu
Microsoft (general archive)	ftp.microsoft.com
Arts & Farces (Visitors Center)	ftp.farces.com

Windows Internet Tour Guide Visitors Center

Access *The Windows Internet Tour Guide* Visitors Center by FTP at ftp.farces.com, using Gopher at gopher.farces.com, and using Mosaic at www.farces.com.

Current versions of interesting Windows programs for use on the Internet are available via anonymous FTP. The latest versions of all the key shareware and freeware programs discussed in this book will be available for downloading.

Author

Michael Fraase
Arts & Farces
2285 Stewart Ave, Suite 1315
Saint Paul, MN 55116
612/698-0741 (voice)
612/698-5106 (fax)
mfraase@farces.com

Publisher

Ventana Press
110 East Main Street
Carrboro, NC 27510
919/942-0220 (voice)
919/942-1140 (fax)

DISK PREVIEW
The Windows Internet Tour Guide Companion Disk

The software on the companion disk accompanying *The Windows Internet Tour Guide* is distributed with the permission of its authors and is provided here for your use. Ventana Press and the author provide this software for your use as is and make no guarantee or warranty regarding its performance or compatibility.

Before you begin, we suggest making a careful backup of the contents of your hard drive and a backup of the companion disk. To install the software from the companion disk, you will need about 2mb of free space on your hard drive.

Chameleon Sampler

The Chameleon Sampler software allows you to route Internet information over a standard telephone line with a modem. The software suite also provides some basic client services you need to access the Internet. E-mail, FTP, TELNET, TN3270 and Ping programs are all included. A complete implementation of the Windows Sockets (WINSOCK.DLL) interface for TCP/IP is included. Installing the Chameleon Sampler software package is straightforward and very simple; step-by-step instructions are provided in Chapter 2, "Getting Connected."

Important Note

The Chameleon Sampler software included on *The Windows Internet Tour Guide Companion Disk* is fully functional and not limited in any way. NetManage, the company that created the Chameleon software, markets a complete line of Windows Sockets–compliant software tools for navigating the Internet. To purchase a full copy of Chameleon—including a network news reader, a Finger client, an e-mail client that supports MIME and a Gopher client—contact NetManage directly.

NetManage
20823 Stevens Creek Boulevard
Cupertino, CA 95014
408/973-7171
408/257-6405 (Fax)
sales@netmanage.com

Glossary

access method: The rules that manage how all the computers and other devices on a network can send information through the same physical medium in an orderly fashion.

access privileges: The privileges to open and make changes to directories and their contents; they are given to or withheld from users. By setting access privileges, you can control access to confidential information stored in directories on a server.

acronym: A word formed from the initial letter or letters of the main parts of a compound term, such as ROM (read-only memory).

activate: To make a nonactive window active by clicking anywhere inside it.

active window: The frontmost window on the desktop; the window where the next action will take place. An active window's title bar is highlighted.

addressing: A scheme, determined by network protocols, for identifying the sending device and destination device for any given item of information traveling on a network.

administrator: The person who sets up a network resource, registers users and their passwords, and maintains the resource.

alert: A warning or report of an error in the form of an alert box, a sound from the computer's speaker, or both. See also **alert box**.

alert box: A box that appears on the screen to give a warning or to report an error message. Its appearance is usually accompanied by a sound warning such as a beep.

alias: (n.) An alternate name used to invoke or identify a command, a network host, a list of users or some other applicable entity. (v.) To provide an entity with an alternate name.

American Standard Code for Information Interchange: See **ASCII**.

Archie: A network service used for locating files that are publicly accessible by anonymous FTP.

ARPANET: A wide area network that linked government, academic, and industrial installations around the world. Primarily connecting research sites, the ARPANET was developed in the 1960s by the Advanced Research Projects Agency of the U.S. Department of Defense.

ASCII: Acronym for American Standard Code for Information Interchange (pronounced "ASK-ee"). A standard that assigns a unique binary number to each text character and control character. ASCII code is used for representing text inside a computer and for transmitting text between computers or between a computer and a peripheral device.

asynchronous: Not synchronized by a mutual timing signal or clock. Compare **synchronous**.

asynchronous transmission: A method of data transmission in which the receiving and sending devices don't share a common timer, and no timing data is transmitted. Each information character is individually synchronized, usually by the use of start and stop bits. The time interval between characters isn't necessarily fixed. Compare **synchronous transmission**.

bandwidth: The range of transmission frequencies that a network can use. The greater the bandwidth, the greater the amount of information that can travel on the network at one time.

baseband: A transmission method in which a network uses its entire transmission frequency range to send a single communication or signal. Compare **broadband**.

baud: (1) A unit of data transmission speed: the number of discrete signal-state changes (signal events) per second. Often, but not always, equivalent to **bits per second**. Compare **bit rate**. (2) The maximum speed at which data can be sent down a channel, such as a telephone line; often confused with the actual speed at which the data is transmitted between two computers, measured in bits per second.

BBS: See **bulletin board system**.

bit: A contraction of **binary digit**. The smallest unit of information that a computer can hold. The value of a bit (1 or 0) represents a simple two-way choice, such as yes or no, on or off, positive or negative, something or nothing.

bit rate: The speed at which bits are transmitted, usually expressed as **bits per second**, or bps. Compare **baud**.

bits per second: See **bit rate**.

bridge: (1) A device that lets you connect two or more networking systems together. (2) A combination of hardware and software that connects two or more networks in an internet. Bridges are used to increase the number of devices and the distances covered in a network. See also **internet**.

broadband: A transmission method in which the network's range of transmission frequencies is divided into separate channels and each channel is used to send a different signal. Broadband transmission is often used to send signals of different kinds simultaneously, such as voice and data. Contrast with **baseband**.

bulletin board system (BBS): A computerized version of the bulletin boards frequently found in grocery stores—places to leave messages and to advertise things you want to buy or sell. One thing you get from a computerized bulletin board that you can't get from a cork board is free software.

bus topology: A layout scheme in which devices on a network are connected along the length of a main cable, or **bus**, rather than in a daisy chain or a loop.

byte: The number of bits used to represent a character. For personal computers, a byte is usually eight bits.

cable: An insulated bundle of wires with connectors on the ends. Examples are serial cables, disk drive cables and LocalTalk cables.

carrier: The background signal on a communication channel that is modified to carry information. Under RS-232-C rules, the carrier signal is equivalent to a continuous MARK (1) signal; a transition to 0 then represents a start bit.

CCITT: Abbreviation for **Consultative Committee on International Telegraphy and Telephony**; an international committee that sets standards and makes recommendations for international communication.

CIX: Abbreviation for **Commercial Internet Exchange**; an agreement among Internet service providers that allows them to account for commercial network traffic.

Clear To Send: An RS-232-C signal from a **DCE** to a **DTE** that is normally kept false until the **DCE** makes it true, indicating that all circuits are ready to transfer data. See also **Data Communication Equipment, Data Terminal Equipment**.

client: A computer that has access to services on a network. The computers that provide services are called **servers**. A user at a client may request file access, remote log-in, file transfer, printing or other available services from servers.

communications protocol: See **protocols**.

configuration: (1) A general-purpose computer term that can refer to the way you have your computer set up. (2) The total combination of hardware components—central processing unit, video display device, keyboard and peripheral devices—that make up a computer system. (3) The software settings that allow various hardware components of a computer system to communicate with one another.

configure: To change software or hardware actions by changing settings. Configurations can be set or reset in software or by manipulating hardware jumpers, switches or other elements.

connect time: The amount of time you spend connected to an information service.

data: Information, especially information used or operated on by a program. The smallest unit of information a computer can understand is a bit.

data bits: In the stream of bits being sent from your computer to a peripheral device or another computer, the bits that contain meaningful information; distinguished from bits used to indicate that a character is about to start, has stopped or is correct.

Data Carrier Detect (DCD): An RS-232-C signal from a DCE (such as a modem) to a DTE (such as a PC) indicating that a communication connection has been established. See also **Data Communication Equipment, Data Terminal Equipment**.

Data Communication Equipment (DCE): As defined by the RS-232-C standard, any device that transmits or receives information. Usually this device is a modem.

Data Set Ready (DSR): An RS-232-C signal from a DCE to a DTE indicating that the DCE has established a connection. See also **Data Communication Equipment, Data Terminal Equipment**.

Data Terminal Equipment (DTE): As defined by the RS-232-C standard, any device that generates or absorbs information, thus acting as an endpoint of a communication connection. A computer might serve as a DTE.

Data Terminal Ready (DTR): (1) One of the handshake lines in a data transmission interface. See also **hardware handshake**. (2) An RS-232-C signal from a DTE to a DCE indicating a readiness to transmit or receive data. See also **Data Communication Equipment, Data Terminal Equipment**.

default: A value, action or setting that a computer system assumes, unless the user gives an explicit instruction to the contrary. Default values prevent a program from stalling or crashing if no value is supplied by the user.

Defense Data Network (DDN): A single, wide area, packet-switching network that integrated the ARPANET research network and the MILNET defense network.

device: (1) A hardware component of a computer system, such as a video monitor, a disk drive or a printer. Also called a **peripheral device** because such equipment is often physically separate from, but attached to, the computer. (2) A part of the computer, or a piece of external equipment, that can transfer information. (3) Any piece of equipment that can be attached to a network—a computer, a printer, a file server, a print server or any other peripheral device.

dialog box: (1) A box that contains a message requesting more information from you. Sometimes the message warns you that you're asking your computer to do something it can't do or that you're about to destroy some of your information. In these cases, the message is often accompanied by a beep. (2) A box that a PC application displays to request information or to report that it is waiting for a process to complete.

download: To transfer files or information from one computer to another.

electronic mail: A network service that enables users to send and receive messages via computer.

Ethernet: A high-speed local area network that consists of a cable technology and a series of communication protocols. The hardware (cable) provides the physical link to connect systems together. The TCP/IP protocol allows different computers to exchange information over a network. The Ethernet specification was developed by Digital Equipment Corporation, Intel Corporation and Xerox Corporation. Ethernet is a registered trademark of Xerox Corporation.

Ethernet backbone: A network topology with separate AppleTalk networks interconnected to Ethernet gateways that are, in turn, connected to a single, continuous Ethernet cable.

Ethernet cable system: A system of high-performance coaxial cables widely used in the communications industry. Ethernet cables can be part of an AppleTalk network system.

even parity: The use of an extra bit set to 0 or 1 as necessary to make the total number of 1 bits an even number; used as a means of error checking in data transmission. Compare **MARK parity**, **odd parity**, **space parity**.

FAQ: Abbreviation for **Frequently Asked Question**; a list of frequently asked questions (and their answers). Most mailing lists and all network news newsgroups provide FAQ postings on a regular basis.

file: (1) Any named, ordered collection of information stored on a disk. Application programs and operating systems on disks are examples of files. You make a file when you create text or graphics, give the material a name and save it to disk; in this sense, **file** is synonymous with **document**. (2) For UNIX operating systems, an array of bytes; no other structure is implied by UNIX systems as they even treat devices like files.

file server: (1) A network device, usually consisting of a computer and one or more large capacity disks, on which network users can store files and applications in order to share them. (2) A specially equipped computer that allows network users to store and share information. (3) A combination of controller software and a mass-storage device that allows computer users to share common files and applications through a network.

file transfer protocol: A protocol that exchanges files with a host computer.

flame: A noxious and usually personal attack against the author of a network news article.

FTP: (n.) (1) Abbreviation for **File Transfer Protocol**; a protocol that determines how files are transferred from one computer to another. (2) A software program that transfers files using FTP. (v.) The act of transferring files using FTP.

full duplex: A four-wire communication circuit or protocol that allows two-way data transmission between two points at the same time. Compare **half duplex**.

full-duplex communication: A method of data transmission where two devices transmit data simultaneously. This method allows the receiving device to echo back each character of your message as it is received.

gateway: A device that connects networks that use different protocols. In effect, it translates between the protocols so that devices on the connected networks can exchange data.

Gopher: A menu-based means of exploring information resources.

half duplex: A two-wire communication circuit or protocol designed for data transmission in either direction but not both directions simultaneously. Compare **full duplex**.

half-duplex communication: A way of communicating between your computer and another computer or a peripheral device in which you can only send data or receive it at one time—not both. The other computer cannot echo back each character of your message as it is received.

handshaking: The exchange of status information between a **DCE** and a **DTE** used to control the transfer of data between them. The status information can be the state of a signal connecting the DCE and the DTE, or it can be in the form of a character transmitted with the rest of the data. See also **Data Carrier Detect, Data Set Ready, Data Terminal Ready, XOFF, XON.**

hardware handshake: A protocol that tells the computer to start or stop sending data by setting the DTR (Data Terminal Ready) line logic state. Also known as the Data Transfer Ready protocol. Compare **XON/XOFF**.

host computer: (1) A multi-user computer, such as a minicomputer or mainframe, that serves as a central processing unit for a number of terminals. (2) The computer that receives information from and sends data to terminals over telecommunication lines. The computer that is in control in a data communication network. The host computer may be a mainframe computer, minicomputer or microcomputer.

IAB: Abbreviation for **Internet Architecture Board**; the "council of elders" that makes decisions about Internet standards.

IETF: Abbreviation for **Internet Engineering Task Force**; a subgroup of the Internet Architecture Board that concerns itself with solving technical problems on the Internet.

internet: A network made up of two or more interconnected local area or wide area networks.

Internet: A worldwide, interconnected group of networks. Internally, the internet is composed of heterogeneous networks (such as ARPANET and CSNET) that use different message formats and protocols. Through the use of gateways that convert formats and protocols between networks, the internet appears externally as a single network, with hosts on interconnected networks appearing as interconnected hosts.

internet address: (1) An address for a computer on a network. The internet address consists of a network number and a host number that is unique for that network. (2) The AppleTalk address and network number of a socket.

ISOC: Abbreviation for the **Internet Society**; an organization formed to support a worldwide information network, and the governing body of the Internet Architecture Board.

K: See **kilobyte**.

Kbit: See **kilobit**.

Kbyte: See **kilobyte**.

kilobit (Kbit): A unit of measurement, 1024 bits, commonly used in specifying the capacity of memory integrated circuits. Not to be confused with **kilobyte**.

kilobyte (K): A unit of measurement consisting of 1024 (2^{10}) bytes. Thus, 64K memory equals 65,536 bytes. The abbreviation **K** can also stand for the number 1024, in which case **Kbyte** or **KB** or is used for kilobyte. See also **megabyte**.

Knowbot: A knowledge robot; a software program that provides information retrieval.

LAN: See **Local area network**.

local area network (LAN): A group of computers connected for the purpose of sharing resources. The computers on a local area network are typically joined by a single transmission cable and are located within a small area such as a single building or section of a building. Compare **wide area network**.

local system: The computer from which a user originates a network command. Compare **remote system**.

local system administration: Management of a single computer. This includes such functions as starting up and shutting down the system, adding and removing user accounts, and backing up and restoring data. Compare **network administration**.

login name: In UNIX systems, the name of a user's account. Used for identification purposes.

login prompt: The prompt (usually login: on UNIX systems) by which a system tells you it is ready to accept your login name.

log off: To indicate to a system or network that you have completed your work and are terminating interaction.

log on: To indicate to a system or network that you are starting your work and are beginning interaction.

login: To identify yourself to a system or network and start to use it. Usually logging on requires a password, depending on the system. Same as **log on**; opposite of **log off**.

MARK parity: A method of error checking in data transmission in which the most significant bit of every byte is set to 1. The receiving device checks for errors by looking for this value on each character. Compare **even parity**, **odd parity**, **space parity**.

megabit (Mbit): A unit of measurement equal to 1,048,576 (2^{16}) bits, or 1024 kilobits, commonly used in specifying the capacity of memory ICs. Not to be confused with **megabyte**.

megabyte (MB): A unit of measurement equal to 1024 kilobytes, or 1,048,576 bytes. See also **kilobyte**.

modem: Short for **modulator/demodulator**; a peripheral device that links your computer to other computers and information services using the telephone lines.

modem command: An instruction to a computer system, usually typed from the keyboard, that directs a modem attached to the computer to perform some immediate action.

multi-user: (adj.) Characterizes a mode or ability of an operating system to support several people using the same computer at once.

multi-user system: An operating system, such as UNIX, that allows many users to access application software simultaneously.

name: The name presented to users of a network to identify a given network service.

naming protocol: A protocol used by AppleTalk to associate a name with the physical address of a network service.

network: A collection of interconnected, individually controlled computers, together with the hardware and software used to connect them. A network allows users to share data and peripheral devices such as printers and storage media, to exchange electronic mail and so on.

network administration: Management of the software and hardware that connects computers in a network. This includes such functions as assigning addresses to hosts, maintaining network data files across the network and setting up internetwork routing. Compare **local system administration**.

network administrator: The person who is responsible for setting up and maintaining the network.

network connection: A combination of hardware and software that lets you set up a particular implementation of the AppleTalk network system, such as LocalTalk or EtherTalk.

network device: A computer, printer, modem, terminal or any other physical entity connected to a network.

Network File System (NFS): A protocol suite developed and licensed by Sun Microsystems that allows different makes of computers running different operating systems to easily share files and disk storage.

network manager: The person responsible for maintaining and troubleshooting the network.

network number: A unique number to each network in an internetwork that has been assigned by a seed router.

network system: A family of network components that work together because they observe compatible methods of communication.

NFS: See **Network File System**.

NIC: Abbreviation for **Network Information Center**; an organization that's responsible for supplying information for any of the component networks that make up the Internet.

NOC: Abbreviation for **Network Operations Center**; an organization that's responsible for the day-to-day operation of the component networks that make up the Internet.

node: (1) A device that's attached to a network and communicates by means of the network. (2) Any network device that has an address on the network. (Some network devices, such as modems, may be connected to a network but not be a node themselves.)

node number: A number that distinguishes one node from all others on the network.

NREN: Abbreviation for **National Research and Education Network**; an effort to combine the networks operated by the U.S. government into a single high-speed network.

odd parity: The use of an extra bit in data transmission set to 0 or 1 as necessary to make the total number of 1 bits an odd number; used as a means of error checking. Compare **even parity**, **MARK parity**, **space parity**.

offline: (adj.) Not currently connected to or under the control of the computer. Used to refer to equipment such as printers and disk drives, information storage media such as disks, and the information they contain. Compare **online**.

online: (adj.) Currently connected to and under the control of the computer. Used to refer to equipment such as printers and disk drives, information storage media such as disks, and the information they contain. Compare **offline**.

OSI model: The Open Systems Interconnection (OSI) reference model for describing network **protocols**, devised by the International Standards Organization (ISO); divides protocols into seven **layers** to standardize and simplify protocol definitions.

packet: A unit of information that has been formatted for transmission on a network.

port: (n.) (1) A socket on the back panel of a computer where you plug in a cable for connection to a network or a peripheral device. (2) A connection between the central processor unit and main memory or a device (such as a terminal) for transferring data. (3) A unique number that identifies a particular Internet service. (v.) To move software from one hardware architecture to another.

PPP: Abbreviation of **Point-to-Point Protocol**; a protocol that enables a computer to communicate with other computers using TCP/IP over standard telephone lines and high-speed modems.

protocols: The rules that govern interaction on a network. Protocols determine where, when, how and in what format information is transmitted.

random-access memory (RAM): The part of the computer's memory that stores information temporarily while you're working on it. A computer with 512K RAM has 512 kilobytes of memory available to the user. Information in RAM can be referred to in an arbitrary or random order, hence the term random access. (As an analogy, a book is a random-access storage device in that it can be opened and read at any point.) RAM can contain both application programs and your own information. Information in RAM is temporary, gone forever if you switch the power off without saving it on a disk or other storage medium. An exception is the battery RAM, which stores settings such as the time and which is powered by a battery. (Technically, the read-only memory (ROM) is also random access, and what's called RAM should correctly be termed read-write memory.) Compare **read-only memory**.

read-only memory (ROM): Memory whose contents can be read but not changed; used for storing firmware. Information is placed into read-only memory once, during manufacture. It remains there permanently, even when the computer's power is turned off. Compare **random-access memory**.

remote: (adj.) At a distance. Unable to be connected directly using local wiring only, but requiring communications devices. Compare **local**.

remote computer: A computer other than your own but in communication with yours through telephone lines, network wiring or other communication links. A remote computer can be at any distance from your computer, from right beside it to thousands of miles away.

remote site: A computer or network that is accessed through a long distance communications medium, such as telephone lines, network wiring, ISDN or a satellite.

remote system: On a network, any computer other than the local system.

RFC: Abbreviation for **Request for Comments**; a collection of papers that define the Internet standards and proposed standards.

server: A computer that provides a particular service across a network. The service may be file access, login access, file transfer, printing and so on. Computers from which users initiate the service are called **clients**.

service: A specialized function that a network provides to users, such as file sharing and electronic mail.

service provider: An organization that provides connections to the Internet.

signature: A text file, usually five lines or less, containing your identification and contact information that is added to your network news articles and e-mail messages.

SLIP: Abbreviation for **Serial Line Internet Protocol**; a protocol that enables a computer to communicate with other computers using TCP/IP over standard telephone lines and high-speed modems.

socket: On a network, a communication mechanism originally implemented on the BSD version of the UNIX operating system. Sockets are used as endpoints for sending and receiving data between computers.

space parity: A method of error checking in data transmission in which the most significant bit of every byte is set to 0. The receiving device checks for errors by looking for this value on each character. Compare **even parity**, **MARK parity**, **odd parity**.

standard: A set of specifications for designing hardware or software that is recognized by multiple vendors, an official standards organization or both.

synchronous: Able to perform two or more processes at the same time, such as sending and receiving data, by means of a mutual timing signal or clock. Compare **asynchronous**.

synchronous transmission: A transmission process that uses a clocking signal to ensure an integral number of unit (time) intervals between any two characters. Compare **asynchronous transmission**.

TCP/IP: Abbreviation for **Transmission Control Protocol/Internet Protocol**; a suite of networking protocols developed at the University of California for the U.S. Department of Defense.

TELNET: A terminal emulation protocol that enables you to login remotely to other computers on the Internet, using a command line interface.

terminal: A keyboard and display screen through which users can access a **host computer**.

terminal emulation: Software that enables a personal computer to communicate with a **host computer** by transmitting in the form used by the host's terminals.

topology: The physical layout of a network.

traffic: Transmissions travelling across a network.

tty: A terminal; abbreviated from teletypewriter, which was the first terminal device used on UNIX operating systems.

USENET: a network of about 3 million users (mostly UNIX users) that communicate using the UNIX-to-UNIX Copy Protocol (UUCP).

WAIS: Abbreviation for **Wide-Area Information Server**; an Internet service for looking up specific information in Internet databases.

WAN: See **wide area network**.

wide area network: Computers and/or networks connected to each other using long distance communication methods, such as telephone lines and satellites. Compare with **local area network**.

World Wide Web (WWW): A hypertext-based Internet service used for browsing Internet resources.

XOFF: A special character (value $11) used for controlling the transfer of data between a **DTE** and a **DCE**. When one piece of equipment receives an XOFF character from the other, it stops transmitting characters until it receives an XON. See also **handshaking, XON**.

XON: A special character (value $13) used for controlling the transfer of data between a **DTE** and a **DCE**. See also **handshaking, XOFF**.

XON/XOFF: A communications protocol that tells the computer to start or stop sending data by sending the appropriate character: either an XON or an XOFF. Compare **hardware handshake**.

Bibliograpy

Benedikt, Michael, ed. *Cyberspace: First Steps*. Cambridge, Massachusetts: MIT Press, 1991.

Brand, Stewart. *The Media Lab: Inventing the Future at MIT*. New York: Viking, 1987.

Cerf, Vinton G. "Networks," *Scientific American*, vol. 265, no. 3, pp. 72–81. New York: Scientific American, September 1991.

Comer, Douglas E. *Internetworking with TCP/IP: Principles, Protocols, and Architecture, Volume I*. 2d ed. Englewood Cliffs, New Jersey: Prentice Hall, 1991.

Engelbart, Douglas C. "A Conceptual Framework for the Augmentation of Man's Intellect." In *Vistas in Information Handling*, edited by Howerton and Weeks. Washington, D.C.: Spartan Books, 1963.

Gibson, William. *Burning Chrome*. New York: Ace Books, 1986.

———. *Count Zero*. New York: Ace Books, 1986.

———. *Mona Lisa Overdrive*. New York: Bantam Books, 1988.

———. *Neuromancer*. New York: Ace Books, 1984.

Gore, Al. "Infrastructure for the Global Village," *Scientific American*, vol. 265, no. 3, pp. 150–153. New York: Scientific American, September 1991.

Greif, Irene, ed. *Computer-Supported Cooperative Work: A Book of Readings*. San Mateo, California: Morgan Kauffman Publishers, 1988.

Hiltz, Roxanne. *Online Communities: A Case Study of the Office of the Future*. Norwood, New Jersey: Ablex Press, 1984.

Kapor, Mitchell. "Civil Liberties in Cyberspace," *Scientific American*, vol. 265, no. 3, pp. 158–164. New York: Scientific American, September 1991.

Karraker, Roger. "Highways of the Mind," *Whole Earth Review*, no. 70, pp. 4–11. Sausalito, California: Point Foundation, Spring 1991.

Krol, Ed. *The Whole Internet User's Guide & Catalog*. Sebastopol, California: O'Reilly & Associates, 1992.

LaQuey, Tracy, and Jeanne C. Ryer. *The Internet Companion: A Beginner's Guide to Global Networking*. Reading, Massachusetts: Addison-Wesley, 1993.

Laurel, Brenda, ed. *The Art of Human-Computer Interface Design*. Reading, Massachusetts: Addison-Wesley, 1990.

Licklider, J.C.R., Robert Taylor, and E. Herbert. "The Computer as a Communication Device." In *International Science and Technology*, April 1978.

McLuhan, Marshall, and Bruce Powers. *The Global Village: New Science*. Toronto: University of Toronto Press, 1988.

McLuhan Marshall. *Understanding Media: The Extensions of Man*. New York: McGraw-Hill, 1965.

Quarterman, John S. *The Matrix: Computer Networks and Conferencing Systems Worldwide*. Burlington, Massachusetts: Digital Press, 1990.

Toffler, Alvin. *Powershift: Knowledge, Wealth, and Violence at the Edge of the 21st Century*. New York: Bantam Books, 1990.

Turoff, Murray, and Roxanne Hiltz. *The Network Nation: Human Communication via Computer*. Reading, Massachusetts: Addison-Wesley, 1978.

Index

D

E

F

G

H

I

J

K

L

M

R

S

T

U

V

W

Colophon

The Windows Internet Tour Guide was produced using PageMaker 5.0 on a 486-50 PC-compatible with 16mb of RAM. The video system used is a Cornerstone Dual-Page 120 grayscale monitor driven by an ImageExcel controller. The body copy is set in Adobe Palatino, sidebars are DTC Futura and headlines are DTC Kabel. The cover art was produced on a Macintosh Quadra 800 using Adobe Illustrator.

Pages were proofed on a LaserWriter Pro 630. Final output was produced on film using a Linotronic 330. Internet software was tested on a Gateway 486 using a Practical Peripherals 144000 FAX modem.

Notes

Notes

RIDE THE WINDOWS™ WAVE

WITH BOOKS FROM VENTANA PRESS

Voodoo Windows

$19.95
282 pages, illustrated
ISBN:1-56604-005-1
Work Windows wizardry with productivity-enhancing tips. Organized by subject, this book offers a wealth of Windows techniques, shortcuts and never-before-published tricks that will streamline your daily tasks and save time. A great reference for beginners and experienced users alike.

The Official America Online for Windows Membership Kit & Tour Guide, Second Edition

$27.95
460 pages, illustrated
ISBN: 1-56604-128-7
This book takes Mac users on a lively romp through the friendly AOL cyberscape. Bestselling author Tom Lichty, a.k.a. MajorTom, shows you how to make friends, find your way around, and save time and money online. Complete with software to get you started. BONUS: 20 free hours of online time for new and current members and a free month's membership.

The Windows Shareware 500

$39.95
417 pages, illustrated
ISBN: 1-56604-045-0
The best Windows shareware available, from thousands of contenders. Includes utilities, sounds, fonts, icons, games, clip art, multimedia and more. BONUS: Four companion disks featuring top-rated programs, and an America Online membership disk along with 10 hours free online time!

DESIGN AND CONQUER!

Looking Good With QuarkXPress

$34.95
350 pages, illustrated
ISBN: 1-56604-148-1
Harness QuarkXPress's superior publishing power with an emphasis on good design and using the right tools. Looking Good With QuarkXPress makes "looking good" a practical matter, combining design ideas with tips on using XPress's tools to achieve special effects. Tough topics are cleared up, shortcuts and commands are grouped in easy-to-use tables and practical examples abound. Available in November.

Advertising From the Desktop

$24.95
427 pages, illustrated
ISBN: 1-56604-064-7
Advertising From the Desktop offers unmatched design advice and helpful how-to instructions for creating persuasive ads. With tips on how to choose fonts, select illustrations, apply special effects and more, this book is an idea-packed resource for improving the looks and effects of your ads.

The Presentation Design Book, Second Edition

$24.95
320 pages, illustrated
ISBN: 1-56604-014-0
The Presentation Design Book is filled with thoughtful advice and instructive examples for creating business presentation visuals, including charts, overheads, type, etc., that help you communicate and persuade. The *Second Edition* adds advice on the use of multimedia. For use with any software or hardware.

The Gray Book, Second Edition

$24.95
262 pages, illustrated
ISBN: 1-56604-073-6
This "idea gallery" for desktop publishers offers a lavish variety of the most interesting black, white and gray graphic effects that can be achieved with laser printers, scanners and high-resolution output devices. The *Second Edition* features new illustrations, synopses and steps, added tips and an updated appendix.

Looking Good in Print, Third Edition

$24.95
412 pages, illustrated
ISBN: 1-56604-047-7
For use with any software or hardware, this desktop design bible has become the standard among novice and experienced desktop publishers alike. With over 300,000 copies in print, *Looking Good in Print* is even better, with new sections on photography and scanning. Learn the fundamentals of professional-quality design along with tips on resources and reference materials.

Newsletters From the Desktop, Second Edition

$24.95
306 pages, illustrated
ISBN: 1-56604-133-3
Now the millions of desktop publishers who produce newsletters can learn how to improve the designs of their publications. Filled with helpful design tips and illustrations, as well as hands-on tips for building a great looking publication. Includes an all-new color gallery of professionally designed newsletters, offering publishers at all levels a wealth of ideas and inspiration.

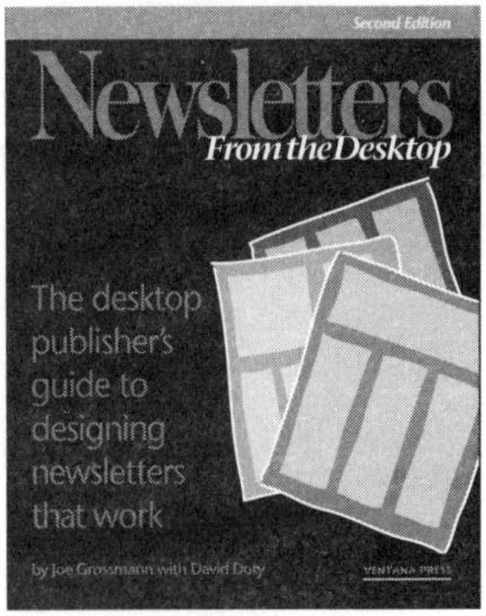

See your local bookstore or software retailer for these and other bestselling titles, or call

800/743-5369 (U.S. only)

WELCOME TO
VENTANA
HELP
CENTER
VISITOR
CENTER
VENTANA LIBRARY
Search

Yes! I want to Stay Plugged In!

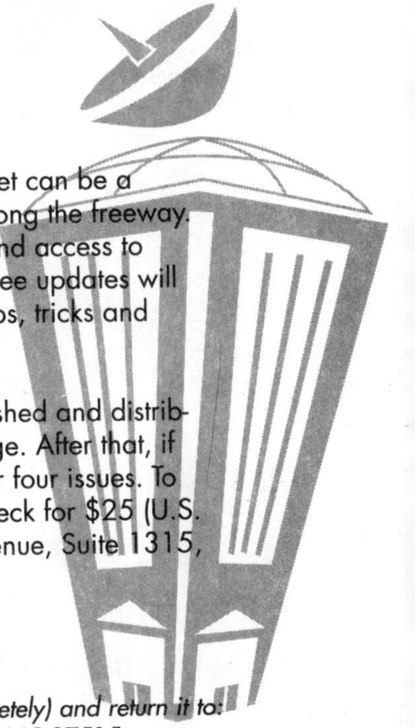

Send Me My Two Free Electronic Updates:

Navigating the strange and confusing highways and byways of the Internet can be a daunting proposition. New services spring up like fast food restaurants along the freeway. By sending in the card below, you'll receive two free electronic updates and access to ***The Windows Internet Tour Guide*** "Visitors Center." Your two free updates will feature the latest information about new Internet resources, file reviews, tips, tricks and pointers on finding and making the most of everything great on the Net.

The Windows Internet Tour Guide electronic updates are published and distributed on a quarterly basis. You'll receive the first two updates free of charge. After that, if you wish to continue receiving the updates, the yearly rate is only $25 for four issues. To subscribe now to a full year of updates (for a total of 6 issues), send a check for $25 (U.S. funds only) payable to Arts & Farces to: Arts & Farces, 2285 Stewart Avenue, Suite 1315, Saint Paul, MN 55116.
For more information, send e-mail to: tour-guide-request@farces.com
(For more details, see Appendix A)

To receive your two free updates, fill out the card below (be sure to fill it out completely) and return it to: Ventana Press, Attention: Windows Internet Tour Guide, PO Box 2468, Chapel Hill, NC 27515

YES! ❑ Send me my two free editions of ***The Windows Internet Tour Guide*** electronic update.

Here's my e-mail address:
(in the standard format of username@domain.top-domain)

____

❑ Keep me up to date on future offers and information about other Internet and Windows books and related materials.

Name ________________________________
Organization or Company ____________________
Address ________________________________
City __________________________________
State ________ Zip ____________________

Ventana Press
PO Box 2468
Chapel Hill, NC 27515

Ventana Press
PO Box 2468
Chapel Hill, NC 27515

Attn: Windows Internet Tour Guide